Rob␣␣ Lewis is from the Black Mountains, in the Brecon Beacons. *The ␣ast Llanelli Train*, his first novel, was nominated for the 2006 Bol␣␣␣␣er Everyman Wodehouse Prize for Comic Fiction; *Swansea Terr␣␣al* and *Bank of the Black Sheep* completed the critically acclaimed seri␣␣ *Dark Actors* is his first non-fiction book. It deals with a subject that ␣s haunted him for a decade.

D1330217

12585136

DARK ACTORS

The Life and Death of
Dr David Kelly

Robert Lewis

**SIMON &
SCHUSTER**

London · New York · Sydney · Toronto · New Delhi

A CBS COMPANY

First published in Great Britain by Simon & Schuster UK Ltd, 2013
This paperback edition published in Great Britain by Simon & Schuster UK Ltd, 2014
A CBS COMPANY

Copyright © 2013 by Robert Lewis

This book is copyright under the Berne Convention.
No reproduction without permission.
All rights reserved.

The right of Robert Lewis to be identified as the author
of this work has been asserted by him in accordance with sections
77 and 78 of the Copyright, Designs and Patents Act, 1988.

1 3 5 7 9 10 8 6 4 2

Simon & Schuster UK Ltd
1st Floor
222 Gray's Inn Road
London WC1X 8HB

www.simonandschuster.co.uk

Simon & Schuster Australia, Sydney
Simon & Schuster India, New Delhi

A CIP catalogue record for this book is available
from the British Library

Paperback ISBN: 978-0-85720-918-4
Ebook ISBN: 978-0-85720-919-1

The author and publishers have made all reasonable efforts
to contact copyright-holders for permission, and apologise
for any omissions or errors in the form of credits given.
Corrections may be made to future printings.

Typeset in the UK by M Rules
Printed and bound by CPI Group (UK) Ltd, Croydon, CR0 4YY

For everyone who was left behind

CONTENTS

My father, who worked for the US government, told me that he once received a memo from the Pentagon stating that too many trivial documents were being classified TOP SECRET and that the practice must stop. The memo was labelled TOP SECRET. He told me this story, he said, for two reasons: to remind me that a sense of irony is not commonly found in the military, and to persuade me never to work for the government.

GREGORY A. PETSKO

It is a corrupting thing, to live one's real life in secret.

GEORGE ORWELL

An Inspector Falls

One July afternoon in 2003, a scientist went out for a walk and never came back.

The day had started without obvious trauma. David Kelly and his wife Janice had woken up in their Oxfordshire cottage a little later than usual, but not too late for breakfast, or for him to miss his usual nine o'clock start in the study. It was a welcome return to the normal routine after a trying couple of weeks. According to his wife he seemed subdued, still tired maybe, but not depressed.

'He had never seemed depressed in all of this,' she later said.

By all accounts he had a busy and productive morning that Thursday, replying to a backlog of emails, dealing with a number of phone calls, and finishing what Andrew MacKinlay of the Foreign Affairs Select Committee had dubbed his 'homework'.

On Tuesday, the day of the Kellys' wedding anniversary, he had appeared before the Committee, accused of anonymously briefing a BBC reporter that the government's case for the Iraq War had been deliberately exaggerated. The MPs who interviewed him concluded otherwise, but MacKinlay had still demanded from him a complete list of all the journalists Kelly had spoken to, 'outside of an authorised briefing', from 2002 onwards. At the time, Kelly had told MacKinlay that he should make a formal request to the Ministry of Defence, while assuring him that 'basically it is very few people'.

MacKinlay had already requested this information from the

MoD direct and it had stonewalled him. Now that the MP had asked for it from Kelly during a televised hearing, the Ministry finally accepted its obligation. Kelly was instructed to supply the list to his bosses by ten o'clock that morning, so it could be scrutinised before being released to the Committee and thence to the public. He made his deadline with over half an hour to spare, sending the list to his line manager, Dr Bryan Wells, and also to an RAF Wing Commander called John Clark, who shared office space with Kelly at the Foreign and Commonwealth building.

'Basically very few people' actually turned out to be almost thirty, although Kelly explained that there might have been contact with other journalists of which he had 'no record'. He emailed the list to the Ministry of Defence via a secure channel used for classified information, and in order for Clark to receive it he had to walk thirty yards down a corridor to a special 'Internet machine', so Kelly rang him around ten o'clock to say he had sent it.

It seems odd that such basic information should have been treated so sensitively, especially considering much of it could be deduced from the public domain. To those few insiders who had been party to the true nature of Britain and America's involvement with Iraq over the preceding twelve years it was no surprise at all, but such voices were silent in the summer of 2003.

'We had a general discussion about developments,' Clark subsequently recalled. 'He was still very tired but in good spirits.'

They also talked about Kelly's next trip to Iraq, now only a week away, for which flights were already booked. At eleven the weapons inspector came out of his study for a coffee, and to exchange some quiet words with his wife about nothing in particular, before returning to his desk and an inbox still bulging with sympathy and solidarity from friends and colleagues who had not failed to notice his headline-grabbing contretemps with Westminster.

'It has been a remarkably tough time,' Kelly admitted in his replies, 'but I have a lot of good friends who are providing support.

Hopefully it will all blow over by the end of the week and I can get on with the job.'

It was not hope without foundation. However brusquely the MoD had treated Kelly, they were still standing by their man, despite the righteous indignation of the Tory shires. At the Foreign Office, Bryan Wells had received that morning a series of parliamentary questions from the Shadow Defence Secretary Bernard Jenkin, who demanded to know what disciplinary measures the Ministry was going to take against its out-of-favour inspector. In Wells's absence, his deputy James Harrison forwarded them to Kelly himself, so the inspector need not fear any more unpleasant surprises.

'More PQs!' Harrison emailed. 'But plenty of time for a reply [the deadline wasn't until September]. I expect Bryan will deal with this tomorrow.'

Wells had already assured Kelly that despite any political pressure he need fear nothing more than a written warning. And even that could probably have been challenged, if Kelly felt inclined to do so. The Ministry had been perfectly aware of his media appearances over the years, and had been careful never to take any kind of official position on them whatsoever. In fact, to borrow a time-honoured term from the CIA, Kelly's 'unauthorised' briefings with journalists had a distinct ring of plausible deniability about them, as far as his various masters were concerned.

It is in this light we must consider another email in David Kelly's inbox that morning, from the *New York Times* journalist Judith Miller. For years, Miller had been writing alarming stories about the increasing dangers of WMD attacks by rogue states, specifically Iraq. All of these were based on often unnamed intelligence contacts supplied by a Bush administration eager to bolster support for its foreign-policy objectives. So Miller was an establishment writer who owed her so-called scoops largely to the fact that the White House felt it could rely on her to act as a largely unquestioning conduit for manipulated and inaccurate intelligence. When her reporting proved false, she defended both the government line and her own career with equal vehemence, for they had by then become much the same thing. And that made her a worrying character to be dealing with if you really were a whistleblower.

Kelly and Miller had been in contact for years. He had helped her put out the US–UK line on a number of occasions.

'I heard from a member of your fan club that things went well for you [yesterday],' she had emailed him. 'Hope it's true.'

Kelly's circumspect response to this obvious player showed little of the good cheer displayed in his other replies.

'I will wait until the end of the week before judging,' he typed. 'Many dark actors playing games.'

Who these dark actors were, he didn't specify. Miller would presumably have understood. She was at the time busy helping and protecting Bush's Chief of Staff Scooter Libby in his illegal outing of the CIA agent Valerie Plame Wilson. It was the White House's revenge for her husband's refusal to corroborate a spurious British intelligence assertion that Saddam Hussein had sought uranium from Niger. When former US Ambassador Joseph Wilson reported the claim was based on 'obvious forgeries', the administration swiftly ended his wife's intelligence career by exposing her in public, an act that would eventually see Miller and Libby incarcerated. Except for the punishment of the guilty, the parallels between this and David Kelly's own Downing Street-induced media exposure are obvious.

Of all Kelly's email correspondence that morning, or rather, of all those that became public through Lord Hutton's subsequent inquiry, his terse reply to Judith Miller was perhaps the most revealing. The rest is fairly innocuous stuff: an expressed eagerness to get back to work, tentative plans for an imminent return to Iraq. On the face of it, Miller's optimism wasn't entirely unwarranted. The Foreign Affairs Select Committee had been entirely uncritical. Having fled their house the previous week to avoid being doorstepped by curious reporters, the Kellys were home again, and things seemed to be settling down.

Janice also seems to have sensed that a return to normality was at last under way. Certainly, she felt sufficiently untroubled to pop out a little before twelve to visit a fellow member of the local historical society. The Kellys had both settled comfortably into village life: yesteryear for her, cribbage nights in the Boar's Head for him. Outside, everything seemed the same as ever. There were no waiting photographers, no London reporters brandishing Dictaphones. She came back with some old photos after about half an hour and went into her husband's study to show them to him, but he only smiled and said he wasn't finished.

And then the official account turns abruptly hysterical.

Moments later, according to his wife, he went and sat in the sitting room on his own, which she describes as 'unusual'.

'He just sat there and looked really very tired,' she said. 'By this time I had started with a huge headache and begun to feel sick. In fact, I was physically sick several times at this stage because he looked so desperate.'

Nevertheless, Janice still made lunch for them – sandwiches and glasses of water – and they sat down to eat it together. If there was anything more substantial than her husband's suddenly stricken visage that caused her to become ill with worry, she has never revealed what it was.

'I tried to make conversation. I was feeling pretty wretched, so was he. He looked distracted and dejected. Oh, I just thought he had a broken heart. He really was very, very – he had shrunk into himself. He looked as though he had shrunk, but I had no idea at that stage of what he might do later, absolutely no idea at all. No, no. He could not put two sentences together. He could not talk at all.'

So some nameless, unspoken crisis appears to have quickly descended. David and Janice, married for thirty-six years, sat opposite each other, munching sandwiches, and said nothing about it. According to his wife.

'What are you going to do?' was the closest she came to broaching the subject.

'I am going to go for my walk,' was the answer, as understated as the last words of Captain Oates. Yet at the same time, it was nothing out of the ordinary. Kelly had become a habitual stroller of the Oxfordshire countryside around his home; apparently it helped with his bad back, but perhaps also it was a way of reconnecting, of reassuring himself he was home. He had, after all, spent much of the last two decades working away, in London or New York or Siberia or the Middle East. In all that time the house had remained something of a constant. The Kellys had lived in it since 1974, and raised three daughters there.

Janice responded to this oblique reply by going upstairs to bed – 'something I quite often did to cope with my arthritis' – and David returned to his study. He came up a little later to ask his wife if she was OK, and of course she said she was 'fine'. And then he changed into his jeans and put on his walking shoes and went downstairs. From what little we know of David and Janice it seems this was fairly characteristic of how the couple dealt with episodes of stress and division, not with heated argument but with one tramping around the fields and the other quietly abed upstairs. Except this was the last time she ever saw him alive.

The phone continued to ring. We know that the Counter Proliferation people at the Foreign Office with whom David Kelly sometimes worked were still brooding over his list of journalistic contacts. The nuances and implications of what was being disclosed here, or withheld, have never been made clear, but suffice to say at least three colleagues were vetting it before it would be passed to the Foreign Affairs Select Committee. The last person to be consulted about any changes to this list was of course Kelly himself. Wing Commander John Clark rang him again six minutes before three o'clock to explain the latest redraft, and once more at twenty past three.

When Clark rang back that second time, David wasn't in the house and Janice had to answer it. She described this at the subsequent Hutton Inquiry as 'a return call for me', which is at odds with Clark's account, but either way the records for the house phone show an incoming call at exactly three-twenty, and both Janice and Clark agree that Kelly was no longer there.

If Janice had a premonition that something had gone very badly wrong for her husband, then Wing Commander Clark sensed some looming disaster too. When he found Kelly had switched off his mobile he kept ringing it every fifteen minutes for the rest of the working day. But there was no answer. David Kelly had left his home for the last time.

At least one person saw him on his walk, an elderly neighbour called Ruth Absalom, who recalls seeing him 'around three o'clock' at the top of Harris Lane about a mile from his house, in the neighbouring village of Longworth, and they exchanged pleasantries between the hedgerows.

He was 'just his normal self', she said, 'no different to any other time when I have met him'.

The papers reported he had also been sighted by farmer Paul Weaver, walking through the fields north of the A420 not far from his home. Weaver said Kelly appeared happy and waved at him. What time Weaver saw Kelly, what he saw Kelly wearing, or what direction he was walking in, are things the police have kept to themselves.

Back in the cottage, Janice was still feeling 'extremely ill'. She sat down in the sitting room and put the television on, 'unheard of for me at that time of day'. There were a few callers at the front door and she had a short chat with each of them (she never said who, and Hutton never asked). Later, she became 'rather worried'. David's walks were usually on the short side, normally as little as a quarter of an hour according to his wife, although this could stretch to twenty-five minutes 'if he met somebody'. If he was going to be any longer he would say where he was going and when he would be back. She became concerned that 'something was wrong' in the late afternoon.

One thing it appears David Kelly sometimes did on his brief walks was use the phone box in the village. The *Sunday Mirror* obtained phone records for Southmoor's single public phone box and later duly reported that somebody had used it shortly after three o'clock that afternoon to ring a national newspaper in Canary Wharf.[1] Procuring confidential phone records was common practice in Fleet Street at that time, albeit that it was illegal. The journalist and author Nick Davies has written how somebody supplied the Kelly's landline bill for that period to two broadsheets within forty-eight hours of his disappearance. But bar that brief, quickly buried mention in the *Sunday Mirror* these intrusions have shed no light on the events of that day. Lord Hutton showed no interest in examining them, although he could have requested official access.

It was less than a month after midsummer when David Kelly set off that afternoon, but the weather was typically British: partly overcast with the promise of very light rain. There had been a thunderstorm the night before. Despite this, Thames Valley Police (after spending several hours searching his house and talking to his family) later reported that David had set off wearing only jeans and a white cotton shirt. Perhaps he never expected to be gone long, or perhaps he just didn't care. Either way, he had still not returned when their daughter Rachel arrived at the cottage around six-thirty that evening.

The night before, the Kellys had stayed with Rachel and her boyfriend in Oxford, and David had promised her they would go walking together that evening to see a foal in a nearby field. Instead she got a phone call from her mother in the late afternoon to say that David had gone walking by himself, and had not returned. Rachel reminded Janice that he was under a bit of stress, and probably seeking comfort from a little solitude. But when it proved impossible for Rachel to contact her father on his mobile, she too grew anxious.

When Rachel came over after work she was initially torn between staying with her mother, by now visibly distraught, or leaving to search for her father. So she rang her older sister Sian, who immediately offered to drive over from her home in Fordingbridge, Hampshire, a journey of seventy miles (Rachel's twin, Ellen, could only remain in distant Fife). Encouraged by this, Rachel decided to take her car up the lanes her father would normally walk: first to the track at the foot of Harrowdown Hill, where she called him from the gate, then along to Hinton and down to Duxford, a small hamlet on the banks of the Thames. When she got to Duxford it was starting to get dark, which suggests it was around nine o'clock, and for the first time it occurred to her that her father might not be coming home. She considered searching some nearby barns, but by now she had succumbed to the same crippling dread that had seized her mother, and she was too nervous to get out of the car. Instead, she returned to the house, upset and afraid, and phoned her two sisters.

On arriving in the village, Sian and her partner Richard also began combing the area by car, stopping to look in churches and bus shelters and other possible locations that a lone and desperate man might find himself. They gave up the hunt a little later than Rachel, returning to the cottage at around eleven, by which time night had well and truly fallen.

A decision had to be made.

'We delayed calling the police because we thought we might make matters worse if David returned when we started to search,' Janice Kelly explained. 'I felt he was already in a difficult enough situation.'

By twenty to midnight, the Kelly women felt they could put it off no longer. Sian rang the police. Three local officers arrived within fifteen minutes.

'I explained to them the situation that David was in,' Janice told Lord Hutton, 'and it seemed immediately to go up to chief-constable level.'

For a grown man of sound mind, who had been missing less than nine hours in clement weather, the scale of the police response was unprecedented. It was clear right from the very start this was about something more than a missing person. There was a rapid and awful escalation on all sides, one that made little sense without the presumption that something terrible had happened. Janice was hysterical by mid-afternoon, by six Rachel was concerned enough to mount a three-hour search (and grew too frightened to be outdoors alone), Sian immediately set off from distant Fordingbridge and then spent almost another three hours searching herself; by one o'clock, the police had a search heli-copter from RAF Benson surveying the surrounding area with heat-seeking equipment and a communications team had erected a forty-five-foot mast in the Kelly garden. Tracker dogs were called in, and by half-four in the morning Janice Kelly and her two daughters were shivering outside while the cottage was searched and her husband's study was cleaned out.

Officially Thames Valley Police were the investigating force, but at five o'clock in the morning Assistant Chief Constable Michael Page met with the head of the local Special Branch at Abingdon police station to ensure their officers would also be present, which allowed for liaison with the Security Service and the Secret Intelligence Service. In all likelihood (as we shall see), these depart-ments had their own men on the ground too, but they have never featured in any official account.

By seven-thirty the following morning, forty policemen were searching the area together with the South East Berks Emergency Volunteers and the Lowlands Search Dogs Association. A mounted unit from Milton Keynes was in transit, and an underwater search team was on the way. Missing children would be lucky to get such a swiftly assembled task force.

Amongst the arriving police were two qualified search advisers, a Sergeant Paul Wood and another sergeant from Milton Keynes, both regarded as national experts. Their task was to gain some understanding of the missing person's condition and habits, and hopefully establish a likely shortlist of locations that could be searched first. At the same time, Special Branch began to seize any potentially sensitive information from the cottage (local eyewit-nesses also said that the wallpaper was stripped, which would almost certainly have been part of an MI5 bughunt). Meanwhile in London, the Metropolitan Special Branch sealed off Kelly's office in the Ministry of Defence and seized its contents.

Back in Oxfordshire, the Thames Valley Police were preparing to launch a public appeal for help. According to their statement, made a little after half-seven, the police were particularly concerned for Kelly because he had been out all night in only jeans and a shirt. But by the time this was announced, Assistant Chief Constable Page had just received the shortlist of search locations from his two specialist advisers, and teams of volunteers were duly dispatched. Harrowdown Hill, which had been Rachel's first port of call, was number two on that list.

Louise Holmes, a hearing-dogs trainer, and Paul Chapman, who worked for Prudential in Reading, both of the South East Berkshire Emergency Volunteers, parked their car at the bottom of Common Lane in Longworth at eight o'clock. With them was Brock, a border collie crossed with an Australian shepherd. They walked north towards the Thames, following Brock's nose, until they discovered a boat moored on the riverbank, but none of the people on it seemed to know anything about David Kelly and their identity remains unknown.

Turning back from the river, Holmes and Chapman were approaching Harrowdown Hill from the north when Brock picked up on another human scent and dashed off. The dog was trained, on finding a missing person, to return to the handler and bark, then lead his owner to the find. This time he just came back and lay down.

'At which point,' said Louise Holmes, 'I realised this was obviously not quite the same as a normal training exercise.'

Louise went on ahead, leaving Paul and the dog at the treeline. She had gone about two hundred metres into the undergrowth when she shouted to Paul that he should ring control. She had found him. He lay in a small clearing, circled by a dense bank of brambles, at the base of a tree. Tentatively she drew nearer, until she was standing only a few feet away, and then froze there as if unable to move for a couple of minutes. It was the first time Louise Holmes had seen a dead body.

'He was at the base of the tree with his head and his shoulders just slumped back against it. His legs were straight in front of him. His right arm was to the side of him. His left arm had a lot of blood on it and was bent back in a funny position. He matched the description we had been given, and I was happy in my own mind that he was dead and there was nothing I could do to help him.'

She rejoined Paul and Brock and they headed back down to the car, where they had arranged to meet the arriving policemen and guide them on. But before they could get to the rendezvous point, three men were already walking briskly towards them from the southern end of the field, only two or three minutes after Paul had made the call.

The identification and appearance of these three men, who just happened to be heading towards the body so soon after its discovery, go some way to illustrating how unreliable the official account can be. Louise Holmes described them as police officers. How did she know they were police officers? Lord Hutton made a point of asking. Because 'they identified to us who they were', said Holmes. Her colleague Paul Chapman described them specifically as three police officers from CID. Hutton asked him the same question: 'How did you know?' 'They showed us their Thames Valley Police identification,' said Chapman. Hutton, who seemed to have anticipated that these three men could prove a tricky matter, went as far as to ask Chapman if he could remember their names. 'Only one of them was DC Coe,' was Chapman's rather peculiar reply.

The three men were led to Kelly's body by Paul and Louise and were then left alone with it for almost half an hour while the two volunteers returned to their car and brought back the police officers from the official search team. Of these, one of the first to arrive was PC Dean Franklin of Thames Valley Police, shortly after ten o'clock.

Franklin describes the three men he found standing around David's corpse as 'two uniformed police officers' and one DC Coe. Hutton asked Franklin what this Detective Constable Coe was up to.

'I have no idea,' Franklin told him. 'He was just at the scene. I had no idea what he was doing there or why he was there.'

But Coe and his colleagues had been up to something. When Louise Holmes discovered Kelly's body, he was slumped against the trunk of a tree. When the two police constables arrive, he is stretched out flat on his back on the ground, in the clear by several feet. Exactly who was with Coe that morning and why did they feel compelled to move the body?

The truth emerged, in part, during the Hutton Inquiry. The only one of the three men to appear before Lord Hutton was indeed a Detective Constable Graham Coe, as identified by the volunteer searcher Paul Chapman. But Coe obfuscated when replying to Hutton, who almost certainly knew Coe was dissembling, and was happy for him to do so.

Coe said that only himself and a DC Colin Shields were with the body on Harrowdown Hill that morning (Shields was never called to appear at the Inquiry). The third man – the man whom each of the four eyewitnesses told the Inquiry they had seen – now disappears from view. Hutton never challenges Coe about the existence of this third man; never asks about him once. Nor, although it must have been perfectly clear to him that the body was moved, did he ask why. And this is all of some consequence, because Coe and Shields were not CID but Special Branch, and their first priority in Oxfordshire that morning was not to find a missing person or cordon off a suicide scene or anything so mundane, but to protect national security, which is the only and entire purpose that Special Branch serves. It is a secretive and unaccountable part of the British police force that acts as public liaison for the intelligence services, for whom it really works. It has often been said that Special Branch exists as 'a force within a force', and that it owes greater loyalty to the spymasters than to any chief constable. Its conduct in the wake of David Kelly's death typifies this.

Coe told Hutton that he had been called to Longworth to make 'house-to-house inquiries', although he does not say by whom or why. Work like this would ordinarily have been carried out by conventional police officers. He also claimed it was Ruth Absalom, the woman who bumped into Kelly in the lane that Thursday afternoon, who told them to go to Harrowdown Hill. Yet Absalom herself makes no mention of this interview, and in her own testimony she explains that when Kelly left her he was walking in a totally different direction from where his body was later found. It seems unlikely she would have directed anyone there on a wild hunch.

Coe maintains that his encounter with Louise Holmes and Paul Chapman was a simple coincidence, which is perfectly possible, but the fact is that if it wasn't, he was under no obligation to tell us why. And Hutton's easy acceptance of his patchy testimony reminds us there are questions even a law lord is reluctant to press upon a working officer of Britain's intelligence community.

For seven years Coe maintained, despite everything, that there was no third man with him and DC Shields that day. Then, interviewed in his retirement by the *Daily Mail*, he took a step closer to disclosing the whole truth and admitted there was indeed another man, but that he was 'a trainee police officer who had since left the force', and refused to name him. But rookie officers do not cut their teeth on Special Branch duties. Neither do they need protection from publicity or from public inquiries. Almost certainly this third man was an agent of MI5 or MI6; and plainly, during the time this agent was with Kelly's body, it was (at the very least) moved, searched, and 'wiped' – because over seven years later, police responses to freedom-of-information requests showed that no fingerprints were found on the knife, the watch, the bottle, or even Kelly's mobile phone.

So the scene of death was demonstrably disturbed by individuals that had nothing to do with Thames Valley Police, for reasons that remain unclear, one of whom was likely an unaccountable intelligence officer whose very existence has been denied – to the extent that several witnesses claimed he was a uniformed police officer, while his Special Branch liaison, DC Coe, maintained for seven years that he was never there at all.[2] The regular police, by comparison, took the issue of forensic contamination so seriously they did not move the body until seven o'clock that evening, when a fingertip search of the surrounding area had been completed.³ This was no ordinary suicide, any more than it had been an ordinary missing person's search.

At twenty to ten, while our unnamed intelligence officer was rifling through Kelly's pockets, paramedics Vanessa Hunt and Dave Bartlett got a call at Abingdon ambulance station telling them to mobilise for a male patient. As they made their way over, the data screen in their ambulance updated them with the information that there was a 'Kilo 1' – a deceased male – at Harrowdown Hill. By the time they arrived, Coe and his colleagues had left, and Thames Valley Police had regained some nominal authority of the scene. While policemen stood around taking photographs that would shortly be classified for the next seventy years, Hunt attached four electrodes to Kelly's chest for a cardiogram reading and obtained the inevitable flat line.

Vanessa Hunt and David Bartlett had over thirty years' experience as working paramedics. They had been called out to hundreds of suicides, they had seen dozens of wrist cuttings. More than anyone else who saw David Kelly's body that day, they had first-hand knowledge of what a self-inflicted death looked like. And to them, something was very obviously wrong.

'There was no gaping wound ... there wasn't a puddle of blood around,' said Vanessa Hunt, whose first thought on seeing Kelly was that he had hanged himself and fallen from the tree. 'There was a little bit of blood on the nettles to the left of his left arm. But there was no real blood on the body of the shirt. The only other bit of blood I saw was on his clothing. It was the size of a fifty-pence piece above the right knee on his trousers. There wasn't even any blood on his cutting hand. When somebody cuts an artery the blood pumps everywhere. You would get a spraying, five or six pints of it. I've seen it hit the ceiling, and even then the patient survived.'

Wrist-slashing is a difficult and painful way to commit suicide, especially if you're not in a bath of hot water. The body's self-defence mechanisms will kick in immediately, and a severed vein or artery will start to contract and close as soon as it's been opened. Wrist-cutting has a high survival rate for this very reason, and is normally associated more with self-harm than suicide. There was a US study of Carolina jails that looked at inmates' suicide attempts over a nine-year period, and found that out of 275 wrist-cuttings, only one ended in death.[4] People who are genuinely intending to kill themselves through slitting their wrists will usually seek to cut those arteries that lie close the surface of the skin, while in the bathroom; somehow, David Kelly missed these but succeeded in completely and lethally severing a single ulnar artery when he was in the middle of a thicket.

Of all the arteries in the human body, the ulnar is one of the shortest and the most difficult to get to. It's buried deep within the wrist, hidden behind nerves and tendons you would have to painfully hack your way past, and it's as thin as a matchstick, which means it's less likely to kill you if it's damaged. According to the Office of National Statistics, between 1997 and 2004 only three people managed to commit suicide by cutting the ulnar artery (one of them presumably being David Kelly himself).[5] If wrist-cutting is already one of the most unsuccessful ways to attempt suicide, aiming for the ulnar artery lengthens the odds even further. Particularly if, like David Kelly, you only attempted to cut one of your wrists.

The knife David Kelly chose to use to do this, the knife that was found at the scene, was a folding pruning knife with a hooked blade. It may have been sharp but its inwardly curving hooked tip made it an impractical tool for an already difficult job. Possibly Kelly made no attempt to cut his right wrist because of the damage he had already inflicted on the tendons and nerves in his left arm with the blade. What's more, he appears to have attempted to cut his left wrist while he was still wearing his watch, because a blood-stained watch was found placed on top of his knife on the ground beside his body. That is to say, it appears David Kelly took a pruning knife to his left wrist while his watch was still on it, and only removed that watch during or after the act. All suicides are an act of violence, but Kelly's was an incomprehensibly sudden and brutal one. And yet, as the retired DC Coe admitted to a British newspaper seven years later, 'there wasn't much blood around'.

What little blood was visible could be seen in some funny places. Inside the lining of a discarded Barbour cap, on the abandoned digital watch, on a bottle of mineral water, left standing neatly upright not six inches from his left arm. The blood on these objects is described as smeared rather than sprayed, which not only reinforces the idea of sub-lethal blood flow but also suggests Kelly had actually handled all these things after he had cut himself. Yet in some of the places you would expect to find blood it seemed there was little or none at all.

'I didn't see any blood on his right hand,' said Vanessa Hunt. 'If he had used his right hand to cut his wrist, from an arterial wound you would expect some spray.'

As members of the emergency services, Bartlett and Hunt expected to go back on shift once death had been formally pronounced. Instead they were kept on site for over an hour, during which they weren't even allowed to radio their control room. The police had established a communications blackout over the entire area.

'It's the only time I've ever seen that happen in my entire career,' Bartlett said. 'We only found out it was because the body was David Kelly's when we were leaving.'

As far as we know, the next person of any significance to arrive on Harrowdown Hill was the Home Office pathologist Nicholas Hunt. Thames Valley Police had rung him that morning to request his presence and he arrived around midday.

Hunt had been a practising pathologist since 1994, and on the Home Office list since 2001, which made him one of the most senior in Oxfordshire. He was a busy man that year, and would remain so. The base where all dead British bodies were repatriated from the Iraq War, RAF Brize Norton, was in the same county.

By British law, every serviceman or -woman killed overseas is flown back to the UK for an inquest, and the jurisdiction for that inquest derives from where the body physically lies, so for almost all of the Iraq War, this was Hunt's office.

The coroner, Nicholas Gardiner (Hunt's boss), could have transferred jurisdiction for these inquests to coroners closer to the next-of-kin, but decided not to. So because of a quirk of law, a provincial coroner's office provided the only public hearings into almost the entire British war dead.[6] As the death toll mounted, it was beset by controversy as a matter of course. Friendly-fire incidents and frequent equipment shortages all played their part, but its most famous case was not flown in by RAF Hercules. As Hunt made his way onto the crest of Harrowdown Hill that morning, he came face to face with the first wave of that war's fatalities, and its most haunting death of all.

Hunt's first impressions were the complete opposite to the paramedics'. Within minutes of turning up, he offered to Assistant Chief Constable Michael Page his opinion that David Kelly had died from a slashed wrist. And then, having stuck his neck out, he waited on procedure and the arrival of the forensic biologist Roy Green and his assistant Dr Eileen Hickey, while a tent was erected over the body.

It was Hunt who performed the first official, recorded search of the body. Amongst the everyday items in Kelly's pockets (a car key, glasses, a Yale key, a Nokia phone, but no wallet), he found three blister packs of co-proxamol (also wiped of fingerprints). Each blister pack normally held ten tablets but they were all empty, except for a single remaining pill. Janice Kelly told Hutton she took co-proxamol for her chronic arthritis, and it has always been assumed that the blister packs found in David's jacket came from her supply.

Not for nothing did the Greeks use the same word for 'medicine' as they used for 'poison'.

Co-proxamol is a potent painkiller, part paracetamol, part something called dextropropoxyphene, an opioid that forms by far the most dangerous component. Whereas an untreated paracetamol overdose will take days to lethally damage your liver, excess dex-tropropoxyphene can kill you in hours, either through respiratory depression or heart failure. When combined with heavy alcohol use it is thought that as few as ten tablets have proven fatal, albeit in an isolated case, and the maximum therapeutic usage is eight tablets per day, so co-proxamol has always been a dangerous drug. Concerns were first voiced about it in the seventies, and today it is only available in the UK on a named-patient basis.

When the toxicologist Richard Allan began his investigations the following morning, he found that David Kelly's stomach con-tained the remains of two tablets and his blood showed 'above therapeutic levels' of dextropropoxyphene, so we know (as the empty blister packs suggest) that he had taken more. But the actual level of dextropropoxyphene found in his blood was well below what was considered a fatal amount: one microgram per millilitre of blood, compared to almost five. Considering that the teetotal David Kelly had no traces of alcohol in his blood whatsoever, this level puts him at the absolute statistical extreme for a possible co-proxamol overdose.

It must be said that measuring the level of toxic substances in a dead person's blood is still an extremely inexact science. Many tox-icologists believe the attempt itself leads to 'the abuse of process, almost certainly to the miscarriage of justice and possibly even to false perceptions of conspiracy'.[7] Either because of this, or because of the low drug levels the tests showed, forensic pathologist Nicholas Hunt stuck with his first impression and concluded in his post-mortem report that the primary cause of death was loss of blood from a slashed wrist. But of course, statistically at least, David Kelly's severed ulnar artery was equally unlikely to have done for him.

The real irony is that he should have survived. Given the relative inconsequence of his cut wrist and his very minor overdose, a fitter person, one who was perhaps not under such incredible levels of stress and exhaustion and isolation, had every chance of pulling through. Instead, alone on Harrowdown Hill, Kelly's overburdened body surrendered him, and he left us, his face fixed on a cloudy English sky, glimpsed through the branches of the ash trees. What answers did it give him? The weapons inspector's open eyes would still be staring upwards when they found him.

According to the body-temperature readings taken by Nicholas Hunt, he expired sometime between four o'clock on the afternoon of his disappearance and a quarter past one the following morning. When his youngest daughter was calling his name from the gate at the bottom of the field, he may already have been ebbing away. Or did he really spend the intervening hours in a copse not three miles from his home while the sun set and the night came on, waiting to bring about his own end?

If David Kelly had been anonymous, if he had been a plumber or a postman, a coroner might have recorded an open verdict, or death by misadventure. In some parts of the country many coroners still adhere to the old-fashioned belief that the dead should not be pronounced suicides unless it is beyond reasonable doubt, unless for example there is evidence of prior attempts or a statement of intent. Instead Tony Blair's political appointees did what was asked of them. The Lord Chancellor, Blair's ex-flatmate Charlie Falconer, adjourned the inquest indefinitely and used a legal loophole to replace it with a non-statutory inquiry that dispensed with a jury and couldn't put witnesses under oath. That too was headed by an unelected peer, one who had launched his legal career by acting as barrister for the Ministry of Defence in the most widely discredited inquest in British history: that of Bloody Sunday.

At the age of seventy-two, Brian Hutton began his first-ever major inquiry by proclaiming David Kelly a resounding and definite suicide in his opening statement, and then proceeded to spend most of his efforts lambasting the BBC and exonerating the Blair government, both in its treatment of Kelly himself and in its machinations to justify the Iraq War. Before he started he had already secretly ordered the post-mortem report to be sealed for seventy years, and all other evidence not presented to be classified for thirty (which partly explains why he was so keen to disallow much of the evidence available at his own inquiry, such as scene photographs).

In 2010, it emerged that although the inquest was cancelled, a death certificate was still somehow secretly completed less than three weeks after the Hutton Inquiry began, the cause of death listed as haemorrhage. The certificate refers to a nonexistent inquest that supposedly took place on 14 August, and unlike every other death certificate in existence, it is signed by neither the coroner nor the pathologist. While Hutton was splashing the vetted testimony of pre-selected witnesses across the newspapers he knew full well the state had already delivered its furtive verdict.

There would always have been doubts, and there would always have been conspiracy theories, but in the government's cynical efforts to produce convenient certainties out of a shady and sordid reality, speculation flourished. Little of it was helpful, but nevertheless all of it constituted an attempt to reach for the truth.

Of those who cried murder, perhaps the most convincing was Mai Pedersen. A Kuwaiti-born USAF translator who struck up a close relationship with Kelly while working with him in Iraq, Pedersen is described by both her ex-husbands (one of whom is a former Green Beret) as a US spy.[8] She has been incommunicado since Kelly's death.

'She doesn't tend to want to get involved any more,' her New York attorney told me.

Even so, in 2008 she released a statement to the *Daily Mail* via the same lawyer, claiming Kelly couldn't have killed himself in the way described because firstly he suffered from 'unexplained dysphagia', a condition that makes swallowing pills extremely difficult. According to Pedersen, he hadn't taken pills of any kind in years. Second, and perhaps more importantly, she claimed he would have been unable to wound himself in the way described because 'he had hurt his right elbow and was incredibly weak in that arm. He couldn't cut a steak with it.' The claim gained credibility when the post-mortem report was released two years later and revealed Kelly did indeed have 'an old curving scar around the outer aspect of the right elbow'. In 2003, Thames Valley Police flew out and spent two days interviewing her, yet Assistant Chief Constable Page (a former Special Branch officer himself) told Hutton that she added 'nothing of relevance to my inquiry at all'.

Pedersen aside, there were plenty of details that begged for a fuller investigation, or pointed to a bigger story. The telephone call from the public phone box. The absence of fingerprints on his personal belongings. The acquisition from his home of his Barbour jacket when the first police report specifically stated he was wearing only his shirt. The helicopter that flew directly over Harrowdown Hill at one in the morning with thermal cameras and yet detected no signs of any human body.

Doubts about Kelly's final movements resurfaced when it was discovered his secret death certificate didn't specify his place of death, only where the body was found. Yet Thames Valley Police could have used his mobile-phone signal to track him by filing a simple request to the Home Location Register. Instead, it appears they preferred not to, an omission they attempted to keep secret until the Information Commissioner forced its disclosure seven years later. Was this casual, or deliberate, negligence on their part? Is it possible there were things about Kelly's death that Thames Valley Police didn't want to know?

If the constabulary were careful not to look into Kelly's suicide too closely, perhaps it was because Special Branch and British intelligence were all over it. The weekend after his death, Ministry of Defence security guards spotted personnel putting Kelly-related material into 'burn bags' and notified Thames Valley Police, who in typical fashion never supplied them to the Hutton Inquiry, or anybody else. What were they trying to hide?

Even stranger is the break-in at David Kelly's dentist's and the resultant theft of his dental records in the days preceding his disappearance, records that strangely reappeared once he was found. Similarly, the paramedic Vanessa Hunt's patient-report form, essential to any proper inquest, vanished from NHS archives, never to return. And there is too the enduring and total silence of his family, who even after almost a decade of controversy have said absolutely nothing to the public or the media concerning any aspect of his life or death. Rumours that his widow was considering suing the government ended in January 2004, when it was reported that Janice had accepted a £180,000 lump sum with an £11,000 annuity. She was under police guard at the time, and had been since David's death – but to protect her from what? And what conditions, if any, were attached to the settlement?

As the Afghan poet Latif Nazemi wrote, silence is itself a sound. Because above and beyond all of this, of course, lies David Kelly's lifelong involvement with intelligence agencies, with despotic regimes, with dangerous weapons, with secret technologies, with illegal wars and dishonest governments and state-sanctioned journalists like Judith Miller. It must be remembered that if any aspect of Kelly's death could be considered harmful to national security then there were men on the ground who were professionally obliged to hide it from us, and we know that those men were there from the outset, shaping much of the narrative that would follow.

In fact it seems that the volunteer searchers Louise Holmes and Paul Chapman may not even have been the first to find his body. According to the post-mortem report that was released by the succeeding coalition government, the vomit trails on Kelly's face ran over the top of his left ear, which means he must have been sick while he was flat on his back (nausea is a possible side-effect of a co-proxamol overdose). Physiologically this was an 'agonal event', occurring while Kelly was deeply unconscious and at the point of death – otherwise, his reflexes would have spurred him to clear his airway. Yet the searchers found him sitting against a tree.[9] Who put him there, and why, and what were they doing there? It's probably no coincidence that as soon as Special Branch and their unnamed spook had an unobserved moment, they returned him to a position that was consistent with the forensic evidence.

The truth behind David Kelly's death has yet to be told. He was financially secure, respected in his field, and eminently employable:

when he died he was a year away from early retirement, and he had already received job offers in Europe and the US. The attentions of the press were doubtless disturbing, but not overmuch: he had appeared in newspapers, books and television programmes for over a decade. As Patrick Lamb of the Foreign and Commonwealth Office told Hutton at the Inquiry, he was an accomplished media performer.

Kelly was not, as Hutton would have it, compelled to suicide by personal shame at betraying his employers. As Jeremy Gompertz QC put it, in his closing statement for the Kelly family, he had betrayed no one, least of all in talking to journalists.

'The reality of the situation is that there was an ad hoc, informal arrangement which had existed for many years and which reflected Dr Kelly's special position.'

Even if the government had thrown the book at him for some alleged breach of code, they couldn't have done so without incurring a massive political cost. It was why they never prosecuted the GCHQ worker Katharine Gun when she leaked that Britain was spying on UN members before the vote on military action in Iraq. They dropped the charges on the courtroom steps on the morning of the trial. As with Gun, any legal action would have seen the state exposed by cross-examination in a criminal court, and Downing Street had too much to hide. No, David Kelly was driven by the trigger of some secret terror. In all likelihood it was a terror he had very deliberately been subjected to.

And we're not supposed to know anything about it.

If we want to know how Britain came to lose its greatest biowarfare expert, we must understand not his death but his life, and the shadowy world in which he lived. It isn't a matter of artery diameters and dextropropoxyphene densities, but a journey. And for me it began not twelve miles from my own home, in a depressed town in the Welsh valleys, at a time when Britain was worried about WMD attacks from a dictator in Berlin rather than Baghdad.

2

Dai

Just because you don't take an interest in politics, it doesn't mean politics won't take an interest in you.

PERICLES

'Well the man from the BBC asked us if we were going to,' said the chair of the Rhondda Civic Society, 'so we thought we had better say yes.'

The next day, which was six days after his death, the BBC duly reported the news that Dr David Kelly was to be honoured with a memorial in his native South Wales. But there is still no plaque to honour the achievements of Britain's most famous weapons inspector, in Wales or anywhere else. And he will first have to wait his turn, for there are a whole host of boxers, rugby players, politicians and other local notables on the list ahead of him.

'We'd bump him up a bit, you know, if someone gave us the funds,' the chair told me. 'Mind you, I think he was actually from Ponty.'

He was.

Pontypridd never felt like much of a town to me. It was two hillsides full of terraces on either side of a motorway; you cast a glance over its uninviting rooftops and hastened gratefully to your destination. All I could remember was a centre that was the usual British bombsite, concrete edifices erected in the days of central planning, a shopping centre with boarded-up façades, discount off-licences, a doomed youth enjoying the twilight of the West in ever-circling third-hand hatchbacks. I had a drink there once with a girlfriend in 1996, and until now I had not been back.

It is a valleys town like my own father grew up in, and although he (as did Kelly) moved out as soon as he was able, for me it seemed a promising starting point. This unprepossessing place twelve miles north of Cardiff was David Kelly's hometown: he was born here, he was schooled here, and until he got married, all the family he ever really had lived in this shrunken and shrinking community. If you wanted David Kelly the man you needed David Kelly the boy, and so I went to Pontypridd to find him. But he had vanished too.

The basic details are easy enough to establish. David Kelly was a war baby, born on 14 May 1944, the day the British army got its operational orders for the D-Day landings. There is a village near Pontypridd called Llwynypia where the Cambrian Coal Combine accommodated its managerial class in a building called Glyncornel House. The year war broke out it was, in the collectivist spirit of the age, converted into a maternity hospital. So David Kelly, together with half the Rhondda, came into the world at Llwynypia: for the rest of the century it was the only maternity ward in the valley, despite the village having streets so narrow they are in places impassable by car. I got stuck there myself, on a thick bank of ice at the end of a steep cul-de-sac, and only got out thanks to a tow from a passing local.

'I've lost count of the number of times I've seen that happen to people who come round here,' he said.

Like everywhere else in the valleys I've been too, Pontypridd and its environs are full of friendly and talkative people, even if they populate a fallen and foreboding landscape. While I was returned to traction, Glyncornel House hospital looked on darkly from high up on the hill opposite, closed down and fenced off. The looters hit it sometime last year, stripping the lead from the roof and the piping from the walls.

David Kelly's parents were two locals who tied the knot in a quiet ceremony three days after Christmas 1940. Tim, formally Thomas, is listed on the certificate as being in His Majesty's Forces. In actual fact he had signed up to become a flying officer with the RAF during the Battle of Britain, which must have provided a rare streak of glamour. He came from a long line of Kellys that had arrived from County Cork just as the Industrial Revolution was rocketing Pontypridd into booming existence, and if their share of the new prosperity was modest, they had at least stayed out of the pits and the Poor House. Tim Kelly's father was a fruiterer, selling his goods from a horse's cart and later a stall in the indoor market. Margaret Kelly's father was Morgan Williams, a man who carved tombstones and memorials, while her mother's family were retailers, or members of the local shopocracy, as the poet John Barnie would have it. He was twenty-four and she was twenty-three.

Ill-fortune seems to have befallen the family before it had really got started. While Tim Kelly was stationed in the Home Counties he met Flora Dunn, a pretty farm girl seven years his junior. Margaret must have sensed that trouble was brewing, because in a reverse evacuation she took the two-year-old David with her into the South East of England, so they could live near the base in Tunbridge Wells. It didn't work. Margaret and David returned a few years after, and she eventually divorced him in 1951. Tim brought Flora home to Ponty for his second marriage within weeks of the papers coming through, and then they left town for good. They started a new life in Northamptonshire, where Tim eventually became headmaster of one of the largest schools in Britain. He and Flora had three children of their own, and adopted a fourth, but none of them ever got to know David until after Tim died in 1983. He left nothing in his will for his first son.

Kelly was left to grow up with a heartbroken mother and her aged parents in their house on Berw Road opposite the River Taff, a three-bedroomed granite terrace with a sunless back garden sloping impossibly up the rocky hill behind. His mother never remarried and kept her ex-husband's name until the day she died, and neither does she seem to have ever moved out, although she found work as a teacher in the local girls' school. Being an only child herself, there were no aunts and uncles for David in this small and compact household, no cousins to play with. Yet it was still a home, for all that. I spoke to a woman four years David's junior who was taken to visit the family as a young girl, and she described a polite and happy boy who indulged her with a few childish games beneath the trees on that rising lawn. It was all she ever saw of him, however. By all accounts, David had few friends in Pontypridd, and no close ones.

On his father's side of the books there were aunts, uncles and cousins aplenty, most of whom lived mere streets away. His Uncle Leslie, in family lore forever changed by the battle of El Alamein, kept the Kelly fruit stall going until the seventies. But as Tim's new family got under way, his prolonged absences grew into a lifelong estrangement, and the Pontypridd Kellys seem to have grown distant in turn. David Kelly had three cousins on his father's side, and one described how a very young David would come by during Tim's increasingly rare visits, hopeful for some contact with his father. His most abiding memory of these appearances was when David turned up and the boys hid from him as a joke, spying on him from behind boxes in the garage while the future weapons inspector searched fruitlessly for company. In adult life they did not keep contact.

David's luck changed for the better when he was admitted to the Boys' Grammar School, which back then was one of the best in Wales. By the time he started there it had already turned out its fair share of bishops and generals. At the end of Berw Road there is an old chapel that has been saved from ruin by its conversion into the town museum, and it was there, underneath the dusty flags, that I was led past photos of jubilees and tramlines into the basement, where the school's records were kept.

'David Kelly was from Ponty, was he? The bloke that hung himself? Well there's something fishy going on there.'

There were detailed registers for every year since the school was founded, all in meticulous copperplate, the details of generations upon generations of young hopefuls on their way up through selective education. Every year except David's. Even that, like so much of his paper trail, is no longer in the public domain. According to the museum manager, the last person to have looked at it was a journalist down from London who visited during the Hutton Inquiry: eager to make contact with Kelly's old classmates in the shadow of some looming deadline, he obviously stole it. And it was sitting in the basement of that old Tabernacle that I felt for the first time the sinking feeling that biographers must sometimes have when they sense how much their subject has already begun to slip away from them; how much a person might be eclipsed for ever by a single story. The same day, I heard a rumour that Kelly's few surviving relatives in Pontypridd, despite having seen nothing of the man for decades, had been visited by Special Branch during the Hutton Inquiry and instructed to remain silent about their distant cousin. If this was true, it wasn't something they admitted to me, although one said they had decided not to talk to the press because they were 'worried about the government'.

Those old schoolmates I did track down had, much like David's cousins, practically no memory of him at all. Several were surprised to find they had shared a classroom with the bearded, bespectacled man who had dominated headlines the year of the Iraq War. Alan Elkan, now an architect in Bristol, perhaps remembers him best, largely by virtue of living a few doors down from him, although neither ever visited the other's home. Elkan described the young David Kelly as a quiet boy with a gentle voice who was bright 'but not in a way that made him stand out'. Kelly's grandparents seemed 'very old' (Morgan would have been seventy-one the year he started grammar school, Ceinwen sixty-three), and he isn't sure he ever met his mother Margaret at all.

'Compared with the other schoolmates I had,' Elkan told me, 'I had virtually no contact with his family at all.'

By the time the boys entered adolescence they no longer shared classes, and they saw very little of each other from then on.

Outside of school the fifteen-year-old Elkan and his friends were teenagers about town, rigged out in white raincoats and 'Robin Hood hats' (as Elkan describes the fashion of the time), mixing with the local Teddy Boys and catching the odd glimpse of the neighbourhood superstar Tom Jones as he started to cusp on his rapid rise to fame. David, with his close but withdrawn family, played no part. There were no rock-and-roll nights at the YMCA for him, no teenage dalliances.

'Lost all contact with him from then on,' Elkan said. 'Then I saw him on telly during the Gulf War – the first one – and I recognised him. And I actually wrote to the BBC to get in touch with him, and he rang me up. We kept meaning to meet each other, but it never happened. Still, we kept in touch on and off through the years since then. The last time I spoke to him was the summer before he died, he said he had to rush off to a UN meeting in New York, but he still found the time to talk to me. He did say to me that he was pretty busy because he was working for two bosses, for the MoD and MI6, but that's all he said. I was gobsmacked at his suicide. He'd never shown any sign of hysteria or anything like that.'

But perhaps David Kelly was never the type to show much sign of anything. If his childhood seems isolated, by the time adolescence arrived he had developed a self-containment so profound he is hardly discernable at all. The obituarists from the national newspapers certainly found little to work with; and ever eager for a story, more than one of them settled for the tale of the coalminer's son who rose to become head boy.

It's a heroic narrative but it's entirely untrue. A history of the school does mention him as a fine and promising long-distance runner, and one can easily see how that solitary sport would appeal to a teenage loner like David Kelly much the same way it did to the boy in Alan Sillitoe's celebrated short story, written the same year Kelly would have been pounding the bleak hills above his home.[1]

There were reports too that he was active in the school's Air

Training Corps, although I couldn't substantiate this. If it's true, it could only have reaffirmed the absence of his ex-RAF father. It was while he was at school he learned to play the saxophone – again, it must be said, something of a solo instrument. The school's music teacher, known as 'Cuke' to the boys, was ostensibly in charge of running the school orchestra but could not repress a proclivity towards jazz. Cuke was involved in the Air Training Corps too, although he seems to have been largely motivated by the opportunity to borrow the band's instruments and put them to a less martial use.

Beyond these details, David Kelly's upbringing is an unknown. The school itself is another ambiguous memorial, its frontage of once-grand buildings now behind wire, its unlit rooms with their smashed windows the preserve only of rodents and the occasional vandal. The council has been trying to sell it off for decades. The school motto carved above the main entrance, *Ymdrech a Llydra* – Perseverance Will Succeed – is barely legible, something to which time has added its own invisible question mark.

Alun Richards, the Welsh novelist, attended the Grammar in the forties, and he too was brought up by his grandparents. He always maintained that his experience of being 'a fatherless child' in that orderly and insular town was the making of him as a writer.

'I learned at an early age to lie low, to watch, to gauge a mood, to know when it was time to speak,' he wrote. 'I also learned to listen, to eavesdrop, gathering what bits and pieces of information I could. I listened from corners, behind doors, on tramcars, to hushed voices drifting out of the vestry after chapel, to the gossip of neighbours talking in the street.'

Discreetly observant, necessarily self-contained, a masked vulnerability: these are the traits that can draw a life towards literature, but they apply equally to Kelly as to Richards, and you can see how such a youth would shape itself just as well to the world of intelligence.

Kelly's final year in Pontypridd certainly held one truly seminal event for the young scientist-to-be. Smallpox broke out in South

Wales. It had been brought unwittingly to Cardiff by a man visiting from Bangladesh, and from there had spread quickly up the valleys. In a frantic effort to halt the disease, firemen burned down the hill-top hospital in Penrhys, a few miles up the Rhondda, and townspeople lined up to watch as the distant flames licked the sky. In desperation an experimental drug was trialled on elderly female patients at Blackmill Hospital in Bridgend, almost certainly without their informed consent. Half of them didn't survive.

Shopkeepers kept tubs of disinfectant by the tills to clean the money they were given. Those who worked with the ill, or who had ill relatives or friends, were often refused service outright, and people with valleys accents were looked at askance if they travelled outside the area. Health inspectors played detective, chasing down people's movements and inoculating those who had been exposed. Affected households were evacuated and their contents removed for incineration. If you worked for the health board you kept damn quiet about your job, such was the level of public hostility and suspicion.

Fear ran rampant. Snaking queues began to form outside doctors' surgeries as people angrily demanded their jab.

'When Trealaw clinic announced only so much was left, panic set in and they were fighting to get the last dose,' said the former health inspector Vernon Bryant.[2] 'People were panic-stricken. People in Pontypridd wouldn't open the door.'

More than once the police were called out. In all, twenty-five thousand local people were vaccinated. Even so, forty-seven contracted the illness, and nineteen of them died. It was the last major smallpox outbreak in the UK. David Kelly's first introduction to dangerous viruses came long before he ever gazed down a university microscope. He had seen first-hand what they could do outside the lab, he had waited in the uneasy line at the clinic in Pontypridd Park for his injection, and he had seen too that fighting such pathogens was a job that won you few friends.

In the future, when he worked to expose those who sought to spread disease by design, he earned a reputation for persistent questioning and dogged pursuit. Even the smallest risks were gravely serious to him, and this was an attitude that had formed in Pontypridd in 1962, the year of the outbreak. The spectre of smallpox would haunt him throughout his life. It visited him in an unsafe lab at the University of Birmingham, in a freezing factory in Siberia and in a dusty storeroom in Iraq, but it never revealed itself to him as it did here.

David made it out of Ponty when Leeds granted him admission to study for a bachelor's in chemistry, botany and biophysics in 1963. After his schooling was over his family seem to have had little use for the town either: they moved to a three-bedroomed apartment in Albany Court, a newly built block in Penarth, a genteel seaside suburb of nearby Cardiff. But the freshman Kelly still couldn't cut loose. Back home there were difficulties that were not spoken of. His mother Margaret appears to have experienced some sort of ongoing nervous or physical debilitation. There was talk of a stroke, or depression, or even, as an old member of her chess club remembers it, of a lobotomy. Certainly she seems to have gone through bouts of infirmity and recuperation throughout David's childhood.

He was driving back to Penarth on the eve of his twenty-first birthday when he found out she was dead. For some time she had been prescribed barbiturates for her nerves, and the inquest found she had died from overdose-induced bronchopneumonia in the Williamses' new flat. The death certificate listed her as a college lecturer but this promotion, along with the move to Cardiff and David's progression to university, appears to have done nothing to abate her black dog. Officially it was an open verdict, but David was never under any doubt that she had committed suicide. It was kept out of the papers, unusually for the time, perhaps because the family had not long been in Cardiff.

One of his friends at Leeds also had a mother who killed herself at around the same time, and it saw the two of them form a close bond. When Kelly later left academia to work for the defence establishment, he nominated this old undergraduate friend as a referee for the necessary security vetting, during which Margaret's suicide came up. In the opinion of the MI5 assessor doing the interviewing, Kelly 'appeared to ride the period well, remaining engrossed in his studies, and at no time did he display any mental reaction to this unfortunate matter. In fact the referee said he can be considered a well-balanced person.'

And yet such an event must have been deeply traumatic. We know from medical records unearthed by the Hutton Inquiry that in the following weeks, Kelly was prescribed tranquillisers for insomnia by the university doctor, and he was given an extra year to complete his degree. And thus David Kelly passed into his age of majority with one parent dead by her own hand and the other permanently estranged, but as his vetting officer was to observe (in a faintly approving tone) it served only to drive him harder, just as it must have added another lacquer to his protective shell. In adult life, he never spoke of either of his parents.

Another contemporary of Kelly's at Leeds was Jack Straw, who was elected chair of the university's Labour Society in 1966, whereupon he rebranded it the Socialist Society and then withdrew its support for Labour because the party was insufficiently left-wing. Straw gained further notoriety on campus when the British Council selected him to go on a student trip to Chile, where, instead of building a youth club, he spent his time quarrelling with his colleagues, posturing as an insurgent communist, and demanding an audience with the opposition leader Salvador Allende.[3] All of which he made up for in later life, when as Foreign Secretary of the Thatcherite New Labour party he helped ensure safe passage home for Allende's murderer Augusto Pinochet at a time when Spanish relatives of the Chilean 'disappeared' were demanding he be tried in the Hague for crimes against humanity.

To his credit, Kelly had as little to do with Straw as possible.

'He won't remember me,' he later told his half-sister, 'because I wasn't a political animal, but I remember him.'

And so it proved. Kelly and Straw met professionally for the first time in 2002, when the former supported the latter in a hearing before the Foreign Affairs Select Committee about UK foreign policy in the wake of 9/11. The Foreign Secretary made a point of complaining to his department that they had sent a nobody along to accompany him. The following year, when Kelly became drawn into the farrago over the government's claims of an Iraqi WMD arsenal, Straw was a part of the Downing Street cabal that secretly exposed him to the press and then belittled him in public.

Luckily, David Kelly's spare student hours were filled by someone far more important. Janice Vawdrey was distantly related to the Vawdreys of North Wales, an aristocratic family that had once owned Tushingham Hall in Cheshire, as well as tracts of Snowdonia. She was studying at the teacher-training college twenty miles away in Bingley, but one of her courses was taught at the university. Between the city campus and the country college, which had only just opened its door to male students, an intense romance quickly blossomed.

David graduated in 1967 with a 2:2 in bacteriology, a classification that is probably just another reflection of his terrible loss. Certainly Birmingham University thought so, because they happily accepted him to do a master's in virology. Jan Vawdrey opted to complete her own education degree in the same institution, but before the two joined each other there they got married in St Mark's Church in Crewe, near the Vawdrey family home.

The death of his grandfather Morgan Williams after a long illness the following year did nothing to break his stride. Happily married, secure, and embarked on a subject that would prove a lifelong vocation, he made it into the hallowed halls of Oxford in 1968, to begin a doctorate in insect viruses at Linacre, the university's newest college. It was only three years old at the time, and without any wealthy patrons to back it had started life as a wooden hut under a mulberry tree. Populated by older graduates and eschewing the social pretensions of Oxford's grander colleges, Linacre was a fitting springboard for the quiet, hard-working Kelly's vault into academia.

After the doctorate, there were two years' post-doctoral work on the influenza virus at Warwick. Jan found work as a teacher, gave birth to their eldest daughter, Sian Elizabeth, and the young family moved into their first home in the village of Eynsham. Then Oxford called him back, this time to become Senior Scientific Officer for the Institute of Virology. The twins, Ellen Rhiannon and Rachel Angharad, arrived shortly afterwards, and the Kellys moved one last time into Westfield, a beautiful five-bed-roomed eighteenth-century house that had been the home of the local poet Wilfrid Howe-Nurse. The Institute promoted him to Principal Scientific Officer in 1977 and then again to Senior Principal Scientific Officer in 1982.

Even if Kelly's academic career never achieved a fame of the first order it was clearly a successful one. In part, he was the right man at the right time. Leeds was one of the few institutions with a for-midable microbiology department that allowed its undergraduates to specialise. At Birmingham he studied under two of the biggest names in the discipline, one of whom was Peter Wildy, who founded and then edited the British *Journal of General Virology*, and went on to chair the Department of Microbiology at Kelly's first university. Kelly's research at Warwick was done alongside the vac-cine supremo Nigel Dimmock, now a professor whose name regularly appears in the press whenever a new flu pandemic breaks out. And the Institute of Virology at Oxford, where he ended up, can be considered the pinnacle. His colleagues there included Tom Tinsley, a Lancashire farmer's son who was instrumental in its creation, and whose name was carved on the keystone above its entrance. And all the while Kelly found the time to continue pub-lishing papers as well as supervising students, one of whom went on to become Professor of Virology at the University of Glasgow.

To become a virologist when David Kelly did was to join the ranks of the pioneers, when names were made and careers were shaped. Microbiology, and viruses in particular, were still very much an emerging field. Many of its greatest experts were still active and remain so today; some of its greatest achievements lay ahead, and some would argue they still do.

For a man who was by all accounts habitually reserved, those years saw him make a large number of lifelong friendships, often with people who rose to some prominence themselves. After his death the scientific journals were full of fond and personal reminiscences from notable scientists who considered him something more than just a peer.

'He was a distinguished microbiologist, a family friend, and a former colleague of thirty-five years' standing,' wrote Chris Payne, Professor of Horticulture at the University of Reading. 'I will remember him as a loyal friend, someone who could be a private person yet convivial in company, with a gentle sense of humour.'

'There's no doubt that the UK has lost a formidable scientist,' wrote Emeritus Research Professor Willie Russell of the University of St Andrews. 'He was one of the very few microbiologists who had real expertise in bioweapons. His professional colleagues will miss his courtesy, his quiet humour, and his ability to make friends easily.'

Even those who knew him only from his time after Oxford said much the same thing.

'David Kelly never sought the limelight and I salute his professionalism, his humility, and his warm loyalty as a true friend,' wrote Terence Taylor in the *Independent*, a former weapons inspector and assistant director of the Institute of Strategic Studies. 'He was a scientific civil servant of the highest calibre who became the UK's leading authority in the effort to prevent the proliferation of biological weapons around the world.'

In a *Telegraph* obituary, which described Kelly as someone who 'in the opinion of his peers was pre-eminent in his field, not only in his country but the world', Alastair Hay, Professor of Environmental Toxicology at Leeds, was quoted as saying 'there was no other person I would have gone to as such a source of unvarnished truth – and such funny asides. But he was the complete professional, he had such an eye for detail that nothing got past him.'

Hay had already experienced his own run-in with the

establishment when his anti-war, anti-apartheid activism meant his appointment as senior lecturer was blocked for seven years by his university's promotions committee, despite the fact he was backed by two Nobel Prize winners. He was amongst the few to hint that the values of David's first career, those of truth, objectivity and shared knowledge – in short, the principles of academia – would not exactly be treasured in his second.

However big the culture clash Kelly encountered when he finally left Oxford, his passion for his subject never receded. In fact, it isn't hard to see how the man's interests mirrored his personality: he believed that the truths of life never lay on the surface, and that its biggest changes occur invisibly to the human eye. The virus is perhaps the most mysterious of organisms, the smallest of them all and of entirely unknown origins, as old as life but yet not quite alive itself. The virus can only replicate robotically within a host cell, which it then consumes to form a legion of doppelgängers that soon set about invading every cell that surrounds it in an entirely unconscious quest for its brutally meaningless existence. Throughout the sixties and the seventies and the eighties, thousands of new viruses were classified, some quite benign, some so monstrous they could reduce a living body to a bloody pool within days.

The most famous examples endure as humanity's invisible bogeymen. In 1967, thirty-one laboratory staff fell violently ill in the German town of Marburg, where it was discovered a pathogen from infected Ugandan grivet monkeys had made the leap into human hosts. The Marburg virus broke out again in the Congo, killing 128 of 154 victims before it ground to an unexplained halt. In 1976, from some oblivious bat or insect deep in the ancient caves of Mount Elgon in Kenya, Ebola bounded suddenly across the species. With the highest fatality rate of any known virus it swiftly wiped out a mission hospital before it could be stopped. In 1981, the US Centers for Disease Control examined five gay Los Angeles men and discovered that AIDS had crossed over from the chimpanzees of sub-Saharan jungles and was spreading, discreetly and lethally, around the world. Such was the nature of the bio-logical agents on which David Kelly spent his quiet labour.

If, inside of himself, there were dark caves where the memory of a painful childhood waited to burst fatally forth, they were never discovered. Hutton was careful to weave his mother's suicide into the narrative of his Inquiry, and leave us with the implication that Kelly's end can be found largely in his beginnings, that his fate was sealed internally before he ever set out into the world, as if by genetics. But David Kelly married happily and well, fathered three children, gained a master's and a doctorate, and launched on two successful careers. He was fifty-nine when he died. While there was no denying the sad turbulence of his early years there was no changing it either, and in the light of his adult life it appears – like smallpox – to have been successfully contained.

If he never felt the need to talk about his youth, perhaps that isn't so much because he was repressed as that he was the product of an earlier age. He belonged to what *TIME* magazine dubbed the 'silent generation', born in a time of crisis, reared in the shadow of the bomb, and characterised as 'grave, fatalistic, morally confused, pessimistic, and searching for faith ... working fairly hard and saying nothing'.

All observations on generational difference are arbitrary gener-alisations, and sweeping ones at that, but the stoic, diligent, modest Kelly genuinely seems cut from an older cloth. Especially when you compare him to the demographic bulge of baby boomers who followed hot on his heels. This was the fate of the Silent Generation, to be overtaken by a wave of competitive individu-alists who believed ardently in their own exceptionalness. And this itself might be of no consequence except that by the end of his life, everybody David Kelly worked under, from his line manager to his department's permanent secretary and right through Cabinet up to the Prime Minister, was of that brasher, more self-centred stripe.

In the political imbroglio that was to engulf them both, Kelly personified the Silent Generation in much the same way that Tony

Blair, with his healing crystals and 'birthing' mudbaths, personified his. It's hard to picture Blair receiving his Congressional Gold Medal up on Capitol Hill (where he received a standing ovation before he even opened his mouth) on the very same day Kelly took his final walk and not see the yawning chasm of an awesome generation gap. And it's equally hard to imagine Kelly, as Blair's office did, demanding his medal be recast with a more flattering image of the recipient. Even if there was less than nine years between them, David Kelly was born in war and Blair was not.

In truth, the war must have loomed almost as large over Kelly's formative days as his family's break-up. His father and his father's brother both went away to fight, as did both his grandfathers in that earlier war against the Kaiser (they got married during wartime, too). His infancy was half spent in blackouts, his hometown was threatened ominously with visits from the Luftwaffe in Lord Haw Haw's infamous broadcasts, and if nothing else it's a remarkable coincidence that the man who would become Britain's authority on biological weapons was issued with his own gas mask at birth.

The spectre of the war was ever present at his grammar school too. More than half the staff were veterans, and there was a roll of honour on the wall of the Assembly Hall dedicated to the teachers and old boys who never made it back. The headmaster, E. R. Thomas, more commonly known as 'Napoleon', would periodically drag errant pupils out before it and try to shame them before its illustrious ghosts. He tried it once with Alun Richards.

'A family of heroes,' he barked, 'and what are you?'

But the young Richards had already developed a bohemian streak.

'Alive!' he quipped.

If Napoleon ever took a similar interest in the young Kelly it's hard to imagine him coming up with such a self-affirming reply. More likely, the school's extracurricular sacrifices had infected him with the attendant sense of obligation. After all, decades later, it was war and the prospect of war that absorbed him.

He was shaped, in many ways, by the state, from the fifties post-war grammar to the sixties universities of Harold Wilson's technological white heat. He came to adulthood in a crumbling Empire where the British government told its people that the loss of their global power would be compensated by bold new territorial claims on the frontiers of science. And if any single institution embodied such a spirit, it was Porton Down.

Sprawling, labyrinthine and highly secretive, Britain's military laboratory complex in rural Wiltshire has been since its foundation the source of fraught controversy, grim legends and spectacular advances. At one time, its biological warfare expertise was without parallel in the world, having amassed such a level of knowledge that the government were able to trade it for thermonuclear technology with the Americans. In the seventies, through a combination of political pressure and budgetary constraints, Porton Down's biological wing was shut down. But events were soon to unfold that showed its closure had been dangerously premature. As the eighties came on, and the Cold War reheated, the Ministry of Defence realised Porton needed a biowarfare division again – and fast – and the man they chose to head it and recruit it was David Kelly. He was forty years old.

Ceinwen Williams, David's grandmother, had died in 1970, a few months before the birth of his first daughter, while he was still a doctoral student. She was the only member of the family he grew up with that he ever really mentioned, and he spoke of her with fondness. She lies with his grandfather and his mother Margaret in a shared and unconsecrated plot at Glyntaff Cemetery, a mile or so south of Pontypridd. With her passing, David's last link with South Wales was severed. Her funeral was almost certainly the last time he was ever in town.

It was said that to his family and his oldest friends, David Kelly was always Dai. Perhaps. Certainly, if you listen carefully to his old television appearances, you can just detect now and then the faint traces of a valleys burr, underneath his received pronunciation. In his obituaries his friends often mentioned his fondness for rugby and his passion for the red jersey, but I suspect these traits were largely token attributes. The adult Kelly was his own invention, cut off from his home and also, although it is taboo now to mention such things, his class. He built himself anew in science and public service, read his own name on the honours list, wore linen suits in summer and abroad, took succour from tending his English country garden. Just as much as his missing father and his dead mother, these things are indicators of a powerful transition.

Before I left Pontypridd, I too visited Glyntaff, on a suitably grey and rainy day, and with the plot number from the burials index went off to read their headstones. Except there was nothing there but three wet grassy tumps. Morgan Williams, just like his father before him, was a monumental sculptor whose signature graces hundreds of resting places on that hillside, even several in his own row. But his wife and daughter lie with him uncommemo-rated. David Kelly never bought a marker for the family that had brought him up. It was the sort of fate his new masters would later wish on Kelly himself, once they had quickly rubbished him: to be seldom spoken of and soon forgotten. And in this they have been at least half successful.

In the Bunch of Grapes down the road, no one had any idea who he was.

3

Vectors

The scientists engaged in this work suffer from a sense of sin which makes them itch to justify what they are doing. Some months ago they sought authority to release a statement that it is more merciful to kill a man by inducing a disease than by blowing him to bits by explosive.

CABINET SECRETARY NORMAN BROOK

It has been known by many names, and certainly there will be more to come. It is the nature of things here, this reclassification. Conceived in the cataclysm of the Great War so that the Special Brigade could return the poison gases wafted over no-man's-land by the Kaiser's army, it was christened the Experimental Ground. Today it is the Defence Science and Technology Laboratory, or DSTL. It has reinvented itself at least a dozen other times in between, setting and resetting its sails to steer a course against the prevailing winds of political pressure and popular opinion. In this it has been successful. It endures. Porton Down, as it's always been commonly referred to, has for almost a century been the home of Britain's biological and chemical warfare research, as symbolic of those dark sciences as Shakespeare's Globe is of theatre.

Since its beginnings it has believed itself to be a necessary evil, and so it has always acted accordingly, careful to present the right face to the public while concealing that which would cause outcry.

This has led at times to an institutional dishonesty, to obfuscation, to cynicism.

Sometimes its name has been the only thing to change. When in April 1930 the government ratified the Geneva Protocol, which banned first use of poison gas and germs, openly developing such weapons would have brought widespread condemnation. So Porton responded simply by altering its nomenclature. Its Offensive Munitions Department, for example, became the Technical Chemical Department. As its own official history admits, 'warfare' was 'expunged from official language and titles' and 'defence' substituted in its place.[1] 'Thereafter all offensive work was done under the heading "study of . . . weapons against which defence is required".'

Even the generic name of Porton Down is not entirely accurate. The labs and ranges it describes are nearer the village of Idmiston than Porton, which would perhaps be of no consequence, except it turned out Idmiston had the better pub. Neither was regularly frequented by any of the DSTL workforce, as far as I could make out.

'It doesn't really have any kind of social life,' a former scientific officer had explained to me, a man whose job interview, in fact, had been conducted by David Kelly. 'I mean because of where it is. Once you finish your day you just get in your car and drive home.'

How right he was. On a cold Spring day I arrived at the front gate not much after four on a Friday afternoon and watched them leave in a steady stream of traffic, good civil servants knocking off early for the weekend. Before long it was just me and the security cameras. I didn't much fancy lingering alone under the lenses of the Ministry of Defence police, and so I parked under the steeple of All Saints Church in nearby Idmiston, and set out to trudge the surrounding fields, to glimpse what I could of Porton Down's distant rooftops and smokestacks from the perimeter of its seven-thousand-acre estate.

It has always felt like haunted country to me, Wiltshire and the Salisbury Plain. Its empty rolling landscape is open but occluded by low hills and bands of forestry, its halting expanses marked by the vestiges of unknowable history. Stone circles and primitive earthworks and chalk horses abound, but what they mean can only be guessed at. The people who built them have long disappeared, leaving behind only riddles. The terrain here is rich with secrets, and not all of them ancient, not now that the military has made it their home.

Around Porton, the armed forces are everywhere you look. RAF Brize Norton, the largest Air Force station in the country, is ninety minutes' drive north, the Royal Navy base at Portsmouth, home to two-thirds of the surface fleet, an hour south. The headquarters of the British infantry is in nearby Warminster, as is the Small Arms School. In the northeast of the county lies the mysterious subterranean Corsham Computer Centre, which a Secretary of State for Defence once told Parliament was 'a data-processing facility in support of Royal Navy operations'; if true, most likely to do with our submarine-based nuclear deterrent.

Much nearer, on the other side of the Hampshire border, five minutes down the A343, lies the School of Army Aviation. Nearer again, on Porton's western skyline, is Boscombe Down, the air-craft-testing site now run by QinetiQ, which has one of the longest military runways in the UK. Locals can remember when an experimental US spy plane crashed there in 1994, an incident that has always been strenuously denied in Whitehall. Ten miles north is the tiny town of Tidworth, transformed by the hulking presence of the army's 1st Mechanised Brigade, and there are yet more barracks in the neighbouring village of Bulford. Just beyond those is the Royal School of Artillery at Larkhill.

Civilian life in this swathe of England feels like an intrusion, the quiet villages like foreign bodies against which an immune system is slowly working. They are encroached upon by military land, by trespassing notices and barbed wire, or else they have been taken over, as with Tidworth, their tiny high streets and flinty cottages overwhelmed by a brutalist sea of MoD building, cheap and stark and off limits. Imber, in the middle of the Salisbury Plain Training Area, was evacuated entirely. Surrounded by a hundred and fifty square miles of MoD property, Imber's pub and post office and church and houses have stood lifeless for over sixty years. Stranger still are the villages like Copehill, built solely to train soldiers in urban fighting, never once inhabited. A few years ago, the army erected an Iraqi settlement somewhere out there for the same reason, a shanty town devoid of Shia, with no muezzin but the wind in the trees.

There could be no doubt in the mind of anyone who worked in Porton Down that they had left civvy street behind them. Red triangular road signs that would elsewhere warn of wandering cows or slow-moving tractors here show silhouettes of tanks and helicopters. Academics have waved goodbye to their quad, scientists bidden adieu to unhindered publication and open peer-group review. David Kelly, permanently based here from 1984 to 1991, never moved to the area. He kept the home he lived in when he worked at the Institute of Virology, preferring to stay closer to the spires of Oxford than the empty prohibited plains around Porton, even if it meant he had to spend three hours in a car every day.

Kelly worked in universities, or research centres affiliated to universities, until he was forty: for half his working life, in other words. There was always a touch of the academic about him, and he remained, even on the other side of the Official Secrets Act, something of a quiet educator. His relationship with some colleagues at Porton was not unlike the role he played in supervising doctoral students. He helped guide much of their research, read their drafts, signed off on their final papers. More than any other employee, perhaps, he was a fairly regular attendee of public and not-so-public conferences, in Britain and abroad.

Often these were hosted by academics specialising in the discipline of arms control. He rarely spoke publicly at such events, although he probably knew more than anyone else present. But sometimes, if he felt someone had said something especially egregious, if an opinion had been expressed that was completely misinformed, he would privately offer them a better understanding of the subject afterwards. It was a generosity that did not go unnoticed. The principles of shared knowledge and collaborative effort, the building blocks of science and of learning, remained important to him. If he felt his second life was exciting and important, he sensed some of its limits too: that advances were not progress if they were kept in silos, that truth was not discovery if it stayed behind the wire.

By the railway bridge at the end of Church Road, I found a bridleway that climbed up out of the village and into a series of long fields, all arable, mostly oilseed rape. I saw no ramblers or riders, no one else at all, in fact. The footpath ran atop a railway cutting for the West of England Line, and on the far side of its high embankment, beyond the brambles and the ubiquitous chain-link, began the Porton Down estate. Two white-tailed deer glanced at me from the other side of the fence and then darted off into the depths of the ranges. Three army helicopters buzzed by in loose formation. A single RAF Typhoon took off from the Boscombe Down airstrip up on the other side of the valley.

The week before, two mysterious explosions had triggered a string of 999 calls over eastern England, until eventually the MoD announced that a helicopter near Bath had transmitted an emergency hijack signal. It was a couple of months before the London Olympics, and the authorities were eager to put on a show of strength, so air command had scrambled a pair of Typhoons from a base up in Lincolnshire with the all-clear to go supersonic on a rapid intercept mission. The explosions were the RAF's new Eurofighters shattering the sound barrier. And in the end the signal was no more than a data-entry error by the helicopter pilot, who was ferrying punters back from the Cheltenham Gold Cup and had keyed the wrong numbers into his transponder.

More often than not, when Kelly engaged in his private asides to speakers and students, it was to downplay sensationalism and excited speculation. To delicately correct people when they went too far, to remind them that Official Secrets Act or no, there were things that were scientifically impossible, or that lay in the distant future. There were some feats no military's technology was yet capable of, or ever would be. The laws of nature have sovereignty over the rule of governments.

By all accounts, he was a rare and calming presence because the spectre of biological warfare, clandestine, frightening, seen by a sentimental public as innately evil, has always been the subject of feverish conjecture. People got carried away with themselves. This is a cultural reaction, not just the consequence of government policy, and behind it lie the ancient dread of disease, which has been distilled in us over millennia, and a very modern distrust of science, as something meddlesome and hubristic. The way these traits affect our attitude towards germ warfare is mentioned in most books about the subject. But what these accounts omit is that our outlook is shaped by something else too: namely, a simple vicarious thrill. There is pleasure.

Secret weapons, mad dictators, evil geniuses, doomsday by design: we have lived with these fantasies for generations. They were the stuff of film and fiction long before Downing Street drafted them into dossiers. Porton Down or some variation of it has found its way onto the pages of many an airport thriller; it has been recreated on countless television-studio screen sets. I had seen it portrayed on the small screen and the written page a dozen times before I arrived there that afternoon. But in real life there were no slobbering guard dogs, no armed patrols, no minefields or search-lights or watchtowers; just me, alone in a field, and an endless chain-link fence.

Most of the buildings can be seen, at least in part, from outside the complex, and all of them can be seen in their entirety from Google Maps. They exude no sinister aura. Most look a bit like the sort of units you would see in any out-of-town industrial estate or business park. One of them, a large silver-and-blue construction just visible on the northwest edge, looked like Swansea leisure centre minus the water slides, although actually it was Porton's new maximum-security lab complex. The only reminder of its real purpose was the constant humming of its fans, reverberating through the country air, keeping the rooms inside at negative pressure. So that in the event of a breach, air will flow in only one direction: inwards. The agents inside those labs – nerve gas, anthrax, mustard – cannot be allowed to reach the outside world. If anything leaks – anything at all – you want it sucked back inside, biological agents in particular. Viruses and bacteria are living things, if one microbe escapes it can grow, spread, renew its population, exceed it. Much the same thing, of course, can be said of ideas.

People can perhaps be forgiven for getting the odd notion about a highly classified military research station that works on lethal pathogens. Even those who sit in the House of Commons.

'We visit it, but with eleven members of Parliament and five staff covering a labyrinthine department like the Ministry of Defence and the Armed Forces, it would be quite erroneous of me and misleading for me to say that we know everything that's going on in Porton Down,' Bruce George MP, one-time Chairman of the Defence Select Committee, told the BBC in 1999. 'It's too big for us to know, and secondly, there are many things happening there that I'm not even certain Ministers are fully aware of, let alone Parliamentarians.'

It doesn't help, of course, that Porton Down has felt obliged, as its patriotic duty, to be economical with the *actualité*. When it was working to amass a biological and chemical arsenal, it obscured the fact, to escape controversy. When it finally abandoned such efforts and concentrated instead on defensive countermeasures, it concealed that too, lest it projected weakness. When Tam Dalyell MP revealed that Porton Down had ended its offensive research in 1968, he was nearly expelled from Parliament by the Speaker.

'For years, I believed the Ministry of Defence stitched me up over Porton Down in revenge for other issues I had embarrassed them about,' Dalyell told his biographer, Russell Galbraith. 'Now it's dawning on me that they did it because they were desperate to keep me away ... They wanted to make the subject a no-go zone.'

Most politicians don't need to be kept away from Porton Down. They want as little to do with it as possible, which I suspect is perfectly fine by Porton. No government department likes suffering the close scrutiny of its ministers. So Westminster gives it a wide berth, and in turn Porton Down tries to keep a low profile, which is a lot easier than it used to be. The protesters who periodically appeared outside its front gates are no more. The Quakers, the pacifists, the antivivisectionists and animal-rights people and general assorted lefties, none of them have been seen for decades. For a long time now, the public has been too worried about what strange weapons might await them at the hands of mysterious lunatic foreigners than to fret about what's being formulated in its own labs. Happily, this time the official line is almost certainly correct. Dalyell was right: by the seventies, all offensive-based research here had ended.

Porton these days is no longer the military monolith that it was. Instead it hails itself as a science campus. A third of the complex now belongs to the Health Protection Agency, which is supposed to deal with outbreaks of infectious disease, and another chunk of the estate was carved off in the Thatcher years to become a private-enterprise science park, although all of it stands behind the same high-security perimeter. When the working day ends, the gates come down and the roads are sealed. The Defence Science and Technology Laboratory, all that remains of the old Porton Down, is officially 'the headquarters of a trading fund for the Ministry of Defence' and employs less than eight hundred people, very few of them actual scientists.

The vast majority of the Porton workforce are, in the manner of most bureaucracies, auxiliary: technicians, clerks, bookkeepers, cleaners, security guards. To these, in recent years, have been added a number of positions that grumbling taxpayers would now tend to call non-jobs: diversity officers, conservation managers, green-travel-plan coordinators ('Must have a sound understanding of the environment as it applies to transportation,' read the job ad, 'experience of managing resources to deliver outcomes, and be competent at communication both verbally and in writing'). Unusually for a secret military research base, it even has its own communications team, staffed by public-relations people whose job it is not to talk to the public. I rang one of them up, just on the off-chance, when I was setting about this book.

'Is it about those servicemen we tested on?'[2]

'No,' I said, grateful not to be in the first tier of undesirables.

'No? What is it about then?'

'I was interested in David Kelly.'

'Well we don't want to have anything to do with that.'

Then she spoke enthusiastically about some decontaminating paint they were developing and we hung up. No, Porton Down doesn't want anything to do with David Kelly any more, but there was a time when it did. He played an integral part in re-establishing it as a centre of military biological research after a hiatus that almost saw it closed down entirely. How and why he came to do so is not a simple story. Kelly ended up in Porton because he was carried there by the tug of power politics in far-off places. His transplantation from academic science was a butterfly effect of the private struggles of ambitious men in London and Washington and Moscow. Without these vectors – 'great men' or historical forces, take your pick – his life would have been quite different.

It could so easily have been otherwise. For a brief spell in the seventies, it looked as if the world might break off its dysfunctional love affair with germ warfare for good. In 1969, with the US military mired in Vietnam, President Nixon made a bid to win over war-weary voters with a dramatic surprise speech at Fort Detrick, the home of the American biological-weapons programme.

'The US shall renounce the use of lethal biological agents and weapons, and all other methods of biological warfare,' he announced to the crowd. 'The US will confine its biological research to defensive measures. Mankind already carries in its own hands too many of the seeds of its own destruction.'

It was a shock to most of the military scientists who had turned up to hear him speak, many of whom felt belittled and betrayed, but Nixon's move was good politics. After all, even the US chiefs of staff were no big fans of bioweapons. The Pentagon consensus was that they were impractical and unreliable.

'We'll never use the damn germs,' Nixon confided in his speechwriter William Safire, 'so what good is biological warfare as a deterrent? If somebody uses germs on us, we'll nuke 'em.'[3]

Nixon's view, whether it reflected a moral conviction or not, prevailed beyond the term and a half of his blighted presidency. The British had already abandoned biological weapons, albeit in secret, not long after they had developed their own nukes, and the year before Nixon's announcement they had circulated a draft convention for banning them entirely. The President's unilateral renunciation created sufficient goodwill for over eighty countries to sign up, including the USSR, and so the Biological Weapons Convention (BWC) was born, the first treaty to ban the use, development and stockpiling of an entire category of armaments. But there was no way of checking that countries were actually complying with it, and no penalties for any that demonstrably weren't. Privately, Nixon called it a 'jackass treaty'[4] and 'a silly biological warfare thing which doesn't mean anything'.[5] But it played well to the American electorate.

In its laudable intentions the BWC chimed with the spirit of the times. The Cold War seemed to have reached a crescendo and rolled back. Mutually assured destruction was no longer inevitable. In the West, and in the Soviet Union, there seemed to come a pause for breath. The vast nuclear arsenals poised on either side of the Iron Curtain, already well beyond apocalyptic in size, slowed in their growth. The bushfire wars in Third World countries, the fighting by proxies, the coups and counter-assassinations, that whole strange and secret pantomime, hit a natural intermission. It was the age of détente, of disarmament and diplomacy.

The first Strategic Arms Limitations Talks were followed by the Anti-Ballistic Missile Treaty, then the Biological Weapons Convention, and then the Helsinki Accords. Trade between the communist bloc and the Free World began to pick up from its habitually morbid levels. Much was made of the millions of tonnes of wheat and other grain that were now bought each year from US farms by the USSR, a country that was supposedly the champion of collectivised agriculture. The era's symbolic highpoint was probably Apollo–Soyuz, when Russian and American spacecraft docked in orbit, and cosmonauts and astronauts shook hands in space.

Back on earth, Dr David Kelly was in Warwick on a Medical Research Council fellowship, studying flu with Nigel Dimmock and Roger Avery. It is an unassuming, perhaps even a modest sort of scientist who focuses his or her attentions on something as mundane as flu. There are a host of other diseases that grab more headlines and garner greater funding, yet the influenza virus kills between three and four thousand people in the UK every year, and ten times that number in a major epidemic; but it tends to kill the elderly, and so takes its toll without comment. This was especially true in the seventies, which was long before the NHS began its programme of winter vaccinations, or tabloid stories of Chinese swine flu stoked public hysteria.

Kelly and his colleagues looked at what the flu virus needed to replicate inside the human cell, at the microscopic building blocks it needed to work with if it was going to make you ill. They studied a number of agents that would inhibit its growth: ultraviolet light, an antibiotic called actinomycin D, and more exotically an alkaloid extracted from the 'tree of life', native only to the barren uplands of southern China and Tibet. Camptothecin, as it's called, was then being tested as a possible cancer treatment, and still is today in some parts of the US, although so far it has proved too toxic to be of much medical use.

Kelly's time at Warwick saw no bounding advances but the flu papers he published there have been cited a decent number of times by other academics. The research he helped carry out on the tree of life proved a dead end but it allowed those who followed to better direct their labours. This is the collaborative nature of science, and always has been, a field where all great discoveries are made 'standing on the shoulders of giants', to quote Newton's famous dictum. Kelly was happy to help quietly build a body of knowledge. He didn't need to be the one who rode the crest of the wave into fame and fortune. He knew that such honours were mostly a matter of chance. When his fellowship ended in 1974, he went back to Oxford, where he was able to focus on what had been his primary scientific interest: insect viruses. They absorbed him for the next ten years.

Tom Tinsley, one of the founders of Linacre College, had now set up a Unit of Invertebrate Virology in the city. Tinsley had spent his working life in Britain's West African colonies, studying how exotic plant diseases affected crops and forestry. As Nigerian independence drew near, he came home, settled in Oxford, and focused his studies on the insects that spread these diseases, or which acted as plant pests themselves. It was Tinsley who had supervised Kelly's PhD, and on Kelly's return he appointed him Senior Scientific Officer at his Unit. Tinsley was twenty years Kelly's elder, well known in his field, an accomplished fundraiser and a useful patron. Under Tinsley's leadership the Unit eventually morphed into the Institute of Virology, and the older man made sure to bring Kelly along as a senior member of the inaugural staff.

The invisible infecting the tiny, this was the scale of detail in which Kelly habitually liked to work. He studied a world that was beyond our perception and yet lay all around us, full of unseen forces and hidden signals. Intricate and evolving as this world was, it was only ever apparent to others when it became grossly unbalanced, when microscopic cataclysm tipped it into the realm of the physically observable, when bad harvests or crop failures or ravaged landscapes brought about poverty and hunger. The rest of the time, you needed special knowledge and skills and patience to see it. In some regards it was not unlike the intelligence world he would later join, but it was a peaceful and scholarly pursuit, at a time when lasting peace seemed a likelier prospect than it had for years. That, however, was set to change.

In the States, Gerald Ford had become the first President since Eisenhower to govern an America that was not at war. The party he belonged to was split by a resurgent right, who said that détente was not peace but surrender. These youthful right-wing Republicans believed in propagating a vision of an America in mortal danger, facing an untrustworthy enemy hell-bent on its destruction; all the treaties were therefore lies, all the talk was subterfuge. Communist Russia was out to take over the world. It was old-school fear-mongering of the sort that has launched countless political careers, and at its forefront were two men: Donald Rumsfeld, Ford's Chief of Staff, and Rumsfeld's assistant, Dick Cheney.

What happened next was a presage of things to come. Rumsfeld, Cheney and the new right claimed America was gravely endangered by a foreign country, but the intelligence didn't back them up. The CIA didn't believe that Russia had any significant military advantage at all, let alone one big enough to seek a war with NATO, and it said so. The neoconservatives responded by demanding to see the CIA's actual intelligence which, being intelligence, the CIA was not overly keen on sharing, and so a rather quiet fight broke out.

The Agency was a little different in those days. Its Director was a man called William Colby, no white knight by any means, but a lifelong spook who had started his spying career behind enemy lines in occupied Europe. He wasn't the type of Director who felt compelled to cosy up to the White House, and neither was he prepared to grant politically partisan amateurs unprecedented access to highly classified material. Colby stood his ground, and his staff backed him up.

'Most of us were opposed to it because we saw it as an ideological, political foray,' said Howard Stoertz, the CIA's national intelligence officer for the USSR. 'We knew the people who were pleading for it.'[6]

Consequently, Ford sacked the uncooperative Colby and replaced him with a man so partisan he was actually chair of the committee running the Republican party, a man called George H. W. Bush, a candidate with no intelligence experience but lofty ambitions for personal advancement. Bush promised a worried Congress he wouldn't use the appointment for party politics and was rubber-stamped in. Within months of taking up post he instructed a senior spook, John Paisley, to open up the Soviet files to a select group of neocons. This was dressed up as a 'competitive analysis exercise' for the CIA's benefit, with Agency analysts ('Team A') going up against external analysts ('Team B') to keep staff sharp and fresh. But within the halls of the CIA HQ at Langley, Virginia, few were fooled.

'It is hard for me to envisage how an "independent" ad hoc group of government and non-government analysts could prepare a more thorough, comprehensive assessment of Soviet strategic capabilities than the intelligence community can prepare,' Colby wrote.[7]

Others were more forthright. To Admiral Stansfield Turner, the CIA's Deputy Chief, Team B were 'outsiders with a right-wing ideological bent'.[8] Ray Cline, head of the CIA's analytical branch, called them 'a kangaroo court of outside critics all picked from one point of view'.[9]

They included names like Paul Wolfowitz and Richard Pipes, who, like Dick Cheney and Donald Rumsfeld and George Bush, would come to exert a profoundly negative influence on the world of intelligence men like David Kelly. Unrestrained by civil service protocol, and supported from on high by the party leadership, they used a highly selective and deeply speculative reading of the CIA's intelligence to buttress their own peculiar, endangered vision of the world. And they rode roughshod over any quiet, objective intelligence professional who stood in their way.

'They ate us for lunch,' said CIA officer Sidney Graybeal. 'It was like putting a high school football team against the Washington Redskins. I watched poor GS-13s and -14s [mid-level CIA analysts] subjected to ridicule. They were browbeating the poor analysts.'[10]

'If I had known how adversarial they were going to be,' Stoertz reflected, 'I would have wheeled up different guns.'

According to Graybeal's colleague Melvin Goodman, 'Cheney wanted to drive the Agency so far to the right it would never say no.'[11]

Cheney got his wish. After Colby had left, it never said no to the White House ever again.

Team B was supposed to be secret, but it started leaking within days. Of course it did. Leaking was its main purpose. Without press coverage for their frightening 'findings', Team B would have been unable to lend its hollow credibility to the neoconservative claims. Now, when the new American right cried wolf, they could say that the intelligence bore them out.

After Jimmy Carter won the election for the Democrats, the leaks became a river. According to John Paisley, the CIA officer who liaised with Team B, CIA director Bush was briefing the media personally on Team B's reports by December. Stories about Soviet military superiority swiftly began to fill the front pages. Once Bush found out Carter intended to replace him at the Agency, he even guested on the NBC TV show *Meet the Press*, giving credibility to the Team B analysis.

'No doubt exists about the capabilities of the Soviet armed forces,' Rumsfeld announced, two days before Carter's inauguration. 'The Soviet Union has been busy. They've been busy in terms of their level of effort; they've been busy in terms of the actual weapons they're producing; they've been busy in terms of expanding production rates; they've been busy in terms of expanding their industrial capacity to produce additional weapons at additional rates.'

Alarmism became a cottage industry, even if the details were at times a little vague, or contradictory. The threat of imminent Soviet world domination was chorused by a string of conservative lobbying firms, not least of which was the Committee on the Present Danger, a hawkish interest group from the fifties, reconstituted with many of the Team B analysts on board ('Present

Danger?' its receptionists sang when they answered the phone). The Heritage Foundation was another such entity. Congress began to accept the views of Team B as objective, informed testimony when they were nothing of the sort.

As was their wont, the neocons beat the drum of imminent imaginary war. The CIA's staff, bound by their code of conduct, could only look on in silence. The actual, hard intelligence Team B had seen remained classified, so there was no way of publicly checking their claims, or even finding out specifically what they were. Anne Cahn, a Carter-administration Arms Control official, finally got to read most of the Team B reports in 1992, after a long litigious struggle.

'All of it was fantasy,' Cahn later told the BBC filmmaker Adam Curtis. 'If you go through most of Team B's specific allegations about weapons systems, and you just examine them one by one, they were all wrong.'

Amongst other things, Team B had said that a radar station in Krasnoyarsk was actually a laser weapon. It claimed that Russia was developing charged-particle beams to shoot down satellites. It asserted that because the Soviet navy had no way of acoustically tracking US submarines, it must have secretly invented technology that was far superior. It inflated the number of Soviet Backfire bombers by over 100 per cent. It criticised the CIA for placing too much importance on 'hard data' while arguing that the absence of data to support its own claims was only further proof of the Russians' aggressive duplicity. After all, the Soviets treasured military power 'to an extent inconceivable to the average Westerner', one Team B report informed its readers.[12]

'I don't believe anything in Team B was really true,' Cahn said. But it didn't have to be. The seed of fear had been successfully sown. Ronald Reagan romped to victory in the 1980 presidential elections with a whopping landslide, his foreign policy campaign taken wholesale from the neoconservative playbook.

The scaremongers got their rewards. George H. W. Bush finally became Vice President, Donald Rumsfeld became a Special Envoy to the Middle East, and a massive thirty-three members of the Committee on the Present Danger went on to become officials in the Reagan administration.

'Defence is not a budget issue,' Reagan was to tell his advisers. 'You spend what you need.'

By the end of Reagan's first year, America had the largest peacetime military budget in the history of the world, and over the next four years it increased even more, by over a trillion dollars, all to defeat a creaking communist country that was slowly imploding of its own accord.

Team B's old CIA liaison officer John Paisley wasn't around to see any of it. He had taken his sloop out for a solo sail around Chesapeake Bay one night, and not come back. The Coast Guard found the boat adrift and empty the following day, and a week after that, at the mouth of the Patuxent River, Paisley's bobbing body, weighed down with diving weights and an eight-pound anchor, a bullet hole behind his left ear. Police said it was a suicide brought about by the breakdown of his marriage, though his widow thought otherwise. In America the story was front-page news for a couple of days, then just news, and then finally, unlike John Paisley himself, it sank without trace. Nobody speaks about him any more.

All of this had a knock-on effect in the UK. Although she had far fewer resources to marshal, and would initially be preoccupied by a right-wing junta in the South Pacific, Margaret Thatcher was obliged to follow Team B's lead in exaggerating the Soviet threat. Like the neocons, she too climbed to power portraying the country she wanted to lead as threatened, vulnerable and lost.

'Rarely in the post-war period can our standing in the world have been lower or our defences weaker,' she said, while leading a vote of no confidence against the Labour government of Jim Callaghan. 'The international position is graver than at any time since the 1930s.'

A committed Atlanticist and a radical conservative herself, Thatcher also boosted Britain's defence spending when she came to power, and thus on both sides of the pond the Cold War restarted with a vengeance. In British academia it triggered a renaissance of military research. By 1982, just over seventy university science departments were working on Ministry of Defence research contracts, many in secret.[13] Oxford had several of them. So Kelly didn't join the Cold War: the Cold War came to him. He was swept away from the campus and the quad, from fighting flu and crop pests, and into the defence sector by manufactured alarm, massaged intelligence and militaristic politics. And for the rest of his life these things would never be far from him. They were never far from any of us.

A Gallup poll conducted in 1980 showed that 39 per cent of the UK population believed a nuclear war – that is to say, the end of the world – would occur in their lifetime. Whatever your views, left or right, hawk or dove, the neoconservative vision of impending Armageddon, of civilisation in the balance, had become the prevailing reality. For an apolitical microbiologist like Kelly, this could have been no more than background, but given the West's paranoia about Soviet strength, about Soviet advances, about Soviet strategy and intention, there came, inevitably, fears of Soviet germ warfare.

The same year that Team B got access to raw CIA data, anonymous intelligence sources began briefing journalists that the Russian military was working on lethal viruses and microbes in six different germ factories.[14] American spy satellites, they said, had captured images of guarded complexes with railway lines for special tanker carriages. Anonymous sources spoke of yet more anonymous sources, who they said had discovered the Soviets were working on anthrax, smallpox, plague, tuberculosis, yellow fever and diphtheria. Yet more unidentified experts said they believed the Soviets were also experimenting with the recently discovered deadly super-viruses Lassa, Ebola, and Marburg.[15] Journalists began to write of the 'germ warfare gap' the same way they had of the 'missile gap'.[16] The media, then as now, never turned down a scare story about the country's enemy *du jour*. It was fed to them entirely by unnamed Washington contacts and it was never corroborated, but this didn't seem to bother anyone. It was as Team B had told the CIA: the absence of evidence reinforced their claims, it didn't undermine them. If America really did have a mortal foe hell-bent on world domination, then it was taken as read such an enemy would want to keep its WMD secret, so it could launch a surprise attack. Any enemy of America was, by definition, believed to be grimly oppressive and inherently duplicitous, so hiding WMD would be well within its capabilities as well as its character.

Jimmy Carter's administration refrained from stoking these fears. Such suspicions were still perhaps a tad too nebulous in substance, too bleak and belligerent in their outlook. But by the dawn of the Reagan Revolution, two very different stories from two very different parts of the world had emerged to support the idea the Soviets were breaking the Biological Weapons Convention. Like the stories that had come before them, they were born out of hearsay, out of a mishmash of second- or third-hand accounts, but they would trigger official accusations and reignite biological-warfare research in Britain and America. They were the justification for David Kelly's new job. Two stories, but only one of them was true. The other was a fabrication.

The first was picked up in Frankfurt, from East Germans recently returned from Russia. They told of how deep inside the Motherland, far beyond the Ural Mountains, dozens or hundreds of people had suddenly taken ill and died in the city of Sverdlovsk in April 1979. Their bodies had been either speedily cremated, carried off to Leningrad in lead coffins, or disposed of in mass graves and covered in concrete. The Soviet news agency Tass eventually announced they had died from eating uninspected meat from anthrax-infested animals, but everywhere people wondered. Sverdlovsk was a major military–industrial centre, full of heavily guarded factories that could easily lend themselves to bioweapons production.[17] If that was their purpose, then anthrax would surely be the organism of choice for its military scientists, just as it had been in Britain and America.

Tass decried such speculation as 'poisonous propaganda'. Russian health authorities had responded instantly by warning citizens to eat only officially inspected meat and to stay away from stray animals. Scores of soldiers had been dispatched to shoot all wild animals in the area, and every uninspected carcass had been incinerated. A team of investigating Soviet doctors had published their findings in a Moscow medical journal, having traced the outbreak to two families who shopped at an illegal market, and a third who had eaten infected sheep. And it was pointed out that naturally occurring outbreaks of anthrax were not uncommon in the Sverdlovsk area: there had been over 150 in the last thirty years. The locals called it 'Siberian ulcer'.

Diplomatically, the Sverdlovsk situation now reached an impasse, but in the West doubts lingered. Contaminated food should have caused a more random distribution of deaths. If the outbreak wasn't a natural epidemic then the narrow spread of fatalities could only have been caused by a release of highly processed, finely powdered, extremely virulent anthrax. This wasn't a case of somebody knocking over a test tube or pricking themselves with a needle. It pointed to an advanced biological warfare programme gone badly wrong.

The US State Department stated simply that it believed the deaths weren't natural. The House Intelligence Oversight Committee held a series of classified meetings and then reported that the Tass account was 'incomplete at best' and that the likelihood Russia was breaking the Biological Weapons Convention was 'fairly good'. The Senate's Foreign Relations Committee passed a resolution urging the President to push the Russians for a fuller explanation, but Jimmy Carter, preoccupied with negotiations on nuclear weapons, let the matter lie. The truth behind the Sverdlovsk anthrax lay buried with the bodies it had killed, nine hundred miles from Moscow, far from prying Western eyes.

The second set of allegations about Soviet biowarfare began on the other side of the world, in the teeming refugee camps and covert guerrilla bases that sprang up on Thailand's hot, wet, mountainous borders after the Pathet Lao seized power in Laos in 1975 and the Vietnamese invaded Kampuchea three years later. The displaced communities in these overnight shanty towns represented the last remaining pro-Americans left in Indochina, and they were tended to by a miscellany of right-wing US outfits who desperately believed their country's long and bloody relationship with the area could still, somehow, be made good. The Heritage Foundation had a presence there, and so too did several missionary and humanitarian groups with ties to the CIA.

Amongst this chaos, these organisations hit upon a story that would draw attention to these people's plight, and point too to the hidden hand of the evil Soviet Empire, wielding a new and mysterious weapon. Camp workers told how Hmong tribesmen, the CIA's indigenous mercenaries in its Secret War in Laos, had been sprayed with strange substances from enemy helicopters and artillery. Symptoms ranged from chest pains, shortness of breath, clouded vision, vertigo, vomiting, dizziness, diarrhoea and dermatitis to sudden convulsive death through massive haemorrhage. The gas was described alternately as being yellow, blue, red, black, white, green or colourless; sometimes it was referred to as smoke, other times as powder; one man said it killed plants within three days, a second said it left plants untouched, a third that it only hurt people if they ate food or drank water that the gas had contaminated.

Eager American officials visited the camps from 1979 onwards and collected testimony in a credulous and haphazard way, without attempting to cross-question or even indentify eyewitnesses. The Hmong, much like the Montagnards before them and the Afghan mujahideen who came after, were romanticised by right-wing Americans into noble savages who fought communism out of an innate natural goodness. Their puzzling testimony was accepted without question. At the end of the year there was a presentation to Congress, but it neither excited nor convinced. A subsequent UN investigation found little by way of physical proof, and there the affair might have ended, had Reagan and the New

Right not risen to power in Washington. For them, proof had never been something to stand in the way of politics, and this unverified but clearly illegal technology was happily and officially added to the catalogue of communist sins.

In September 1981, Reagan's Secretary of State, Alexander Haig, was in West Berlin, trying to placate the Federal Republic. Living right on the front line of the Cold War, which had divided their country, West Germans had been alarmed by American rhetoric about the need to confront the Evil Empire. Contrary to neoconservative policy, Bonn still favoured détente, and so Haig's visit was marked by the biggest anti-American demonstrations in Germany since the Vietnam War. When he spoke at the city hall there were thirty thousand chanting demonstrators outside. Haig decided to warn them about what Ivan was capable of: this strange, 'lethal' weapon that was being used in Laos and Kampuchea and (he added) in Afghanistan.

'We have now found physical evidence,' he announced. 'It has been analysed and found to contain abnormally high levels of three potent mycotoxins – poisonous substances not indigenous to the region and which are highly toxic to man and animals.'

Finally the Western media ran with the story, and it was probably a journalist's touch that reduced the Hmong's confused and multicoloured descriptions of this mystery weapon to a simple, headline-grabbing nickname: Yellow Rain. The Soviet Union dismissed it out of hand: Haig was 'a mean and vicious slanderer' and his story had been contrived to provide a pretence for Reagan's military build-up. Then it became a simple matter of us versus them, with loyal neoconservative appointees in and outside the State Department lining up to parrot Haig's accusations. James A. Phillips at the Heritage Foundation told the papers the evidence was now irrefutable.

'The Soviets have crossed a line that even Adolf Hitler, in the darkest days of World War Two, refused to cross,' Phillips added. Very soon the mainstream American media were making the same assertions.

'Except to the willingly obtuse, the evidence is conclusive,' editorialised the *Wall Street Journal*, on Haig's return to Washington. 'The Soviets have long been engaged in the development and production of chemical and biological weapons.'

The UN promised to mount a second, more thorough investigation, and Haig said he would soon present his own detailed report to Congress, so the world waited. But the second UN team came back from South East Asia as nonplussed as the first, and by the time Haig spoke to Congress in March the science behind his claims was looking a little shaky. It turned out that mycotoxins occurred naturally in plant fungus. They were harmful, but only in large doses: a human would have to snort a spoonful of the stuff to be affected by it on the battlefield, which made it an unusual choice for a biological warfare agent.

Haig never did produce his 'physical evidence' before Congress. Instead he made it exempt from the Freedom of Information Act, but the truth crept out, slowly. Someone – it was never quite clear who (possibly the Pentagon or the State Department or the CIA or the Thai government) – had gathered twig and leaf samples from the site of an alleged Yellow Rain attack, where the foliage had been speckled with a strange yellow residue. The gunk was promptly circulated for testing. Some samples had no mycotoxins at all while others contained only a few parts per million, a truly negligible presence. However, in a few cases toxin levels were so high that scientists wondered if the material hadn't been tampered with. The Australian Defence Department came right out and said they thought they were fakes. They were. Quizzed by *New Scientist* magazine on the matter, a State Department official later admitted some samples had been deliberately spiked, but only to 'test the scientists' analytical procedures'.[18]

Didn't that raise doubts about US impartiality?

'People must trust the credibility of the State Department,' was all the source said.

But if this residue wasn't a toxin, then what was it? The State Department, the CIA and the Pentagon weren't telling. So a

collection of British, Australian, Canadian and American civilian
scientists met in Ottawa and quickly figured it out: they were
pollen deposits. Just the sort of thing on which plant fungus likes
to grow.

Undeterred, Fort Detrick said the Soviets had obviously incor-
porated pollen into the design of their mystery weapon because
its grains were small enough to be inhaled, and it made an excellent disguise: proof, once again, of how advanced and duplicitous
the Russians could be. In fact, as the scientists discovered, the
pollen from the samples was native to the trees of South East Asia.
So according to the US, the Russian deception had involved
covertly harvesting tonnes of pollen from Indochina, taking it
back to secret bases in the Motherland, infusing it with near-
harmless levels of naturally occurring mycotoxins, loading it into
munitions, training foreign soldiers in its use, and then shipping
it back to Vietnam – all without anyone noticing. It was a ridicu-
lous hypothesis, not least because no trace of these munitions had
been found.

No toxin-carrying shell, rocket, missile or grenade has ever been
discovered in Kampuchea, Laos or Afghanistan, not even a fragment of one. Neither, in terms of military evidence, had the
Americans been able to turn up any surveillance photos, nor any
relevant signal intercepts, nor any supporting Soviet or Vietnamese
documentation. The Australian Secret Intelligence Service, desperate to discover what was really going on in its own back yard,
paid an agent in Kampuchea ten thousand dollars because he'd
stumbled upon an RPG with a liquid payload. It turned out the
device was a perfectly normal RPG that had been dumped in a
paddy field; the liquid inside was nothing but swamp water. Even
then, the Reagan administration remained adamant that the
Soviets were using a new toxin weapon. How else, asked the true
believers, could you possibly explain these strange pollen deposits
without attributing them to a secret communist biological warfare
unit?

Eventually the Professor of Natural Sciences at Harvard,

Matthew Meselson, and Tom Seeley, Professor of Biology at Yale, visited the camps and found out. It was bee shit. Under the microscope the pollen grains were empty, some had collapsed outer shells, and further tests showed high levels of uric acid: all this stuff had passed through an insect's digestive tract. The Massachusetts Institute of Technology and the Australian intelligence service both agreed. It led to a heated war of words.

Chester Mirocha, Professor of Plant Pathology at the University of Minnesota, told journalists that Meselson had jumped 'a large abyss from science to politics ... I think he went out there oriented as a political animal, and this to me is a little bit dangerous in terms of good science.' He dismissed the 'bee theory' as 'childish' and 'absurd', and said tens of thousands of the insects would have needed to defecate in an area en masse, which was 'ridiculous'. Yet this was exactly how bees behaved. If high winds have confined them to their hive they will swarm for a 'cleansing flight', defecate an appropriate distance away from their home, and return. As it happens, Mirocha could have found this out just by walking across his own campus, as the University of Minnesota has had one of the world's leading bee research labs since the twenties. Anyone there could have told him the truth, but instead he preferred to talk to the papers.

Mirocha was one of the very few real scientists to publicly defend the existence of a 'Yellow Rain' weapon, but then he had also been the US military's primary tester on their foliage samples from Kampuchea. He remained a fierce supporter of this supposed Soviet toxin spray even as the science suggesting it was widely discredited. He is retired now, and the communists are gone. There is peace in South East Asia, even if the Hmong remain a people in limbo (many, as it happens, were resettled in Mirocha's Minnesota). I wondered if maybe, after all this time, the professor had become a touch less ardent in his analysis. We exchanged a few polite emails on the subject before he came clean on his outlook.

The real issue wasn't whether there was a weapon or not, he told me. The real focus was on the welfare of civilian populations suffering under communistic regimes, on minorities like the Hmong, who were being shot and bombed by their new government.

'If publicity on possible mycotoxin involvement decreased these attacks,' Mirocha told me, 'then a humanitarian purpose would have been served.'

It was the nearest he came to an admission that for him, as for so many others, perhaps even for most of us, the consequences are more important than the truth. To this day, the location of the lab that secretly spiked the foliage samples for the State Department remains unknown.

Rod Barton, one of Kelly's fellow United Nations Special Commission (UNSCOM) inspectors, was a junior analyst at Australia's Department of Defence when America told the world it had discovered a new Soviet toxin weapon. He attended meetings with British and American intelligence at which Mirocha was present. At a round-table meeting hosted by the UK's Defence Intelligence Staff in late 1982, Barton's attempts to make sense of the Hmong's bizarre accounts were rudely shouted down by the Americans.

'How can there be doubts?' a senior CIA officer yelled at him. 'How can you question the refugees who are the victims in this?'

It was at that moment, Barton said, that he understood that intelligence analysis was not about science but politics. It was something that Kelly himself would later come to learn.

In the end, despite the bold assertions of ambitious politicians and a supine State Department and a much cowed CIA, despite a great number of stern, patriotic editorials, the truth became known. Journalists beat their way to the refugee camps, where they discovered first-hand how problematic the Hmong's testimony was. This isolated people had always been prone to archaic beliefs and superstitions, but a decade of war had abruptly exposed them to modern technology in the most brutal of ways.

The Hmong lived in a world of evil spirits, and phenomena like planes and helicopters were simply added to the pantheon. They had an almost mythological fear of aircraft and anything that fell from them, because, and Chester Mirocha was quite right about this, the Hmong had been the victims of relentless and over-whelming aerial attacks. But not from the communists. Decades later, the US Air Force admitted to dropping more ordnance on Laos than it had throughout the whole of the Second World War. America's Secret War had turned that tiny country into the most bombed place on earth.

Little wonder that in the teeming, traumatised exodus that fol-lowed American withdrawal, strange tales abounded. Years before the Yellow Rain story broke, Walter M. Haney, a camp volunteer, heard talk of 'gold and silver poisoned paper' that made people drunk when they touched it. Days after their exposure, he was told, they would fall sick and die.[19] Working a full decade before the Reagan government's Cold War paranoia about Yellow Rain, Haney was able to soberly reflect that it was probably just metal-lic radar chaff from American planes.

Similarly, the Australian author and anthropologist Grant Evans arrived in the camps in 1982 and found them aflame with gossip about a communist-made disease called Rohk Yued. Vietnamese spies, Evans was earnestly informed, were rubbing a special powder onto the Hmong's underwear which would cause the vic-tims' genitals to expand to over ten times their normal size. Drinking dog's blood apparently worked as an antidote.[20] Unsurprisingly, Haig hadn't seen fit to mention poisonous paper or Rohk Yued in his speech at Berlin or in his report to Congress.

The evidence the State Department had amassed for Yellow Rain attacks in Kampuchea and Afghanistan was even flimsier than what they'd obtained from the Hmong in Laos. A gas mask with a Soviet star on it, two defecting Vietnamese soldiers singing for their supper, a couple of vague mujahideen eager for arms: that was it.

The US government has never retracted its Yellow Rain claims. In fact it repeated them throughout the eighties, even claiming it had spread to Iraq and Iran, and right up until the late nineties papers published by both the USAF and the US Army Medical

Department referred with absolute certainty to the use of Soviet mycotoxins. The existence of such weapons was routinely used to justify the Pentagon's chemical and biological warfare budget. In the scientific world Yellow Rain was comprehensively rubbished within two years of Haig's speech, but this didn't really seem to matter. The media and the masses had been given a story, and it never quite went away. After all, a secret toxin weapon can command our imaginations far better than a poison-producing plant fungus growing in bee excrement. In parts of South East Asia Yellow Rain has gained a mythic, folkloric status. Many Kachin in northern Burma, who have been fighting a long struggle for independence, insist the Burmese junta attacked them with Yellow Rain in 2011.

'All the green leaves which were affected by the unusual rain were burnt up and most of the insects were killed a couple of days after the rain,' reported the *Kachin Post*. Children had apparently developed an inexplicable cough. Photos of leaves affected by Yellow Rain were posted online. They look identical to leaves shat on by bee swarms.

This, as Carl Sagan has observed, is the practical definition of pseudoscience: that it is more easily contrived than real science, more easily presented, and that it pushes real science out, often because at some level it relies on an emotional appeal. In the months preceding David Kelly's recruitment by Porton Down it was precisely this blend of wilful self-delusion and deliberate propaganda that was being propagated by the leadership of Britain's most powerful ally. Porton Down, characteristically, stayed compliantly silent, though it knew full well the truth. It let itself be marginalized. The politics of the age were plainly changing, and Porton's scientists tried to keep out of the way.

Weapons of mass destruction, especially biological ones, which are little understood, were becoming more useful as headlines than as bombs. They were at their most potent in the minds of the masses than in military arsenals. The idea was becoming more important than the reality; the fear more important than the threat;

the consequences more important than the truth. Intelligence stopped becoming a way to know your enemy and became a way to convince your electorate.

In the short term, Sverdlovsk and Yellow Rain were good for Porton Down. They were the catalyst behind Downing Street's decision to restart Britain's biological warfare research. Unfortunately, Whitehall had only just finished shutting it down. The month of the Sverdlovsk anthrax outbreak the Ministry of Defence had handed Porton Down's entire Microbiological Research Establishment (the MRE) over to the Department of Health and Social Security.

When the MRE was built after the Second World War it was the biggest brick building in Europe. Its laboratory benches accounted for over 90 per cent of the country's teak imports, at a time when the country was not exactly overflowing with foreign currency reserves. In a period of national austerity it was given considerable operational freedom and significant funding: until Britain acquired the bomb in 1957, biological warfare was the only meaningful weapon of mass destruction it could wield. By 1980 all this had gone, the MRE had been transferred out to Public Health, and its ex-director, Professor Robert Harris, had been sacked. Porton Down intended to whittle its military microbiologists down to ten, the smallest number thought necessary to maintain the minimum knowledge base.[21] But sacking military microbiologists can lead to a lot of classified knowledge floating around. In the end, the MoD just gave the scientists nothing to do and hoped that most would eventually seek jobs elsewhere. The more conscientious of them tended to sit in the staff library and read. There were no labs for them to work in.

By the time Sverdlovsk and Yellow Rain germ warfare appeared in the papers, the MoD had all but extinguished its biological weapons expertise. It had done so with such bureaucratic ineptitude that its former scientific employees could not easily be lured back. So behind the scenes, individuals untainted by any association with the facility's controversial closure began to put out discrete feelers to people they considered viable candidates. One such recruiter was a Cabinet-level insider called Harry Smith. He was a well-known scientist and academic in his own right, but he was also ex-Porton Down himself, having worked there as a Senior Scientific Officer during its fifties and sixties Cold War heyday, under its Chief Superintendent David Henderson. Overlooked for promotion as successor to Henderson, he quit for academia, and was soon offered the chair of Birmingham University's Microbiology Department. He accepted, on the condition they built him a high-security lab for working on highly contagious viruses.

Freed from the secrecy of Porton Down, Smith's star shone. He was elected to Fellowship of the Royal Society, and became president of both the Society for General Microbiology and the International Congress of Microbiology, but he never left the military entirely behind him. He continued to help out, to advise, to take care of 'little things'. He had his own locked office at Birmingham, with its own special locked filing cabinet to which only Smith had access. His secretary was given a name to contact at the MoD if he ever went missing, and two male colleagues at the university were given instructions as to what to do with the cabinet if Smith or his Department experienced any kind of sudden emergency.[22] These are standard security measures for any scientist who has ever done classified work for the Foreign Office or the Ministry of Defence.

'That's exactly what it's like,' said a former chemist and retired professor, with a sigh of recognition, when I spoke to him about Harry Smith. 'You do a little bit of secret or sensitive work for the government and it follows you around for the rest of your life.'

I wonder sometimes how many of them there are, in science departments and research councils up and down the country; I spoke to several.

Smith's tenure at Birmingham was not without incident. In 1966, smallpox escaped from his labs, probably through a service duct, and twenty-five people ended up in hospital. It happened again in 1978, and killed an anatomy photographer called Janet Parker. People wondered if perhaps this might have been related to some sort of secret military research.

'There is the deepest suspicion that Janet Parker did not die of variola major [smallpox] and we feel there might have been unauthorised experimentation,' said Clive Jenkins, General Secretary of the lab technicians' trade union to which Parker belonged. 'We feel there might have been unauthorised experimentation with other dangerous pathogens or recombinant techniques.'

The official inquiry was headed by Sir Keith Dumbell, who said Parker had died from a rare but natural strain of the virus. Yet Dumbell was an old research colleague of Smith's lab manager, Professor Henry Bedson, and the pair of them had already published research papers about how they had engineered a smallpox–cowpox hybrid, 'a distinct new type of virus', while at Liverpool.[23] When Bedson heard there was going to be a government inquiry into the Birmingham smallpox outbreak, he slit his throat in his shed with a pair of gardening shears. Intrusive media attention was held to be a contributing factor. His wife told the coroner he was 'tired, weary, concerned, but not depressed'. Janice Kelly would describe David at the Hutton Inquiry in almost the same words: 'tired, subdued, but not depressed'.

Whatever the dangers of Smith's labs, it was his pioneering presence at Birmingham University that attracted young postgrads like David Kelly, who did his master's in virology there. How much Smith and Kelly had to do with each other is hard to say; the university was unable to find his master's thesis in the archives, but if David wasn't aware of Porton when he arrived at Birmingham he certainly was by the time he left. During Kelly's time there Smith invited Dr Thomas Inch, a former colleague from Porton Down, to come and speak to the science students, and when Inch arrived he was met with a sit-down protest (it was 1968, and campuses everywhere were angry). Undergrads demanded to know why Porton Down was allowing its patented CS gas to be used against Vietnamese villagers and student demonstrators in Paris.

'Because we need the money,' Inch is reported to have replied.

By the early eighties, Harry Smith was, on top of his other duties, senior microbiology adviser to the Ministry of Defence, and from 1982 onwards he was sniffing out potential candidates to lead Porton's new microbiology lab. When he reconnected with Kelly, now the number two man at Oxford's Institute of Virology, he knew he had found a contender. Kelly might not have been tempted, but the previous year Tom Tinsley, the Institute's founder and director, had suffered a triple heart attack while attending a conference in Strasbourg. The board had begun casting around for his replacement, and Kelly had a feeling it wasn't going to be him. It was the same situation Harry Smith had been in at Porton Down when Henderson quit. Smith, at roughly the same age Kelly was now, had responded by changing his sector, a decision that he had never had cause to go back on. He persuaded Kelly to do the same, albeit in reverse: to go from academia into defence.

It's interesting to reflect that Smith, Tinsley and their protégé Kelly were all grammar school boys from provincial working-class backgrounds. Tinsley, as noted earlier, was the son of a Lancashire farmer, Smith the son of a Northamptonshire bookmaker, Kelly's closest equivalent to a father figure carved gravestones in the Welsh valleys. Both Tinsley and Smith were roughly the same age as his real, absent father.

Recruitment adverts went out to a few select publications in late 1983. The *New Scientist* ran one in November, only a few months after it had published an ad for Tom Tinsley's successor.

The Ministry of Defence (it read) wanted a Superintendent for its Defence Microbiology Division at the Chemical Defence Establishment, Porton Down, 'to be the focal point for work on the hazards of attack by microbes including viruses and microbial products and for defence against them. Work includes oversight of broadly based microbiological research, liaison with Civil Service departments and keeping watch on all developments in the microbiological field.'

'Experience in the molecular biology of toxin production or toxin action would be advantageous,' the advert added. Even if the British secretly knew that Yellow Rain was spurious, Soviet agents had recently made a series of assassination attempts using the castor-oil protein ricin. Most famously, the Bulgarian dissident Georgi Markov died after he was shot by a tiny, perforated, ricin-filled bearing which his killer had apparently fired from a converted umbrella on Waterloo Bridge. Ten days before, assassins had tried to kill another Bulgarian defector, Vladimir Kostov, on an escalator in the Paris Metro, using the same technique. Boris Korczak, a Lithuanian–Pole who the CIA may have run as a double agent inside the KGB, was allegedly hit by an identical ricin pellet in a supermarket in Virginia. It was the work of Frank Beswick at Porton, a fellow Welshman and future Kelly colleague, that helped police and intelligence make the link. Without the eagle eyes of Scotland Yard's scientific officer Robin Keeley, who spotted the 1.7mm pellet, and Beswick's forensic testing at the Porton labs, Markov's death might have been judged a natural one. Instead there was an inquest and the coroner ruled he had been unlawfully killed.

According to the advertisement, Kelly's new job was at the Senior Principal Scientific Officer level, with an upper pay scale of £19,315.[24] This was exactly the same rank and salary that he commanded at Oxford, so it seems clear his motivations for moving weren't mercenary. What he heard at last was someone asking him to take the helm. The glamour of classified work, the vigour of the military world, as well as Porton Down's scientific reputation, all probably helped convince him too. He told Smith he was interested, the ministry offered him the job, and MI5 set about his 'developed vetting', a process that would take up the next six months.

When Kelly came he brought a number of his Oxford staff with him. It shows not just how urgently Porton Down sought to rebuild its biological expertise, but also how trusted Kelly was both by his colleagues and by his new employer.

'It was a big scalp,' a friend of Smith's told me, when we discussed the deal he'd struck with David Kelly. 'It was a coup.'

Kelly's first task was to ensure that the Chemical Defence
Establishment had the right laboratories and facilities for the study
of dangerous microorganisms, and from there he went on to
direct and formulate their entire programme of research. He
began work in the summer of 1984, and he was from the very
outset of his second career Britain's most senior practising military microbiologist.

It seemed to me, on the face of it, a rather sudden transition. I
pored through the papers Kelly published before he disappeared
from public view, searching for a sign that his career had already
touched upon the world of biological warfare. Had Kelly any deal-
ings with Porton Down before he became its Superintendent? It
seemed unlikely, considering the man spent most of his time
working with insect viruses, but the strange truth is that military
scientists have long been interested in insects.

In the thirties and forties, Britain, Germany and France all
researched the crop-destroying Colorado beetle as a strategic agent
(it was the Nazi effort to develop insecticides to defend against
an Allied crop-pest attack that led German scientists to discover
nerve gas). When the Imperial Japanese invaded Manchuria, the
infamous Unit 731 under General Ishii Shiro dropped ceramic
bombs filled with plague-infected fleas or cholera-carrying flies
onto Chinese cities, triggering epidemics that killed over a
quarter of a million people.[25] After hostilities ended, Ishii faked
his own death to escape a war crimes trial, but he was found by
the Americans, who offered him immunity from prosecution
in exchange for his expertise, and soon the US was secretly developing its own insect biowarfare programme, funded by hundreds
of millions of dollars from the Department of Defense.[26]

In 1954, the US army tested specially designed bombs packed
with payloads of fleas in the middle of the Utah desert. The next
year in the wetlands outside Savannah, Georgia, they tried the
same thing with mosquitoes, and found the insects bit targets over

half a mile from the drop site. These insects weren't intended to be mere irritants. The US had discovered a way to infect mosquitoes with yellow fever, an incapacitating disease that causes fevers and nausea and in almost a fifth of cases, death, after organ failure, bleeding from the eyes, and massive intestinal haemorrhaging. A single bite is sufficient for transmission and there is no known cure. By 1960, Fort Detrick had purpose-built facilities that could rear half a million fever-carrying mosquitoes a month, and had drawn up blueprints for a production line that could increase that output two hundredfold.[27] Meanwhile, engineers were designing plant that could produce 50 million fleas every week.[28]

Tests like this continued in Utah, Georgia, Florida and elsewhere throughout the sixties. The US navy became involved in 1965, when Operation Magic Sword, conducted off the US southeastern seaboard, showed that swarms of yellow-fever mosquitoes could be kept alive for ocean crossings, and, with the right winds, could travel almost four miles from ship to shore. Entomological warfare (or EW) was a going concern right up until President Nixon unilaterally banned the US biowarfare programme. But all this remained top secret until a partially redacted US army report entered the public domain in 1997. Costs per EW death, the report noted approvingly, could be as little as 29 cents or less.[29]

Some governments suspected that America's EW programme hadn't been entirely experimental. The Colorado beetle arrived in Soviet farmland for the first time in the early years of the Cold War, and in large numbers, which several communist countries attributed to covert US activity. Equally controversial were the accusations made during the Korean War that the States had attempted to spread disease above the 38th parallel, through a menagerie of air-dropped insects. The US has always decried these charges as propaganda, although the Koreans were able to back their claims with more evidence than the Americans were later to supply in support of Yellow Rain. The possibility that the USAF dropped disease-ridden bugs on North Korea is still bitterly contested by both sides today.

In 1997, Cuba officially protested to the UN that the US had repeatedly and covertly attacked it with crop-destroying insects. The following year Iraqi state media blamed US agents for a screw-worm infestation it said had infected fifty thousand farm animals in a month (screw worm is native to Central and South America and had never been seen in Iraq before). Who do you believe? Which side are you on? This vortex of conspiracy and counter-conspiracy is the sine qua non of biological warfare. It inhabits a grey plane full of allegations and rebuttals, where everything is contested, and every argument has an element of propaganda on each side. But what cannot be denied is that entomological warfare can be horribly effective, and it was the subject of extensive research and development by several countries.

Insects as disease delivery systems? In a way, it was brilliant. The mosquito, the tick, the fly: these are abundant, dirt-cheap, naturally occurring miniature homing missiles, self-designed to perfection over tens of millions of years of evolution. Load them with a pathogen, and epidemics would ensue. Gas masks would be no protection. The enemy might never know he had been attacked. Should suspicions arise, they would be almost impossible to prove. 'Vectors' became the biowarfare buzzword, the big thing: using a legion of natural hosts and forces to turn a planted pathogen into an epidemic.

Because of Britain's intelligence-sharing arrangement with the US, Porton Down would certainly have known about Fort Detrick's work on vectors, but did it ever do any research of its own?

David Kelly's unofficial recruitment officer, Harry Smith, left the MRE because he was beaten to the top job by a man called Gordon Smith.[30] Gordon Smith was a well-known authority on insect viruses, appointed at a time when Fort Detrick's EW studies were in full swing. Before arriving at Porton, Smith had spent years in Kuala Lumpur studying how a certain mosquito transmitted yellow fever, and testing vaccines on Malaysian soldiers. Ostensibly this was entirely a civilian study, but it was conducted at the same time the US military were testing the same species of mosquito as a way of spreading yellow fever deliberately, and what's more, outbreaks of yellow fever had never occurred in Malaysia. The country had no reason to fear the disease. It isn't hard to perceive a possible military dimension to Smith's research.

Smith was only at Porton Down for four years before he left to become Dean of the London School of Hygiene and Tropical Medicine, but one of his lasting legacies was the Arbovirus Epidemiology Unit he set up there.[31] It continued to research insect vectors up until Whitehall closed down the MRE. On 19 February 1975, *The Times* reported that it was working in collaboration with the Unit of Invertebrate Virology, where Kelly was senior scientific officer.

'Safety tests are nearly complete on a group of viruses that are to be released to infect pests responsible for much of the damage to cereal crops and grasslands,' the article said. It explained how as much as a third of the food production in developing countries was destroyed by pests, how this affected the world's poorest and disadvantaged peoples, and how using viruses instead of pesticides would be a lot cheaper, given 'the growing shortage of the chemical substances' used to make such things.

Rather than spraying fields and farms with dangerous chemicals like organophosphates (from which the Nazis had invented nerve gas), the idea was to perpetrate germ warfare against the insects instead. Viruses could be released that would kill only specific crop pests and leave other organisms untouched. It was eco-friendly and potentially it was safer too, although the safety tests to release such viruses were incredibly strict. They needed a good amount of specially demarcated land and a high-security perimeter.

'That's why there are so few viral pesticides available,' Professor Hugh Evans explained to me. Evans was a colleague of Kelly's at the Oxford Unit, and is now Head of Forest Research in Wales. 'It costs so much money to do the checks. If Porton hadn't offered to help I doubt we would have been able to do it at all.'

After that, the biggest challenge was infecting the unwanted insects in a way that would spread the virus as quickly and thoroughly as possible. It's this which explains why the military had taken such an interest in a project intended to benefit impoverished countries, because if you can infect insects with a virus that will kill them, you can infect insects with a virus that will kill people. The methods are exactly the same.

'If you were a microbiologist at a foreign intelligence agency, for example, and you went through the open literature it wouldn't be difficult to infer what Porton Down's points of interest might be,' said Philip Entwistle, another Oxford entomologist who worked alongside Kelly and Evans.[32] 'At the time it never crossed my innocent little mind.'

Kelly and his team in Oxford were refining techniques that had already been secretly researched decades ago by the military for far less peaceful purposes. They were bumping up against the hidden world of biological warfare: America's secret deal with General Ishii, and the hundreds of millions of dollars it had subsequently spent on entomological warfare, were still classified. The *Times* article mentioned that Kelly's Unit were studying three possible infection techniques: spraying an area with an aerosol of the virus in a liquid suspension, spraying larvae with a virus in solution so they would hatch into infected adults, and luring insects to virus-contaminated bait which could be placed in situ.

Most of it had been done before. Twenty years ago, Fort Detrick found that if you exposed mosquito larvae to sufficient amounts of virus-infected plasma, they would grow into virus-infected adults, capable not only of killing humans but of turning other mosquitoes into killers too. It wasn't something you tended to see in nature, but it worked in the lab. Even earlier than that, Dr Guilford Reed at the Defence Research Laboratory in Ontario found that rather than rearing and stockpiling millions upon millions of infected flies, and then packing them into specially designed bombs, you could just lace insect food with a pathogen and lob that behind enemy lines instead.[33] The insects who fed on it would then become lethal virus-carriers. The Canadians found canned salmon worked pretty well: it was a protein-rich growth medium for germs to propagate in, and as it rotted it attracted large numbers of bugs.

What the Oxford team brought to the table was ultra-low-volume aerosol spraying. This was a new and devilishly complex application method, but it proved incredibly efficient.

'At the time,' Evans told me, 'we were cutting edge.'

'We could isolate the virus, purify it, suspend it in solution and load it into equipment we could calibrate to give us what we knew would be the optimal amount of virus in every droplet,' Entwistle explained. 'We knew exactly how much to spray and what coverage we would get, either from helicopters or from the ground. It worked very well. I can easily see how that could have a military application.'

Neither Evans nor Entwistle was ever told that Porton had any military interest in their work, and presumably Kelly was treated just the same. But at the very least, Porton knew of him. Was this what put him on the radar? Was there anything specific about him that made Kelly especially suitable for Porton Down? What vectors carried him there? I asked a professor that Harry Smith had once talked to about the superintendent vacancy, and I asked another professor who had worked alongside Kelly at Porton Down. Both gave me the same answer.

'Look,' said one, when we were going over Kelly's published papers, 'I'm a bacteria guy, and David was a virus man, so we didn't interact all that much. But I think it probably really came down to two things. He had experience of running a top-end, large-scale microbiology lab. There aren't too many of those people about.'

'And what's the second thing?'

'He could keep his mouth shut. Believe it or not.'

I dare say he could. Whatever he told Andrew Gilligan or Susan Watts or any other journalist in the weeks and months before he got slandered in Downing Street and hauled before parliamentary committees, there was a lot more he never said. Despite his gentle asides at conferences, despite the numerous media interviews he gave throughout his second career, there were topics he never broached, subjects he didn't speak of. Kelly died keeping dozens of secrets, weeks of headlines that never once saw the light of day. It could not have been otherwise.

For everyone that works at Porton Down, keeping your mouth shut is a basic job requirement, even if you have very little to say. A year or two after my initial contact with them, I asked if the Porton Down conservation team might let me come along on one of their field trips. They organise between twenty and thirty a year, escorting interested visitor groups over the ranges, or parts of them. The housewives of Hanham, the twitchers of Trowbridge, local nature societies and the like are taken through the grounds, the flora and fauna pointed at. It's a box-ticking exercise for the Ministry of Defence Estates, to evidence good stewardship of the land.

There are seven thousand acres behind that chain-link fence, and Porton Down hardly uses any of it. During the First World War, when they were testing poison gas, things were different. Clouds of chlorine and mustard would waft periodically over its chalk grasslands. Health and safety standards were a little laxer in those days, and there was a war on. The last open-air trials of anything remotely hazardous took place in the fifties. Why keep so much land? Because it acts as a security buffer, because it might one day be needed again, because if it was sold off there are no guarantees a developer wouldn't find a stack of rusting phosgene shells buried somewhere in the thin soil. Anyway, this is how government departments work. If left unobserved they will grow, like fungus, as they absorb staff, property, responsibilities, funding; such are the miniature empires that mandarins build.

The irony of all this is that the land behind the wire at Porton, purposeless and disused for most of a century, has become one of the richest natural habitats in Britain. It teems with all kinds of wild flowers, endangered birds and rare insects, butterflies in particular. Almost four-fifths of British butterfly species can be found here, the White Admiral, the Purple Emperor, the High Brown and Dark Green Fritillaries, any number of lovelies to get the lepidopterists excited. The insects Kelly had to work with, cabbage moths and fruit flies, colourless and commonplace, are pretty dull in comparison. If he ever found the time on some sunny day to wander the uplands above his lab, I am sure he would have appreciated it – the way life can flourish if it finds a space, even in a chemical and biological warfare centre.

There is too in Porton Down an awesome amount of archae-ology, as you would expect in this corner of the country: Bronze Age barrows, Neolithic flint mines, Saxon spearheads, the pottery and burial grounds of the prehistoric Beaker people. Submerged in a coppice of hazel trees is Benson's Folly, the remains of a tower built by the grasping eighteenth-century Whig William Benson. Benson connived against Sir Christopher Wren to steal his job, and also that of Wren's assistant, Nicholas Hawksmoor, so Benson could give the post to his brother. After he had dislodged two of Britain's greatest architects to become Surveyor General, Benson enriched himself by telling Parliament that certain important buildings were in a state of murderous disrepair, and desperately in need of his attention. This led to him sacking his ablest sub-ordinates, falling out with his friends, and, when he claimed the House of Lords was about to fall down, earning the enmity of the Treasury, and so finally the sack. He died mad and alone and in much reduced circumstances. His Folly, a testament to the dangers of alarmism for self-advancement, was a ruin long before the War Office bought it up for their Experimental Ground. It lies in pieces in its own thicket on the northern slopes, a metaphorical warning for anyone who works around biolog-ical weapons.

I had hoped there might be some small chance I could see a bit of this. Every couple of years Porton Down's conservation team shows a journalist from one of the London papers around, as long as they promise to keep to the nature angle. It's a nice bit of PR,

I suppose, to suggest the military are keeping the countryside beautiful, but I didn't have a newspaper they could strike a deal with, so I was palmed off in a fashion typical of the Ministry of Defence. First they said they were too busy to take me around, then they denied they took anyone around at all, then they admitted that they did but they didn't want to have me there, then they refused an interview, then they stopped responding to my emails. It was no more than secrecy for secrecy's sake. Secrecy is the oxygen of institutions like Porton Down, and the lifeblood of the Ministry of Defence. It takes a rare soul to break through that, whether you're looking in or looking out, although Kelly managed it, however briefly.

'You need a better cover story, Rob,' said a friend who worked at GCHQ, but bugger it, I thought, I'm not infiltrating the North Devon Butterfly Society for this. A man has his limits. Which is what they count on, I suppose.

After a couple of miles, I drew up opposite some sort of maintenance yard halfway along the northwest perimeter, a patch of dusty tarmac with a couple of shipping containers on it, surrounded by a semicircle of huts. The railway line stretched interminably ahead of me to Andover and beyond, and the sky above had turned from a spring blue to a foreboding concrete slab. Rain was coming. I turned around and came back the way I had come, along the same empty bridleway into the wind, following the endless fence, the concrete and chain-link construction that surrounds almost the entire complex, and I thought briefly of my own father.

'I got nearer to Porton Down than you ever will,' he said, when I told him I was writing this book.

He had been the contractor that had built the fence.

And he was right.

I didn't know it at the time, but in a field six miles away Special Branch were standing guard over the body of Dr Richard Holmes while they waited for the coroner's ambulance. He had left his house on Wednesday morning, for a walk, and not been seen since. The police had put out an appeal earlier that Friday after-noon.

'We believe that he has been looking at information on the Internet regarding self-harm and the use of toxic substances, and people are urged not to approach him for their own safety,' Sergeant Paul Franklin told the local press. 'Richard has recently been under a great deal of stress and may behave unpredictably.'

After an absence of over forty-eight hours, Holmes, aged forty-eight, was found by police that lunchtime in a field only half a mile from his home, near a path popular with joggers and dog walkers. The police appeal and the discovery of the body happened within an hour of each other, as was the case with David Kelly.

He left behind a wife and a young daughter. The family put a notice in the *Salisbury Journal*, announcing that Richard had died 'tragically after recent dark days'.

It was a week later when news finally broke that Holmes had been a Senior Principal Scientific Officer for the chemical wing of the Defence Science and Technology Laboratory at Porton Down. He had recently resigned, but nobody was prepared to say why. His widow also worked at Porton Down, although not as a scientist. There were reports in the local press that the police appeal had annoyed the family, who knew that Richard was a nerve-gas expert who didn't need Google to tell him about toxic substances, and that he would never present any danger to any-body. But it's standard procedure when someone goes missing from Porton Down for the police to downplay their work links and give reasons for people to stay away from them.

When Jean Baxter, who was twenty-nine, vanished in 1974, the public were told she was a clerk who 'worked in a computer office outside the security area' and had 'no access to confidential infor-mation'.[34] Her car was soon found abandoned on the Wessex coast, but it was over a fortnight before the press reported her dis-appearance, and four months were to pass before Dorset and Bournemouth Police finally found her decomposed body on the cliffs at St Aldhelm's Head, not far from where she had parked. The local constabulary admitted to *The Times* that they had been advised 'to take as little action as possible' if they found her because she could have been 'carrying secret chemical warfare data', or have been 'infected by contact with experimental farmland'.[35] Dr Baxter had been a Senior Scientific Officer. The inquest recorded an open verdict.

When the black dog visits the scientists at Porton Down, it seems he tends to lead them outside, into nature and seclusion. The same year that human guinea-pig Ronald Maddison died in a Porton Down gas chamber, the head of the chemical department took cyanide in a field outside his home.[36] His name was Leslie Williams. His wife told the coroner that he was prone to strolling the countryside and often came home late.

'He stayed out until he felt civilised,' she said. 'He got frightfully depressed. It was the materials he was working with that caused this depression.'[37]

And there have been others. Leigh Day & Co., a solicitors' firm who helped a number of volunteer test subjects finally win compensation – and the same firm that would later mount an unsuccessful High Court challenge to get an inquest for David Kelly – know of at least twelve test volunteers who committed suicide after exposure to nerve agents and hallucinogens. Flight Lieutenant William Cockayne tried to kill himself three times. He ended up spending several long spells inside mental institutions. When he tried to claim a disability pension for nervous exhaustion in 1969 and, again unsuccessfully, in 1973, the Ministry of Defence chose to paint Cockayne as a feckless alcoholic and chronic gambler, and said his debilitation was self-imposed. Local workers from the nerve gas factory that Porton Down ran in Cornwall have similar stories.

How many members of Porton Down's permanent scientific staff have ended their own lives? Who knows? I heard talk of a woman doctor discharged from a mental hospital who paid one final visit to her colleagues at the lab before going home to kill herself. If true, that death went unreported. One suspects there are probably others. Secrecy for secrecy's sake. Who benefits, really?

'You ask any GP in town,' said one Old Portonian I talked to. 'Over half the Prozac prescribed in Salisbury is for people who work at the DSTL.'

At the time, I took it as a joke. You don't have to be mad to work here, but it helps. But the more you know, the more you wonder.

I found my car by the church steeple as the sun was setting behind the airstrip at Boscombe Down, and got myself out of the county. As I've said, its landscape has always felt a little haunted to me, open and unknowable at the same time. All that ancient history, all that private land. It affects you a little bit. It certainly seems to have rubbed off on the soldiers stationed here during the Great War. While they waited to go off to the Front, or were recuperating from the wounds it had given them, they carved their own chalk patterns into the low hills. Regimental cap badges, mostly. The average design took fifty men the best part of six months and used perhaps fifty tonnes of chalk.

Some of these hillside badges are being preserved, like the eight at Fovant, but most are slowly fading away. They are, I think, just as esoteric as the white horses and standing stones, and certainly far more complex in their symbolism. If some future anthropologist came upon them, divorced of context, would he be able to construe from their crowns and laurels and initials the massed ranks stood flinching in the trenches of another country? Could he read from them the burning gases from which Porton Down was born? I doubt it. How strange, how terrible, that we might strive so hard to mark our passing, to be remembered and understood, and leave behind only mysteries.

Rarely had I been so grateful to join the busy headlights of the M4.

4

Superintendent

Beware.
MOTTO OF THE CHEMICAL AND BIOLOGICAL
DEFENCE ESTABLISHMENT, PORTON DOWN

From the very beginning, British intelligence kept a close eye on Kelly. They found out things about him and his family that he didn't know himself. A private and compartmentalised man, he was regarded by the Security Service as someone who knew what secrets were. Kelly lived with secrets. He kept them. He was one.

Developed vetting is the lengthiest and most expensive form of routine security screening available to the British state. The process takes an average of six months, but it can go on for far longer. Officers went over Kelly's personal finances, his family, his friends, the friends of his friends, his previous employers and his work colleagues; his political associations and leanings, his finances, his sex life. They investigated how much he drank, if he'd ever taken drugs, if he'd ever displayed any mental instability or financial irresponsibility, if he had any secret vulnerabilities or dependencies. Psychologists and detectives spoke not just to nominated referees but also to anyone they felt like in their probe for potentially damaging secrets. Developed vetting is invasive. It's not unknown for agents to speak to a previous sexual partner about the candidate's behaviour in the bedroom, and neither is it unusual for interviews to last more than three hours.

We know Kelly discussed his mother's suicide but the most difficult subject would have been his father, and his father's new family. Thomas Kelly had died the previous year, and David would have been asked to supply details of his estranged father, the young stepmother he hadn't seen, the step-siblings he hadn't met. Thomas and Flora Dunn had three children of their own and adopted a fourth, by which time contact between father and son had completely broken down. It's possible Kelly didn't know about his step-siblings until he was told about them by MI5.

However emotional it may have been, Kelly passed his vetting without trouble, and as security officers pored over the minutiae of his life, the world turned. The resurgent Cold War so beloved of the Republican right showed no escalation at the centre, but on its fringes proxies rose and fell. In the Middle East the Iran–Iraq War entered its fourth gruesome year. Saddam's forces finally halted the Iranian counter-offensive but it was obvious to everyone that they'd used WMD to do it. After years of Iranian complaints, the US State Department finally admitted that 'the available evidence' showed Iraq had used chemical weapons. The State Department's representative in Baghdad, William Eagleton, cabled back to say 'the Iraqis have been stunned by our condemnation'.[1]

The Baathists had every right to be surprised. The US had been one of the countries that helped Iraq put its chemical arsenal together in the first place. In 1982, Iraq began ordering brand-new crop-spraying helicopters and planes from US manufacturers, for the sort of low-volume aerosol dissemination perfected by Evans and Entwistle at Kelly's Oxford Institute in the seventies. The Iraqis hadn't yet mastered it to the same degree, but they were trying.

Privately, Iraq told the State Department that it urgently needed to triple the size of its spraying fleet because the 'demand for pest control' meant they had some 'upcoming major jobs'.[2] The request was made by the Iraqi director of agricultural aviation, but there can have been little doubt the imports were intended for military use. 'Insecticide' was a common euphemism for 'chemical weapons' in Iraq, perhaps because nerve gas and insecticide share the same chemical precursors, or because pesticide and CBW (chemical and biological weapons) could be dispersed using the same equipment.

'The invaders should know that for every harmful insect there is an insecticide capable of annihilating it whatever their number, and Iraq possesses this annihilation insecticide,' an Iraqi military spokesman publicly announced.[3] Major General Maher Abd Al-Rashid, head of the Iraqi Third Army Corps, was equally lyrical:

'If you gave me some insecticide I could squirt at this swarm of mosquitoes, I would use it so they would be exterminated,' he said, 'thus benefiting humanity by saving the world from such pests.'[4]

All this none-too-subtle language was a cynical and knowing wink at the purported morality of the international community.

'The international community?' as "Chemical" Ali Hassan al-Majid was known to have said. 'Fuck them! The international community and those who listen to them.'[5]

If nothing else, the Iraqis were at least open in their disregard for the moral censure of other countries. They had a war to fight, and little time for the sort of 'psalm-singing defeatists' (as Churchill once called them) who said a country could kill one way but not another. After the US authorised the crop-sprayer sale, chemical attacks on Iranian troops quickly escalated, and Iran sent scores of its dying soldiers to European hospitals so the West could witness the effects for itself. Secretly, the US had known Iraq's chemical warfare had been an 'almost daily' occurrence for at least five months, but now it was obliged to offer some official criticism.[6] At first the Iraqis mistook this hypocrisy for sincerity, and they were shocked. Donald Rumsfeld visited Baghdad later in the month to assure them that despite the rhetoric they could still count on US cooperation.

The Iranians had tried repeatedly to get the UN to investigate Iraq's WMD, but to no avail. One visiting UN delegation did conclude that chemical weapons had been used, but bizarrely, it refused to say by which side. Even so, some sort of formal UN response now seemed inevitable. The US State Department met with the Iraqi Ambassador, Nizar Hamdoon, to see how the damage might be mitigated. Hamdoon said that if the UN had to raise the matter then a simple statement would be less troublesome than a Security Council resolution.[7] It could be drafted, he suggested, so as to mention chemical weapons generally and only in passing, and then it could focus instead on points beneficial to Iraq, such as the need for an immediate ceasefire. Under US influence, that was exactly how the UN statement turned out.[8]

Of course it wasn't just the US that had armed Baathist Iraq. The East Germans and the Russians were both blamed, but it was the West that gave it its WMD capability – the Americans, the British, the Dutch, the Spanish, the French and the Germans who supplied the parts and experience. Without them its chemical arsenal would never have got off the ground. And as Kelly started his second career, these countries began to assist in Iraq's biological warfare programme too.

America alone shipped over a hundred strains of dangerous pathogens to Iraq from private companies like the American Type Culture Collection in Maryland, but also from government offices like the Centers for Disease Control head office in Atlanta, which provided (amongst many other things) military-grade anthrax from Fort Detrick. Iraq ordered everything on the menu, and the US Department of Commerce approved every sale. From Western Europe came fermenters and spray dryers and tonnes of growth medium to grow the pathogens in, although it was years before any of this became known to the public. Instead a familiar and entirely spurious story resurfaced, spun by operators on the fringes of the intelligence world, that would point people's attentions in quite a different direction. As suspicions grew that the West had helped supply Saddam with WMD, the media began to report that the Iraqis had actually been using Soviet-supplied Yellow Rain.

The source of these claims was a Belgian professor of toxicology at the University of Ghent, whose name was Aubin

Heyndrickx, hitherto a scientist of sound standing, much like Chester Mirocha. Halfway though Kelly's vetting he announced he had found traces of mycotoxins in the blood and urine samples of Iranian soldiers being treated at a Viennese hospital.

'We can confidentially assume that the identification of myco-toxins in the Iran–Iraq war represents yet another Soviet violation of the Biological Weapons Convention,' the *Wall Street Journal* duly reported.[9] But others vehemently disagreed. Sweden, which was also caring for a number of Iranian soldiers, said it had found no mycotoxin traces whatsoever, and that the men were clearly suffering from mustard gas poisoning (manufactured in plants built by Western engineers using Western plans and Western parts).

'From the way he's presented his results, I don't believe him,' said Professor Mats Ahlberg, of Sweden's National Defence Research Institute. 'He hasn't proved the existence of mycotoxins.'[10]

The Harvard professor Matthew Meselson was equally uncon-vinced. In fact on its second outing, in the Iran–Iraq War, the Yellow Rain story was dismissed even more roundly than when it had been spun in Afghanistan and South East Asia. Heyndrickx's accusations went nowhere, but they grabbed the headlines for a spell. As with all allegations of biological warfare, the charges served a political purpose, and for Aubin Heyndrickx, serving a political purpose became a new occupation. Just as David Kelly was changing his career, so too was he.

While Kelly was saying his goodbyes at Oxford, Heyndrickx hosted a special conference in his hometown of Ghent. In the tradition of Belgian cities, Ghent is picturesque, sleepy, orderly, criss-crossed with rivers and canals. Cobbled squares, creeping ivy and stepped gables abound. But that May, the walls of the univer-sity hall were incongruously draped in massively enlarged photos of chemical warfare victims. In attendance were Iranian doctors, whose burnt patients lay dying in hospital beds as they spoke; rep-resentatives of Afghan guerrillas, keen to vilify the Soviets; and from all over the world, industrialists and salesmen and government officials with a stake in the shady world of chemical and biological warfare. By the entrance were display stands of gas masks and NBC suits, which gave the whole thing the air of a trade fair. Vendors of protective equipment said sales were surging. One marketing manager estimated that the number of big contracts offered by governments had tripled in the last five years.[11]

Heyndrickx himself downplayed any financial motivations for organising the conference. 'We are trying to do something for the freedom of man,' he said, when quizzed. For Heyndrickx, like Mirocha, the consequences were becoming more important than the truth. Peer review was something to steer clear of. Heyndrickx deliberately chose the smallest room in the building to give his presentation on Iraqi Yellow Rain, but in the cramped audience was Professor Meselson, who had already debunked the weapon in a dozen different publications.

'This isn't science,' he was heard mumbling to himself, as the Belgian delivered his speech. Heyndrickx didn't hang around to take questions from the floor.

Among the other attendees were two South Africans whose interest in all this was far from academic. One was stocky, bearded and balding, with a round face and an upturned nose. The other was a taller, older, clean-shaven man with a long stride. Quietly they networked with sales reps and scientists, they listened to speeches and sales pitches, and said as little as possible.

For three years, they had been visiting similar conferences around the world doing just this; listening, watching, studying, for any information they could gather about chemical and biological weapons. They told anyone who asked them that they were plain-clothes policemen. The younger one was Brigadier Wouter Basson of the elite 7th Medical Battalion, later known as Dr Death. The other was an actual South African police general with two doctorates in chemistry, one Lothar Neethling. Born in Hitler's Germany, Neethling had been a member of the Nazi Youth before his adoption by a Cape Town doctor after the fall of the Third Reich. Later the papers would call him 'the South African

Mengele'. They were the architects of Project Coast, Apartheid South Africa's secret CBW programme.

Coast was the product of 'total strategy', the belief that South Africa's white supremacy was a front line in the war against communism, and that the clamour for racial equality was actually Soviet-sponsored subversion, or 'total onslaught' as P. W. Botha called it. It had to be met with 'total war'. So when Botha ascended from the Ministry of Defence to the office of Prime Minister he signed off on plans for the secret development of biological and chemical weapons, to safeguard the Afrikaner ascendancy.

Basson, a fast-rising star within the South African military, had been an early advocate of germ warfare, and so despite his relative youth the generals picked him to head up their programme. It was a position that required a degree of tact, as there was a UN resolution in force banning the sale of military equipment to South Africa. Yet wherever he went, the clubbable and lavishly funded Basson was able to find allies and partners. In one of the bars off the Vrijdagmarkt, Heyndrickx quickly became one of them.

Basson says he paid Heyndrickx almost 4 million Belgian francs to go to Iran, get hold of some shrapnel from Iraqi chemical attacks, and open up channels with Iranian intelligence. Heyndrickx went that same year with four BBC *Newsnight* staff in tow, claiming to be part of the UN investigation.[12] The idea, apparently, was to bring the bomb fragments back and plant them on South Africa's borders, to suggest the country had been attacked with chemical weapons. For whatever reason, the plan was never executed.

Instead Heyndrickx secretly ordered and received a number of chemical agent monitors, designed to detect the presence of poison gas, from a British company that listed his university department on the end-user certificate. But in reality, he brought them with him to South Africa.

A civil war was then raging in neighbouring Angola. Like most conflicts of the period, it was subsumed in the wider Cold War, with the Cuban military fighting for one side and the South African and the CIA on the other. The Angolan that Washington and Johannesburg were backing was Jonas Savimbi, a murderous warlord who commanded little global sympathy, so rather helpfully Heyndrickx announced that Savimbi's opponents had resorted to using mustard and nerve gas. He said he had tested soil, leaf and water samples and found traces of these terrible weapons on all of them, though he refused to share the data. The only actual physical evidence he cited was the serendipitous discovery of chemical agent monitors, which he claimed had been seized from captured Cuban soldiers.[13]

For all of this, Basson testified to paying the professor 90 million francs.

Just as the Yellow Rain story allowed the Pentagon to publicly justify boosting its CBW budget, Heyndrickx's Angolan allegations gave the South African military an excuse to green-light Project Coast, and gave its scientists a working rationale too.

'My moral stance was if you had an enemy that would chuck chemicals on you, you could chuck it back at them,' Dr Johan Koekemoer, one of Coast's heads of research, later explained.[14]

This was disingenuous at best, because the biological and chemical weapons that Coast ended up developing were not intended for the battlefield. They were meant for assassins. Under Basson's leadership, Project Coast weaponised an impressive arsenal of poisons, toxins and microbes. Thallium, a highly toxic metal, was one, the herbicide paraquat was another, the pesticide aldicarb a third. All of these could be bought off the shelf. Microbial agents like salmonella, cholera and botulinum toxin, on the other hand, were grown in the lab. Other substances weren't particularly difficult to come by but were sophisticated in their effect: an overdose of the antibiotic monensin is largely untraceable and will trigger heart failure. Brodifacoum, another pesticide, is an anticoagulant that can cause strokes and haemorrhages and is equally hard to detect in a dead body. And they were all used, routinely.

That we know any of this at all is only because of the Truth and

Reconciliation Commission, which gave Coast scientists a chance to come clean and claim amnesty, and thus afforded the world a unique glimpse into the secret world of black ops and wet jobs. Schalk Van Rensburg, Coast's laboratory director, was explicit about the nature of his work:

> Mr Chaskalson [staff lawyer for the Truth and Reconciliation Commission]: Are you aware that two of the substances we discussed, Brodifacoum and monensin, cause acute heart failure in the human and also have the dubious merit of not being traceable?
>
> Dr Van Rensburg: That was a very highly sought after merit, Mr Chaskalson.
>
> Mr Chaskalson: Can you elaborate as to why you say that?
>
> Dr Van Rensburg: The most frequent instruction we obtained from Doctor Basson and Doctor Swanepoel was to develop something with which you could kill an individual which would make his death resemble a natural death, something that was not detectable in a normal forensic laboratory. That was the chief aim of Roodeplaat Research Laboratories' covert side.
>
> Mr Chaskalson: That's quite a startling admission or statement.
>
> Dr Van Rensburg: That's the most frequent repeated need that I heard or instruction given.

Equally startling is that there was little considered ground-breaking or pioneering about the work undertaken by Project Coast. For the most part it was playing catch-up with the advances of other nations. As the US Senate's Church Committee discovered in 1975, the CIA had already developed a silent dart gun, replete with telescopic sight, which could shoot a tiny projectile that would feel like an insect bite, if it was felt at all, and leave no trace besides a small red welt.[15] The dart itself would melt away in the bloodstream, Mary Embree, who worked in the CIA's technical services, later explained, and the Agency's research library listed at least one undetectable poison that could mimic a heart attack.[16] South Africa confined itself to using whisky bottles, beer cans, clothing, cigarettes and screwdrivers as delivery systems. Every British expert I spoke to considered the weapons of Project Coast laughably primitive, but they worked well enough.

When Kelly's clearance came through in the summer of 1984, these were his global peers, though they were of very different stripes: Iraq and South Africa. Iraq concentrated on battlefield applications, all the better to defeat the Iranians. Apartheid South Africa sought them for the discrete disposal of troublesome individuals or groups. Britain, officially, studied biological warfare only to determine how it might defend against it. Between them, these three countries covered every major aspect of bioweapons research, and they began in earnest within the same calendar year.

David Kelly arrived at Porton Down, in the rolling plains of Wiltshire, to head up its new Defence Microbiology Division in the summer of 1984. Meanwhile, on a dusty, sun-baked peninsula on the banks of the Tigris, Iraq's Military Industrialisation Commission were putting the finishing touches to the new Salman Pak biological research facility. At the University of Baghdad, a short drive northwards, a number of microbiologists and chemists were soon about to follow Kelly on his one-way journey from academia to military research. And that winter in South Africa, on a farm not far from the Roodeplaat dam, Wouter Basson's scientists and special forces officers ramped up their bio-research with the construction of a new laboratory in the highveld overlooking Pretoria.

The question begged by the synchronicity of these three complementary programmes is how much did they know of each other? The governments behind them were loosely allied, even if they couldn't shout about it. Thatcher, like Reagan, believed in 'constructive engagement' with the Botha regime, and she allowed 'defensive' exports to Saddam's Iraq throughout the Iran–Iraq War.

Did these programmes interact? The world's military microbiologists form a small pool indeed. In his criminal trial, Wouter Basson even alluded to a 'CBW mafia'. Did Kelly or his colleagues ever meet their South African or Iraqi equivalents? Absolutely not, is the official answer. The government has always denied contemporaneous awareness of either programme, let alone admitted to any form of collaboration. Yet there is evidence that suggests otherwise.

In June 1986, in a London club, Basson rendezvoused with Roger Buffham, formerly a major in the Army Ordnance Corps and one-time officer in Northern Ireland's Special Military Intelligence Unit. Buffham's business sold surveillance equipment to South African special forces through a network of sanctions-busting front companies, and, it seems, he provided Basson with his ticket to Porton Down.

Project Coast received a lot of help from the Wiltshire white-coats. They provided restricted NATO software and classified studies on hallucinogens and incapacitants. When Basson needed a new, safer laboratory to work on more highly dangerous pathogens, two 'consultants' from Porton Down advised on the construction.[17] Buffham arranged a visit to Porton for Basson's nominal superior, Surgeon General Niel Knobel. Basson, the man in charge of Project Coast, claimed at his own criminal trial that he was granted repeated access to Porton Down himself. And in 2009, he told Bob Coen of the Canadian Broadcasting Corporation that he knew its late Superintendent pretty well.

'I met Mr Kelly on three or four occasions. Purely from an information exchange point of view.'

'Did you ever meet him in Porton Down?'

'That I can't answer. But we did meet him on a few occasions.'

'You were able to visit Porton Down and Fort Detrick?'

'Yes, we did that. I wouldn't like to talk about it. The next question I get asked is who arranged it and why and what and where, and I already have hassles with the UK and American governments. I don't need any more, thank you, that's enough for me.'

The directors of covert biological warfare programmes rarely get to retire peacefully. Unlike the academic Kelly, Basson was a combat doctor before joining the biowarfare world, and when Project Coast was rolled back his life retained the same taste of adventure it always had. After Apartheid ended, Basson began to turn up in a lot of strange places. It seems he was being put to use by someone. Like agents generally are, he was probably alternately induced and compelled; sometimes it was the carrot, other times the stick, hence the hassles.

A shady deal was done in Croatia, apparently to buy a vast quantity of black-market sedatives. There was talk of a small-arms deal with Pakistan. Basson was arrested twice in Switzerland, apparently for intercepting $40 million or more of Vatican bearer bonds. He was in and out of Libya all the time, under some quite implausible covers: opening a cigarette factory, constructing a railway line, founding a heart hospital. Miraculously, each time Basson came back home alive and at liberty. A charmed life indeed, for a man who isn't a spook. A lot of the Afrikaners who dabbled in the WMD business didn't live beyond the end of Mandela's presidency.

British-born Alan Kidger, sales director for Thor Chemicals, was found dismembered in the boot of his BMW in Soweto, smothered in a strange oily substance, shortly after being drawn into a red-mercury scam. Four days after the body was discovered, arms dealer Don Juan Lange decided to inform police about an upcoming caesium 137 deal; he was later found dead in his Durban flat with a bag over his head, connected to a cyanide-gas canister. 'The gas bottle was a decoy,' a detective later told a Reuters stringer. 'There was no trace of gas in his blood. His head had been bludgeoned. We think he was killed because he was about to spill the beans.'

A fortnight later, a colleague of Kidger's, John Scott, director of Wacker Chemicals, was discovered gassed to death in his car. His wife and his two daughters were found fatally stabbed at the family home. He left a suicide note that said 'I made a big mistake five weeks ago and this was the only solution. I had everything, and I

blew it because of ten minutes of irresponsibility.' Five weeks earlier Scott had gone on a business trip abroad. Police found out he
had been in Zambia at the same time as Kidger. They wondered
about those ten minutes. They wondered about the fresh wounds
on Scott's hands too, visible in the scene photos but not mentioned
in the post-mortem, which were more consistent with defending
against a knife attack than committing one.

A chemical engineer called Wynand Van Wyk was bludgeoned
to death in a Cape Town hotel, having been lured there for an
unspecified business meeting. Dirk Stoffberg, an out-and-out play-
boy arms dealer who seems to have sold anything he could get
his hands on to anybody who would pay, a former Project Coast
assassin with self-proclaimed links to US Marine Colonel Oliver
North, was found shot dead with his seventh wife on the balcony
of their luxury home in the Magaliesberg mountains. And there
were others, perhaps fourteen or fifteen cases, according to off-the-
record police estimates.

Sometimes killing wasn't necessary. Project Coast's banker,
Samuel Bosch, had a prolonged and violent psychosis triggered
(Basson believes) by a poisoned chocolate. Basson and his Coast
colleague Philip Mijburg smuggled him to England, where Bosch
was taken into custody after he made repeated attempts to buy a
woman's house with a derisory amount of Polish currency. Bosch
told the Pretoria High Court in 2000 that he'd spent spells in clin-
ics ever since.

Whatever the exact body count, it was clear that in the aftermath
of Apartheid somebody was going through South Africa's discarded
arms dealers and weapons scientists like a scythe through long grass.
The police openly speculated that it was Mossad, but they never
provided any evidence. There were never any arrests, never any
eyewitnesses, never any forensic matches. This is the sort of thing
that can very occasionally happen to weapons experts, when they
can no longer count on the protection of their government.

On the surface Basson was as rogue as they come, yet he
survived. Someone was looking after him. Dr Death's Libyan

sojourns were probably fishing expeditions for the CIA and MI6. It's hard to imagine that he could have been up to anything else: he certainly wasn't advising on fag factories or railway track, and if he'd gone there unsanctioned, earnestly intending to flog WMDs to Gaddafi, he would have been signing his own death warrant. Which isn't Basson's style. The opposite to David Kelly in many ways, Basson is extroverted, easy-going, and morally flexible. Dr Death is a natural survivor.

Arguing that Basson was a lesser risk if brought back inside the system, representatives from the British and American governments privately pressured President Mandela to reinstate him in the Defence Force at his old rank and salary. So, incredibly, Mandela re-employed the man whose staff once considered using thallium to poison the future president while he was still incarcerated, and Basson became Head of Cardiology at the military hospital in Pretoria. Perhaps, on the part of his high-placed foreign friends, it was payment due for services rendered. Whatever the real reason, it looked like he had landed on his feet in the new South Africa. But he couldn't walk on water for ever.

His luck changed when the Truth and Reconciliation Commission received amnesty applications from two former Coast colleagues, guilt-ridden over their involvement, and eager to avoid a criminal sentence should their past ever come to light. It meant that the programme, still a closely guarded state secret, was about to explode into the public domain.

Michael Kennedy, deputy director of South Africa's National Intelligence Agency, said the CIA offered Basson and his family protection in the States under an assumed identity. The Bassons refused to go. The CIA imposed too many restrictions: who they could meet or talk to, where they could live, where they could travel, what they could do for a living. They decided to stay put, which made Wouter a worrying loose end for Western intelligence. So in the parlance of John le Carré, they burned him. Burned him rotten.

On 4 February 1997, the following month, he was arrested for selling Ecstasy under the willows in Magnolia Dell Park, not far from the family home in an upmarket suburb of Pretoria. The supposed buyer was a former colleague of Basson's called Grant Wentzel, who was waiting there to meet him in a white Nissan, with a detective hiding in the boot and several more loitering nearby. Basson arrived to hand over some boxes of wine and the police pounced.

Basson's immediate response was to make a run for it. There was a river in Magnolia Dell just a short sprint away from the car, and the sunlight on its sparkling waters beckoned to him from between the trees. He put on a burst of speed and dived in, fully clothed, but the Apies River at that point was only about two feet deep. As Basson quickly discovered, real life is not an action movie. When he staggered back out of the water, muddy and dripping, Giel Ehlers, head of the city narcotics division, put the cuffs on him. Ehlers said that when Basson found out he was a city policeman and not a foreign assassin he was so relieved he almost broke down.

The police said they found several thousand Ecstasy tablets in a plastic bag inside one of the wine boxes. When Basson's name finally appeared in the newspapers it was as a drug dealer, a military scientist 'at the end of a long decline', as the *Observer* portrayed him.[18] It has the ring of a classic smear sting from start to finish. It also meant Basson's 'insurance' got cancelled: when police raided his house immediately afterwards, they found and seized a number of sealed trunks and drums containing all the data he'd copied from the Project Coast files before his exile into the wilderness.

Sometimes, if they cannot kill you, they will cow you. After his arrest Basson was bailed into the protective custody of South Africa's National Intelligence Agency.

'His biggest concern was a kidnapping or an assassination,' said Mike Kennedy.

They were understandable fears. Once his name began to appear in the papers, Basson said, 'the local CIA agent in Pretoria came up to me on the sidewalk, outside the US Embassy on

Schoeman Street, and threatened he would tell the Libyans I was a double agent'.

It was, in effect, a death threat by proxy. Basson caught the next plane to Tripoli and begged for his life. The Libyans held him for fourteen days. Whatever he said, or whatever was said on his behalf by parties unknown, it worked. He came back again in one piece, as always. But broadly speaking, Basson appears to have got the message. When it came to the Truth and Reconciliation Commission, he barely said a word.

First he asked for a hearing in camera. When that was refused, he stalled them with legal arguments, aided by his loyal and pugnacious barrister, Jaap Cilliers. Meanwhile, the clock was ticking: the Commission's mandate expired on the last working day of July 1998, which was when Basson finally turned up. He spurned the offer of possible amnesty out of hand and spent the best part of the morning debating technicalities. The leader of Project Coast played it as close to his chest as he could, but those who worked under him had already said more than enough.

'It cannot be doubted that without some level of foreign assistance this programme would not have been possible,' the TRC's summary read.

Basson wasn't much more communicative at his criminal trial, which began the following autumn and dragged on for three years. It may have started with a single drugs bust at Magnolia Dell but over sixty other charges quickly piled up, mostly relating to murder, conspiracy to murder, and fraud. The prosecution called almost two hundred witnesses. Basson, who was facing life imprisonment, called none.

It turned out that Basson's incriminating former friend, the supposed drug dealer Grant Wentzel, had been arrested in Florida in 1990 for attempting to export missile technology, along with yet another Coast colleague, Jerry Brandt. Brandt told the court that Wentzel had been held separately and given preferential treatment, and Wentzel himself testified that he hadn't even ended up going to court for sentencing. The implication was clear: Wentzel had become an American agent. He never denied it. Judge Hartzenberg ruled the drugs bust a set-up, and after thirty months, dismissed all charges against Wouter Basson and granted him amnesty. A small coterie of generals from the old regime clapped him from the gallery as he walked free (Hartzenberg and the generals, it must be said, came from the same sort of background).

After that, Basson gave up on South Africa. He lived in Switzerland for a while, not far from Lake Geneva, practising cardiology and doing the odd bit of guest speaking. I couldn't figure out why he would move to a country that had arrested him twice before; somebody there must have liked him too. After a couple of years, the Swiss government came under pressure to launch its own inquiry into the secret support it had given Apartheid South Africa, and Basson decided to come home. I found him listed as a cardiologist for a medical practice out in Durbanville on the Western Cape. When I contacted him, it was, by chance, the tenth anniversary of his acquittal at Pretoria High Court. He was in a good mood, even if his homecoming had raised the usual legal wrangles. South Africa's Health Professions Council were taking him back to court to see if they could get him struck off the medical register for unethical conduct.

'Life goes on,' he told me. 'It's one last battle to fight.'

Basson seems resigned to his lot: eleven years at the helm of Project Coast followed by a lifetime of periodic exile, perpetual vilification, constant press attention, and regular court cases. I think the old soldier in him even relishes the tension. He is famed for his cavalier attitude in the courtroom, and no Basson trial is complete without a photo of him winking at the camera. In this he is the complete antithesis, again, of David Kelly, or rather the Kelly persona we are asked to believe in: a man who was fatally crushed because he had to spend a single afternoon with eleven MPs.

Basson is known for being talkative, even gregarious, with writers and journalists, but I asked him about Kelly, about his British links, and he clammed up. I said if he was worried about repercussions, I could go through Jaap, his long-term legal advocate.

'Good luck,' he said. 'You'll have more luck going through the Blue Bulls forward pack.'

And that was the last I heard of Dr Death. But I wasn't the only person interested in him. Despite sworn testimony from its senior scientists that the South African chemical and biological warfare programme had had British help, only one British MP has ever asked about Project Coast in Parliament. That was Andrew MacKinlay, who sat on the Foreign Affairs Select Committee that grilled Kelly two days before he killed himself.

'I reckon you are chaff,' he famously told Kelly. 'You have been thrown up to divert our probing. Have you ever felt like a fall-guy? You have been set up, have you not?'

After the body was found there was speculation it was MacKinlay's 'aggressive questioning' that had driven Kelly up Harrowdown Hill. The MP even got hate mail about it. On balance, I find it more plausible that Kelly was somehow secretly assassinated than compelled to kill himself because the MP for Thurrock had been insufficiently polite. If anything, MacKinlay was trying to offer Kelly a lifeline, albeit in gruff tones. That people ever thought otherwise is only a sign of how badly they thirsted for answers, of how sorely we needed a reason for the inspector's final walk.

MacKinlay was still an MP when I left a message about Project Coast with his parliamentary secretary. To my surprise, I got a return call within minutes.

'What are you after?' MacKinlay asked me, and I told him about this book and David Kelly.

'Who do you think killed him?' was the next thing he asked me. A lot of people asked me that question, or some variation of it. Some asked me because they thought he was murdered, others because they couldn't countenace talking to anyone who did, but for years pretty much everybody asked me.

'I don't know,' I said. 'I've only just started researching this.'

'Well, keep digging. You know what the South Africans were working on, don't you? Poisons that could kill someone undetectably, and his death would look entirely natural.'

It was alarming, to hear a Member of Parliament talk like this. After all, nobody had found any traces of poison of any kind whatsoever in Kelly's bloodstream. But then, it turned out, nobody had really looked for any. When New Labour finally fell from power, the incoming Conservative government resisted the mounting legal pressure to hold a proper inquest into Kelly's death by releasing the post-mortem reports instead. They showed that the toxicology tests had been no more than the standard police set: the toxicologist Allan Richard had checked for traces of alcohol, recreational drugs and 'chemically basic' medicines like paracetamol and antihistamines. As if David was a recruitment consultant or a sales manager or a solicitor, and not the former head of Britain's secret biological warfare laboratory. They treated him like he'd been a rock guitarist, not an active and experienced member of the international intelligence community. Even the crude weapons of Project Coast, the outdated programme of a developing country, would have escaped notice.

MacKinlay hadn't read the post-mortem reports, but he sensed the presence of something hidden, and in Parliament, although he was met with obfuscations, denials and lies, he kept pressing. Some of his constituents began to wonder if MacKinlay had gone mad, and as I searched through Hansard I wondered if maybe he really was a little haunted by the hard line he'd taken with Kelly that afternoon. I knew he'd made a point of contacting the family afterwards to offer his condolences. But whether his quest to unearth a Coast connection was propelled by some sense of personal guilt or not, he exposed a deal of dishonesty.

MacKinlay asked what information the government had on Project Coast and was given an answer so vague as to be pointless: 'a variety'. He asked if the information could be put in the members' library, and was given instead, on the floor of the Commons, the web address of the Truth and Reconciliation Commission.

MacKinlay asked when the government had first learnt of Project Coast, and Parliament was told that 'initial reports were not received until 1993' and that even then they were 'inconclusive'.

In reality, MI6 have had a file on Basson since at least 1985. In that year, Peter Martin and Jim Shortt, ex-soldiers, were approached by Basson at a military medical exhibition in Bloomsbury, where they were representing a firm called Special Training Services. Basson began to ask some very technical questions, so the two tipped off MI6. To their surprise the intelligence service actually sent them on a training course at Winterbourne Gunner, a few miles south of Porton Down, to help them land the contract. Peter Martin, incidentally, died of a stroke seven years later, but his fiancée Rosemary Durrant is convinced he was killed because he knew about Project Coast.

'He was terrified of being assassinated,' she told the *Oxford Mail*. 'The suggestion is they used untraceable poisons.'

Durrant subsequently moved to London and began screening her calls. At the time of her interview with the *Mail*, she refused to pose for a photograph.

Far from receiving initial and inconclusive reports in 1993, the British government actually knew more about Project Coast than the South African President. When President De Klerk took over from the Apartheid hardliner Botha in 1989, Coast's secrets were so closely guarded he had to commission a special inquiry to find out what had been going on.[19] In the meantime, the UK and US governments issued De Klerk with a private démarche telling him 'they were fully aware of the contents and extent of the Defence Force's CBW programme, and that they had certain reservations'.[20]

As both Basson and General Knobel told the Truth and Reconciliation Commission, Washington and London had wanted Coast closed down before it could fall into the hands of the coming black government.[21] On coming into power, President Mandela let the matter lie. He had already been warned that asking too many questions 'could jeopardise relations with countries which may have assisted the programme'.[22]

MacKinlay's next attempt to get at the truth was more tactical. Seeing he couldn't get any answers in the Commons, he filed a request with the Foreign Office under the Data Protection Act to see what records the department had held on him ever since he'd started asking questions. Over a dozen officials had held a 'handling strategy meeting to deal with Andrew MacKinlay's questions', and the names, job titles and departments of most attendees were redacted, which meant they were MI6. This was an extraordinary response if there really was, as the government insisted, nothing to reveal.

'They know,' MacKinlay said. 'They know there was some kind of illicit, probably illegal involvement by our security and intelligence services with Wouter Basson, so they don't like being asked about it.'

And still he kept pushing, from the backbenches, as backbenchers are sometimes wont to do. Often the government said that providing an answer would 'incur disproportionate costs', or that there were no records, or simply that they couldn't answer. Eventually Kim Howells, MP for Kelly's hometown of Pontypridd and then Minister of State at the Foreign Office, admitted that 'in the course of their normal duties some Government officials and scientists did have contact with their South African counterparts'.

It was the most the government were prepared to reveal. There was no need for further concern, Howells said, because a full investigation had taken place in secret, and found no evidence of wrong-doing. When MacKinlay asked if the investigation might be placed in the Commons library he was told the sources were too sensitive. Consequently, we know nothing about it, and ministers were only too happy to see the whole affair remain in the shadows, where MI6 and Porton Down habitually reside, and whence, having investigated themselves, they announced themselves irreproachable.

Whether or not MacKinlay found the answer he was looking for, he had found a secret. It was just one of many secrets that Kelly carried and never spilled. Another was Britain's early knowledge of Iraq. Officially the UK professed virtually no knowledge of the Iraqi biological weapons programme until Iraq became an enemy, and then, quite suddenly, it was certain that it had one. After the invasion of Kuwait, one of Kelly's biggest worries was ensuring that Porton Down could produce enough vaccine to inoculate the troops against Saddam's weapons. By the time of the Gulf conflict over a third of the Porton workforce had been transferred to work on biological defence, and it had proved one of his biggest challenges.[23]

Just as Porton Down had known of Project Coast, it knew too of Iraq's germ warfare programme, and it was knowledge gained through something approaching tacit cooperation. A year or two after Kelly became Superintendent, his lab at Porton received an order from Iraq for dozens of lethal pathogens.[24] Apparently, the order was refused, because it appeared too obviously military in nature. The Iraqis were referred instead to the Pasteur Institute in Paris and the American Type Culture Collection in Maryland, but the order form gave Kelly and his colleagues, and all the intelligence officers who were involved, a clear idea of exactly what the Iraqi bioweaponeers were working on. Nothing was done to stop them. The opposite, in fact.

When Iraq's military scientists sought to protect themselves from the obvious dangers of working with anthrax, the safest solution seemed a vaccine, but outside of the Soviet Union there was only one laboratory in the world that was licensed to manufacture and distribute one: Porton Down. And so Kelly's Defence Microbiology Division sold 150 doses of anthrax vaccine to a country it had already judged to be developing an anthrax weapon.[25]

In 1988, in Winchester, Kelly's staff held a special three-day workshop on anthrax.[26] There were almost ninety people there. Kelly was present, so was the man who had helped hire him, Harry Smith, and so was Dr Nasser Al Hindawi, one of Iraq's most senior microbiologists. It was Hindawi, at the University of Baghdad, who had convinced Saddam Hussein to start a germ-warfare programme in the first place. With him was Abdul Rahman Thamir, a biologist affiliated to the state security organisation. They sat and listened and learned all they could. They asked questions and were answered. In between lectures they wandered the high street, admired the Buttercross and the cathedral, posed under the statue of Alfred the Great. On the first evening, they were invited into Porton Down itself. On the second, everyone went to the Theatre Royal. Kelly would meet them both later in quite different circumstances, not to educate them but to interrogate them, about a programme he already knew they had. There was always an element of charade to UNSCOM.

Iraq's germ-warfare experts learnt a lot from Britain. Rihab Taha, later known to the popular press as Dr Germ after UNSCOM started briefing journalists about her, had studied plant pathology at the University of East Anglia. It had been her name on the order form that had come in to Porton Down.

'It was a measure of her innocence, really,' her tutor told me. 'She didn't think they'd turn her down. She didn't think there would be any problems.'[27]

Amer Rashid Al Ubaidi, Taha's boss and later her husband, had a doctorate in chemistry from the University of Birmingham, where Harry Smith had taught and David Kelly had studied. Dr Hazem Ali, who several UNSCOM inspectors maintained was in charge of developing Iraq's virus weapons, had gained his doctorate at Newcastle. Professor Shakir Al Akidy, supposedly a toxin expert, had done a master's in pharmacology at Imperial College and a PhD at Cardiff before taking up a job at Porton Down itself. He left the same year that Kelly arrived.[28]

Such were the numbers of Iraqi scientists studying microbiology in Britain that even civilian academics grew concerned. Joe Selkon was the director of an Oxford lab when he received what he thought was a distinctly unusual postgraduate application.

'He had a superb CV, he was going to work for us for free, and we would receive £20,000 from the Iraqi government,' he told *File on 4*.[29] But Selkon's team were studying bacterial resistance to antibiotics, work with distinct biowarfare potential, so he asked around. Was this how Iraq always sent its students abroad? Only in microbiology, it appeared. After talking to his academic peers Selkon contacted the security services about the application and was told they already knew of nine or ten Iraqi scientists studying sensitive microbiology subjects under similar arrangements, in universities up and down the country. Nothing was done to stop them.[30] The flow of knowledge was encouraged right up until Iraq's invasion of Kuwait, and then, as the Gulf War drew closer, the students were rounded up and returned home.[31]

Perhaps most damningly of all, it appears that, knowing all of this, the UK government approved the sale of twenty-two tonnes of bacterial growth medium from a company called Oxoid in Basingstoke. This was the soup you grew germs in. Hospitals might get through a kilo or two of the stuff every year for testing and research, but twenty-two tonnes was unheard of, a truly industrial quantity. In a roundabout way, through another former employee, I tracked down the sales manager who had signed off on the deal. As he explained it to me, it was two transport planes' worth, one of the biggest orders the company had ever delivered. He had been in and out of Baghdad in 1988 to clinch the deal, and the Ministry of Defence, he told me, were clearly involved in the purchase.

Yet the sale went through. The Department of Trade and Industry green-lighted it, the Defence Intelligence Staff did not intervene, Customs and Excise raised no objection. The sales rep, who I shall not pseudonymise (aliases are tiring), told me he had no contact with British intelligence, but I am inclined to have my doubts. He lives in another country now, and gives occasional lectures on how microbiology businesses can avoid unwittingly aiding arms programmes. At these he has a habit of referring to MI6 as 'our matey-bobs down the road'.

He was lucky he wasn't arrested, and so were his directors. In the aftermath of the Gulf War, Customs and Excise hadn't hesitated to go after businessmen who had broken the arms embargo against

Iraq, even when they had government clearance. Prosecutions started against three firms. Matrix Churchill, for machine tools; Ordtec, for a fuse assembly plant; and Atlantic Commercial, which had exported machine-guns. Consequently, men very much like Oxoid's former sales rep had been facing long prison sentences, until it transpired they had all been reporting to MI6, something the government and the Secret Intelligence Service had been keen to suppress. Alan Clark, Minister of Trade at the Department of Trade and Industry, admitted in court to misleading Parliament over the matter.

That in turn triggered the Scott Inquiry, which was supposed to examine in detail Britain's arms sales to Iraq. But Oxoid was kept out of that, just as it was kept hidden from Customs and Excise. It was concealed from UNSCOM (but not from Kelly) for a few years too, until MI6 decided it was time to build the case against Iraq. It seemed incredible to me that Oxoid hadn't had a channel to British intelligence.

'Yeah,' the sales rep said. 'Ah, I'd rather you keep my name out of this, actually.'

And what of Kelly himself? What was our Superintendent doing, while Project Coast was surreptitiously smearing women's underwear with parathion,[32] and Iraq was busy brewing vats of anthrax?

Not all the research at Porton Down is classified. The scientists there do publish some of their work, and it shows that Kelly maintained a relationship with his old Oxford Institute, with which he personally oversaw a genetic study on a highly infectious insect virus, NPV. A few years after this, US intelligence speculated (rather wildly) that NPV might make a good base vehicle for a new generation of genetically engineered bioweapons.[33] If you could splice NPV with something that was lethal to humans, like smallpox, you could produce a very powerful, easily transmissible, vector weapon.

Porton Down's interest in civilian vector studies continued under Kelly's tenure, but whatever his relationship with Oxford's

Institute of Virology, it doesn't seem he was able to offer his successor there the same level of support. The man eventually appointed over Kelly to become director of the Institute was David Bishop. Whereas Porton Down had previously allowed Institute scientists to use its grounds for safety tests, under Kelly's stewardship it seems Bishop was forced to look elsewhere. When he developed a biopesticide that blended poison-producing scorpion genes with an infectious caterpillar virus he was forced to trial it in Wytham Woods, three miles outside of Oxford. It was harmless to humans, but when the press found about it Bishop and his team found themselves at the centre of a scandal, and after much public protest the project was abandoned.

About a year afterwards, for reasons that have never been explained, Bishop was relieved of his duties as director. His six-month notice period was reduced to the two minutes it took to march him out of the building. He since moved to France, where he spends his retirement in quiet solitude, and nobody has heard much of him since. He is, I suspect, like Chester Mirocha and Harry Smith and so many others in this tale, a scientist with secrets.

'The Russians were interested in this too, you know,' he wrote to me. 'I made a visit in the nineties to one of their ex-secret research facilities in Siberia and the extent of their research into various viral pesticides and delivery systems surprised me. I suspect perhaps it was this that led to Porton's interest, or vice versa.'

While Porton retained an interest in vectors, what really excited it in the eighties was genetic engineering. DNA had been physically altered for the first time at the start of the seventies, and it triggered a revolution that sent shockwaves through the life sciences. Kelly came to Porton just as the labs there were acknowledging its impact. Biological agents didn't have to be harvested from nature any more. They could be built from scratch. The Defence Microbiology Division no longer had to counter simply what existed, but what could be invented. It was a task limited only by the scope of its own imagination.

This was the culture at Porton when Kelly commenced his second career. It was an environment that encouraged speculation, and shrank from putting a ceiling on any possible threat. This was where his first years in military biology were spent, and they were formative. He and his colleagues worked not just in lab but in an echo chamber, filled with whatever fears they could devise.

The invisible had become infinite.

We knew from published literature that Kelly supervised the genetic mapping of the toxins produced by a bacterium called *Clostridium perfringens*. *Clostridium perfringens* is everywhere in nature. It can be found wherever there is decaying vegetation. In terms of human harm it leads to little more than food poisoning, of which it is a common cause, but when it feeds on dead flesh it secretes toxins that cause gas gangrene. In a wound, if the gangrene is untreated, these toxins will kill. The bacteria become deadly. Cell death will creep throughout the body. Living flesh will blacken and bubble as pockets of gas inflate. A thin, sweet, putrid pus discharges in quantity. If it is not possible to excise or amputate, the bloodstream fills with poison, the immune system becomes overloaded, all tissue grows inflamed, shock sets in, and death follows soon after.

Kelly and eight of his subordinates learnt how to make these toxins. They studied how to clone them on the molecular level, how to produce and purify and crystallise them. Very possibly, for experimental purposes, they tested them as an aerosol spray. At a certain density, inhalation of aerosolised *perfringens* toxins would prove fatal within forty-eight gruesome hours. At a greater density, inhaling the bacterium itself would be sufficient.[34]

Kelly and colleagues also mapped and cloned the simian Herpes B virus. Herpes B is endemic to macaque monkeys, the most widespread genus of primate, where its symptoms are the same as normal herpes, but it is transmissible to humans, and if left untreated it will kill four out of every five people it infects. If you are bitten or scratched or spat at by an infected macaque, if you get faeces flung in your face, if you handle one and pick your nose or rub your eye, you should assume the worst. If an infection isn't treated quickly enough it will cause permanent neurological impairment. If it is treated too late, or not at all, you will die from a spasming, shattered nervous system, or a swollen bleeding brain. You will develop a headache, then a fever, then confusion and fatigue and ever worsening tremors until you expire in a hallucinogenic fit.

Officially, all this was called 'maintaining a watchtower capability'. In practice, it meant inventing weapons to defend against them. When the scientists of other countries pursued similar avenues, it was assumed they were simply inventing weapons with which to attack. From a watchtower, everyone starts to look like an enemy.

Ironically, Kelly's most commonly known contribution while at Porton Down was the work he did at the other end of the country. The decontamination of Gruinard Island was widely reported, and eventually it became something of a media circus. For the team at Porton it also meant a good deal of man hours. A lot of time was spent on it, but then in cleaning Gruinard[35] they were dealing with a legacy almost half a century old.

Wester Ross is a stretch of mountainous coastland in the northwest Highlands, a series of bays and lochs sheltered from the full brunt of the Atlantic by the Isle of Lewis. It is one of the few remaining parts of rural Britain where the term 'countryside' is inappropriate. There are no neat hedgerows here, no ploughed fields. It is remote, rugged, and almost entirely unchanged by the small population that subsists in its isolated villages and lonely crofters' cottages. It is also, and this surprised me, outstandingly, breathtakingly beautiful. It is a land of high snow-capped ranges and pink sands and heather and calm blue waters.

Porton Down's entire biological department came here for the first time before David Kelly had even been born. After continental Europe had fallen to the Nazis, America had fled the Philippines, and German panzers had begun another devastating blitzkrieg against the Soviet Union, the British government began to wonder if breaking the Genera Protocol might not be such a bad idea. Could illegal germ warfare change the tide? Churchill demanded to know.

In utmost secrecy, a very powerful committee was formed to evaluate possible agents. Anthrax was the obvious choice. Biological warfare had always had its detractors, not just on a moral level but on a practical one. Critics considered it inefficient and unproven, but even the nay-sayers couldn't discount the power of anthrax. *Bacillus anthracis* is a hardy, spore-forming bacterium that can withstand extremes of temperature and prolonged submersion in saltwater. In can survive in the soil, even in quick-lime, for decades. Occasional outbreaks had always presented a lethal hazard to livestock, but it was known to have killed people just as easily.

A skin infection brought up large black lesions, an unpleasant but obvious symptom that could be safely treated. Eating anthrax-infected meat would have you vomiting blood in a couple of days, and so unless it was promptly diagnosed gastrointestinal infection could easily prove fatal. But most dangerous of all was pulmonary exposure, and cases of this had been observed in wool-sorters, brush-makers, leather-workers and the like. Anthrax spores are seldom any bigger than a hundredth of a millimetre, and if you inhaled any, you were in trouble. For a few days, it would feel just like flu, and then you reached a toxic tipping point that triggered complete respiratory collapse. It killed just about everyone it infected.

The central difficulty was figuring out how to get the spores inside German lungs. In the best ad hoc, make-do traditions of British wartime boffinry, Porton's biologists brewed up batches of anthrax using milk churns and Marmite. Glass flasks were filled with the resultant slurry, loaded into an Austin van, and driven from Wiltshire to Wester Ross, under orders to avoid major highways and not stop unless instructed to by the police.[36] In Gruinard Bay, it was poured into bomblets and anti-tank bullets, and these were ferried out to the flat, lozenge-shaped island half a mile offshore, where they were tested against flocks of tethered sheep. All of them died.

The trials were recorded by the Porton biological department on colour film, and it's possible for the public to see portions of this in some video archives.[37] A few edited minutes have found their way onto the Internet. It all looks oddly futuristic, to see these men in their hazard suits and rubber gloves and gas masks plodding through the bracken. It could have been filmed last year. A very modern fear was felt for the first time at Gruinard, and it is still with us.

It was all considered a great success. The committee shared its secrets with the Americans, who in return accepted an order to produce and deliver half a million British anthrax bombs.

'We should regard it as a first instalment,' Churchill wrote.

It never arrived. Instead, later that year, after a lot of old-fashioned attrition, the Russians beat the Germans back at Stalingrad. By the time the US army had the production lines in place, the course of the war had already changed. But after it was won, the factories and laboratories were left standing. Fort Detrick and Dugway Proving Ground in Utah were born at Gruinard – the entire American programme was. The scientists Stateside and at Porton kept furtively working on further refinements, on different diseases and better means of delivery. The secret tests continued, in more controlled environments, on millions of animals, and tens of thousands of volunteers too, most of whom were never told what they were exposed to. The genie got out of the bottle at Gruinard Island. Over forty years later, Kelly and his colleagues came here to try and stuff it back in.

The first lot had tried. When their experiments had ended, they burnt off the island. They put on their protective suits, lit a series of fires, and retreated to the mainland to watch it spread through the heather. The flames crept from one end to the other, charring every inch of topsoil and sending a thick curtain of black, anthrax-infested smoke up into the cold Scottish sky. It made no difference. The anthrax, in its natural protective coat, proved impervious. So they nailed up some warning signs, prohibited landing, and left it alone. It became an open secret. Locals didn't really talk about it. Visitors were few. Farmers found their sheep came down with it every now and again, so Porton put a man in nearby Aultbea to verify claims and dole out compensation, and life moved on. Except on Gruinard.

Just why it became so important to clean up Gruinard Island when it did has really never been properly explained. Nobody needed to use it. The family that had owned it were in no hurry to get it back. I spoke to some of the senior personnel who worked alongside Kelly on the job, and they didn't know either, or at least they didn't tell me if they did. Yet strangely, one very obvious explanation was all over the papers at the time.

In October 1981, anonymous letters began to arrive at the offices of various broadsheets. They were from an outfit calling themselves 'Dark Harvest', who said they had 'brought back the seeds of death to where they had come from'.

'In 1941 the government took our island away,' they had written. 'We want it back.'

Claiming to have received assistance from local people and microbiologists from two Scottish universities, Dark Harvest announced they had removed 300 pounds of infected soil from Gruinard Island, and promised to distribute it at 'key points' over the next twelve months if their demands were not met. Asserting (hysterically) that Gruinard would be uninhabitable for the next two hundred to one thousand years, they called for a comprehensive survey of the area and asked for the island to be buried under reinforced concrete. The first load of anthrax-infected soil had apparently been left at Porton Down.

The press rang Porton, who confirmed the story. Reports differ, but the soil was either flung into the grounds from a passing train or deposited at the front gate. It had been analysed; the soil was indeed from Gruinard, and it contained anthrax spores.

It made for a great story.

A few days later, after a tip-off, Lancashire police found a sealed tin box on a rooftop near the Conservative Party Conference being held at the Winter Gardens in Blackpool. *The Times* received another mysterious communication, a shop-bought bereavement card with its incongruous pre-printed message left inside: 'Thanks for your sympathy and flowers.'

This handwriting underneath was considerably more cryptic:

DARK HARVEST
The Answers:
1) Priest
2) Ewe
3) Broom
2 islands and a loch or 2 lochs and an island.

What it meant is anyone's guess, although those familiar with Gruinard will know that Loch Ewe and Loch Broom are a few miles either side of Gruinard Bay, and Priest is a small uninhabited island a little further out to sea.

Porton Down analysed the soil left at Blackpool and said that while it had come from Gruinard Island, it was anthrax-free. The police said a thorough investigation was under way. Then absolutely nothing happened. No more letters were sent. No more containers of soil were found. No one was ever questioned, let alone arrested. And the following month the Ministry of Defence announced it was reviewing plans to decontaminate the island, and the whole affair just melted away.

It remains a very curious affair. Just how the soil was delivered to Porton in the first place is hard to say. I have walked the railway track that borders Porton Down, I have stood there and watched the trains pass at the bottom of the cutting. There is no one, not even an Olympic shot-putter, who could throw a bucket of soil from a speeding train up a thirty-foot embankment and over the twelve-foot fence atop it. I don't see how it could have happened. Similarly, the front gate at Porton is permanently manned by the Ministry of Defence police. Suspicious cars would have their licence plates taken as a matter of course (mine was). A pedestrian or cyclist who approached, left a parcel, and then left would draw even more attention, and could well expect to be stopped and questioned.

It was also reported that when Highland Police made their initial inquiries at Gruinard Bay, there had been no strangers in the area except for the usual visits from Porton Down itself. The small community in that part of the country is, as you might expect, reasonably tight-knit. The only people with a boat were the two Flett brothers, paid to row over to the island every year and repaint the warning signs. Yet nobody had seen anything. More curiously, staff and students at the microbiology departments of Scottish universities weren't even questioned at all, although they would have presented a reasonably small pool of people.

Years later came off-the-record briefings claiming that Dark Harvest was actually an offshoot of an entirely unknown nationalist movement called the Scottish Civilian Army. The Scottish National Party has certainly never heard of them, and from what I could gather, the misfits who comprised the Scottish National Liberation Army are equally ignorant. In any case, taking a 1400-mile round trip to drop a lethal bacterium off at a guarded government research facility shows a level of motivation far beyond anything ever evidenced by the small bunch of eccentrics who formed the extremist fringe of Gaelic nationalism.

The 300 pounds of anthrax-infected soil were never found. Neither does it appear to have led to a single instance of anthrax poisoning amongst its handlers and keepers, which would have been automatically reported by any doctor or hospital to the Public Health Agency.

The Highland Constabulary have no records at all relating to Dark Harvest, not in their archives or at the nearest station.

'That was a Special Branch job,' I was told. 'We wouldn't be able to tell you a thing.'

The presence of Special Branch, as ever, points to only one thing. Dark Harvest was a matter for British intelligence, and that made it nobody else's business. Given the lack of any serious investigation, the inconsistencies in reported accounts, the nonexistence of the Scottish Civilian Army and the absence of any official written records, it's hard to discern what their interests were, but it may be that the Sverdlovsk anthrax leak helped shape events.

The incident at Sverdlovsk happened only two years before Dark Harvest. Dark Harvest made the study of anthrax-infected soil a high priority both for MI6 and for Porton Down, which sent up a team to survey the island shortly after it heard the news. It would have been important to know what terrain exposed to military anthrax activity looked like, how the spores could be detected and what form Russian decontamination efforts might have taken. After the Soviet anthrax accident there were scientists in Wiltshire and spooks in London who would have been desperate for Sverdlovsk soil samples. Ironically, if the Dark Harvest story is true and not some sort of cover, they got a couple from somewhere far closer to home.

Until then the government had simply ignored the problem. John Alec Macrea, one the neighbourhood's more community-minded members, had once left a petition to be signed at Laide Post Office.[38] It demanded only three simple things of the government: it asked if experiments were still being carried out on Gruinard, if it was being retained for future experiments, and if there were any plans to decontaminate it. It amassed seventy signatures in a matter of days before the police confiscated it. Macrea protested that he had been an officer in the Royal Navy for twelve years, was on good terms with his MP, and swore there had never been 'any subversive activity' in the Bay, but he never received any official response.

After Dark Harvest, Porton Down mooted several methods for cleaning up Gruinard. One option was to irradiate it, but the community were sounded out on that, and they didn't consider making the island radioactive would constitute a great improvement. Apparently they also considered encasing it in cement, just as Dark Harvest had demanded, but it was deemed impractical. A variety of chemical treatments were tested, but it was only after Kelly took charge that a solution was settled on. The plan was to douse Gruinard in formaldehyde. They would restore the island by embalming it. A private contractor was appointed to provide the labour, and in 1986, two years into his appointment, the clean-up commenced.

It was no small task. The budget ran into the millions. They removed the affected topsoil in sealed containers and sprayed the earth underneath with over 800,000 litres of formaldehyde in solution. Twenty-four tanker loads of it were driven up and ferried over. At the petrol station in nearby Tarvie someone noticed one of them was leaking, and the roads had to be closed down for six hours while the fire brigade mopped up, formaldehyde being a highly toxic carcinogen. The local MP, Charles Kennedy, complained that it should have all been brought up by boat.

By the end of the summer, they were done. Kelly and his colleagues left it alone for the winter, for the solution to seep through and do its work, and came back the next year to take more samples and check that the process had worked. It hadn't, not entirely. They still found some low concentrations deep in the soil at the spots where the bombs had been dropped or the sheep had been buried. So they injected yet more formaldehyde into the soil.

In a final test, the Ministry of Defence paid a man called Steve Lynn to tend a flock of sheep on the island for the whole of that summer. Whether he was vaccinated or not nobody knows, but the sheep weren't, and they all survived. Kelly's crew took yet more samples. At even lower levels, the anthrax was still there, so they pumped the earth with yet more solution, but there wasn't much more they could do. Gruinard Island is a little over a mile long and about half a mile wide, and it had been drenched in 260 tonnes of formaldehyde.

No one was especially eager to announce mission accomplished. It took another three years of cautious waiting and sampling before it became official, and there was a small ceremony to mark the occasion on the island's jetty, with news crews and journalists in attendance. The press had been offered several tours of the island throughout the long decontamination process, and plenty of foreboding articles had been penned about what it was like to set foot on Britain's anthrax island.

It wasn't a bad junket for a London reporter; the broadsheets all sent people, so did some of the regionals, and a couple of magazines. Occasionally it had been a bit of a scrum. On one open day the man from *The Times* turned up in his own chartered seaplane, for which he earned the jealous derision of his peers.

Jack Melling had been at Porton Down for sixteen years before he ever ventured up to Gruinard. 'I'm not sure why Gruinard became so important,' he told me, 'but it *was* a way of demonstrating some public benefit. Porton Down had always done a lot medically, but environmentally, I don't think it had done anything. And environmentally, it was a unique job. It wasn't like cleaning up a farm after an agricultural outbreak. Decontaminating Gruinard was interesting, challenging work. Nothing like it had ever been done before.'

Not, at least, outside the Soviet Union. For Porton Down, it carried positive PR value, and Kelly had been on hand to help deliver it. His earliest exchange with the media that I could find was a letter to the *New Scientist* in 1986, explaining how the formaldehyde on Gruinard wouldn't affect the area's sea life (there was very good salmon fishing in the rivers off the bay, and locals didn't want it disturbed). Dealing with journalists and public perception had been an important part of his job from the very beginning.

A ceremony of sorts finally took place one bright blustery afternoon in April 1990. Michael Neubert, the junior Defence Minister, turned up and made a big show of pulling down the ministry's warning sign. Flashbulbs duly popped. The event was hijacked to a certain extent by a Glaswegian sculptor called George Wyllie, who turned up with a bottle of Scotch and laid a commemorative plaque before installing one of his trademark 'spires'.

It would be easy to dismiss this as self-promotion, but Wyllie was ex-Navy, and he'd been in Hiroshima after the bomb dropped. He had seen the havoc that weapons of mass destruction can wreak. What's more, Hiroshima had regained its population by 1958, and continued to grow, whereas Gruinard had been off-limits for half a century. Rex Watson, the former director of the Chemical Defence Establishment at Porton Down, had earlier said that if the RAF had bombed German cities with anthrax they would still be uninhabitable.[39]

'For air, stone and the equilibrium of understanding,' read the plaque. 'Welcome back Gruinard.'

Judging from the photos, David Kelly appears to have been distinctly unimpressed. Yet later, at a formal dinner in Edinburgh to mark the occasion, he was in good form. The speech he gave to the committee that had overseen the decontamination was, apparently, quite funny. Yet I wonder how much he believed it:

'Welcome back Gruinard.'

The island remains unused. The trust that owned it used to send some sheep over every summer, but that soon stopped. It was too much trouble. The island's soil is mostly peat, full of the organic material on which bacteria like to grow. A single seal or seagull or black rabbit or white-tailed eagle, if it comes into contact with just one infinitesimally small spore, will give *Bacillus anthracis* all the opportunity it needs to burst forth once again. One of the types of anthrax tested on Gruinard was Vollum, the most virulent non-engineered strain then known to the West. It came, coincidentally, from a dead cow not far from Kelly's house in Oxfordshire, where it was discovered in the thirties, and it would cross his path again, in a different country, in a different part of the world.

When the US began its own independent biological weapons programme after the Second World War, it avoided the dilemma of creating another Gruinard by building a test sphere the size of a small moon. Most famously known as the Eight Ball, Fort Detrick's million-litre steel sphere has walls an inch and a quarter thick, stands five storeys tall, and weighs 131 tonnes. It's so big that aerosol clouds can stratify inside it. It has its own microclimate. The building that housed it was demolished decades ago, but the extraordinary Eight Ball is still standing, and incredibly, has even been added to America's National Register of Historic Places. So it will long remain, another seldom visited monument to the legacy and containment of germ warfare.

This is the problem with fighting germs: there is no victory. They don't surrender. They don't make peace or sign treaties or become your ally. A lethal bacterium will always remain an enemy, and you can never be sure it is not holding out a pocket of resistance somewhere, waiting to launch another offensive. On Google Maps, higher-resolution images of Gruinard Island have been blurred out at the request of the British government. The annual Ministry of Defence estimates still carry an indemnity 'in relation to the disposal of Gruinard in the event of claims arising from the outbreak of specific strains of anthrax on the island'.[40]

The abiding unease people feel over Gruinard surfaced once more in the months after 9/11, when a tabloid newspaper ran a story claiming Scottish terrorists could supply anthrax from Gruinard Island to Osama Bin Laden.[41] It would be tempting to investigate this as some sort of government disinformation, but the propensity of the British tabloid press to print absolutely any old rubbish makes it rather a moot point. It disinforms its readers as a matter of course.

Fear and disinformation are the two corollaries of biological weapons. They travel together. Where there is disease there is fear, and where there are weapons of mass destruction, there are lies. But shortly after David Kelly had finished pumping formaldehyde into Gruinard, he heard a story that would frighten the most stoic and cynical of listeners.

The British government knew about Project Coast, and they knew about Iraq's biowarfare efforts at Salman Pak, but in all that time the Soviet Union had remained the same blank, unreadable monolith. That was about to change. The curtain was about to be lifted on the most extensive biological weapons programme in the world.

A man had walked into the British Embassy in Paris. His name was Vladimir Pasechnik, and he said he was a senior Soviet microbiologist and that he wanted to defect. What he offered in exchange was an insider's account of how a military superpower had been secretly beset by bleak, apocalyptic lunacy. It was a glimpse into the heart of a nightmare.

Back in Belgium, Aubin Heyndrickx went on to carve out something of a career as a 'discoverer' of chemical and biological weapon attacks. After his business in Iran, South Africa and Angola was concluded, he sounded the same siren again in Romania, where he said the security forces of Ceausescu's crumbling regime had poisoned a water tank with sarin or VX. No one else ever unearthed any supporting evidence. He claimed alternately to be a UN adviser or a consultant to the European Commission, which gave him a certain credibility, but in practice this seems to mean he just sent them unbidden letters.[42]

By the mid-nineties, he had overstretched himself. He was convicted in 1991 for libel and forgery, and was forced to quit his post at Ghent. He left his university post the same year, as a US Department of Defense cable described, 'totally disgraced in his field. All of his studies turned out to be nonsense.'[43] The year before, he had received a three-month suspended jail sentence for defrauding his employer, which he promptly compounded by starting rumours that his ex-mistress's new boyfriend was a drug trafficker, which earned him another three months' suspended for libel. At his own criminal trial Basson dismissed Heyndrickx as a mercenary agent provocateur and propagandist.

Heyndrickx countered all this by pointing out that whatever his detractors claimed, chemical and biological weapons were horrible. He said a delegation of world experts would vouch for his findings and his competence, but in the end he could cite only two 'authorities' who backed him. Neither were laboratories, and one was the Institute for Credit Risk and Analysis run by Evelyn le Chêne, a fellow Belgian who would later become well known to Britain's activists and demonstrators as a private-sector spymaster for corporations like BAE Systems.[44] In 1995, Heyndrickx found himself in court again, where he was convicted for falsifying lab results, and also unable to adequately explain the presence of a large sum of money in his bank account.

At that point you might have expected Heyndrickx to fade away, but before the decade was out he was back in the fold. He turned up in Kosovo, where he said the Serbs had used nerve gas against thousands of children, and he was hereafter referred to without reservation by people who should have known better. *Jane's Defence Weekly* cited him, and so too did David Kelly's old Porton Down boss, Graham Pearson. In 2002, the US Senate Committee on Foreign Affairs was informed that Heyndrickx was a 'world-renowned' 'senior United Nations consultant' whose 'scrupulously documented' evidence proved that Castro's Cuba had a WMD programme.[45] And with a sad inevitability, after the invasion of Iraq he ended up on the front pages of the *International Herald Tribune* and the *New York Times*, posing in his white coat in his study, surrounded by jars of pickled flesh he said were samples from the gas attack at Halabja, offering his services as an expert witness for any upcoming trial. He was seventy-nine years of age.

Truth versus consequences? Heyndrickx made a career out of it, always playing the latter off against the former, a dark actor if ever there was one. There are others like him, but as far as I can tell he was the only one who freelanced, hence his trouble with the law. Those with a government to protect them can always hide their test results behind the chimera of national security. Those who work for their country can always count on a quiet retirement, unless they fall from grace.

5

Vladimir Takes a Walk

As we Russians say, free cheese can only be found in a mousetrap.
IGOR V. DOMARADSKIJ, SOVIET BIOWEAPONS
RESEARCH DIRECTOR

Nobody can really say why he did it, but one October day in Toulouse a military microbiologist went out for a walk and never came back. Somewhere along the banks of the Garonne, or in some winding medieval alleyway, or under the falling leaves of some tree-lined boulevard, all that can be said is that something happened. Something that prompted Vladimir Artemovich Pasechnik to leave his hotel, his colleagues, his job, his family, his home – his life, basically – behind him, and walk off a plank.

A few hours later, he was four hundred miles to the north, standing in the lobby of the Canadian Embassy in Paris, asking to defect. The Canadians stalled him with paperwork, either because they didn't know what they'd got or because they sensed that Pasechnik was perhaps already somebody else's boy. In the end, he resorted to the British Embassy on the rue du Faubourg Saint-Honoré. It was only round the corner but it was under constant surveillance, which made the short walk a one-way trip.

Vladimir Pasechnik was fifty-two years old and the director of the Institute of Highly Pure Biopreparations in Leningrad, a civilian laboratory that had been providing covert assistance to the

Soviet military's secret germ-warfare programme. He had only been given permission to leave Russia so that he could visit a French biotech company. Now, in plain view, he had strolled into the British Embassy, in a totally different part of the country. This was 1989, and during the Cold War such acts were terminal events. Life as you knew it was over. Go home to the Motherland, where you now risked interrogation, impoverishment and imprisonment, or fall into the arms of your handlers, and hope you got a good deal. There was no going back. Like David Kelly, Pasechnik had a wife and three children. He cannot have known what would happen to them, or if he would ever see them again. He had left all of them, left everything and everyone he had ever known, with no more than the clothes on his back. What Pasechnik committed that October afternoon in Paris wasn't suicide, but it was something almost as drastic.

Inside the Embassy, he was passed very quickly to the MI6 station chief who immediately flashed a message to HQ, which in those days was Century House, then a grey, brutalist tower block by Lambeth North tube station. London said to bring him in. Ever since the Sverdlovsk anthrax leak their analysts had been poring over blurry satellite photos and Soviet yearbooks, trying to unlock what the Russians were up to. Now they had the key: human intelligence from the heart of the programme. Operational protocol meant MI6 was supposed to ask the French for permission before picking up Pasechnik, as the defection occurred on French soil, but not in this instance. Instead his British officers quickly issued him with a false passport and escorted him on that evening's British Airways shuttle to Heathrow.

Whoever had been handling Vladimir in Toulouse had done a thorough job. When he arrived on English soil Pasechnik embarrassed his bodyguards by bursting into tears. The Russian was apparently inconsolable. Almost all defections occur at levels of intense personal stress, and this was no different. After all, from an intelligence standpoint, stress has its uses. Those trained in recruiting and handling defectors are taught that it is important to establish psychological control, and by the time he arrived in Britain Vladimir Pasechnik had become convinced he would face serious criminal charges for his work with biological weapons.[1] It's not an impression he would have formed inside the Soviet Union: most of Russia's military scientists later said they had never heard of the Biological Weapons Convention. It wasn't an accurate impression either, since only countries, not people, can be considered in breach of the BWC. Yet despite his painful illusions, or perhaps because of them, Pasechnik had apparently acquiesced in his own removal.

According to one account, his wife Natasha was waiting for him at the airport outside Moscow when his flight got in.[2] Only his assistant was on board (Pasechnik was apparently supposed to have caught an earlier flight). The two of them waited for him in the arrivals lounge until the end of the weekend, and then, fatefully, as they were obliged to, they informed the authorities. Pasechnik's absence became a matter for the KGB, and hope petered out.

Years later, when the defection became public knowledge and MI6 arranged a few interviews for a very select number of approved journalists, it was put about that Pasechnik came to the West because he had been ideologically motivated.[3] That he had come to feel biological warfare was morally wrong, that he couldn't sleep at nights, that he was courageous and noble and self-sacrificing. The same things were generally said about all Soviet defectors, and perhaps every defector, as a matter of course: that they came here because their country was wrong, and ours was right. No mention is ever made of bribes or blackmail, although such ruses certainly played their part on occasion. Defections and defectors, then and now, have always been used as propaganda. But as intelligence officers know, ideological defections are the rarest kind.[4]

Let it be said, as no one has until now, although it seems all too obvious, that whoever convinced Vladimir Pasechnik to walk out of his own life must have leaned on him pretty hard. Whoever it was, and however they got to him, the pressures they expertly applied must have been immense.

The *Times* journalist Nick Rufford once met David Kelly in his local pub, the Waggon and Horses in Southmoor, and asked him straight out: what had MI6 really done to convince Vladimir Pasechnik to come over?[5]

'Who knows what those James Bond chaps get up to?' Kelly had said.

'But,' Rufford added, 'there was a twinkle in his eye and he was clearly enjoying a secret.'

I wondered what Pasechnik's widow Natasha had to say about it. I asked an American UNSCOM colleague of Kelly's, who had come to know the family reasonably well, if she would talk to me about her side of the story, about the reasons for her husband's defection, and how his treatment by British intelligence looked from her perspective.

'Hey,' he told me, 'I can ask, but she's never done interviews. She won't. It's a rule of hers.'

He was right. She won't and she didn't. But whose rule is it really? Hers, or MI6's? Like Janice Kelly, Natasha Pasechnik leads a quiet life, careful of who she meets, sets limits to all her conversations, and won't go on the record for anybody.

Whatever prompted Pasechnik to come over, his obvious personal distress led many of his handlers and debriefers to believe he was genuine even before his bona fides could be verified. Intelligence people are instinctively suspicious of defectors as plants or fantasists, but Pasechnik's tormented emotional state seemed all too sincere, and other, smaller details added up as well. He had a fondness for Mozart sonatas that would have been rare outside the *nomenklatura*, and he couldn't drive, which was another sign of high social standing.[6] Later, he would marvel at the fact Kelly owned his own home computer.

Typical defector debriefings would have started with the humdrum, with reassuring banalities. Photos and fingerprints would have been taken, there would have been a medical exam, an IQ test, and questionnaires to be filled in on work history and personal life. Nothing too sensational was expected at this stage. Bona fides did not build themselves overnight. You took down a series of prosaic details at the outset and you came back to them after a few weeks. If everything still held together then, without contradictions or changes, you were on your way to validation.

For a few nights, Pasechnik was bounced around London hotels. Taking him to Century House would only have advertised his whereabouts to the world's intelligence agencies, all of whom covertly scrutinise each other's headquarters. Eventually MI6 found him a safe house. I haven't been able to find out where – no one would tell me – but details from various accounts suggest it was an old house, somewhere nondescript, by the sea.[7] Weston-super-Mare, perhaps. Southend, possibly. Safe houses in both places would feature later in Kelly's last, haunted days.

The CIA preferred debriefings to take place in safe houses fitted with two-way mirrors and audio bugs and hidden cameras, so that body language could be monitored at all times. More than one fabricator, having deftly deflected a barrage of particularly probing questions, has been exposed by a sly and incongruous smile when they believed they were unobserved.[8] Whether MI6 kitted out the Pasechnik safe house in the American fashion is unknown, but in other respects they seem to have followed the US approach reasonably closely (that we know anything about Western debriefing procedures at all is because of CIA declassifications; British intelligence has always remained characteristically and entirely silent on the subject, and so have the individuals interrogated, Pasechnik included).

The CIA believed that defectors should be debriefed by big teams, with at least two interrogators.[9] A single defector would be handled by a couple of experts in his field, a counter-intelligence officer to spot doubles and plants, and some sort of friendly handholder figure (also in practice an interrogator, sometimes the most efficient). On occasion, if it seemed appropriate, they would bring in a member of the opposite sex for company. Then there would be a guard or two and, crucially, a psychiatrist: nervous collapses of defectors were not unknown, and many had growing psychological problems to begin with. Sedation had sometimes been required in the past.

As soon as Pasechnik touched down in Heathrow, MI6 began putting its team together. A request for debriefers with biological expertise went out to the Defence Intelligence Staff (DIS) in the Metropole Building on Northumberland Avenue, off Trafalgar Square. The Metropole had once been one of the grandest Victorian hotels, but by then had been worn down by fifty years of government occupancy. To say it had a faded grandeur would be too kind. Its drab interior was cramped, poorly lit, and not overly clean.

Then as now, the DIS was not a spy agency, like MI5 or MI6 or GCHQ, but the intelligence wing of the Ministry of Defence. It didn't run agents, win defectors or intercept communications, but if the secrets such activities uncovered were military in nature, it analysed and assessed them for distribution to ministers and their departments. Topical, reliable, or politically sought-after 'product' got sent to Cabinet via the Joint Intelligence Committee. Everything else got shoved in a filing cabinet. The DIS did (and does) technical desk work, far from the glamour and frisson of espionage. Similarly, the officers in MI6 may very well have been able to compromise, convince, and compel with aplomb, but they knew practically nothing about the ins and outs of military microbiology. They had no real idea about the finer details of what Pasechnik was telling them. Problematically, at that time the DIS wasn't much more clued up either.

In 1989, the man in charge of the chemical and biological weapons desk at Defence Intelligence was Brian Jones, and he had a grand total of two staff: one man to deal with the chemical stuff, and another for biological. The biological expert was a man called Christopher Davis. Early details of Pasechnik's disclosures came through on the wire; the way Davis tells it, it was a grey, rainy Friday afternoon not long before five o'clock when the news came

in. Davis and Jones were looking forward to crowded train carriages and warm homes and the weekend.

Instead, DIS was informed that MI6 had acquired a senior
Soviet source – codenamed TRUNCATE – from a biological lab
in Leningrad who claimed the Russian military had been carrying out secret research on, amongst other things, a bacterium
called *Yersinia pestis*, which the generals hoped could be made
resistant to antibiotics. The source claimed to have once been part
of a team that modelled how *Yersinia pestis* could be aerosolised and
sprayed from a cruise missile.

Davis and Jones exchanged glances.

Yersinia pestis had once wiped out a third of Europe. The population had taken a century and a half to recover. It is better
known to most people as the Black Death.[10]

What Davis said next has been mentioned in almost every
retelling of this story.

'Oh shit,' he said.

Christopher Davis was a doctor in the Royal Navy, and Brian
Jones had been a metallurgist in the Admiralty Research Labs in
Portsmouth. Neither had any first-hand experience of biological
weapons. Davis suggested they bring in David Kelly. Jones had first
met Porton Down's new biology superintendent on a Ministry of
Defence management course three years earlier, and had seen him
periodically since – 'I recall that I found him quite hard going,' he
later wrote, although if Jones's future performance at Hutton was
anything to go by we would all have benefited if he'd been rather
more hard going himself.[11] Jones spoke to Graham Pearson, the
director of the Chemical Defence Establishment at Porton Down.
He asked, while giving as little away as possible, 'if David Kelly
could be nominated for additional security clearance and provide
us with some assistance'.[12]

While being told next to nothing about the task in hand except
that he would be away from home for some weeks, Kelly agreed,
and was swiftly granted top-secret clearance and 'access to sensitive intelligence material, *subject to indoctrination*'.[13] It was a status

he would continue to hold right up until his tumultuous final weeks fourteen years later.

Defector briefings, at least during the Cold War, were intense. The initial period, when the subject was at his most vulnerable, was considered to be the most important. It is in those early few weeks or months that an intelligence service must decide if their man really is who he says he is, and to what extent he can be relied upon. For the CIA this could sometimes be determined in two to three weeks, although 'generally it is more like two to three months', and Kelly's debriefing of Pasechnik sits comfortably within this timespan.[14]

Internal CIA manuals talk a great deal about the importance of maintaining psychological superiority, of poses and impressions and behaviour. Often a little drama or two was staged to test the subject, and I doubt that Kelly would have refrained from such ruses if asked (later, in UNSCOM, these tactics were routinely used by senior inspectors). In any case, everyone involved in the debriefing had to maintain a steady, integrated front. Kelly was hurriedly brought up to speed by MI6 on what and what not to say, on what kind of language to use, on how to present himself for maximum effect.

The CIA always lodged its interrogators away from the defector and his safe house as 'it is better not to have to eat, sleep and play with a person whom you are trying to squeeze dry'.[15]

British intelligence were of the same opinion. David Kelly later told his stepsister, Sarah Pape, that he was lodged in a hotel for weeks on end, 'although nobody in my family knew anything about that at the time. He just did not discuss it with us'.[16]

Staying at a remove enabled the debriefers to talk in private, to compare notes and answers to questions already put, to chart emotional gambits and trajectories and, not least, to give themselves some time off.

Interrogators needed to be alert, self-controlled, and quick on their feet in order to spot and exploit any change of mood. Anger, anxiety, jealousy and homesickness can all be played on.

Interrogators, Kelly quickly found out, cannot afford to be easily impressed or emotionally open, while at the same time they need to be very emotionally perceptive.

'The pressures on them are great,' advised the CIA training officer John Ankerbrand. 'Otherwise promising apprentice intelligence officers have more than once found their undoing in the handling of a defector.'[17]

The safe-house debriefing began in early November. The key team appears to have been Christopher Davis from DIS, David Kelly form Porton Down, and a Russian 'translator' who has never been named, and is almost certainly an MI6 officer. They positioned themselves around some sparsely furnished room in the safe house, their defector was brought in (it's always better to have him brought to you than to go to him) and finally they laid eyes on their quarry.

He was a short, stocky man with a round but well-defined face, dark hair and a bald pate. His build seemed too muscular for your average scientist, his large hands could have belonged to a builder. And he was sullen, confused, dazed. He spoke with hesitation. Kelly and Davis had been instructed to call him by an assumed name – Michael – but Davis says they knew who he was. And slowly, as the weeks passed, as the questions in their thousands were asked and answered, Vladimir Pasechnik slowly began to emerge, his life reconstructed entirely in a quiet room in a secret house on the English coast.

Kelly's first foray into the world of intelligence set the pattern for much that would follow. So much of his future work would depend on precisely this, on conversations both unobserved and recorded, on secret discussions in sealed rooms. What was said and concluded during these exchanges always remained the exclusive property of Her Majesty's Government. Kelly only ever spoke about Pasechnik once, although Davis has gone on record several times. Each occasion, one assumes, occurred under instruction or licence. Every disclosure, then, may have had its own agenda, and not every admission was necessarily true. It is the fate of the handlers to be handled in turn. Years later, lies were told about all of this. What follows is largely what remains uncontested by researchers outside the intelligence community, or by those who have left it.[18]

Slowly, but with growing confidence, Vladimir spoke. Halted only briefly by odd interjections from Kelly and Davis and their spook, his tale found its own pace and momentum, almost as if it was unfolding on its own. In a sense, it was. All stories have their own intrinsic, organic shape, something as natural as truth, and which is always deformed by secrecy. Only with the telling, with exposure to air and space and the ears of others, do facts finally realign, and things make sense. Everyone has their story, and every story yearns to be told.

Far off, from behind the curtains of that room, came the stark, territorial cawing of the gulls. Nearer, and much quieter, was the constant whirring of a tape recorder. Out of sight and earshot were the crashing of waves and the pull of the tide and Vladimir Pasechnik shifted in his seat and took a long breath and began to beat his own way up to oxygen and sunlight and the world.

He was born in Stalingrad in 1937, in the midst of Stalin's Great Purges, which may be why his family soon relocated to their native Leningrad. If the move offered them any respite, it was brief. By the time Pasechnik was eight years old he had lived through the most terrible siege in the history of mankind. With the Third Reich's Army Group North outside the city gates, the Pasechniks and their neighbours were reduced to eating cats, sawdust, and wallpaper paste. The city police were compelled to form a special unit to deal with the spread of cannibalism, and it ended up making over two thousand arrests.[19] By the time the siege was lifted, over a million civilians had died or gone missing, as well as over a million Red Army soldiers, with two million more wounded or sick.[20] According to his obituary in the *Telegraph*, Pasechnik's parents were among the dead. Like David Kelly, he grew up in the care of relatives.

He remained in Leningrad after the war, excelling at school, and then graduating top of his class at the city's Polytechnical Institute. A young and rising star, he went on to work and study the biological use of polymers at another Leningrad academy, the Institute of High Molecular Compounds, where he rose to deputy director. Then, in the early seventies, the moribund world of Soviet science experienced a belated renaissance. Since the days of Stalin it had been blinkered by political bias, most severely in the field of biology, where evolutionary theory and genetics had been banned as capitalist heresy. In their place stood the dubious doctrines of apparatchik Trofim Lysenko, whose fudged arguments that living things could acquire characteristics from their environment within only two or three generations found favour with the Soviet project to perfect the working man. He rose to greatness on the back of them, and although Lysenkoism was transparent bunk to his successors, if they wanted to work as scientists they were obliged to accept it as truth. Then, at the start of the seventies, everything suddenly changed.

The Central Committee of the Communist Party made the bold and open statement that the Soviet Union would finally commit its resources to a new wave of genetic research in molecular biology, to let the nation and the world know 'we had at last awakened and resolved to overcome our backwardness in this field'.[21] Lysenko, as Trotksy once had been, was airbrushed out of the picture.

New committees were founded, a new umbrella organisation was created, and a network of new research institutes, called Biopreparat, was proposed, each lab to be built from scratch. The following year Vladimir Pasechnik was asked to head one in his native Leningrad. He was thirty-seven years old, younger even than Kelly had been when he made his fateful transition from Oxford to Porton Down. Pasechnik was promised a provisional budget so high as to be practically unlimited. He was told he would be free to recruit the best staff he could find, and was given permission to import whatever equipment from the West he thought necessary. The wages of Biopreparat scientists would be much higher than other civilian researchers, their housing would be better, and they would be given access to special shops that allowed them to buy consumer goods unavailable to the average Russian. Also, he was informed, he would be doing his patriotic duty.

Unsurprisingly, Pasechnik accepted the offer. Yet all was not as it seemed. His job interview was conducted by the head of Biopreparat itself, who turned out to be one Lieutenant General Ogarkov, with KGB officers present. It was explained he would be forbidden to talk about any aspect of his work with non-Biopreparat scientists. Neither, as a Biopreparat scientist, could he subscribe to academic journals or visit libraries, in case spies discerned the direction of his research. Lab security would be handled by the KGB, which would have offices and staff in the institute itself, as in every Biopreparat facility, to monitor staff and communications. And, as with every other Biopreparat lab, his most senior staff would typically be military officers, always dressed in civilian clothes, sometimes even under assumed names.

'Officially,' Pasechnik told his debriefers, 'we were involved in two problems which we could publicly talk about. One was vaccine development and the other was producing preparations for protecting crops. Biopesticides.'[22]

Kelly's ears must have pricked at this. His colleagues at his old Institute of Virology had worked on biopesticides too, and Porton Down had always taken a very helpful interest. Behind his poker face, he must have sensed what was coming next.

'In fact,' Pasechnik confessed, 'we were developing methods of production and equipment for a biological weapons programme.'

Four years after he spoke to David Kelly, on the two occasions when he was invited to talk to journalists, Pasechnik gave the impression he had been hoodwinked. That he had wanted to work only in public health, to make vaccines and cure cancer, and that he had unwittingly fallen victim to a Faustian pact with the corrupting Soviet military. According to this narrative, he worked for years without realising the ugly consequences of his labours, and as the truth dawned and the real, military nature of his research became evident, he grew disgusted, and yearned to escape.

Perhaps. Much later, speaking to the former UNSCOM inspector Raymond Zilinskas, he said he knew about the military nature of his work from the day he moved into his new labs. Given the circumstances of his recruitment and the conditions of his employment, Pasechnik must at the very least have suspected the truth from the start, even if those under him remained in the dark. And I doubt the orphan of Leningrad would have turned down the chance to help defend his motherland.

It was another six years before Pasechnik's Institute of Highly Pure Biopreparations (IHPB) opened for business in its purpose-built lab complex on a back street in Leningrad's desirable Petrogradsky district, a dozen blocks away from the State Medical University (where he worked in the interim nobody knows, or if they do, they aren't saying). Pasechnik told his debriefers that the majority of his workforce weren't told the true nature of their work and never asked about it either. Like most Soviet employees, perhaps like most people anywhere, they were happy to accept their privileges, concentrate on their job and not ask too many difficult questions.

Those of Pasechnik's staff with high enough security clearance were told by the KGB that their work was military in nature, but purely defensive. The Americans and the British, the KGB explained, were secretly researching biological weapons and so the Soviets had to as well, if only to counter them. It was the exact same rationale that Porton Down and Fort Detrick used. Except even this was just another cover, or 'legend' as the Russians called it, a second lie within the first.

Only those at the very top of Biopreparat's pyramid, of whom there were exceptionally few, were told the truth: they were part of an ultra-clandestine project called 'Ferment', or Problem F, its objective to design and develop what were termed 'weapons of special designation', Kremlin-speak for the next generation of genetically engineered biological weapons. It was the military, not the Academy, who had finally convinced the politburo to ditch the embarrassment that was Lysenkoism, and they were eager to make up for lost time.

The scale of it all was staggering. Pasechnik's Institute had a staff of over four hundred.[23] He knew, too, of five other Biopreparat institutes of equal or greater size across the country, and countless sub-institutes and research stations. Joined to this, he said, were the three biological labs of the military itself, at Sverdlovsk (where the anthrax leak had occurred), Kirov and Zagorsk, run by the 15th Military Directorate, a new wing of the Soviet army dedicated purely to biological warfare, and even more secretive still. By the most conservative estimate the number of Russian scientists working on Project Ferment ran well into the tens of thousands. Meanwhile, despite being allowed to make a few new hires, David Kelly's Defence Microbiology Division wouldn't have filled the top half of a double-decker bus.

'The information was so stunning,' said Davis. 'A whole ministry exposed, millions of roubles spent, a complete organisation shown to be a front. It just went on and on.'[24]

Ferment was so compartmentalised that Pasechnik found it difficult to say how advanced the overall programme was, but his experiences had afforded him a pretty good partial impression. Davis again:

'He spoke about what he knew personally, or as a result of data that he was aware of, and what he had been told, and what he had found out just chatting with other people. He never, ever stretched things.'[25]

No, the stretching came later, and it was not Pasechnik who did it.

Leningrad's Institute of Highly Pure Biopreparations was tasked with developing formulations for the agents weaponised at two other Biopreparat labs. These were the State Research Centre for Applied Microbiology (SRCAM), in the newly built science settlement of Obolensk, just south of Moscow, which handled bacteria, and Vector, deep in western Siberia, which handled highly contagious viruses.

It was no good engineering and growing lethal microbes and then just scooping them out of fermenters and stuffing them into bombs. These biological agents had to be treated, and given a form that offered longevity and protection, which would keep the payload both biologically pure and highly dispersible if burst or sprayed. The military kept asking for increasingly concentrated formulations, with higher kill counts per kilogram, and Pasechnik's staff worked endlessly at finding the techniques and fillers to do it.

His first job was to do with a bacterium called *Francisella tularensis*, which caused rabbit fever, first discovered in Californian squirrels in the early twentieth century. It can cause nasty skin lesions for those handling infected animals, which tend to be the smaller mammals, but like all microbes it does its most damage in the lung. In everyday life, this is something that rarely happens, except when a gardener might run his mower over an infected rodent corpse and inhale enough of the disturbed particles for pulmonary infection. In these cases, after a couple of days incubating inside the body, fever will set in and perhaps mild septicaemia. The body will inflame as the immune system kicks into overdrive. It's nasty, and it's highly infectious, perhaps the most infectious bacterium known to man, but it's rarely fatal and a blast of streptomycin or a similar antibiotic will knock it out.

Non-contagious and non-lethal, *F. tularensis* might seem a strange choice of pathogen for Pasechnik to prepare into powder, but then the Soviets weren't intending to use your common garden strain. Over in Obolensk the Biopreparat scientists were labouring to genetically design a new, lethal variant, one that couldn't be stopped by medicine.

'[*F. tularensis*] was an effective agent in many ways,' Igor Domaradskij, the SRCAM research director, later explained. 'It has a low infective dose, it's very stable, and it's easy to aerosolise. A strain of tularaemia that could overcome vaccine immunity and be resistant to antibiotics would make a formidable weapon. And because it's a non-contagious infection, the Ministry of Health granted us research permission for it.'[26]

An unstoppable strain of tularensis would blow out your lymph nodes in less than three weeks, and then, if you were still alive, go to town on your lungs, your liver, your kidneys and your spleen. Everyone it didn't kill it would incapacitate, perhaps for months. That was the theory, anyway. In practice Pasechnik had by far the easiest part of the job. Preparing a suitable powder was easy, but mastering the genetic code for tularensis proved all but impossible. Domaradskij's team spent years just learning its biochemistry. Eventually they managed to transfer into it some genes that gave it a little resistance to antibiotics, but there was a side-effect, as there often is with genetic engineering: code an organism with a new trait, and it loses an old one.

'Having become resistant to several antibiotics, the strain lost its virulence, which was unacceptable to the military,' Domaradskij said. 'If a test monkey took so much as an extra day to die they took it as a serious setback. The strain they wanted had to be fully virulent. One germ cell had to be enough to start a lethal infection, and it had to be incurable. These goals were not at all easy.'

In fact, these goals were so difficult they were never achieved. After years of fruitless research at Obolensk the military biowarriors of the 15th Directorate, who had always been inclined to see the civilians at Biopreparat as untrustworthy long-haired rivals, came along and shut the project down.

'We are not playing here!' shouted Domaradskij's boss, General Urakov, a Moscow hardliner with little time for academics. 'We are making weapons!'

Once the generals had canned *tularensis*, they ordered Biopreparat to work on *Yersinia pestis* instead, the bacterium that had caused the Great Plague, but they asked for exactly the same genetic modifications, and unsurprisingly Domaradskij and his crew ran into exactly the same problems.

'The loss of biological activity during all technological processes was quite high,' Pasechnik told Kelly. 'Extremely high, I would say. This problem is quite complicated, and as far as I know it was never really solved.'[27]

As well as the plague bacterium, Biopreparat was also instructed to focus on the microbes that caused anthrax, and the horse infections glanders and melioidosis. It was a tall order. Some of the senior staff began to wonder if the military were simply setting them up to fail, but the research continued. The workforce could hardly complain, seeing that most of them didn't know what they were really supposed to be doing in the first place. Like the majority of civil servants they were happy to turn up and take the money. A quiet cynicism endured.

'People used to say, we're in a highly paid job, there's no reason to change it,' Pasechnik said. 'But at the same time there were sad feelings about the uselessness of the programme and its vicious characteristics.'[28]

For Kelly and for Davis, and for all the Cold War Kremlinologists in Whitehall, the hawks and the maximalists who never stopped fretting about the Russian bear, Pasechnik's revelations described something far more vicious than useless. However short the Soviet scientists fell of their goals, they were skating over a biological Armageddon.

There were a couple of flashpoints in Pasechnik's debriefing. The first was when he said he had been told to prepare a powder treatment for *Y. pestis* that would enable it to be efficiently sprayed from a subsonic cruising altitude of two hundred metres. As ever, further details were need-to-know, and Pasechnik wasn't on the list, but he could guess why he'd been asked. So could everyone in his debriefing room. They could only be the dissemination specs for a Soviet cruise missile, of which the Russians had thousands. Difficult to detect and even harder to intercept, a cruise missile could be programmed to spray its payload over multiple targets before it ran out of fuel. Waves of disease could be triggered by just a single fire-and-forget launch. Work on the project had begun the year before Pasechnik defected, and was unfinished when he left. Despite several years of effort his Leningrad institute hadn't found a way to turn plague into a powder dry enough for aerosol dispersal. But how long would it be before it did?

Elsewhere in the system, there was worse for Kelly to worry about. Although Pasechnik and his peers were forbidden to communicate openly with each other, he had become friendly with Lev Sandakhchiev, the director of another Biopreparat institute. They were the same age, and although very different in almost every other regard, the two of them got on. Pasechnik was a broad and placid person with little appetite for the limelight, while Sandakhchiev was a twitchy, chain-smoking bird of a man festooned with an ever-growing list of qualifications and accolades. He had been awarded a professorship, elected to the Academy of Sciences, and appointed to lead Vector, the new virus research station in Siberia.

Vector was one of the few places in Biopreparat, perhaps the only place, where the civilian scientists were really allowed to run things, and consequently it was considered by some to be the finest biological institute in Russia.[29] On the few occasions that Pasechnik had visited, Sandakhchiev had let slip a little about the stuff his staff had been working on in their icy fastness. It was a catalogue of the most lethal and exotic viruses known to man. In the freezers at Vector were flasks holding Ebola from the Congo, Zaire and Sudan; Marburg from the shores of Lake Victoria; Machupo from Bolivia; and a collection of brain-melting equine encephalitis bugs from all over South America. Present too, in an isolated high-security building protected by guards from the Ministry of the Interior, was a collection of smallpox.

Vector scientists had worked hard to build their menagerie of microscopic destroyers. They had visited the graves of a seventeenth-century smallpox outbreak in Siberia, broken through the permafrost, and taken samples. And the quest for new strains would have continued, except the 15th Military Directorate intervened.

Under strictest secrecy, army officers arrived at Vector bearing their own breed of smallpox, and as usual, told the civilians to stop wasting their time.

'They told Sandakhchiev to take it and get on with it. They said they had a fully developed "recipe" already. They said "there's no room for improvement with this strain".'[30]

No one knew where it came from but it was the most virulent smallpox anyone at Vector had ever seen. The top-secret viral military lab at Zagorsk had obviously either found it or built it, and Vector found itself ordered to attempt its mass production. They tried incubating it in eggs, five thousand at a time, but soon progressed to infecting legions of guinea-pigs. After death, high concentrations of the virus nestled in the animals' livers and spleens. The organs were harvested and homogenized in special blenders, and the biomass was then freeze-dried, ready for liquid suspension and testing as an aerosol.

The room in that safe house must have suddenly seemed very small, and as silent as the bare, bracken-clad hills above Kelly's hometown, where as an adolescent he had seen the pox run rampant. He knew Pasechnik's story was plausible. It was exactly how they propagated viruses at Porton Down.

'They haven't completed anything,' Pasechnik ran on, apparently eager to diffuse the tensions his disclosure had created. 'These viruses are very frail. Ebola is killed by sunlight, a lot of these agents are. We couldn't help them with the protective formulations, with the chemical treatments, because my lab was in the centre of Leningrad. We weren't allowed to work on anything as dangerous as that.'

Even with an experienced staff, Pasechnik said, Vector had already seen at least one scientist die from mishandling viruses. Kelly had no problems believing this either. He knew from the deaths at his university in Birmingham that there are no absolute guarantees when it comes to locking down killers like smallpox.

Soon after that the debriefing concluded. Pasechnik checked out, without doubts, and what he had said in a few weeks was more than anyone could believe. It was difficult to know what to do with it all. MI6 would secretly hold him incommunicado for the next three years, while Kelly and others came back to him with more technical questions as events snowballed. The debriefing team withdrew to compile and compare notes, to give some form and coherence to the mountain of frightening information that had avalanched towards them. But they had news for Pasechnik too.

Stuck in his safe house, the defector had been cocooned from the outside world. He had seen no television, heard no radio, read no newspapers, and so he didn't know that barely a week after the Secret Intelligence Service had scooped him up, the Berlin Wall had fallen. The entire Eastern bloc was crumbling; in Czechoslovakia the Velvet Revolution was already well under way. Pasechnik had fled the Soviet Union only moments before its ultimate dissolution began. The Russia he had abandoned was already disappearing into history.

None of this was any comfort to the 'maximalists' in Whitehall. Sudden geopolitical change was always fraught with possible dangers, particularly if it concerned the Warsaw Pact. Thatcher may famously have seen Gorbachev as a man she could 'do business with' but the Kremlin-watchers saw no reason to be optimistic. They urged caution, and trusted no one. After all, in Moscow the same Soviet generals still held command, the same missiles still sat in the same silos, and in the labs of Pasechnik and Sandakhchiev, of Biopreparat and the 15th Military Directorate, the same scientists were still brewing up pathogens with the potential to inflict biblical levels of pestilence on the populations of their enemies.

In the corridors of power, it led to a rare prominence for the BW experts at Porton Down and the Metropole Building. Kelly and Davis helped draft a series of briefings on the subject for their bosses to press on time-pushed politicians. After all, the spectre of the mushroom cloud was immediately understood. Explaining the aerosol dynamics of *Yersinia Pestis* and the military value of *Francisella tularensis* took a little more effort.

'We embarked on a programme of education for anyone in Whitehall who would listen,' Jones later wrote.[31] 'From ministers to chiefs of staff and from select committee parliamentarians to Foreign Office diplomats.'

In February 1990, the fruits of the Pasechnik debriefing were shared with the CIA, and the news about Biopreparat finally reached Washington. But while the twilight of the Soviets triggered a series of high-level summits between East and West, neither Thatcher nor Bush the Elder pushed the issue of biological weapons as much as the hawks had hoped. Despite the efforts of Brian Jones at DIS and Graham Pearson at Porton, the subject was relegated to the sidelines, where it had always resided. It was raised only as an aside. Even this was only due to the pressure put on Thatcher by Percy Cradock, the thorny chairman of her Joint Intelligence Committee, which then as now was the only official channel between Cabinet and the spooks.

Gorbachev told her the programme had been mothballed long ago, as far as he knew. His Foreign Minister said the same thing. They knew nothing about it. There was some research going on into *defence* from biological weapons, they offered, just like at Porton Down, but no more than that. Biopreparat made vaccines and worked for the public health.

'I know where you're getting all this,' muttered the Soviet Defence Minister. 'It's that defector.'[32]

Meanwhile Pasechnik was discreetly traduced by the KGB and others as paranoid and disgruntled, a fantasist with possible mental health problems.[33] The Russian rumour mill ground out off-the-record portraits of Pasechnik as an untrustworthy man working to his own agenda. It was the same treatment Downing Street would dish out to Kelly himself years later, when it described him as 'a bit of a Walter Mitty character'. Then as now, this is the fate of insiders who break ranks, whether in Moscow or in London.

Washington kept a tight lid on the news from MI6's seaside safe house. The Iron Curtain looked to be finally lifting, and at a critical diplomatic juncture few wanted to go public with angry accusations about germ warfare. It could jeopardise the ongoing negotiations over nuclear weapons, which were a bigger danger than the bugs of Biopreparat by far. Discussions about Pasechnik were confined to a secret committee called, in a jokey Orwellian fashion, Ungroup, because it didn't exist. Its members included Team B graduates like Paul Wolfowitz and Stephen Hadley, and they must have been doubly glad that nothing leaked: information like this could be used by an unscrupulous opposition to slam the administration for being too soft. It was, after all, what they had done to Carter, and what they would do to Clinton.

Thatcher herself was never able to believe that Gorbachev had really lied to her. If what Kelly had got out of Pasechnik was true, then perhaps Gorbachev simply didn't know about it. Perhaps his generals were deceiving him.

'That's about as likely as your generals deceiving you,' Cradock told her.

The chairman of the JIC did not let up. British intelligence held fast to their WMD claims, while politicians found other things to prioritise, and in the meantime, nothing and nobody leaked. It was all a far cry from what would later happen with Iraq.

Eventually, after a series of démarches behind closed doors, a solution of sorts was settled on. It was the following summer that Gorbachev first sketched it out, during a visit to Camp David. One clear day, when the Presidents had changed out of their suits and were standing on the veranda in their jumpers, listening to the wind blowing through the aspens, Bush waved off his retinue.

'It was a very private conversation,' Gorbachev later said.[34] 'Just the two of us and my interpreter.'

Once they were alone, Bush brought up what the CIA had been telling him about the Soviet programme. Gorbachev denied it existed, and said the KGB had been telling him the same thing about the Americans: that despite Bush's protestations, the US military were still secretly researching their own biological weapons.

'I believe you,' Gorbachev responded, 'why won't you believe me?'

Bush shrugged.

'Those are the reports I get,' he said.

'Well,' Gorbachev pressed on, 'you are not an expert on biological weapons, and I am not an expert on biological weapons. So let us have some mutual verification of whether these things have been destroyed or not. Let your people come to our weapons facilities, we also know where your facilities are, and we will visit those. Let's have an exchange.'

There were those in Whitehall and Washington that had expected such an approach. They had cautioned against it, because they saw no need for reciprocity. After all, they had Pasechnik. What could the Russians possibly have that would lead them to think the West was breaching the BWC? Why let the Soviets into Fort Detrick? But in the end, as long as the American side got to go first, Bush agreed to the proposal. The Ungroup had changed priority. They didn't need to know the finer details of what exactly had been researched, or crave a public mea culpa about the Biopreparat system – the important thing was just to make sure the damn project was terminated. And this too was vastly different from how things would play out with the nascent programme in Iraq.

Advisers and ambassadors spent another six months thrashing out the details. There was a brief hiatus in August when Saddam Hussein invaded Kuwait, and US–USSR relations hit a pregnant pause. But it soon became clear the situation in Arabia would not be met with any sudden military response, and so negotiations continued.

Snow was falling on the ranges at Porton Down by the time Kelly heard anything else about it. He and his colleagues were frantically busy trying to develop some biological protection for the troops being flown out to the Gulf. It was an urgent and uphill battle, seeing that Porton's vaccines were far from perfect. They had tried their anti-anthrax jabs out on guinea-pigs, and in some trials as many as a third of them still died after exposure.[35] As well as being ineffective, the drug was likely to have severe side-effects too. In the absence of testing on human guinea-pigs, no one could know for sure.

'The speed at which the work had to be done left a little something to be desired in terms of testing', admitted Major General Alexander Harley, who was Assistant Chief of Defence Staff at the time.[36] 'We did obtain UK licensing, but the balance of risk between possible side effects and what might happen if the troops were not protected played a big part in obtaining this.'

If it had simply been for domestic, civilian consumption, the drug would never have been released. It took the threat of Armageddon to get them passed, and then they were shipped out by the thousand. As conflict drew near, the Ministry of Defence did try to sell them on to NATO allies and old Commonwealth countries, but unsurprisingly, there were no takers. The strict conditions of secrecy under which all these vaccines had been developed didn't exactly reassure potential buyers.

'It was all terribly secret,' Harley explained, 'because from the moment you've discovered which weapon strain the enemy are using, it takes time to grow enough for your own use, whereas if the enemy learns what you're doing, they can immediately change the strain to something else.'[37]

The one thing that stood in Kelly's favour was that he knew exactly which anthrax strain the Iraqis were using, because as the US Congress later found out, it was the American Type Culture Collection that had supplied them. For the most part, the vaccines that came out of Porton Down were based on those same pathogens.

'The vaccinations were codenamed Victor, Cutter, Porton and Biological,' according to Sergeant Shaun Rusling, a Parachute Regiment medic with the 32nd Field Hospital.[38] 'Despite being medical staff, we were never told what was in them, or specifically what they were for. After two of my injections, I decided they were so debilitating I wasn't going to take any more. Then my boss told me I had to set a good example, so muggins had his third one and it was even worse than the first two. I had a terrible fever for forty-eight hours, I couldn't even get out of my cot.'

The side-effects of these untested vaccines were so severe that several commanding officers refused to order their men's injections. This was certainly the case with Major General Rupert Smith, who commanded the 1st Armoured Division, Lieutenant Colonel Arthur Denaro of the Queen's Royal Irish Hussars, and Lieutenant Charles Rogers of the Staffordshires.

'We had so much bloody stuff pumped into us I wouldn't be remotely surprised if some people reacted badly,' Denaro said.[39]

'We were used as guinea-pigs, knowingly or unknowingly,' former senior aircraftman Kerry Fuller told the BBC.[40]

Fuller may have been more right than he knew. The most controversial and most debilitating of these injections were the plague vaccines, which arrived at the front only days before the ground attack. Yet plague could normally be treated with simple antibiotics, and it was one of the few pathogens the US never exported to Iraq. Neither UNSCOM nor its successor, the UN Monitoring, Verification and Inspection Commission (UNMOVIC), ever found any evidence that the country had ever developed a plague weapon. Undoubtedly, what was on Kelly's mind was not Saddam Hussein but Vladimir Pasechnik, and the safe house where he had heard the Soviets had engineered a plague strain resistant to pills. To use an army adage, Porton Down was preparing to fight the next war, not the one in the Gulf.

Officially, the Ministry of Defence has always insisted there was no such thing as 'vaccine damage' but thousands of Gulf War veterans would disagree. Campaigners have long insisted the injections played a key part in 'Gulf War syndrome', an illness the MoD still refuses to accept exists. Labour promised a public inquiry in 1997 but never delivered one, and an independent inquiry in 2005 by Lord Lloyd of Berwick was ignored by Blair's government and, bizarrely, even by the Conservative opposition. Consequently, applications for war pensions have been rejected in their hundreds.

Porton Down simply maintained its habitual silence, as it had over forty years of testing on volunteer servicemen.

Graham Pearson, Porton's then director-general, later praised Kelly's competence and enthusiasm in those rushed months of late 1990. He had been an essential part of Britain's biological defence capability in the Gulf, as his CMG citation later read. That capability was 'limited', as Pearson admitted, but it was Kelly's groundwork that allowed Porton Down to develop its 'world-class facilities' in the future.[41] This was another of Kelly's legacies, and like much of what he achieved here, it was mired in controversy from the start. Like most things he worked on, he was never able to talk about it.

Whitehall counted on Kelly's ability to keep a secret. It was all on the same classified, need-to-know basis when Graham Pearson called him into his office that December for a second time, to tell him that the Defence Intelligence Staff required his services once more. As before, it would be for a number of weeks, and Kelly couldn't tell anyone, not even his family, where he was going. Just as he had the previous October, he agreed without being told what he was needed for, although he could probably have guessed. Over the year, he had been dealing with the fall-out from Pasechnik's defection. I heard a rumour, unsourced and unverified, that British intelligence had picked up another Biopreparat defector that autumn.[42] If so, SIS and Porton Down never broke his (or her) cover, and their identity remains unknown, but for Kelly it would have involved another protracted debriefing away from home. When he found out he had the chance to see the Biopreparat labs for himself, it must have seemed something like closure.

In reality, it was to prove anything but.

Kelly and his fellow debriefer, Christopher Davis from the biological desk in the DIS, were among the five British experts chosen to go on the trip. The third was Hamish Killip, who worked on Brian Jones's chemical desk, and the fourth was Peter Davies, a Foreign Office diplomat attached to the Arms Control and Disarmament Department (and whose diplomatic status could very possibly come in handy). The fifth has never been named, and his department has never been specified, but everyone agrees he spoke fantastically fluent Russian.

In Washington they would join seven Americans, led by Edward Lacey from the US Arms Control and Disarmament Agency, before flying out. Before they went they were given some cursory training on tradecraft and operational security by the army's Intelligence Corps and SIS, which would at the very least have included warnings about the sort of Soviet counter-intelligence they might be likely to face – honey traps and covert surveillance being two rather obvious pointers. They were shown, amongst other things, how to check if their luggage had been searched (and it would be). If standard Intelligence Corps field training is anything to go by, they received instruction on how to use things like hidden cameras, as well as how to spot them.[43] On their arrival Stateside, American intelligence brought them up to speed with the procedures and standards they expected of the whole team. The rules for the visit had been painfully negotiated in advance: photos could be taken, but only if the cameras were given to the Russians to use, and the images shared between all three countries. The same went for audio- and video-taping. No electronic equipment could be used without prior Soviet inspection and consent.

Their itinerary was already fixed. The trip would cover four labs, whose unwieldy names formed an alphabet soup of acronyms. The first was the Institute of Engineering Immunology (or IEI) in the small community of Lyubuchany, thirty-five miles south of Moscow. The second was the State Research Centre for Applied Microbiology (SRCAM) in the 'science city' of Obolensk, another short run out of the capital, where Igor Domaradskij and his colleagues were working on bacterial agents. Third was the All-Union Research Institute of Molecular Biology and Scientific-Production Association, more mercifully referred to as Vector, the viral research station of Lev Sandakhchiev, out in Siberia; and finally came

Pasechnik's own Institute of Highly Pure Biopreparations (IHPB), in his native Leningrad. The defector had known and visited the directors at each of the other three facilities; it was Kelly's debriefing that had set the schedule. Two days had been allocated for each location.

The thirteen inspectors touched down in Moscow on 7 January 1992, almost fourteen months after Vladimir Pasechnik had taken his walk, more than enough time for the Soviets to clear up any evidence of military activity. Conversely, Kelly and Lacey's team had less than ten whole days to get at the truth, and they would be working in the heart of a country famed for its secrecy and formidable counter-intelligence. From the outset, it must be said, the odds were not good.

They arrived late and checked in to the Hotel Leningradskaya, one of the 'Seven Sisters', the imposing Stalinist skyscrapers erected on the banks of the Moskva River to demonstrate the collective might of Soviet industry.

'We won the war,' Stalin had said. 'Foreigners will come to Moscow, walk around, and there's no skyscrapers. If they compare Moscow to capitalist cities, it's a moral blow to us.'[44]

Suitably enough, at the time of its opening Leningradskaya was a socialist showpiece, a 28-storey neoclassical monument to the workers' struggle. Its grand gold-leafed lobby had a hand-carved wooden ceiling, glittering chandeliers and a heavy dose of bronze statuary. After Uncle Joe passed away in his locked bedroom, Khrushchev had criticised it for its distinctly unsocialist excess, but by the time Kelly arrived its gold had tarnished. The lights flickered, the décor had dated, and the carpets were threadbare. It seemed like more of a mausoleum than a hotel, a memorial to a doomed experiment.

The team ate a hushed supper in the hotel restaurant before making their way down the dark cherry-wood corridors to their rooms. Conversation was minimal: the only place in the entire country where they could talk with relative freedom was the US Embassy. The colourful lights of Komsomolskaya Square sparkled up at them in the frosty night. From his window Kelly could see

Yaroslavsky Station, one end of the Trans-Siberian Railway. According to Pasechnik, between its two terminals, almost six thousand miles apart, lay hidden the component parts of the largest and most secretive biological warfare programme in the world. By the time Kelly bedded down, his body clock shot, the challenge looming before him must have seemed both deeply daunting and vitally important. He was the lead UK scientist on the first biological weapons inspection in the history of the world.[45]

The next morning they made an early but inauspicious start. The team assembled in the freezing darkness to trek the ten blocks to the lofty Soviet Foreign Ministry, another of Stalin's Seven Sisters, where they waited, sleepy-eyed and shivering in their parkas, for their coach and their Soviet escorts. Their welcoming party, when it turned up, was a mixture of Biopreparat scientists and unidentified KGB officers. One of them, obviously not a Russian but a Kazakh, with Asiatic features, chain-smoked broodily. While everyone else in his party had dressed in suits and ties, the Kazakh wore an old brown sweater.

'We worried about the sweater,' one of the American team later said. 'We thought he wore it to conceal some sort of secret equipment.'[46]

The man in mufti was Colonel Kanatjan Alibekov, though he would later be known by a different name, in another part of the world. Alibekov was present throughout the entire trip, and became the inspectors' bête noire.

'Wherever we went, he knew what was going on in those labs,' Kelly later said.[47] 'Or at least he appeared to know. He would be the one taking a lead in providing an explanation, or he would be stopping the people working there from offering their own.'

Eventually, after the morning rush hour had started, the transport arrived, which turned out to be a lumbering Soviet-made bus. They had hardly left the city limits when its windscreen mysteriously shattered. So the diplomats and intelligence men inside, together with their Soviet escorts, huddled on the back seats for warmth, while the biting wind sent snowflakes up the aisle.

Frank Malinoski, a physician with a doctorate in microbiology who worked in the virology division at Fort Detrick, was the team's US medical officer.

'It must have been fifteen below,' he told me. 'At least.'[48]

After a slow sub-zero crawl to Lyubuchany they entered the gates of the IEI, the smallest of the four institutes they were to visit. It consisted of three laboratory buildings, already familiar to Kelly from the satellite photos he had been shown during his debriefing, and again during the team's pre-trip training. But by the time he arrived there it was clear the roll-back of Project Ferment was well under way. Some of the land at the site had been carved off for a manufacturing plant that made small plastic bottles to serve Kristall vodka in passenger aircraft. When Pasechnik defected the IEI had a staff of five hundred; when Kelly arrived that had been whittled down to a fifth, although even then there were very few of them around to lay eyes on.

'All the facilities we visited were like that,' Malinoski said. 'They were like ghost towns. Everybody had been told not to come in, they were sick, or on holiday. The workforce was never there to interview or observe.'

The morning was taken up by a meet-and-greet and then an interminable speech by the director, Vladimir Zaviyalov, who spoke about his institute's achievements. After all, its scientists had had a number of articles printed in open publications. Already behind schedule, the team sat politely in their seats while the minutes dragged by. After the speech came lunch, a sumptuous Russian affair with caviar and vodka on tap. There was always vodka on tap wherever the team went, generously but forcefully offered. No one ever drank it. Eventually some members resorted to carrying cans of Diet Coke around with them.

Like Pasechnik, Zaviyalov had been another promising thirty-something scientist when Biopreparat snared him in its web. He later said he had had no idea his institute would be anything other than a civilian research centre, which may well be true, given that Zaviyalov had been given permission to travel abroad freely in the early years of his directorship: he would have had no secrets to give away.[49] Only years later did he discover his second 'legend': that his work on immunology had an important defensive dimension for the Soviet military. He was aghast. He considered it impossible to do the best science in a closed system. But worse was to come, when after a few more years in post the KGB granted him higher clearance and he was told the full truth. His role was not just to find ways of boosting the human immune system, but to break through it.

Pasechnik had heard rumours about the place. He knew Soviet genetic engineers were looking at ways to disguise their pathogenic weapons so they could slip through the body's defences. There had even been talk, theoretical gossip, about designing a weapon that could turn the human immune system against itself. Instead of destroying foreign cells, a fake protein could trigger an inflammation that would destroy the host's own nervous system. Effectively, you could induce advanced multiple sclerosis in whoever you sprayed.

Terrifying as the rumours were, Kelly found little evidence to support them during his two days at the IEI. The staff were almost entirely absent and the facility's actual lab space was minimal. There was just nothing to see.

'The Institute of Immunology was an easy stop,' Alibekov later wrote, after he had defected himself.[50] 'Its activities were largely confined to theoretical analysis and defence work, and there were no suspicious pathogens on hand.'

The team left without unearthing any evidence of Project Ferment, though not for want of trying. Sometime on the second day Christopher Davis pulled out a miniature tape recorder, or something that to all intents and purposes resembled one, for which he was immediately reprimanded by his hosts. A long time was to pass before the West ever got anything resembling confirmation of the 'multiple sclerosis' agent, and again that was almost certainly only human intelligence, hearsay or testimony from another refugee fleeing the system. Exactly how close the Soviets (or the Russians) have really got to refining a prototype strain remains unknown.

If the IEI had been a non-starter, everyone knew the next site was a different prospect entirely. They had seen the satellite photos; Kelly and Davis had studied them in minute detail all year. SRCAM, the bacterial institute, was a huge complex of thirty buildings, with a staff of four thousand. Malinoski estimated that it was about ten times the size of his workplace in Maryland. It made the Chemical Defence Establishment at Porton Down look like a scout hut. According to a former research head, it was designed to pass itself off as a sanatorium if viewed from space, but US analysts weren't fooled for long. While they couldn't see inside the buildings, their layout apparently gave the game away, and doubts existed about the place long before Pasechnik disappeared.

Once more they travelled by coach, this one with an intact windscreen, through a forest of snowy pines to the town of Obolensk. The odd elk stared at them morosely as they passed. The settlement was a new town, built in the seventies to house the SRCAM scientists, and it was named after a clan of royal princes who centuries ago had established a quasi-kingdom there, hidden by the dense cover of the trees. But there was nothing remotely quaint or traditional about Obolensk. It was built by soldiers, and its citizenry appointed by the paranoid and prejudiced KGB. Its vetted population referred to it as 'the city without Jews'.

SRCAM's military credentials seemed evident from the start. They counted eleven army checkpoints between Moscow and Obolensk, and the welcoming speech when they arrived that morning was given by the Institute's director, General Nikolai Urakov, from the shadowy 15th Military Directorate. It gave absolutely nothing away about offensive work and, just like the speech at the IEI, the presentation took up an entire morning. The afternoon was spent on a 'familiarisation' bus tour of the complex itself, without the group ever setting foot inside a building. From an intelligence-gathering perspective, it was pointless, but at least the group now knew where they stood. The Russians were trying to stall them into doing as little productive inspection as possible.

The next day the visitors compensated for lost time by splitting up, and the British went off to find an aerosol test-chamber Pasechnik had told them about. Any kind of top-end pathogen lab would have a sealed area for research on the transmission of airborne diseases. But Kelly and Davis reckoned the aerosol chamber at SRCAM was also a blast chamber: the Soviets had been exploding BW munitions in it. Finding ways of delivering biological agents in conventional munitions had always been one of the biggest problems for military microbiologists. The explosion invariably neutralises most of the payload, either through temperature or through sheer physical pressure. US tests showed that explosive munitions killed over 96 per cent of the agent they were designed to deliver.[51] Attempts to improve on that would depend chiefly on how the microbes had been chemically treated, which was one of the things Pasechnik had been working on in Leningrad. Blast-testing in an aerosol chamber would leave very obvious dents in the walls, marks that might be the clearest and easiest way to prove Biopreparat's clandestine military purpose.

At first their Soviet hosts feigned complete ignorance. They knew nothing about a test chamber, or where one could be found, if there was even one there at all. So Kelly produced a map that he had helped put together during Pasechnik's debriefing, and pointed out the building that housed it. On the back foot, the Soviets followed along. At the entrance there was some difficulty about finding a key for the door, but Kelly's team held firm. Somehow they talked their way inside.

The test chamber was a windowless, steel-walled room, and the entrance was a thick double-skinned door like you might see below decks on a battleship. It lay on the other side of a decontamination shower. The team heaved it open and stepped inside.

The walls themselves were pristine. In fact, it looked like they could have been recently burnished. Only the inside of the door told a different story. It was a lighter weight of steel, and it was dented in several places.

Then, it seems, there was some difficulty about the lighting, a power cut, or a blown bulb – in any event, it became difficult to see. One of the team produced a torch and passed it to Chris Davis, who had barely begun pointing it around when he felt a heavy hand on his shoulder.

'Electronic devices not permitted,' said his escort. 'Give it to me.'

For whatever reason, there was no way Davis was handing over that torch. It was the second time the Russians had caught him with unauthorised equipment. The Royal Navy surgeon commander fell back on formalities:

'We are your guests. We are on an official diplomatic mission sanctioned by your president. This is no way to behave.'

The situation became a stand-off.

'It was tense,' Davis said. 'They didn't know what to do, and I wasn't going to back down.'

Eventually, somehow, the impasse was overcome. The lights came back on, if that was really all it was, and the team got their torch back. Had the incident perhaps been designed to shed a different kind of light? Who knows what these James Bond types get up to? as David Kelly once rather knowingly said.

In Obolensk the mood was now serious in the extreme. Davis said the door showed signs of explosives-testing.

'That was the workmen who fitted the door,' said a minder. 'They damaged it a little installing it.'

Kelly pointed out that in his opinion the room showed clear evidence of shrapnel.

'That's just natural wear and tear,' one of the Russians explained. 'Things get worn down and damaged.'

Nobody on the British side was convinced. Yet they were only visitors. They had no powers to exercise beyond the limits of their own perception, and there was nothing they could do but note the answers given to them. In the afternoon the teams met up at Corpus One, a nine-storey building with over five acres of floor space, by far the biggest part of the complex, and the most secure. It had six floors of high-containment laboratories, with more than two hundred filtered labs running at negative air pressure.[52] The top floor had a small-scale production unit with a 100-litre fermenter; underground was a central collection library that held thousands of strain samples. And unlike the Seven Sisters back in Moscow, Corpus One hadn't been built to impress. Every inch of it was functional. It was a truly imposing building.

A few floors up, Kelly was allowed to 'suit up' for a look around one of the labs, but the suits at Obolensk weren't anything like the ones at Porton Down or Fort Detrick. Those had valves that let you connect and disconnect your breathing cord without breaking the seal of your outfit. In Obolensk there were no valves. You just pulled your hose off the tap and held it closed with your thumb until you reached the next oxygen pipe. Kelly watched in amazement as the Soviet scientist accompanying him showed him how the set-up worked.

The lab itself had been cleaned out. There were no materials to look at, no work in progress on the benches. His sweep revealed little but poor standards of Soviet biosafety. As they showered and changed on their way out, Kelly and his disingenuous escort stood naked together in the decontamination room, and he wondered briefly what the hell was going on with his life.

'It was a very strange situation indeed,' he later said, in his final television interview. 'It's very odd to be thousands of miles from home, alone, in a facility, in this sort of situation.'

Then the process ended and the chamber opened and Kelly was back amongst his steely-eyed colleagues and the dissembling Soviets and his moment of introspection was over. He asked for another hot-zone inspection on the floors dedicated to plague research, but General Urakov sidestepped it by claiming he would have to impose a two-week quarantine period on anyone who went inside.

The day ended with a formal complaint from their chief escort, Nikita Smidovich, that Davis's use of a torch had broken the rules of their inspection – something that Edward Lacey had to concede, but it was point-scoring of little consequence. The same thing could be said of the trip so far. There had been no admissions, no breakthroughs, no smoking guns. Their time at Obolensk had given them nothing but further grounds for suspicion.

The next day was Saturday, a scheduled rest day, but leisure time was scarce. They reconvened in the US Embassy for a thorough mid-tour debriefing and returned to the Leningradskaya for an early night. Tomorrow came the flight to Siberia, on an Aeroflot plane the Soviets had dedicated to the inspection team for the duration of their visit. But it wasn't just the Soviet military who were conspiring to stall them. The Russian weather was at it too. They were severely delayed by a heavy blizzard and spent half the day parked on the tarmac before arriving in Novosibirsk in the middle of the night.

They disembarked and stood around in an empty aircraft hangar while they waited for their transport. It was forty below. Then, incredibly, they were shuttled from one extreme to the other, when they found themselves at one of Gorbachev's presidential dachas. Edward Lacey had a grand piano in his room. The beds were king-size, the bathroom fittings were solid gold, the furniture was antique, and decanters of expensive vodka were everywhere. Disorientated and exhausted, Kelly was able to grab only two hours' sleep before the next inspection. On surfacing that morning, life must have taken on the alienating strangeness of a waking dream.

For Kelly, getting inside Vector was going to be the pinnacle of an extraordinary trip. He was a virologist, after all, and the Siberian labs represented the most advanced viral research centre in Russia, and the most secretive, at least on the civilian side of the fence. Like SRCAM and Obolensk, Vector had its own residential town built for it, at Koltsovo. The labs themselves had been cautiously sited a few miles downwind.

Vector was of a similar size to SRCAM, but it had been built by convicts, not soldiers. The brickwork was out-of-kilter and the concrete was uneven. The scientists who worked there joked that the prisoners had deliberately made every step a different size so they could send as many scientists plunging to their deaths as possible. The crudeness of its construction aside, the researchers within these slightly crooked walls were working right at the very edge of some scientific frontiers. Lev Sandakhchiev, the institute's director, began to outline them at length in his welcoming speech, listing the civilian achievements he had overseen, but for once the inspectors cut him short. There was too much at stake to sit there and listen. They needed to see the truth for themselves, if they could find it.

'That was a fast-paced visit,' Malinoski said. 'Everyone was looking in as many different directions as possible.'

Initially the facility offered up little in the way of clues. It had been thoroughly sterilised, documents had been stashed, and everyone had been told to stay at home. The Vector leadership had decided to 'sacrifice' the institute, stripping it of its military role, the previous month.[53] In one of the labs they toured Kelly found a handwritten note left for him on a workbench. It was one of the few bits of paperwork left in view, and it was in English.

'The Eagle does not catch flies,' was all the cryptic message said.

Apparently, neither Kelly nor Davis had any idea what it meant.[54] Perhaps later they found out (one suspects their translator may have had a classical education). It was a proverb from the time of ancient Rome and referred to the ambitions of Empire, and its sentiments are fairly clear: a superpower cannot feed itself by hunting down the insignificant. Had they understood at the time, it's doubtful they would have agreed with its import. They were each engaged in a career-defining exercise, both considered they were on the trail of a weapons system that could slay whole populations, and yet one wonders whether in later life, inside Iraq, Kelly ever thought of it. This brief anonymous note might not have seemed so inappropriate then. The mindset of biological weapons inspectors, however, tends towards another direction.

Kelly's venturing around Vector was limited. Given the arrangements of the inspection, he was only really able to cover one building in the complex. But even then he forced a remarkable admission. Their hosts were keen to show them some software that modelled how clouds of viruses and bacteria might spread over different terrain, something they said they had spent fifteen years developing. When the inspectors returned from Russia they would argue that such software had a clear offensive military potential, although Porton Down had something similar; we know because the floppy discs found their way to Project Coast.

Fed up with watching green grids on a monitor, perhaps, David and his translator wandered off.

Over Kelly's career as an inspector, he became well known for taking time out to talk to the most junior staff. The bottlewashers, the drivers, the undergraduate assistants; it was the underlings he went to when he wanted the truth. It seems that from very early on he was sceptical that the great and the good would ever tell him anything he could rely on. On reflection, this was something that proved to be as true at home as it was in Soviet Russia or Baathist Iraq, and it's interesting that some of his most revealing conversations, in his last year, were not with his bosses or political masters but with a few trusted journalists, most of whom were relatively unknown until his death, or civil servants who really he had little to do with, like David Broucher, the Foreign Office's Permament Representatie to the Conference on Disarmament in Geneva.

Inside the bowels of the main building at Vector, characteristically almost entirely devoid of staff, Kelly found a lab assistant, the sort of lowly personage who might have been overlooked in the KGB's silencing pre-visit briefings. He struck up a conversation with him about the sort of organisms he'd been working on, and with guileless innocence, it seems, the man told him they'd been testing smallpox.

Kelly kept up the poker face of an interrogator, but his mind must have reeled. The UN'S World Health Organisation had eradicated smallpox in 1979. It was a medical triumph of international cooperation, a process that ironically had been partly instigated by a Russian academician. There were now only two places in the world where the virus was supposed to exist, and under the most stringent security: in sample flasks at the Centers for Disease Control (CDC) head office in Atlanta, Georgia, and at the Research Institute for Viral Preparations in Moscow, which was run by the Ministry of Health. Now, finally, came some confirmation of the most disturbing strand of Pasechnik's debriefing. Smallpox was on the loose again, and it had arrived in a secret research lab that had unknown associations with the Soviet military.

Giving nothing away, Kelly casually steered the conversation back to smallpox three times. Once, just to be sure there was no confusion, he used its Latin name. Each time the man repeated it back to him. He showed no doubt, nor any sense of what he was giving away.

Conversations that no one hears. These were the stock-in-trade of Kelly as an inspector.

'I didn't expect smallpox at Vector,' Kelly said. 'And I certainly didn't expect them to be working on it in labs like that.'

The Eagle had caught its fly.

Yet in essence the Romans' proverb still held true. What the little people said hardly mattered. It was the leaders, the directors and the politicians and the generals, that people really listened to. And immediately, they began backtracking. Kelly rejoined his group; they were standing beside an aerosol testing-chamber which, it was being explained, had been used for testing monkeypox.

There was no monkeypox in Russia. Even in Africa its person-to-person spread was limited. In the depths of central Africa, far from medical help, it might prove dangerous, but for the Russians it was no public health hazard, and neither, assuming the worst intentions, would it make a practical weapon. Kelly stood staring at the steel walls of the chamber, his feet planted on the tiled floor, and listened to the lies. He was certain it was a cover story for smallpox development.

Somebody asked if they could go inside and swab for samples. The Russians shook their heads.

'They said our vaccines might not protect us,' Malinoski said later.[55] 'Like they had developed viruses that were resistant to American vaccines.'

And Kelly looked up and began to ask, in an increasingly pointed way, about testing on smallpox, and on the differences between offensive and defensive research, and the use of explosive chambers.

His Soviet guides exchanged alarmed glances. They could see where these questions were going. Whether it would be made here, at Vector, or issued diplomatically, from Washington or London in the coming months, they sensed the accusation that they were building a smallpox weapon. Soon Kelly and Davis found themselves asked to wait in an office while their guides frantically tried to locate staff who were senior enough to placate their visitors' concerns. This took the best part of an hour.

Kelly's questioning led to everyone gathering in Vector's conference room for a round-table meeting. That, at least, was the idea. What it became was a head-to-head between David Kelly and Vector's director, Lev Sandakhchiev. They were by some distance the most knowledgeable virologists in the room, opposite numbers from either side of the Iron Curtain. The others sat back and took notes.

Yes, said Sandakhchiev, there was some smallpox research going on at Vector. But not on live samples. The stuff they had here was inactivated, as the scientists say, unable to recreate itself inside a host. It was killed smallpox, like you'd use to make a vaccine.

'All right,' said Kelly, passing the ball back. 'Why are you spending lab hours on researching dead smallpox? As a disease, the pathogen is effectively extinct.'

'You can't say that,' said Sandakhchiev. 'What about global warming? We've had outbreaks of smallpox in Siberia in the past. If the permafrost melts, and the bodies of smallpox victims are disturbed, well who knows?'

Kelly could only shake his head. It seemed, to him, a nakedly ridiculous argument. But on its own terms, it stood up. The absurdity of it angered him. There was nothing absurd about smallpox. It had killed a third of a billion people that century, until the WHO got it under lock and key. It was still worshipped as a deity in some countries, and feared as a demon in others.

'Have you engineered new strains of smallpox here?' he asked, and there was ice in his voice.

There was no answer.

'Have you spliced smallpox with other viruses?'

Nothing.

'Is there a strain of smallpox here that is resistant to vaccines?'

Silence.

'It was a very tense moment,' Kelly later said.[56] 'It seemed like an eternity.'

Eventually, he tried again, and recapped his line of questioning.

'Smallpox has been eradicated as a disease. No one is developing it is a weapon. The US and the UK have both abandoned biological warfare, and they were early sponsors of the Biological Weapons Convention, which they have signed and ratified, as have you. Yet you claim your research into smallpox is defensive.'

Sandakhchiev's face hardened.

'The US did not give up biological warfare,' he said. 'They continued researching it in secret after they officially renounced it. And we are sure this research would include a smallpox weapon.'

Then he stood up. The questions and answers were over. There would be no more disclosures.

That evening at the dacha, the Russians laid on a banquet, and the Americans and the British joined them around a long dining table in a vast, high-ceilinged hall. The food was served over six or seven courses. The vodka flowed.

Solemnly, the inspectors sipped their Diet Cokes. Conversation did not come easily.

The last stop was Leningrad. Their private Aeroflot jet landed at an airport that adjoined a military base, and it was humming with activity. As they taxied to the terminal they watched as squadron after squadron of MiGs scrambled to the skies. The final stage of the Persian Gulf War had begun: the ground attack that would restore Kuwait to the Al Sabah family. In case Operation Desert Storm spiralled beyond its UN mandate, the Soviet Union was taking the precaution of reinforcing its southern airstrips.

The inspectors must have felt like history was overtaking them.

The Institute in Leningrad held little of interest for its visitors. Being the workplace of the defector, it would have been the first Biopreparat lab to be thoroughly cleaned by the KGB. None of its staff mentioned Pasechnik once. It was as if he had never existed. The only sign he had ever been there at all was a single signature, scrawled at the bottom of some mundane notice, pinned to a board at the end of a dim corridor.

By the time they touched down in Washington, the war was over. The whole team was held for a thorough debriefing by American intelligence. It lasted for weeks, longer than the inspection itself. When it concluded, they had compiled a report over two hundred pages long. It remains classified to this day, but apparently it was unequivocal in its conclusion: the USSR was operating a clandestine and offensive biological weapons programme, and it was concealing the fact.

On returning to the UK, Kelly and the British team put together their own report, which presumably said much the same thing. This one went straight to Percy Cradock at the Joint Intelligence Committee and was circulated to the Cabinet. Not for the first time, and not for the last, the secret life of David Kelly ended up in the lap of the Prime Minister.

Back in Moscow, General Kalinin, the director of Biopreparat, a man conspicuously absent throughout the inspection, was penning a one-page report for Gorbachev. 'The visit passed without incident,' he wrote. 'We were able to ease their concerns about an offensive biological programme. They no longer have grounds for suspicion.'

It was the first inspection of its kind and it led to nothing but totally opposing views on either side; not a meeting of minds but a hardening of differences. It had been born in a climate of constant suspicion, and it was a child of its time. It fed a stalemated cycle of accusation and denial, and afterwards became largely a matter for diplomats and politicians, to be played out invisibly behind closed doors. For Kelly there were still the reciprocal visits to be dealt with, when the Russians would come to Porton Down and Fort Detrick, but before that the Gulf had added another trip to his to-do pile.

That inspection, however, would play out quite differently.

6

Inspection as Archaeology

I have an open mind at this stage.
DAVID KELLY, TELEVISION INTERVIEW OUTSIDE
THE PALESTINE HOTEL, BAGHDAD, AUGUST 1991

August is Iraq's hottest month. The temperature can reach 130 degrees, the single consolation being that the flies, perhaps the only living creatures to flourish in Mesopotamia, die off above 120. The horizon is a haze of heat on a featureless plain, every distant building or vehicle is an indistinguishable blur, people become spectres. Very quickly your skin becomes slicked in sweat, and then caked in dust; the same dust that has collected in your hair, in the folds of your clothes, in between your teeth. There is dust everywhere, it abounds even more than the flies, sometimes the air itself turns thick with it. When the high winds of the shamal blow down from the Taurus Mountains sandstorms can make the air unbreathable, even impassable, as if the earth has risen up against you. The shamal can stretch for miles and last for days and has shut down entire cities. But even without the dust and the sand, prolonged spells outdoors can easily result in heat exhaustion or sunstroke. The sun is fierce and constant here.

'It corrodes all pride,' wrote the imperial journalist Edmund Candler. 'The very air seems to sweat. Strike a match and it will burn dully without a flicker as if the flame were choked.' To stand in the desert when the sun was up felt like 'standing at the edge of a huge fire in a high wind, licked by gusts of flame'.

Worse; you cannot drink the water, and you chance your arm with the food.

When the British first came here in numbers, with Candler in tow, it was to open a front against the Turks at the outset of the Great War, before Iraq even existed. Less than a third of them ever reached the front. In the Highland Light Infantry only twenty-eight men ever saw enemy lines, the rest dropped dead or were invalided out within months of arriving.

'One's skin becomes an affliction, one's blood a curse, one's tongue and throat a torture,' complained General Keary, of the British Indian Army, as he watched the troops around him fall without a shot being fired. 'The sun here is the most relentless, untiring enemy a man can have.'

And not just men, either. It takes an even harsher toll on exposed bacteria and viruses, which are deeply sensitive to extremes of light and heat. The Middle East has always been an impractical environment for the deployment of biological weapons.

Kelly felt this himself for the first time on 2 August 1991, when he led the first UN weapons inspection to deal with Iraq's germ warfare research. As far as the public knew, it was the first bio-logical-weapons inspection in the history of the world. His incredible experiences inside the Soviet Union were still top secret. They had played a key part in his recruitment and they had shaped his outlook as an inspector, but he couldn't talk about them with his colleagues. Very few of them had high enough security clearance.

He led a twenty-eight-strong team on that first visit, a sizeable crew by UNSCOM standards, but then Kelly always tended to lead the larger inspections. They were a curious mix of military microbiologists, biotechnicians, medical practitioners, special-forces soldiers, munitions experts, interpreters, engineers, administrators and, although they pretended to be otherwise, officers of Western intelligence agencies, even of non-Western intelligence agencies too. If they weren't spying on Iraq, they were spying on each other. Intrigue was never in short supply in the United Nations Special Commission.

The Iraqis still treated the inspectors with civility in those days. They allowed UNSCOM free use of Habbaniyah airport, in the heart of the Sunni triangle, some fifty miles west of Baghdad, and let them park their vehicles on the apron so they could be loaded directly from the plane. Germany had offered to provide all flights for the Commission, and the Luftwaffe's workhorse for getting teams in and out of the country was a twin-turboprop Transall in UN white. Kelly and his colleagues sat buckled up in its sideways-facing canvas seats while it made its slow descent. In later years, after Operation Iraqi Freedom, landing aircraft had to make mad spiralling dives to avoid RPG attack from anonymous insurgents, but under Saddam the country was still relatively stable, however ostracised it had become.

The Transall popped open its cargo doors while it was still trafficking down the runway. The passengers blinked as the bright light of the morning desert streamed into the dim belly of the plane, shifting uneasily in their seats as the cargo behind them lurched forward under its straining webbing. In the trunks and crates was a horde of equipment: cameras, video recorders, surveyor's tools, secure communications gear, bomb disposal tools, medical kit for every conceivable emergency, Geiger counters, metal detectors, sensors to test for all manner of chemical and biological agents, and the dreaded protective NBC suits.

Nobody was looking forward to having to put on a protective suit. Like the team's chemical agent monitors and emergency atropine injectors, they had been designed in Porton Down, but they were lined with a charcoal-impregnated felt that made them stifling even in the UK's climate. In the Middle East, they were practically unwearable, as British troops had quickly found out. The slightest physical exertion could cause the wearer to collapse, so the 'doom suits' were a lot more effective in principle than in practice. Likewise the atropine injectors, which were supposed to save servicemen from nerve gas attack, had more to do with morale than medicine. Nerve gas is odourless, colourless, and the most lethal chemical weapon known to man: by the time you have spotted the symptoms of nerve gas poisoning, you are minutes, perhaps seconds, away from death. Even if your spasming hands succeeded in finding and firing the injector, no expert could guarantee how effective the atropine would be.

As with all weapons of mass destruction, it was the fear that mattered most. The great irony of WMD is that they are very seldom intended to be used as weapons at all: nuclear, biological or chemical, their primary payload is always psychological. They don't even have to physically exist to deliver it – the mere possibility of their possession can be used as deterrence or as *casus belli*. Saddam's regime knew this as well as anyone. After gassing Halabja, the crews of Iraqi helicopters found they could empty bags of flour onto rebellious Kurds and instil the same sense of panic.[1]

On an intellectual level, for professionals like Kelly, biological weapons can be a scientific achievement, but for most of us they have nothing to do with the brain. They belong to the gut, the heart. They inspire terror, and that terror is what is politically most useful about them; it can be fanned or doused as strategy dictates. Kelly was a scientist and academic who had worked around biological weapons for seven years at the most senior level. Iraq had nothing to teach him about the intricacies of biowarfare. What it would give him was his introduction to the fear business.

Once the propellers of the Transall had stopped spinning, the passengers' side door opened and its metal stairway extended downwards. Kelly stepped out from the fuselage and into the blazing heat of history. He could feel the roasting air rising off the tarmac. Beads of perspiration formed at his temples. A knot of Iraqi minders waited on the apron, all uneasy smiles and leather jackets, but the noise of the turboprops still made conversation mercifully impossible. The only real welcome came from the UNSCOM members whose lonely job it was to staff the Baghdad field office, who had been at Habbaniyah in time to watch the flight approach, and who were already loading the plane's cargo into the waiting fleet of white UN Nissan Patrols. Kevin St Louis, UNSCOM's Baghdad field director, of necessity a man of some good humour, offered a smile and a wave.

The flight from Bahrain had taken a little over two hours. The team for UNSCOM Biological Weapons 1 (or BW1) had assembled in the lobby of the Holiday Inn in Manama at half-five that morning, in the last of the dark cool before daybreak. Inspections always started early, to get as much work out of the way as possible before the Arabian sun reached its burning zenith. Through the round portholes of their transport they had watched it rise over the sparkling Persian Gulf. Crossing over liberated Kuwait they had counted the black columns of smoke still billowing from the Rumaila oilfield, where retreating Iraqis had blown the wells half a year ago. Firefighters were still capping out the flames.

They arrived on one of the hottest days of the year. Kelly and his team, their arms laden with baggage, walked across the baking tarmac to a low brick building that looked more like a barracks than an airport terminal. Inside, the walls were grubby, the paint was peeling, and the floor was covered in sand. A clerk took their United Nations laissez-passers and ushered them into a waiting room where a framed photo of Saddam Hussein hung on the wall. It had perhaps once been a room for VIPs: the furniture was all leather, although rich veins of dust had collected in its seams. A noxious smell emanated from the nearby WC, but far more pervasive was the musty air of disuse, which was everywhere.

Habbaniyah had been an international airport once, when Iraq could claim membership of the international community. Its immigration office had seen actual immigrants. Now, after the ceasefire, Iraq wasn't even allowed internal domestic flights. The only air traffic Habbaniyah saw and would ever see, until the next war, over a decade hence, were UN transport planes.

The clerk disappeared with the team's travel documents for the best part of an hour, and they were served sweet lemon tea while they waited. It gave the Iraqi minders a chance to pump the inspectors for information, to find out about them personally and operationally. Kelly stood with his usual formal erectness, his face habitually stern, his demeanour civil but unyielding. He had been pressed by intelligence operatives before: inside Russia, at international conferences. It came with the territory. But there was another group present, a small delegation that clearly wasn't part of the heavy mob.

Unusually, one of these was a woman, perhaps not much more than five feet tall, with dark hair worn in a prim bun. She wore a long-sleeved blouse buttoned up to the neck, a skirt that came down past her calves, a pair of flat-heeled shoes and the plain, demure appearance of a village schoolmistress, though she was only thirty-five. Once UNSCOM later exposed her to the press, they dubbed her Dr Germ, a nickname that upset her no small amount. But Kelly never called her that. His nickname for her, though she never heard it used, was the Desert Rose. She was of course Dr Rihab Taha, from the University of East Anglia, who on transferring to Baghdad had written to him asking for strain samples.

Kelly had seen her order sheet in 1986; it had her name and signature on it. He had known what she was involved with, what organisms she was after, and where she was working. To the outside world Porton Down had said what it always said: nothing. But within British intelligence wheels had started to whir, cogs had started to turn, and files were opened. Taha's deputy was there too, Abdul Rahman Thamir, the man Kelly had met at Winchester and invited back to the Porton labs. Did they chat about their previous connections, their small portion of shared time? Not publicly, it appears, not as far as anyone has said. This too, it seems, like the Soviet inspection, was another thing that couldn't be freely talked about. Even so, the three of them must have shared a flash of recognition before they looked away. They danced around it, and it was a dance that would continue until they all disappeared.

'How do you intend to proceed?' Taha asked.

Kelly, mindful of working against a time limit, rolled forward his schedule and asked for a meeting at eight o'clock that evening. Taha suggested the conference room at the Palestine Hotel.

The tea glasses chinked, a bluebottle buzzed, the sun rose higher. Eventually the blue laissez-passers were returned, bearing official entry visas. The laissez-passers were important for UNSCOM because unlike normal passports they revealed neither the bearer's nationality nor his place of birth, which was hoped might disguise the fact that this supposedly supranational organisation was staffed by a disproportionate number of people on the payroll of the British and American governments, two countries which had recently waged war against Iraq and which now openly sought to overthrow its government. Britain and America's troubled relationship with that country dated back to its birth. Between them, London and Washington had created and then recreated Iraq not once but several times, in a violent cycle that was the unhappy hallmark of its history.

Their paperwork processed, the team filed into the blissful air-conditioned chill of the Nissan Patrols. Behind the waiting vehicles stood a line of concrete hangars, their thick domes cracked open by the US Air Force's latest laser-guided bombs. The MiGs caught inside them had since been dragged out and left to rust, burnt-out, on the dunes, where their warped and blackened wings made them look like giant mantids.

The airbase itself had originally been built by the Royal Air Force in the thirties, as Britain sought cheaper ways to exert authority over its still expanding Empire. A young minister called Winston Churchill had championed the new doctrine of 'air control' as an alternative to maintaining expensive infantry garrisons. Rebellious settlements could be attacked from the air, although in practice the RAF had found it difficult to distinguish, from bombing altitude, between good and bad natives. But the administrators were not overly concerned about accuracy. They believed retribution to be a more potent display of power than discernment, and that it was better to respond with indiscriminate violence than with nothing at all.

'The Arab and the Kurd now know what real bombing means,' an RAF squadron leader called Arthur Harris had said. 'Within forty-five minutes a full-sized village can be practically wiped out.'

The young officer who made this far more reliable forty-five-minute claim would later cap his career by masterminding the carpet bombing of German civilians.

Air control created a form of government that was distant and punitive and arbitrary; the form that Iraq's government would always take. After the 2003 invasion, when studio audiences or television presenters questioned Tony Blair's judgement or integrity in sending British forces once more into Iraq, the Prime Minister would often complain, with a studied incredulity, 'But Saddam used chemical weapons against his own people!'

If it had been up to Winston Churchill, Britain would have used chemical weapons against the Iraqis generations before Saddam gassed Kurds at Halabja.

'I do not understand this squeamishness about the use of gas,' he said, in a War Office meeting to discuss the British Mandate in Mesopotamia. 'I am strongly in favour of using poison gas against uncivilised tribes.'[2]

Iraq has never brought out the best in British politicians.

The UNSCOM convoy, followed by its Iraqi minders, pulled out of the airport gates and past the shores of the great Habbaniyah Lake, where in an earlier age Imperial Airways had refuelled their flying boats before the onward journey to British India. Within minutes Kelly's team was travelling down the main highway that linked Amman to Baghdad, heading for the Iraqi capital. Their dusty road ran in distant parallel to the Euphrates, skirting the age-less farms and villages that lay on its fertile banks, where life seemed eternally tranquil. In reality, life in Iraq was anything but.

It was a year to the day since Iraq's invasion of Kuwait. Reeling from a long and expensive war with Iran, Saddam had begun casting about for a way to offset his regime's crippling debts, and military action against its smallest neighbour seemed to offer a possible solution. Kuwait had loaned Iraq billions of dollars to defeat the Ayatollah, and now it was insisting on payment in full, while simultaneously flooding the market with cheap oil, which bankrupted Iraq even further. To add insult to injury the tiny sheikhdom was also slant-drilling into the Iraqi portion of the Rumaila oilfield. Baghdad had been stridently rattling its scimitar for weeks.

Aware of a massing Iraqi military presence on the Kuwaiti border, April Glaspie, the US Ambassador, had met with Saddam and his deputy Tariq Aziz only days before the invasion, and what she told them has since achieved a kind of infamy.

'We have no opinion on Arab–Arab conflicts like your dispute with Kuwait,' she reassured them. 'The issue has no association with America.'

It was seen as a green light, but rather than grabbing a little land, as Glaspie and Washington had expected, Saddam seized the entire emirate. Four divisions of Republican Guard and a division's worth of special forces had crossed the border in the early hours of the morning, and occupied almost all of the country by mid-afternoon. The token Kuwaiti forces fled into Saudi Arabia. The Emir evacuated his family only half an hour before plainclothes Iraqi commandos stormed their residence, his younger half-brother remaining behind to die on the palace steps in a rare gesture of royal honour. The rest of the family had a far more modern grip on events: they checked into a luxury resort in Dhahran and signed a multimillion-dollar contract with a New York PR firm called Hill & Knowlton to convince US voters of the need for military action. Dubious tales of Iraqi atrocities duly abounded.

Saddam's last-minute decision to occupy all of Kuwait apparently shocked the US and the UK, but it came as no great surprise to anybody who knew him, or who knew the Middle East. Iraq had always considered Kuwait to be a sub-district of Basra that owed its independence solely to British interference. It had said so since the thirties, although perennial instability in Baghdad meant not every government had pressed the point.

Iraq, like Egypt and Syria, had long harboured the dream of

creating a greater Arab state; a strong, secular, independent nation that would unite the peninsula. It was a vision that had always been popular with poorer Arabs, and unless they were blessed with royal blood or government patronage, poor was precisely what most Arabs were. They yearned for a country that used its oil wealth for infrastructure and improvement, rather than saw it squandered by a ruling elite which hid behind foreign militaries for protection. They had no love for Gulf State aristocracies like the Al Sabahs of Kuwait. It is remarkable to reflect on this now, after decades of demonisation, but Saddam's invasion was not a wholly unpopular move. There were spontaneous public demonstrations of support not just in Iraq but in Jordan and Palestine too.

With the obvious exception of Kuwait itself, Arab governments initially refused to condemn the occupation. Most countries in the region hoped the crisis could be solved peacefully, and without foreign involvement. Saddam agreed to attend a hastily arranged summit in Jeddah, and said he could withdraw his forces within twenty-four hours of a favourable settlement. His only stipulation was that the Kuwaiti royal family were not restored. For a moment it seemed the conflict might be contained, but behind the scenes the US was already applying pressure. The State Department threatened to cut off all aid to Egypt unless it took a hard and public stance, so President Hosni Mubarak released a statement proclaiming Saddam's invasion illegal and calling for immediate and unconditional Iraqi withdrawal. It effectively cancelled the summit, and with it any hopes of a peaceful Arab solution.

The next day, two-thirds of the Arab League voted to endorse the Egyptian line, although they also called on the West not to send any troops to the Gulf. It was a futile request. Within a week, American forces were arriving in Dhahran. Dick Cheney had apparently convinced a credulous King Fahd that Saddam had seized Kuwait only as a springboard to sweep through Saudi Arabia. Over the coming months, the Holy Kingdom would play host to the biggest influx of armed infidels the Middle East had ever seen. The army assembling there would become one of the biggest in military history, a force five times bigger than the one that landed in Normandy in 1944.

Once the Arab League had turned on him, Saddam annexed Kuwait. Perhaps he found it all too hard to believe. The last time he invaded a country he had met with near-global approval. After attacking Iran, fawning Congressmen and Cabinet ministers had come to visit, embassies had reopened, and foreign governments had fallen over themselves to offer credit and weaponry. Jacques Chirac had called him an esteemed personal friend. Only the year before Kuwait, the US State Department had called him 'a force for moderation in the region'. If the average American thought of Hussein at all it was as a little-known regional ally; brutish, sinister perhaps, not the sort of man you would want as Governor of California, but perfectly acceptable as a far-off, on-side autocrat. Saddam's genocidal campaign against the Kurds was overlooked or even obscured. Then, within days of the invasion, he swiftly became the biggest villain in the world, and would remain so until his death. So too would his supporters, or indeed anyone who had anything to do with his government.

Saddam's fall from grace was something akin to a marvel of the age. It is often said of dictators that they are expert proponents of the personality cult: witness the ubiquitous statuary, the murals, the framed portraits in every palatial hall. But America and Britain subscribed to their own cult of Saddam too. Except, instead of portraying him as some magnificent latter-day Nebuchadnezzar, they cast him as an evil madman who threatened to devour the world. He became America's go-to enemy for the rest of his life.

It all happened within days of invading Kuwait. The most memorable sign of this abrupt metamorphosis, the star above his cradle, was a fifteen-year-old girl called Nayirah, who testified before a pseudo-Congressional committee that she had been in a Kuwaiti maternity ward when Iraqi soldiers entered and removed premature babies from their incubators, equipment which they then stole, leaving the babies to die 'on the cold floor'. Saddam became the blood-hungry overlord of an army of criminal baby-killers.

The committee co-chair, John Porter, said he had never heard of such 'brutalism and inhumanity and sadism'. The episode was frequently referred to by the President and by pro-war politicians. The video footage of the testimony was seen by over sixty million Americans. You can see it on YouTube today. It's moving stuff, which is what effective propaganda tends to be.

Nayirah's identity was concealed from the public when she gave evidence, 'to protect her identity and her family, and we ask the media to respect that', as Porter explained. Actually she was the daughter of the Kuwaiti Ambassador to the US and Britain, himself a member of the deposed Al Sabah family, although the committee chairmen, John Porter and Tom Lantos, denied they knew this at the time.

Amnesty International, Human Rights Watch, the World Health Organisation and Physicians for Human Rights all visited Kuwaiti hospitals after the Iraqi withdrawal and reached the same conclusion: the incubator story didn't stand up. They had been lied to. In fact it's extremely doubtful that 'Nayirah' or her family were even in Kuwait when Iraq invaded. It transpired later that all the committee 'witnesses' has been coached and scripted by Hill & Knowlton, the PR firm the Kuwaiti royal family had hired. Al Sabah money had also gone into establishing a 'Congressional Human Rights Foundation' for Lantos and Porter to run, and Hill & Knowlton had given it office space.

Both Lantos and Porter later justified the unquestioning attention given to 'Nayirah' by arguing that the Baathist regime had done so many terrible things that one hoax didn't matter. It was, again, a case of truth versus consequences, and it was the consequences that mattered to Lantos who, being a Holocaust survivor, had some first-hand experience of evil regimes himself. In the end, of course, it was the consequences that won out. By the time the public discovered the truth, Congress had voted, and Operation Desert Storm – the war to liberate a country that had never known democracy – was already fought and won.

'Come on, who gives a shit whether there were six dead babies or two?' said Hill & Knowlton executive Lauri Fitz-Pegado, when the media caught up with her.[3] Does it make a difference? Whether there were three hundred and twelve dead babies, as was initially claimed? Or zero, as several human-rights organisations and medical charities later found? Saddam's military had killed women and children, it had killed them by the thousand, but years before, and in a different war. It had killed them casually, almost incidentally, and from a distance, through shelling and bombing and gassing, because they had been ordered to evacuate their Kurdish towns and villages but instead had remained.

Does the truth really matter, if lying serves a noble cause? Evidently, plenty of people thought it didn't. Once Saddam crossed into Kuwait, lies and falsehoods about Iraq came thick and fast. Tom King, the UK's Defence Secretary, said 'tens of thousands of civilians' had died during the Iraqi occupation.[4] Middle East Watch later examined the matter and discovered a thousand was the most likely outside estimate.[5] A thousand dead civilians is an atrocity, but it is a fraction of the collateral damage that the coalition caused when they eventually responded.[6]

If the conduct of the Iraqi military was subject to propaganda, so too was its size and purpose. Much was said about Iraq having the fourth-, sometimes even the third-, biggest army in the world. It was nonsense. When journalists started to fact-check, Carne Ross, then a political–military desk officer at the Foreign Office and later a colleague of David Kelly at the UN in New York, was tasked with 'proving' the statement. By his own admission, he did this by pulling down a copy of *Jane's Armies of the World*, adding Iraq's enormous army reserves to that country's total, and excluding the reserves from everybody else's.

'I need not have worried,' Ross later wrote. 'The "fact" that Iraq had the third-largest forces in the world became one of those factoids, believed by everyone, validated merely by multiple repetition.'[7]

Few observed that even with the support of the entire Middle East, the US, Europe and the USSR, this army had still failed to defeat the weakened forces of revolutionary Iran.

Cheney may have won basing rights in Saudi Arabia by frightening its royals that Iraq was about to attack, but satellite imagery showed no build-up on the border. Jean Heller, a reporter for Florida's *St Petersburg Times* and an eight-time Pulitzer nominee, persuaded her editor to commission some commercial satellite imaging of the area. The photos were crystal-clear, and they showed nothing but empty sand. She showed it to two experts at George Washington University: they found some barracks. They had been abandoned. Far from being coiled to spring a second invasion, the Republican Guard, repeatedly referred to by Washington, the Pentagon and the media as Saddam's most formidable fighting force and the linchpin of his rag-tag conscript army, had actually retreated from Kuwait soon after the annexation, something Washington and London kept quiet about for months.

'This aggression will not stand,' orated President Bush, who spoke of 'drawing a line in the sand', and after some expensive lobbying the UN, the Arab League and even the USSR, defanged by its own political turmoil, all backed the American position.

Iraq pointed out that the Middle East was full of disputed or occupied territory, like Israel in the Gaza Strip and West Bank, or Syria in Lebanon (Syria actually consolidated its occupation of Lebanon during the Kuwaiti occupation). It offered 'to withdraw from Kuwait if the United States pledges not to attack as soldiers are pulled out, if foreign troops leave the region, and if there is agreement on the Palestinian problem and on the banning of all weapons of mass destruction in the region'. America said negotiating with Saddam would only 'reward aggression'. Saddam, said Bush, was the 'Butcher of Baghdad' and 'a tyrant worse than Hitler'. The bombing began in January.

The resulting ground war to liberate Kuwait lasted just one hundred hours. There was a single doomed counter-offensive but the vast majority of Iraqi troops surrendered instantly or had already fled. Resistance was less than minimal. Some of the surrendering soldiers were without boots, some were in their mid-sixties, some were fifteen, all were ravenously hungry. The one-sidedness of the conflict found its photogenic expression in the 'Highway of Death', where American pilots bombed and strafed a convoy of routed Iraqis in civilian vehicles. Eleven coalition divisions made deep sweeping lunges, for hundreds of miles, into Iraq itself, and made only – at most – glancing contact with the Republican Guard.

'Remember how it started?' riffed the comedian Bill Hicks. 'They kept talking about "the elite Republican Guard" in these hushed tones like these guys were bogeymen or something? "Yeah, we're doing well now, but we have yet to face the elite Republican Guard." Like these guys were twelve feet tall desert warriors, never lost a battle, they shit bullets. Yeah, well after two months of continuous carpet bombing, and not one reaction at all from the elite Republican Guard, they became simply "the Republican Guard". Not nearly as elite as we may have led you to believe. And after another month they went from being "the Republican Guard" to "the Republicans made this shit up about Guards being out there". It wasn't really a war. A war is when *two* armies are fighting.'

In a more verbose and less amusing way the French intellectual Jean Baudrillard wrote a collection of essays contending exactly that. His book, *The Gulf War Did Not Take Place*, argued the conflict was largely symbolic, the continuation of politics not by war but by bloody pantomime. From the Western perspective, what it gave us was not any shared experience of fighting, but stories, pictures, and propaganda.

Even for Saddam Hussein personally, the war had far less impact than anyone had hoped. However disastrous his miscalculation over Kuwait proved to be, he was right in one thing: Washington needed him, or someone very like him.[8] Bush's coalition left him in power.

'We were not going to get bogged down in the problems of trying to take over and run Iraq,' Dick Cheney told the press the following year. Neither did the US want to create a power vacuum that might advantage Iran, or catapult an independent Kurdistan into existence. But even so, the ceasefire was a one-sided business. Iraq was no longer allowed to fly planes, even inside its own air-space. It remained subject to the strictest sanctions the UN had ever seen, even though it no longer occupied Kuwait. And it became subject to the most intrusive arms inspections in the history of the world. A UN resolution mandated the creation of a Special Commission to carry out these inspections, and so the United Nations Special Commission, or UNSCOM, was born. The sanctions were supposed to be lifted once UNSCOM declared Iraq free of WMD.

Neither the sanctions nor UNSCOM nor Saddam were expected to be around for very long. The CIA circulated a paper that predicted the dictator would fall within six months. Military defeat, the economic blockade, covert CIA activity and the inspections themselves were supposed to create the necessary preconditions for his overthrow. UNSCOM was shown the CIA report, which may be why some of the inspectors thought the Commission would be finished within months. The first official deadline was forty-five days. Kelly himself said he thought the inspections would be over in half a year.[9] Instead they would take up the next seven years of his life, and even after UNSCOM was withdrawn and disbanded, he was never really able to escape the sinister and long-running theatre we have made of Iraq.

We have all of us lived through it.

For those of my generation, the Gulf War is the first war we can really remember. The build-up lasted for months, and several of the boarders at my school had fathers in the forces, many of whom were stationed in Saudi. It was not unusual to intrude upon a worried twelve- or thirteen-year-old boy crying to himself in an empty room. Scare stories about Saddam's secret doomsday weapons were commonplace, and the casualty estimates for the coalition were horrific: two hundred thousand in some news-papers. General Peter de la Billière himself later said he expected at least fifteen hundred British deaths (lives which he felt, 'very privately, . . . we shouldn't be losing').[10] Given all this, I doubt that any of us really understood why we were going to war in the first place. I had no relatives in the Middle East and I wanted to be a soldier, so I didn't mind. The notion that one country shouldn't invade another was simple enough for me to get hold of, and afterwards, like millions of Britons, I was entirely absorbed not by the war's politics but by its tales of derring-do.

The quiet son of an RAF doctor approached me one evening while I was rereading *Bravo Two Zero*, the bestselling account of an SAS unit compromised deep behind enemy lines, which had been authored by its own patrol commander.

'Some of the stuff in that never happened, you know,' he said. I was an adult by the time I discovered he was probably right.

Bravo Two Zero sold over a million and a half copies in the UK, and like just about everything else that has been written about the war in Iraq, contains the customary exaggerations and embellishments, events that other troopers in the unit maintain never took place. Its claim that an eight-man patrol killed over two hundred and fifty enemy soldiers has been roundly dismissed, although at least one of the deaths they inflicted was, it appears, on an unarmed civilian, and some in the regiment have said that those troopers captured by the Iraqi army were not tortured but received medical care. If the book can be boiled down to its single, uncontested element, it is the story of one man's remarkable feat in running away.

Desperate to extricate himself from Iraq, Colin Armstrong would cross one hundred and eighty miles of hostile terrain. And years later, David Kelly would walk three thousand yards of Oxfordshire countryside.

After leaving Habbaniyah airport, Kelly's convoy crossed the Euphrates at Fallujah, using a girder bridge that had somehow survived the coalition's air attacks (the RAF had hit the market instead, in a daytime raid, causing over a hundred deaths[11]). Over a decade later, after occupying American ground forces had killed a number of protesters in the city, Fallujah would retaliate with a grenade attack against four US mercenaries, and hang their bodies from the girders of that bridge. Photos of their dangling corpses were widely circulated by news agencies, and an outraged America would send in the 1st Marine Expeditionary Force, which killed perhaps another five or six hundred of Fallujah's civilians before withdrawing. But all that was in the future, in a war yet to happen. When the UN Nissan Patrols rolled over Fallujah Bridge that morning the only bodies they saw belonged to neighbourhood boys, cooling off in the slow waters of the Euphrates as it meandered around a steep bend.

At Abu Ghraib, they took the expressway to the capital. From the highway you could see the upper floors of Iraq's vast central prison, hidden behind its long concrete wall, a drab brown-grey edifice as lifeless as the drab brown-grey plain surrounding it. Built by British contractors in the sixties, it had cropped up in an Amnesty International report after the Iran–Iraq war, but few had heard of it back then. American antipathy towards Saddam would soon trigger a torrent of horror stories about the place, but few, if any, would ever be verified, until the US Military Police took over 'Grab-an-Arab' and began committing and photographing crimes of their own.

Nearing Baghdad, the reality of the recent war became apparent. The roadside checkpoints, the anti-aircraft emplacements, the fortified barracks all reminded you this was not a country that was truly at peace. The city itself appeared undamaged until they reached the centre, where landmark ministries were either burnt out or completely collapsed. From a distance, some seemed perfectly normal, then you noticed they had no floors, that you could see the sky through their glassless ground-floor windows: further examples of America's new 'smart bombs' at work. The coalition's bombing of Baghdad had perhaps killed only a little over two thousand civilians.

At that time UNSCOM's Baghdad field headquarters was the seventeenth floor of the Baghdad Sheraton, although the Sheraton corporation, like most foreign businesses, had divested itself of the hotel shortly before the Gulf War. The Baathists ran it now. The ex-Sheraton overlooked the Tigris River and Firdos Square, home to the nearby Palestine Méridien, it too dropped by its parent company, which was where that night's conference was being held. Baghdad's tallest buildings were its luxury hotels, its skyline proclaimed it a city open to the world, but Saddam's creaky vision had imploded. The country had become a pariah state overnight, and all those towering hotels were empty. Even the war correspondents, the sorry salvation of many a desperate hotelier, had by now drifted off to disasters elsewhere.

In a foyer deserted except for a few listless and obvious agents of the secret police, the team checked in, and went up to their rooms. Kelly stood alone at his window and looked down at the stream of honking traffic circling below, silent and distant behind the tinted glass. It was a rare moment of solitude in a hectic schedule, and he savoured the calm. There was little else to do but wait. It was impossible to have any meaningful discussion with his fellow inspectors: it was assumed the hotel was bugged, and minders followed them everywhere they went. Neither UK nor US intelligence had any secure areas anywhere in the country; the nearest home embassy was in Kuwait City, and UNSCOM's early countersurveillance was at best a makeshift affair. Secure transmissions out of the Baghdad field office were encrypted with a time-consuming book code, using a biography of George Bush. Kelly quickly checked on his team, then went back to his room to watch some incomprehensible Iraqi television before drawing the curtains and catching up on his sleep. He could hardly have expected that he would be back here another thirty-seven times, usually for weeks on end. It would consume his life.

Contrary to what the CIA had promised, Saddam did not fall – in fact, he would outlive the inspector – and as long as Saddam held power the inspections had to continue. It was the easiest way the US and the UK could maintain diplomatic support for the sanctions, designed both to contain the dictator and to undermine him, so that a suitable replacement might find it easier to take over.

The blockade had begun within days of Iraq's invasion. UN Resolution 661 prohibited every member state of the UN from supplying goods to Iraq unless they were 'intended strictly for medical purposes, [or] in humanitarian circumstances, foodstuffs'. Oil was the only thing Iraq really produced, everything else had to be imported, and so the sanctions hit hard. The US Department of Agriculture predicted 'drastic shortages' of food, warning that 'extreme hardship will likely be apparent by the end of the year'.[12] The global blockade was an extreme measure, but it was justified by being the only alternative to military intervention and 'the slaughter that modern-day warfare brings'.[13]

As a captive, Saddam would later remind his FBI interrogator that America's sanctions had begun even earlier. The Iraq Sanctions Act, which called for an immediate end to all commercial and financial transactions between the US and Iraq, had been introduced to Congress five months before Saddam's troops crossed over into Kuwait. A similar amendment had already been snuck into an appropriations bill and passed as law that April, and Washington had been urging other countries to follow suit since.

'There is nothing for us to buy from America,' Saddam told Ambassador Glaspie that July. 'Only wheat. Every time we want to buy something, you say it is forbidden. I am afraid one day you're going to say we're making gunpowder out of wheat.'

And within weeks, even the wheat was forbidden.

As Saddam neared the end of his life, the FBI Special Agent George Piro asked him if he realised that by invading Kuwait he had doomed his country. Saddam shrugged, and said that America had always planned to destroy Iraq once its war with Iran was over. This is not an unfounded view. Several Middle Eastern governments thought that Kuwait's antagonism towards Iraq after the Iran–Iraq War was incomprehensible without the tacit promise of American military support.

'The Kuwaitis were very cocky,' an aide to King Hussein of Jordan told the American journalist Milton Viorst. 'They told us officially that the United States would intervene if there was trouble with Iraq.'[14]

When Iraqi forces occupied Kuwait, they found documents describing secret high-level meetings at which CIA officials had exhorted the Kuwaitis to put pressure on an Iraq weakened by its war against Iran. Tariq Aziz, the Foreign Minister, distributed copies of them at the United Nations that October and the CIA decried them as 'total fabrications', but it seems likely the Kuwaitis were counting on somebody. The Baathist leadership never shook off the suspicion that they had been led into a trap. Just as Kelly would be. This, as Kelly was to find out, was the nature of politics in the Middle East: secretive, deceitful, indifferent to who got hurt. And everyone was at it.

The UN sanctions, 'more massive in scope than any ever adopted in peacetime against any nation', were supposed to prevent a war, and war came anyway, weeks of relentless bombing followed by a brief pantomime on the ground.[15] In a tent at Safwan in southeast Iraq a ceasefire was quickly agreed on, and the UN Secretary General sent in Martti Ahtisaari, the future president of Finland, for an urgent appraisal of Iraq's humanitarian situation. His report was unequivocal.

'Nothing we had seen or read had quite prepared us for this particular form of devastation which has now befallen the country,' Ahtisaari wrote. 'The recent conflict has wrought near apocalyptic results on the economic infrastructure of what had been a rather urbanized and mechanized society. Most means of modern life support have been destroyed or rendered tenuous.'[16]

Yet a month later, after furious lobbying by the US, the UN passed Resolution 687, and Iraq discovered that although the war was over, the sanctions would continue. Ostensibly they would continue until Iraq could prove to a special UN commission – UNSCOM – that it had destroyed its nuclear, chemical and biological weapons.[17] But this was a fig-leaf. In reality the sanctions had nothing to do with disarmament, as soon became transparent.

'All possible sanctions will be maintained until Saddam Hussein is gone,' the White House press spokesman Marlin Fitzwater told the world's media, once the resolution had been passed.

'We don't want to lift these sanctions as long as Saddam is in power,' said President Bush.[18]

'We are not interested in seeing a relaxation of sanctions as long as Saddam Hussein is in power,' concurred Bush's Secretary of State, James Baker.[19]

'Iraqis will be made to pay the price while Saddam Hussein is in power,' said National Security Advisor Robert Gates. 'Any easing of sanctions will be considered only when there is a new government.'[20]

The Safwan ceasefire had been reneged on. The *Washington Post*, with the bellicosity that post-Kuwait Iraq has always inspired in the English-speaking media, editorialised that this volte-face was 'entirely justified by Saddam's record of treachery', but the only other country to support this line was Britain, John Major having already announced the UK would veto any attempt to weaken sanctions 'for so long as Saddam Hussein remains in power'.[21]

All of this was completely contrary to what had been agreed not at Safwan but at the UN Security Council. It was a policy that would take an epic toll on the people of Iraq as the years passed, children in particular. It would see the UN, at the instigation of the US, contravene both its own charter and the Geneva Convention. At the time of Kelly's first inspection the human cost of UNSCOM's presence may not have occurred to him, but others accepted it from the start.

'We assumed UNSCOM's activities would keep sanctions in place,' admitted Charles Duelfer – then at the State Department, but later an UNSCOM deputy director – 'sort of kicking the rock down the road, which was the traditional US approach with Iraq.'

In his room at the Baghdad Sheraton, Kelly looked at his reflection in the mirror, smoothed down his hair and tucked in his shirt. Five weeks ago, on the recommendation of another old Portonian, Professor Bryan Barras, he had been seconded to UNSCOM and flown to New York. There he met Nikita Smidovich, of all people, one of the Russians who had escorted him around Obolensk, and who was now working for the UN

(Smidovich says he never defected but just sort of left. Whatever the circumstances of his departure, he soon earned the trust of his British and American colleagues, and he still works out of the UN headquarters building today). The two of them put together a questionnaire for the Iraqis, looked over their early declarations, assessed whatever intelligence they could share, and sketched out a training programme for BW1's new inspectors.

A week before, Kelly and his team had flown into the tiny island kingdom of Bahrain for acclimatisation and further training at the CIA's GATEWAY station, a rambling, run-down building in back-street Manama, guarded by US Marines. Hamish Killip, the DIS analyst and former Porton Down staff officer who had also been on the Soviet inspections, was already there on secondment, as was Rod Barton, from Australia's Defence Intelligence Organisation. Both would later work alongside Kelly inside Iraq as inspectors themselves.

Now, finally, Kelly was in Baghdad.

It was almost eight o'clock. He took a final look out of his eighth-floor window, and watched the Tigris, opaque and impenetrable, oozing down towards the Gulf like chocolate. Did he wonder why the river was that colour? Did he know? The huge power station in southern Baghdad, al-Dohra, had been knocked out by bombing, and the sewage had backed up onto the streets. After cannibalising other power plants for parts, the Iraqis managed to get al-Dohra running again, at least for most of the time, and the sewage pumps began churning. But the treatment plants had been bombed too, and in any case, Iraq couldn't buy the chlorine they needed to work, in case they used it to make chemical weapons. So a city of three and a half million people was pumping its effluent straight into the Tigris. Under sanctions, the people of Baghdad faced epidemics worse than any bomb could deliver.

Downstairs in the lobby of the former Baghdad Sheraton, Kelly rejoined his senior inspectors and their interpreters and they crossed the road to the former Palestine Méridien, which was opposite. The sun had sunk, and so the evening was merely hot.

It was pleasant to be outdoors. There was practically no public hostility in the early days of UNSCOM. Inspectors could walk around on foot without worry, and in any case, Firdos was still a quiet, well-to-do riverside neighbourhood, and the city seemed calm.

A few blocks away, in St Fatima's, a Catholic Relief volunteer called Doug Broderick was busy giving food handouts to the church's middle-class parishioners.

'Right now throughout the country, we have a classic response to food shortage, pre-famine,' Broderick had told the journalist Patrick Cockburn the previous week. 'You have people selling jewellery here in Baghdad. Your used-watch market is flooded with watches. Families are pawning their carpets, their furniture, their gold, their silverware. Anything that has any kind of value – their cameras, their videos, their radios – in order to get cash for food.'[22]

Iraq's humanitarian crisis never formed part of the pre-mission intelligence briefings for UNSCOM inspectors. They weren't looking for it, and they didn't see it. On the few occasions when they literally bumped into it, they generally called it something else: propaganda, or melodrama, or plain bad taste. If deep down they ever felt any differently, it was something they kept to themselves, Kelly included.

Around the conference table in the Palestine Hotel, flanked by Iraqi interpreters, assistants and security officers, Dr Rihab Taha was waiting for them. With her was a short man with closely cropped black hair and the ubiquitous thick moustache worn by almost all Iraqi men from middle age onwards. He was introduced as Brigadier Hossam Mohammed Amin, and he was Iraq's chief disarmament officer, the senior liaison point for UNSCOM, and the man entrusted by the regime to oversee inspections, provide minders, authorise declarations, and facilitate interviews. He was forty-one years of age. By the time the weapons inspectors would be finished with him, a long time in the future, his hair and moustache had turned a solid grey. Despite his military bearing he always wore a suit and tie, and he spoke English reasonably well, although his accent was heavy.

Kelly knew from his briefings that Amin, like many senior Iraqis, was a Tikriti, from the same village as Saddam, to whom he claimed a distant kinship, although the Brigadier seemed a far more credible official than some of his ilk. He was an educated man, had been an engineer by profession, and was sometimes so quiet his voice dropped to an almost inaudible murmur. No one ever saw Amin relish his authority. There was an unease about him, sometimes even a sadness. He was the sort of person who could seem awkward even when he was sitting still, and few inspectors thought he liked his job.

Amin, perhaps, was one of the very few people who had some premonition of where all this might lead. Years later, after Operation Iraqi Freedom, in between his 'enhanced interrogations' at Camp Cropper, he would pass the time by writing poetry on paper smuggled into his cell.

'Alas,' he wrote, of his tormentors, 'you don't see that one day you destroyed your life in this place.'

That was all a long way away.

Everyone around the conference table at the Palestine Hotel took their seats, and a suspenseful silence spread around the room. By order of a UN Security Council resolution, Iraq had to unconditionally accept the destruction, removal or rendering harmless, under UNSCOM's supervision, of all its biological weapons, all its stocks of biological agents, and 'all related sub-systems and components and research, development, support, and manufacturing facilities'.

Thus far, Iraq's declarations about biological weapons had been minimal, but concise. It said it didn't have any. And as we all know now, it was right.

In May, it had supplied to Rolf Ekeus, UNSCOM's Swedish chair, a list of all Iraqi facilities related to biological production (for political reasons Washington never suggested an American chairman, but they made sure his deputy always was).[23] For the most part these were vaccine factories, or bakeries, included because they handled large-scale fermentation. About half the sites on the list had been selected as bombing targets during Desert Storm, most famously a baby-milk factory in Abu Ghraib.

The American journalist Peter Arnett had reported the baby-milk bombing for CNN. As well as the bomb-damaged factory, his footage showed tell-tale signage, workers in baby-milk uniforms, a baby-milk production line and large quantities of milk powder, and he was roundly criticised by the White House and then the rest of the media as a result.

'It was a biological weapons facility, of that we are sure,' said Colin Powell, the same day Arnett's piece was broadcast.[24]

'That factory is in fact a production facility for biological weapons,' White House spokesman Fitzwater briefed the press. 'The Iraqis have hidden this facility behind a façade of baby-milk production as a form of disinformation. Everything that Peter Arnett reports is approved by, censored by and reviewed on the spot by the Iraqi government. This is not a case of taking on the media. It's a case of correcting a public disclosure that is erroneous, that is false, that hurts our government, and that plays into the hands of Saddam Hussein.'[25]

Newsweek and others promptly derided Arnett's gullibility in falling for Iraq's 'ham-handed attempt' at crude propaganda. UNSCOM, UNMOVIC and the Iraq Survey Group all went on to visit the factory at Al Kindi. They visited it several times, just in case they had missed something. They installed video cameras inside it to record what was happening, interviewed the staff who worked there, and performed sampling analysis on its machinery. What they all found was that the Baby Milk Factory at Abu Ghraib made baby-milk powder, and nothing else, and always had done, although this wasn't a discovery that was ever press-released.

Only two of the biology facilities on that list were under military ownership. One was Salman Pak, the Iraqi Porton Down, on the banks of the Tigris, fifteen miles south of Baghdad, which had also been bombed. American intelligence had been leaking stories about the place since the invasion of Kuwait, and some papers were able to print satellite imagery of the site.

'Everyone thought they were playing with one or two things at Salman Pak,' as one inspector later said.[26]

The other military centre the Iraqis had declared to Ekeus was virtually unheard of. It was Al Hakum, in a small town called Jurf Al Sakhar, fifty miles out to the southwest, which had somehow escaped the attention of US Air Force planners.

Kelly had been briefed on all of this before he'd even left London: MI6 and the Defence Intelligence Staff had formed a special entity to brief British UNSCOM inspectors, called the Rockingham cell.[27] Satellite imagery of Iraq's declared locations would have been analysed by the DIS, export and import records examined, data from human sources compiled. His meeting with Amin that evening was not unlike his showdown with Sandakhchiev in Siberia: Kelly had a substantial degree of inside intelligence, and it would secretly inform every interview he ever conducted. It was how the game was played. But unlike his visit to Vector, there was no hostility in the Palestine Hotel.

On the Iraqi side, the conversation that evening was open to the point of rambling. It was all Kelly could do to keep to the narrow, pre-arranged plan of his questioning. Like a barrister, an interrogator attempts a formal neutrality, and keeps his knowledge and opinions to himself. His questions are pointed and clear, but they conceal other questions, barbs and feints and traps that can be circuitously returned to. As an UNSCOM inspector, he sought official clarification and declaration, but as an intelligence man the unconscious admission was just as important, and politically, prompting a provable falsehood was at least as valuable as turning up the truth.

So far, while Iraq maintained it had no biological weapons, and listed all its sites, it had said nothing about its research. As Kelly knew, and had known since the anthrax conference at Winchester, if not earlier, Iraq had established a military programme. The Iraqis could stonewall and deny it, or they could open up.

The discussion had hardly begun when Amin offered that yes, Iraq had conducted military biowarfare research, and it had been at Salman Pak.

Kelly began probing into its goals. Was its research offensive or defensive?

'Well,' said Amin, with a candour that would evaporate over the coming months, 'a military programme covers both aspects, doesn't it?'

Around the room a few eyebrows were probably raised, but Amin was not being disingenuous. He was casually wrestling with the problem that had beset biological inspectors and researchers ever since the Cold War. Where and how do you draw the line? In the fifties, Porton Down did it by cynically erasing the word 'warfare' from its official language and replacing it with the word 'defence'. Kelly worked for the Microbiology Defence Division at the Chemical Defence Establishment for the Ministry of Defence. Even so, it was still a classified, high-security military laboratory where scientists bound by the Official Secrets Act engineered lethal pathogens and assessed their viability as weapons. In Russia, as Kelly had found out, Biopreparat had been staffed by thousands of scientists who had been told, who believed, and who argued that they were only protecting their country.

'Well,' asked Kelly, who had spent most of the previous year frantically trying to protect British servicemen from whatever biological weapons Iraq might have developed, 'have you produced any vaccines? What are you giving your own troops?'

'We vaccinate them for cholera and for typhoid,' said Amin, 'and that's all.' Kelly nodded, simply to register the answer, which, again, was something he already knew. The British had taken enough Iraqi prisoners that February to find that out for themselves.

Eventually Amin handed over a typed statement covering half a single page. It explained that 'for military purposes' Iraq had researched anthrax, *Clostridium perfringens* (or gas gangrene) and botulinum toxin at Salman Pak. None of these agents were surprising subjects of study. They were the most commonly researched biological warfare agents in Porton Down, and Kelly had spent time on all of them in the eighties.

What wasn't present on that list was plague. Of all the injections Kelly's lab had sent out to the Gulf, the plague vaccine was the most controversial, and the most hurried. The last booster jabs arrived within days of the ground attack, and, as mentioned earlier, they were so debilitating that several commanding officers refused to issue it to their troops: Major General Rupert Smith of the 1st Armoured Division was one, and Lieutenant Colonel Charles Rogers of the Staffordshires another.

Neither Kelly nor the Ministry of Defence ever publicly admitted their mistake. After UNSCOM had pulled out of Iraq, and the inspectors had little to do but PR about the dangers of Iraqi germ warfare, Kelly would give an authorised (and probably instructed) interview to Tom Mangold for his book *Plague Wars*.[28] By then, UNSCOM had been in Iraq for over eight years, and had never found any evidence of weaponised plague.

'Iraq denies working on plague but I find its absence conspicuous,' Kelly told Mangold, having visited Iraq thirty-seven times without uncovering any plague whatsoever. 'I remain deeply suspicious.'

Hossam Amin had introduced the 35-year-old Taha as head of the research programme. Kelly, and Western intelligence, had already surveyed the open scientific literature that Taha and her colleagues had published. Dr Germ's publication record was not exactly prodigious. She had published only her master's and a doctorate, each in collaboration with John Turner, her supervisor at the University of East Anglia. Both were about plant diseases. Before coming to Britain she had written a paper about salmonella in animal feed with Nasser Al Hindawi, the man who had met Kelly at Winchester in 1989, and who some UNSCOM inspectors maintained was the 'father' of the Iraqi biological warfare programme. None of her three publications had the slightest military application.

'If Rihab really was the head of Iraqi germ warfare research,' Turner told me, 'I don't think they could have got very far. She wasn't especially gifted as a student in the first place.'

Neither, does it seem, were there any bright shining lights amongst her staff. Amin explained that she led a small team of ten scientists and, in response to another question from Kelly, that only three of them held doctorates. A little later he was presented with their research papers, a pile of unpublished and often handwritten notes in a mixture of Arabic and English. There were no lab books and apparently few test results. It all looked decidedly undergraduate, at best.

Years later, after Operation Iraqi Freedom, American forces ransacked Baghdad's government buildings and an intelligence cell called Dragon Hunter unearthed some of these documents. They were partially declassified in 2012. Reading them evokes a certain pathos now. There is a brief history of anthrax in the twentieth century, scrawled in marker pen on unlined paper, that reads as if it could have been cribbed from an encyclopaedia. There is no sign of the sophistication that would be needed to create and run the mythic fleet of ground-breaking, high-containment mobile weapons labs that would later seize imaginations in London and Washington.

'Who does Taha work for?' Kelly asked, reaching above her, perhaps, for someone that might appear credible.

'General Ahmed Murtada Ahmed Khalil,' Amin offered. 'He heads the Technical Research Centre that oversees the labs at Salman Pak. It oversees Al Hakum too.'

As well as holding a high military rank, Ahmed Murtada held a doctorate in engineering.

'Can I see him?'

'I don't see why not. I'll see what I can do.'

It was more than Kelly had hoped for. He reviewed the papers he had been given, or pretended to, while he decided what to say next. He later said that the openness he had encountered that evening had thrown him a little. It certainly wasn't what he was used to in Soviet Russia.

'Why have you chosen to reveal this programme now?' Kelly asked Amin.

'We are concerned the work might be misinterpreted,' said the Brigadier, prophetically. 'Possibly, it could be used for propaganda purposes against us.'[29]

He told Kelly that the programme had been running for only four years. It started in earnest in 1986 and then had been abruptly wound down in 1990, before the invasion of Kuwait, when the entire stock of Iraqi warfare agents had been destroyed. It had been put in autoclaves, sterilising equipment that resembles high-pressure-steam cookers, and killed off as a precaution before hostilities commenced.

It seems that most UNSCOM inspectors, unrelenting in their quest to dig up Saddam's secret germ bombs, never accepted this. Why would you want to destroy your biological arsenal, however embryonic it might be, before going to war? Some, like Nikita Smidovich, found it inexplicable. Yet the US Air Force had already provided the answer to that some months before Kelly ever set foot inside the country, by bombing the baby-milk plant at Al Kindi.

Equipped with an extensive list of hypothetical BW facilities, General Charles Horner, the commander of the US Ninth Air Force, had been troubled by the possibility that bombing them could cause huge civilian casualties, perhaps even outside Iraq. He had been warned that clouds of anthrax from targeted laboratories might drift down the Arabian peninsula, so Dick Cheney, now risen to become the Secretary of Defense, had promptly put his nerves at ease.

'We said, there has to be a penalty to a country that would build and store these horrible weapons,' Horner later related, 'so maybe if some people are killed, no matter how bad that is, it sends the right signal to anybody that would build biological weapons.'[30]

In the event, of course, the planners had exaggerated the size and scope of Iraq's biological efforts by a considerable factor. They had exaggerated everything, almost as if America's mighty military machine sought to find its own justification, although in truth, it was just the prudence of power. In the warped prism that is war, overwhelming force (or violence, to use its true name) can sometimes count as caution. And so cautiously, in a war it suffered rather than fought, Iraq had rolled up its biological programme before the bombs started to fall.

Or so it said.

On his way out of the Palestine Hotel, Kelly was suprised by a television news crew who pressed a microphone into his face. The early UNSCOM inspections were high visibility, and the media reported on them almost every day. They were a glimpse into Iraq itself, albeit with a touch of exciting adventurism, and people wondered what doomsday devices the inspectors might discover. On the nuclear side of things it's true that one or two remarkable stories did unfold, but the novelty soon wore off. The inspections, in their hundreds, would drag on for the rest of the decade, and Washington and London would work hard to generate the right kind of interest.

Some of Kelly's interviews over BW1 were curiously at odds with the media strategy that would follow. Neither London nor Washington nor the staff they appointed to UNSCOM would ever miss the chance to depict the Iraqi regime as a deceitful and dangerous one, and sometimes that 'chance' would be deliberately engineered, but things were different at the start.

Red-faced in the heat, even though the sun had set, Kelly stood blinking in an open-necked blue shirt outside the entrance of the hotel, displaying little of the composure he would exhibit in his future public appearances (including the Foreign Affairs Select Committee).

'How's it been going?' asked the reporter.

'So far it's actually been excellent,' he said, leaning into the microphone, his eyes somewhere off-camera. 'We have had a warm reception. Every request I have made has been met or they have said they will meet it. I have an open mind at this stage. I have an open mind.'[31]

It all sounds entirely off-message now.

The next day, Kelly visited Salman Pak. The complex was spread out over a narrow three-mile peninsula on a sharp bend in the Tigris. Like most of Iraq, the land there was flat, dry and featureless, although there were thick reeds growing on most of it, drawing water from the riverbank. The only landmark on an otherwise empty horizon was the great Arch of Ctesiphon stretching into the sky, the last monumental remains of a city two thousand years old.

The British military had been here before. An expeditionary force on its way to take Baghdad had been beaten back by the Ottomans in the shadow of that arch. After a brief siege, it would end up being force-marched to Turkey in what has been called 'the most abject capitulation in British history', but that too was ancient history. Kelly's team were here as victors, and they had to tread carefully. The ground was still littered with unexploded ordnance from their own air forces.

Salman Pak had been more than just Taha's biology lab. There were scientists here who had worked on Iraq's formidable chemical arsenal too. Elsewhere in the complex there was an electronics research station with its own production plant, and the headquarters of the Mukhabarat's special operations division. Iraqi intelligence used to train counterterrorism forces there, using a parked Boeing fuselage to teach anti-terrorist techniques.

In the build-up to the invasion of Iraq, countless false defectors would emerge from the shadows to claim the Mukhabarat camp was the complete opposite: not a counterterrorist school but an actual academy for terrorists. The more hardline UNSCOM inspectors heartily concurred, although they had each visited Salman Pak enough times to know the truth. Charles Duelfer, of the US State Department, and UNSCOM's second deputy chair, was one of them.

'Of course we automatically took out the word "counter",' he told the *Guardian*. 'I'm surprised that people seem to be shocked that there should be terror camps in Iraq. Like, durr! I mean, what, actually, do you expect? Iraq presents a long-term strategic threat.'[32]

'Many of us had our own private suspicions,' said Richard Spertzel, UNSCOM's other senior biological inspector. 'We had nothing specific as evidence, yet among ourselves we always referred to it as the training terrorist camp.'[33]

As the CIA would later have to admit before Congress, the Mukhabarat centre at Salman Pak was no such thing. It had been built under the supervision of British intelligence in the eighties, and had actually hired instructors from Britain's SAS to run hostage-rescue courses, which might explain why it so closely resembles the same facility in Hereford.[34] Kelly certainly knew all this, but in the fever-struck months that followed 9/11 his voice was silent on the issue, as it was about so many things.

When his team arrived that morning they found themselves walking around a bombsite. The main electronics building had received a direct hit in its elevator shaft, leaving a gaping hole in each of its six floors. It looked like it might collapse any moment, but this didn't stop the inspectors from ferreting around inside it, against the advice of their own demolitions expert. Other smaller buildings had been destroyed entirely, or demolished by the Iraqi clean-up team. Two bulldozers were parked up on site, having already knocked down eight smaller structures. Later, when UNSCOM settled on its official, antagonistic line, the inspectors would argue this was all part of some cunning deception, rather than clear evidence of the programme's end. But no one complained about it on BW1.

Taha's lab had been bombed too, but inside it the inspectors found two small-scale lab fermenters with seven- and fourteen-litre capacities. The filing cabinets were empty, the bookshelves and desk drawers had been stripped, and document bonfires had been lit in the middle of the office floor. Charred paper covered in computer print-out and Arabic script fluttered in the breeze from blown-out windows. By the roadside, expensive lab equipment and machine tools sat uselessly in the sun, awaiting salvage or the scrapyard.

Under ground, Salman Pak was less badly affected. One

basement looked like it might have made a good cold room for the bulk storage of biological agents, all of which would need to be protected from the fierce Mesopotamian heat, but it was completely bare. Wires trailed from the walls, the fittings were gutted, and the electricity was cut. In another dark cellar, the inspectors found what looked like primate cages, but Taha said they were never used. Inspectors later learnt that the officials Iraq had sent to central Africa to procure test monkeys had been ripped off by unscrupulous traders, or absconded with the funds. Taha's scientists were left to test on goats and dogs and horses, all poor substitutes for human physiology.

Kelly was certain that Salman Pak must have had an aerosol chamber, perhaps even a blast chamber, and so Taha took him to the ruined remains of a square, one-storey brick building in its own patch of wasteland. Judging from appearances, the block had never been connected to the sewage system, or even the water mains. Taha told him they had only ever used the chamber about once a year, and so when they did need running water they just parked a trailer outside it. The inspectors could see from the size of the transformer attached to the building's exterior that its power supply had been minimal. It was a far cry from what Kelly had seen in Obolensk and Siberia.

Sifting through the debris, it became clear the chamber itself was absent. Aerosol chambers were not rooms: they were huge, sturdy, prefabricated steel boxes, precision-engineered so they could be hermetically sealed.

'Well, if this is the building that housed the chamber, where is it?' Kelly asked.

'I'm not sure,' said Taha. 'It's been removed and destroyed.'

'It's essential for us to inspect it.'

'I'm not sure that's possible. I'll see what we can do.'

After that, Kelly and his senior colleagues stayed out of the heat, interviewing staff indoors. The rest of the team foraged in the ruins, while their bomb disposal experts attempted to clear the cluster bombs from outside another bunker. It was a task that would take them two days, with the constant fear that unexploded ordnance might suddenly 'cook off' in the sun.

The interviews seem to have yielded little or nothing. A physician appeared who said he had never worked with dangerous pathogens, and one Sinan Abdul Hassan seemed to have done very little work whatsoever. Things picked up a little when Taha reappeared with a vast collection of test tubes. They represented the last sample stocks of every microorganism and pathogen her team had possessed.

'You gave them to us,' she said. 'You can have them back. This programme has nothing now, it's finished. There's absolutely nothing left at all.'

Taha asked Kelly to sign a receipt for them, which he did. He told the press the following day it was 'a symbolic gesture'.[35] Yet it was more than a gesture. Taha was right. No military-grade pathogens would ever be found again anywhere in the country. Kelly took them back with him to Porton Down, where they were analysed and checked in his lab. If, as well as the strains from America and France, they included organisms from Porton itself, no one has ever said.

The next day, Kelly's interviewing was interrupted by a message over the radio. The disposal officers had cleared the entrance to the bunker but their Geiger counters revealed there was something radioactive inside. Kelly went over to discover the source, which was a weight of radioactive Cobalt 60 in a locked metal box.

'He was furious with the Iraqi minders and officials for having put his inspectors in a health-threatening situation,' wrote fellow inspector Tim Trevan, when he came to pen his own account of the UNSCOM years. 'When he returned to the discussions, David was in an appalling mood. He was certainly not about to take any bullshit from the Iraqis.'[36]

But Tim Trevan wasn't on BW1. As with many of his colleagues, UNSCOM's withdrawal had left Trevan obliged to issue dire warnings about the evils of Saddam's regime from the comfort of his own home. When Blair's government issued its second, plagiarised dossier to argue the case for invading Iraq, it would contain a passage lifted directly from Trevan's book.

Was Kelly really as livid as all that? Before breaking into that bunker his inspectors had been tripping around unexploded ordnance, defusing cluster bomblets, picking their way between collapsing six-storey buildings – all hazards his own country had helped create. What's more, it seems now that the Cobalt too was only there in the first place because of British assistance. At the conference in Winchester that Taha's deputy had attended two years earlier, Porton Down scientists had shown the Iraqis how the isotope could be safely used to neutralise anthrax.[37]

However Kelly reacted to the unwelcome gamma rays of Cobalt 60, it did nothing to deter the Iraqis' continuing cooperation. The interview room at Salman Pak was visited that afternoon by Taha's boss, Lieutenant General Dr Ahmed Murtada, the director of the Technical Research Centre.

Kelly pressed him, as he had pressed Brigadier Hossam Amin, on whether Iraq's programme had been offensive or defensive. Murtada refused to be drawn, as Amin had: it's military research, he said. It's got elements of both. But the General was a very different character to the quiet, awkward Brigadier; he was older, more senior, still ambitious, and proud of his office. What he did reveal was that it had all been blessed by Hussein Kamel, who had headed Iraq's Military Industrialisation Commission.

Kelly must have wanted to draw breath. Hussein Kamel al-Majid was the son-in-law and second cousin of Saddam Hussein. Suddenly he could glimpse a series of connections that ran right to the inner circle, from the young man he had met in Winchester, to his lady lab boss Taha, to her boss General Murtada, then to Hussein Kamel and finally Saddam himself. He could see the chain of command in its entirety.

On their last day, Taha found him to say she had located the chamber. Kelly and a carload of fellow inspectors were taken a mile or so back down the Baghdad road to a landfill, where, batting off clouds of bloated bluebottles as they waded through the rubbish, they finally laid eyes on Iraq's aerosol chamber. It was tiny, sized for a single primate, and it had been completely crushed. Kelly reckoned it had been flattened by bulldozer tracks, down to about six inches in places. He recognised it as manufactured by the Karl Kolb company, from a plant just outside Frankfurt. Undamaged, a grown man wouldn't have been able to stand up in it. No one even bothered to swab for samples. The team trudged back to their car and the ex-Sheraton Hotel. The next morning they flew back to New York, two days ahead of schedule.

'We haven't found any evidence that Iraq has biological weapons,' Kelly told the assembled reporters at a press conference in the UN building. One of them asked him why he had called off his inspection.

'The UN considers our mission to be successful,' he said.[38]

Kelly returned to Iraq once more at the end of September 1991, but not as chief. He had been swopped with David Huxsoll, the most senior inspector to accompany him on BW1. Huxsoll was a commander at Fort Detrick, so he was eminently qualified for the leadership of BW2 (on his first trip Rihab Taha had kept asking him about the US biological programme). They conducted a whirlwind tour of any installation that could possibly have handled growing the quantity of pathogens needed for filling weapons.

At Samarra Drug Industries, they discovered a workforce busy making cherry cough syrup. The next day they toured the Agricultural Water Research Centre, or what was left of it after the bombing. Only one laboratory was in anything like working order.

'It was essentially derelict,' Kelly said. 'There was no obvious biological weapons structure.'[39]

They visited a slaughterhouse on an intelligence tip-off that proved groundless, and a defunct bakery that was an equal waste of time. At Al Kindi, near the baby-milk factory, they inspected a veterinary vaccine plant, where strolling through yet more bombed-out buildings they came across an impromptu production line that resourceful staff had jerry-rigged in the ruins. As Iraq's declaration and the roadside sign outside both promised, it was making animal vaccines. Similarly, as Kelly and Huxsoll found out, the medical vaccine plant in Al Meriyah was also making just what Iraq said it did. And at the foot-and-mouth centre in Al Daura, under the easygoing management of Hazem Ali, who had gained his doctorate at Newcastle University, they were making vaccines for foot-and-mouth. The only remarkable thing about that place was its workforce.

'Al Daura was full of attractive young ladies, absolutely full of them, all apparently busy, but busy doing nothing,' Kelly later recalled. 'Every single one of them knew Hazem Ali.'[40]

There was some degree of containment at Al Daura, but only to stop any live foot-and-mouth disease from escaping outside. The ladies themselves were unprotected.

'Nothing struck me as unusual,' said Huxsoll. 'It would have been a last-resort place to make biological weapons.'[41]

The only site to pique the interest of the inspectors was Al Hakum, out in the desert on the other side of the Euphrates. Like Salman Pak, it had belonged to General Murtada's Technical Research Centre, and its remote location made it a perfect site for working with dangerous microbes. Imagery from spy satellites showed the layout was suspect too: the buildings were spaced impractically far apart for a commercial facility, but for a military installation concerned about possible air attack it made perfect sense.

On their arrival, Kelly and Huxsoll were introduced to Nasser Al Hindawi, the institute's director. This was the other Iraqi that Kelly had met at Winchester. Did they talk about their night at the Theatre Royal? Or about his visit to Porton Down? It appears not.

Hindawi explained that Al Hakum made single-cell protein (SCP) for livestock. The British had pioneered SCP at Grangemouth Oil Refinery in the sixties. The 'proteins-from-oil process', as they'd called it, used paraffin wax, a by-product of the refining process, as a medium for yeast, and thus created food out of industrial waste. Al Hakum, the inspectors were told, owed its location to the proximity of a petrochemical refinery called PC2. Kelly had seen the maps, and the explanation was plausible. It was the only thing that Al Hakum was actually near, apart from sand. Its construction had been completed in mid-1990, shortly before Iraq had rolled up its BW programme.

'Everyone thought Al Hakum had just been put into place,' Kelly later said. 'At the time, I didn't believe it had been used.'[42]

Several empty buildings still awaited their equipment. The flasks and manuals in the laboratory were brand-new. The animal house was empty save for a few chickens and a stack of folded-up animal cages that looked like they'd never been used. Hindawi said they would need them for nutritional testing when they got their production line up to speed. And before Kelly left to survey the grounds, he offered one more thing.

'Iraq has no biological weapons,' Hindawi said. 'It had a research programme, certainly. But that is a different matter.'

In the main building, Kelly saw two industrial-scale fermenters, but the interior didn't seem at all suitable for work on dangerous pathogens. No specialised ventilation seemed to be in place, and the layout was entirely open, with no barriers or protection of any kind. It was all decidedly low-containment. The small and largely unqualified staff present spoke openly of their work and the difficulties it presented them with. Swabs were taken from various bits of equipment: none of them would read positive for anthrax or any other agent.

Outside, the distance between the buildings was so huge that Kelly and Huxsoll had to get back in their Nissan, and it was when they decided to see what was inside Al Hakum's air-conditioned warehouse that the pair made their biggest discovery: kegs upon kegs of growth medium from Oxoid in Basingstoke. Tonnes of it. Kelly and Huxsoll were both extremely suspicious and deeply perceptive men, and Kelly in particular could already reasonably be considered the most experienced biological inspector in the world. Yet neither of them raised the matter, either on their visit or in their subsequent report. Britain's secret export was deliberately brushed aside, at least for the time being.

After BW2, the Luftwaffe flew the inspectors back to GATE-WAY, the CIA station in Bahrain, for the usual debriefing by American and British intelligence officers. Hamish Killip and Rod Barton were still there. Their job, and the Americans', was to siphon off whatever information UNSCOM inspectors gathered for delivery to Western intelligence agencies (that, in fact, was GATEWAY's true function). They had to give certain nationalities, like the Russians and the French, a wide berth, but most inspectors came from English-speaking countries and were happy to fall in.

Barton took Kelly out for a Chinese, and over a spicy chicken dinner in Manama's old town the inspector recounted his experiences.

Privately, Kelly told Barton he was convinced the Iraqis had originally intended Al Hakum to be a biowarfare production plant. It had been constructed under the military aegis of the Technical Research Centre, and under some secrecy: Kelly gathered that Iraq's press had never reported on its opening, despite its vast size. All of this was extremely unusual for an animal-feed plant. And there was also the small matter of the incinerator, whose smoke-stack Kelly had spotted on his tour. Why would it have been necessary to burn animal carcasses? Only, he assumed, if the animals were going to be exposed to anthrax.

The intelligence officers in Manama took note. The information was secretly circulated to the British and American governments. Kelly's suspicions never found their way into his UN report. The Iraqi programme, after all, appeared to be ended. There was no evidence of any weapons, or of any continuing attempt to make them – only unanswered questions about the past. But for national intelligence, his discoveries counted as useful 'product'.

Before Kelly went into Iraq, British intelligence had suggested where to look and what for, told him who he might meet, and what he should and shouldn't say to them. When he came back, he told British intelligence what he had seen and heard. The direction and collection of this information occurred under the cover of what was supposed to be a multilateral international disarmament effort under the ostensible authority of the United Nations.

There is a word that intelligence officers have for a person who collects information on their behalf from a foreign country under the guise of another, permitted, activity. That word is 'agent'. Some inspectors, like Kelly, would always publicly deny they were spies. Others argued that liaison with their national intelligence services was the only way they could do their job, and some, like Tim Trevan and Rod Barton, both excused the channelling of UNSCOM information to national intelligence agencies by claiming the UK and US had ample resources to get the information through other channels anyway. A few just accepted it as a fait accompli.

'Every time I returned home I was wheeled in,' Ron Manley, a chemical inspector and Old Portonian, told Daniel Pearl from the *Wall Street Journal*. 'The government is paying for you so they feel they have the right.'[43]

As Manley went on to explain, the practice allowed the government to put out far scarier assessments of Iraq's WMD threat than UNSCOM was prepared to, and this would happen with increasing frequency in the years after Kelly's first inspection.

One inspector, the extraordinary and indomitable Scott Ritter, a former US Marine major, tried to game the system, and formed an independent intelligence cell within UNSCOM that could play the agencies the way they played UNSCOM. He was castigated politically for acting 'above his pay grade', as the then Senator Joe Biden put it, and resigned, citing lack of support from his own government.[44] After leaving UNSCOM, Ritter became a strident critic of Washington's claims about Iraqi WMD, until he was later entrapped in a sex sting by the Monroe County Sheriff's Office, and sentenced to five years' imprisonment for failing to verify that the undercover officer he was role-playing with in an adult chat room was above the age of consent.

Every government ran their inspectors as agents, in the national interest. It was inevitable. Rolf Ekeus has admitted it happened: US inspectors in Iraq would update Washington on secure US-supplied phones with intelligence they had yet to formally submit to UNSCOM, if they ever submitted it at all. Ekeus' successor, the bull-headed Australian Richard Butler, simply denied it entirely, but in the same interview he was forced to confess he had no way of knowing how inspectors and their governments interacted.[45]

Iraq complained about all this for years. No one listened, of course. Nobody wanted to be seen to support the regime. After Ritter's resignation Stateside, the hitherto partisan media finally woke up, and enough political pressure mounted for a few questions in Parliament. In the House of Lords, Baroness Symons was asked if there was any substance to the rumours that the inspectors had been suborned by the spooks.

'In dealing with questions of this nature we get into a little difficulty,' said Symons. 'It is the policy of this Government not to comment on matters which have a bearing on intelligence.'[46]

It was the nearest Britain has ever come to acknowledging the truth.

This was the reality of UNSCOM. The Commission was in no way accountable to the United Nations itself. The Secretary General, whether it was Javier Pérez de Cuéllar, Boutros Boutros-Ghali or Kofi Annan, never had any control over UNSCOM, which was accountable only to the Security Council, and effectively this meant it was dominated by the biggest player on the Council, which was America.

The inspectors who worked for UNSCOM were not United Nations employees but civil servants seconded from their home governments, entities that continued to determine their salary, their conduct, and their careers. The United Nations had little means of influencing them when they breached UN rules, which under the sway of their masters back home, they often did.

It was, however, different at the start. In the early days they came simply to find weapons. When they did, which was almost always because Iraq had declared them, they destroyed them. When they didn't, they said so. But despite the best wishes of the White House, and the covert efforts of Ted Price and others at the CIA, Saddam remained ensconced in Baghdad.

Hunting weapons would no longer be good enough for the CIA and MI6, or for the State Department and the Foreign Office. By definition, it was no longer good enough for the UN Special Commission.

After his tour with Huxsoll, David Kelly would not return to Iraq for three years. Saddam was still in power, and UNSCOM's mission would be transformed.

The game had changed.

7

Intent

The visits were obviously unsatisfactory for both sides.
DAVID KELLY, WRITING FOR
THE VERTIC YEARBOOK, 2000

Kelly's reputation as an inspector rested entirely on the work he did in Russia and Iraq, and the work he did in those countries is widely known. But there was another aspect to Kelly the inspector that has met with far less attention, and it shaped him just as much as the years he spent uncovering programmes in hostile regimes. For a brief window of time, David Kelly saw what it was like to be on the receiving end of foreign suspicions. The inspector was himself inspected.

Within three months of coming back from Iraq Kelly was in Washington. There was a price to be paid for the access he'd had to the Biopreparat facilities inside Russia: the Soviets were entitled to some return visits. They would get to see for themselves the biological facilities of Britain and the United States. The thirteen-man Soviet delegation would be the same size as Kelly's team had been, and as he found out, they would bring with them their own prejudices and political goals. America was the first country on their itinerary, and to maintain its presence in the trilateral process the UK sent Kelly and his DIS colleague Chris Davis along as observers.

The person the Americans had chosen to act as host-in-chief for the visit was a woman called Lisa Bronson. A qualified attorney, having served as a legal officer in the US army's Judge Advocate General's Corps, Bronson became the Corps's first female colonel before she turned thirty, by which time she had already helped negotiate a chemical weapons treaty in Geneva. She left the military soon afterwards, and was promptly appointed as a civilian to the Pentagon's Arms Control desk.

The US had no offensive biological weapons programme to conceal, and hadn't had one since the sixties. Washington and the Pentagon had every hope that an unambiguous, transparent and hospitable reception should allay any worries the Soviets might have. The Russians picked four American sites for inspection, and Bronson had organised multiple 'dry run' practice inspections at each of them before they arrived in the country. All the dry runs had passed without problems, and expectations were high. Once the Soviets saw America had nothing to hide, the whole inspection process should open up.

It was not to be.

The diplomats, scientists and military officers who arrived at Dulles International Airport were sceptics on enemy territory, and their guard was up from the moment they stepped off the plane. During their flight the Soviet Union had ceased to exist. It had become the Commonwealth of Independent States, and so the inspectors entered America bearing the passports of an obsolete country. Inspector Grigory Berdinnikov, from the Soviet Foreign Ministry, expected them all to be turned away at immigration. They had good reason to be uneasy, and the briefing they'd been given before leaving hadn't helped matters.

As was always the case with the British and the Americans too, the Russian inspectors had met with their own intelligence people before coming over. The entire delegation had been briefed by the GRU, the foreign-military-intelligence wing of the Soviet army, at its headquarters in Moscow. An officer there had taken them through the available satellite imagery and ground maps of the four sites they were to visit: Fort Detrick, the Dugway Proving Ground in Utah, the Pine Bluff Arsenal in Arkansas, and the Salk Institute in Pennsylvania.

The Russian team was told that the GRU had secret intelligence that the US was running a covert biological weapons programme and that their trip was probably the only chance the Soviets would get to gather evidence from inside it. A GRU officer pointed out structures that seemed particularly suspicious, like a large, round building at Fort Detrick that looked a lot like a testing chamber. He also explained that surveillance had shown traffic activity at all the sites: surveillance photos from the Pine Bluff Arsenal had revealed 'weapons containers' being loaded into lorries. By the time the meeting was over, nobody had any doubts about what was expected of them. They were going there to find a programme, not assess whether one existed. Their job was not to interpret data but to collect it, and they expected to encounter evasion and deceit.

It was the typical inspector's outlook.

Lisa Bronson was an intelligent, energetic woman who possessed a natural diplomacy and a degree of relevant experience. Nobody in Washington saw her appointment as being at all controversial, but when the Russians found out their chief guide was a lawyer rather than a scientist, an attractive 31-year-old woman with no experience of a biology lab and no affiliation to any US biological facility, they were automatically suspicious. When they saw how senior base commanders deferred to this diminutive lady outsider, their attitude hardened. The Americans had decided that all of their visitors' questions had to be channelled through Bronson so they could receive coordinated answers, but the Soviets thought this a ruse. It stopped them from freely interviewing key personnel. They saw it not as convenience but obstruction, and just like their British and American peers, when the Russian inspectors perceived obstruction they took it for deception.

The UNSCOM experts had felt the same way about Rihab Taha. Few thought she could really have made a serious contribution to Iraqi WMD efforts: she had been thrown up as a barrier, which was why Kelly had nicknamed his first inspection 'the Rihab roadshow'.

'It constrained how information got to us,' Kelly said, years later. 'It made it tough to talk to other people, identify inconsistencies, leverage in and move forward. Of course, it also made it quite obvious to some of us that they were lying.'[1]

If he ever stopped to think about it, he would have known from his experience in America that Taha's presence was simply a practical expediency, and perhaps even a helpful one, but inspectors everywhere are intrinsically disinclined towards good faith.

The Russians arrived on a Saturday. On Sunday morning, Kelly joined them as they returned to Dulles Airport and boarded Air Force Two, the Vice President's Boeing, for the flight to Salt Lake City. They owed this rare luxury not to privilege but to secrecy: in order to keep all the inspections under wraps, the Pentagon had decided civil airlines risked too much publicity. The stateroom, the conference centre and the communications centre on Air Force Two were all out of bounds, and so the passengers took their business-class seats in the rear cabin and settled in for their four-and-a-half-hour flight.

On touching down in Utah, they were put up at the Airport Hilton and that afternoon in the conference room the first official meet-and-greet began. Ambassador John Hawes from the State Department introduced them to Lisa Bronson, representing the Defense Department, and three supporting colonels from the Pentagon's Arms Control desk. The Russians accepted the hospitality but it did nothing to ease their concerns. None of these people were actual scientists, after all. None had worked on the programme, and the Soviets had not travelled half the world to talk to diplomats in an airport chain hotel. It smacked of delaying tactics.

They got cracking on the inspection proper at six o'clock the following morning, when they caught the coach that would take them on their eighty-mile journey to Dugway Proving Ground.

Through tired eyes Kelly watched day break over one of the great empty spaces of inland America, a barren, infinite-seeming mountain plateau dotted with sagebrush and juniper and ever distant snow-capped peaks. The dry blue sky seemed to have sucked all the colour from the ground, leaving it a pale pastel grey with the faintest smudges of purple and red on its low hills. All else was salt flats and sand dunes. They crossed an Indian Reservation where the only living thing they saw was a roadrunner, darting off the tarmac and disappearing into the scrub at the last second; and then traversed the length of Skull Valley, where in 1968 a stray cloud of VX gas had drifted off the Dugway test ranges and killed six thousand sheep. That it didn't kill any people was entirely a matter of good luck, and although the incident was widely reported at the time, the US military didn't officially admit what had happened for thirty years.

In the shadow of Vickory Mountain, they passed the tiny township of Dugway, with a population of less than one thousand, built to accommodate the staff who would work at the Proving Ground. They caught sight of a chain-link fence festooned with hazard signs and then, finally, the grid of low buildings that made up the Proving Ground headquarters.

Kelly sat quietly at the rear of the Dugway meeting room while the local commander gave his morning presentation. It contained nothing he didn't already know. The US had abandoned biological warfare and so the research done here was defensive, evaluating gas masks and protective suits and decontamination techniques. The microbes used for the open-air trials were relatively harmless simulants. In all likelihood none of this was new to the Soviets either. If they felt their time was being deliberately wasted, as the British and the Americans had in Russia, it seems they were too polite to say.

For the rest of the day, and the next, the Russians were let loose to collect soil samples from the ranges. Scientists from Biopreparat and the 15th Military Directorate would perform a careful analysis of each of them, sealed in tin cans and transported back to the

Motherland, to see just what bacteria and viruses Dugway had really been working on. The Americans were only too happy to let them take whatever they wanted. The commander's presentation had been entirely truthful, and what's more, the Dugway Proving Ground covers over twelve hundred square miles of desert, an area almost as big as Cornwall. So for much of their stay the only sign of the Russian presence was a distant plume of dust from the wheels of their borrowed jeep, glimpsed occasionally on the horizon. From the American perspective, it was a painless visit.

After Utah, it was a flight back to Washington on Air Force Two and another six o'clock start to get bussed down the interstate to the outskirts of Frederick, Maryland, and the gates of Fort Detrick, home of the United States Army Medical Research Institute of Infectious Diseases (acronymically, USAMRIID, and pronounced You-Sam-Rid).

In an earlier incarnation, Fort Detrick had been the brains behind America's biological weapons development, the scientific centre of a programme that had lasted twenty-six years, employed thousands of people, owned vast tracts of land and occupied multiple purpose-built facilities all over the continent. It had received billions of dollars in funding. When Nixon canned it in 1969, its annual budget was over $300 million. And as the Russians had observed, despite this change in policy many of these sites remained the property of the US Department of Defense, and had seen continuing construction since. Despite the easy manner of their hosts, they remained wary guests.

As the group entered Detrick itself, they noticed the same high surrounding walls, perimeter fences, security checkpoints, surveillance cameras and armed, uniformed guards that would always arouse suspicion in their American and British peers. They received the usual welcoming speech before suiting up for a tour of the high-containment pathogen labs, during which they discovered a room that had been completely sanitised. They could see from the marks in the floor that the furniture and fittings had recently been stripped out. Given the visit had been arranged months in advance, it looked like a clear case of concealment. The Americans explained that the lab had only held electron microscopes, units that had been moved to another, entirely civilian, lab in Frederick City.

It was not accepted as a convincing explanation.

In desperation, Detrick's overall Deputy Commander David Franz took measurements from the boltholes in the floor and drove the Russians into Frederick to let them see for themselves. When they saw the microscopes, and the complicated furniture and shielding that housed them in their new setting, they were able to check the proportions for themselves. It was a match. An official accusation was avoided, but the suspicions of biological weapons inspectors are not always such an easy thing to assuage. Had the equipment been moved further afield than Frederick, or destroyed, these doubts would have been impossible to dispel. Whenever UNSCOM saw that anything had been moved at any of the sites it visited, almost all of which were civilian, it always reported it as concealment even when inspectors were subsequently shown the equipment.

The next day, Bronson told the Russians they could pick five buildings in the Detrick complex to inspect. The site covers over 1200 acres, so another bus was provided, and Fort Detrick's Deputy Commander for Research, Dr Charles Bailey, acted as chaperone.

'It was a cold, grey rainy day,' he told me. 'We gave them a map with the building numbers on it, and they picked the first one they wanted to see and we set off. Now Fort Detrick is a large place. I didn't know off hand what every building was for, I still don't. They picked somewhere and I had no idea what it was, but off we went. I only realised what they actually wanted to inspect when we got up close. It was a large, cone-shaped concrete building with big double doors, and really it's the sort of structure you see all over Maryland. Virginia too. We keep road salt in there for the winter.'

Bailey left Detrick long ago to lead another biodefence institute in Manassas, Virginia, but he remembers the Soviets well.

'They had their own satellite imagery,' he explained, 'and they'd seen trucks coming and going in and out of this building, and they thought it was some sort of underground base. They could see exactly what it really was without leaving the bus but one of the Russian colonels went out to have a look at it anyway. He actually took a pinch of this salt and tasted it. The civilian scientists just sat there laughing at him. But the military officers? They came with their minds made up.'

The difference between what your national intelligence service tells you and what your own personal intelligence discerns can be vast. Faced with such stark contrasts, to which do you give the greater authority? The inspectors of UNSCOM visited several sites suspected of hiding an underground laboratory, on no other basis than the word of some unidentified informant. Their searches proved equally mistaken, but as far as we know, nobody ever thought it was funny.

The Russians spent the rest of their time at Detrick annoying the staff. There was no outright hostility, as Bailey was at pains to point out, but there were accusations, and as with almost all weapons inspectors, they never shrank from getting in people's way.

'The National Institute of Health is based in Detrick too,' said Bailey. 'They do a lot of cancer research and stuff like that. And we had to take these Soviets into the labs where people were working and watch while they climbed onto work benches and removed ceiling tiles and disrupted everybody. It was deeply frustrating, especially knowing that whatever we showed them, when they got back to Russia they were going to slant their report the way their superiors wanted it.'

Even so, Bailey's visitors could perhaps be forgiven their trespasses. The National Institute of Health was housed in Building 470, the seven-storey Cold War pilot plant for Fort Detrick's anthrax production. The townspeople of Frederick called it the Tower of Doom, and local lore was full of scare stories about its gruesome past. Urban legends aside, three of its workers had contracted lethal infections from the pathogens studied inside it, and a fourth had accidentally released two thousand gallons of wet anthrax slurry while trying to prise open a stuck valve.

As the Russians discovered, while its owners and purpose had changed, Building 470 had not. Its two huge fermenters remained in place, and its exterior was still graced with the same fake windows that had been built to fool passers-by into thinking it was an everyday office. If you scratched its surface the old plant, rusty and cobwebbed, was still there under the skin. The bean-counters had judged that ripping it out was too expensive, an explanation that may not have been entirely reassuring coming from one of the richest countries in the world. In Iraq, UNSCOM would demolish or destroy sites with far less of a 'signature' than Building 470.

The Russians may have been perplexed by the capitalist idiosyncrasies reflected in Detrick's decrepit anthrax factory, but what they saw next must have been an even bigger culture shock. Before leaving Frederick they were taken to see the famous Eight Ball, the million-litre carbon-steel test sphere that America had built to avoid creating another Gruinard. As noted earlier, the building that housed it had long been demolished, although theoretically, with some renovation, the Eight Ball could have been put to use once more. The visitors were shown the plaque at the sphere's foundations, which explained the facility was now a memorial and listed on the US National Register of Historic Places. How much this overcame the Soviets' distrust is anyone's guess, but it's probably safe to say that if David Kelly had met with a similar excuse for an aerosol test chamber in Russia or Iraq he would have laughed about it for years.

After Maryland, the inspection paused for the weekend, which the Russians spent in their embassy in Washington, and then everyone jetted off to Arkansas, to visit the Pine Bluff Arsenal in Jefferson County. They were put up in a hotel in Little Rock, and made another six o'clock start on the Monday morning for the coach ride down the wooded banks of the Arkansas River to see the production labs and storage bunkers of America's old bioweapons programme.

Like every other aspect of America's biological-warfare efforts, Pine Bluff was a legacy of the Second World War. The weapons were designed at Fort Detrick and were tested at Dugway, but it was here that they were made and stored. The bunkers where they were kept, or 'underground igloos' as the staff quaintly called them, still dotted the grounds in their dozens. Their neat staggered rows took up a good chunk of the base's twenty square miles.

In its heyday Pine Bluff could churn out war-fighting quantities of disease. The fermentation plant there was ten storeys high and got through two million gallons of water a day.[2] It produced every pathogen in the programme, including anthrax, tularaemia, brucellosis, Q-fever, botulinum toxin (or BTX), Staphylococcal Enterotoxin B (SEB), and Venezuelan equine encephalitis (VEE). Not all of them had been safely contained. One accidental outbreak of VEE infected fifteen workers.

'It's not lethal,' Bill Patrick, Pine Bluff's Chief of Product Development, later reassured people. 'It just makes you want to die. Your eyes want to pop out of your head.'[3]

As well as brewing up these agents the base was also tasked with loading them into munitions – bombs and spray tanks mostly – and understanding the scale of this operation gives some idea about how complicated germ warfare can be. As the Arkansas scientists discovered, biological weapons aren't inert, like explosives; they're living things, which means they can age and die. You can't just make a load of germ bombs and keep them in a bunker. What you need is the capacity to deliver them, freshly made and in generous supply, when the generals ask you.

In the fifties, the US Air Force asked Pine Bluff to develop brucellosis as an air-dropped incapacitant. Humans infected with the disease come down with undulant fever, constant nausea and frequent vomiting, and are unlikely to pick up a rifle for a good few weeks. Sometimes brucellosis becomes chronic, and relapses occur throughout the sufferer's life, and in almost a third of cases it causes arthritis, but the vast majority of patients survive, which made it a first-class non-lethal agent in the eyes of the military.

So Patrick and his men had to grow the bacteria, concentrate it, and keep it on standby. Every two or three weeks, if they received no further orders, they heat-sterilised it and made another batch. A filling line was ready and waiting at twenty-four hours' notice to stuff the brucellosis into M114 pipe bomblets, little cylinders about twenty-one inches long. The tiny M114s would then be stacked inside half-tonne M33 cluster bombs, over a hundred of them in each one. A fleet of sixty-seven refrigerated trailers had been specifically purchased to take the M33s to the nearest airstrip, where under the supervision of an emergency decontamination team they would be loaded onto a Globemaster transport and freighted across the Atlantic to air bases in the European theatre for loading onto bombers. Via this tortuous process, which today's business consultants would call 'just-in-time' manufacturing, Pine Bluff could potentially deliver 22,000 brucellosis cluster bombs a month, and the infrastructure needed to achieve this was immense. Despite what inspectors would later say about Iraq, military biological warfare programmes are not things that are easily overlooked.

To the Russians' dismay, most of the equipment that Patrick had used to make all these weapons had been left in place. The filling machines that loaded the bombs were all still there, although they hadn't been used for decades. As with Fort Detrick, its removal had been considered a needless expense, and the facilities had been given over to public health, in this case the National Center for Toxicological Research, which was part of the Food and Drug Administration.

The mosquito room, where scientists had bred biblical amounts of disease-carrying insect vectors, was still in place too. The enormous tank the bugs were reared in was now being used to breed catfish, so the FDA could research the diseases that affected intensive fish farming, but it could easily have been put back to its original use. It must have taken Kelly back to his days in Oxford, when his colleagues at the Institute of Virology had conducted their own insect vector trials on the ranges of Porton Down, but of this he said not a word. Instead he stayed characteristically schtum while the agitated Soviet colonels videotaped it all for the GRU back in Moscow.

The next day, the Russians wanted to see inside the igloos, but without explaining why, Bronson told them that half were off limits. Naturally enough, her visitors objected.

'You are denying us access to something that is critical, and you obviously have something to hide,' complained Colonel Berdinnikov.[4]

He was right, at least in principle. The 'igloos' were being used to store the Pentagon's chemical weapons, which weren't covered by the inspection agreement and remained top secret. Bronson couldn't tell the Russians why they weren't allowed inside them, or what they were being used for. Their repeated requests were met with nothing but blunt refusals, even when they pulled out their own satellite imagery, and pointed to the concrete pads outside every bunker. They had been built to support refrigeration units, and so clearly, the colonels argued, the bunkers had been meant for biological weapons. But it was no good. Bronson had been given her orders, and she didn't budge.

After that, the tour turned sour. There was little more good grace on either side. The last stop on the Soviet itinerary was the Salk Institute in Swiftwater, Pennsylvania, a private biocompany sustained by a US Defense contract to make vaccines against biological weapons. It had never had any connection with the offensive programme, and so that, at least, proved uncontroversial, but the damage had already been done. If the Russians hadn't found their smoking gun, they could at least raise the issues of obstruction and capability, just as Kelly and the Americans had raised with them, and just as UNSCOM would raise in Iraq.

These trilateral inspections continued for the next three years, and never broke the impasse they began with. The Russians visited more sites in America, a vaccine plant in Liverpool, and Kelly saw four more facilities inside the former Soviet Union. Footage of one of his inspections found its way into a BBC news report.

'I am not accusing you,' he says, in a fairly accusatory tone, to a blank-faced scientist in some dismal, poorly lit Soviet lab. 'I am stating there is a capability here that can be used for that purpose.'

Capability became a watchword for inspectors. When they couldn't find any weapons, the ability to make them was the next-best thing.

Meanwhile, the Kremlin never admitted to an offensive programme, and the inspectors never found concrete proof that they had kept one running after Pasechnik walked his plank, although they kept pressing. In response, the Russians always seemed to find just enough grounds to suggest it was the Americans who were secretly building a biological arsenal.

'We too have some questions to put to the British and US side,' a general told a Russian press conference.[5] 'We have some complaints to make.'

The inspections created a cycle of suspicion that went nowhere, despite the tens of thousands of hours and the millions of pounds that were spent on them, despite the lives they swallowed up and changed for ever.

Impatient with Yeltsin's apparent inability to ease their anxieties, MI6 went public with Pasechnik in 1993. They put him on BBC's *Newsnight*, where he was interviewed by Mark Urban, and he talked a little about his work on plague. To show this designer of doom was now an acclimatised British citizen, just like any other guy, they filmed him walking out alone one night, to buy a paper from a newsagent that had no other customers. The pathos of this lonely, urban scene is touching when you know a little about Pasechnik's life. He had at that point been living incognito in a foreign country, separated from his family, for four years. The Secret Intelligence Service were able to repatriate them a few months afterwards.

As well as his appearance on the BBC, Pasechnik's handlers

asked him to give one more interview, to James Adams, the former Defence Correspondent of the *Sunday Times*, and after that he returned to something like anonymity. He was given a job of sorts in the public health labs at Porton, and lived modestly in a very small house in a nondescript cul-de-sac in a village outside of Salisbury. He never gave any more interviews until the end of the nineties, when he spoke only to the former UNSCOM inspector Raymond Zilinskas and his fellow academic Milton Leitenberg, who spent years piecing together the Soviet programme as academics.

'He never went into detail about the nature of his defection,' Zilinskas told me, 'but he was a moral person, and I think that was why he left. He just didn't like what he was doing, it wasn't what he thought science was for. I visited his old lab in Leningrad and the staff had put framed pictures of him on the wall. They said he was the best director they'd ever had. And a kind one too.'

Although he escaped Biopreparat, Pasechnik never realised his true ambition to use science for the greater good. At Porton he published only a single paper on the purification of bacterial toxins, and later, as the millennium turned, he filed some patents and left to set up a small biotech enterprise with a wealthy and reclusive astronomer. Nothing came of it. It was all a long drop from the days when he oversaw almost five hundred scientists as director of his own institute.

He died of a stroke in his home two months after 9/11, aged sixty-four. The wider world had no idea he was dead until Chris Davis tipped off a journalist in New York two days later, and a week after that the British papers ran their own obituaries, none of which revealed very much at all about what had happened to him after he left the Soviet Union. The private life of the defector had come to its lonely and unobserved end.

'I was told many times that I should just get on with my work and stay in my place,' Pasechnik had explained to Adams, when he asked him about why he had thrown it all in. 'I realised that you can't do anything when there is someone standing behind you holding your hands. You can't do anything unless you make some other decision.'[6]

So Pasechnik, trapped in a system he could no longer tolerate, made his choice. And years later, with nowhere left to defect to, Kelly would make his.

Nobody could make the inspections that Pasechnik triggered work. For years, decades in fact, diplomats and officials tried to hammer out an agreement whereby the Biological Weapons Convention could be formally enforced. While it was sending inspectors into Russia and Iraq, the official US position in these negotiations was that universal biological inspections were worse than useless. Its diplomats argued that they were too intrusive, that they rendered a country vulnerable to military and industrial espionage, and that even with full access, inspectors could still produce false results.[7] A country that was in full compliance could be painted as being in dangerous breach, and vice versa. After all, a factory that made vaccines and a factory that made weapons could use exactly the same equipment.

'When you're trying to discover an offensive biological programme, the real question is intent,' Frank Malinoski told me. 'We could see inside some of their labs, but what really counted was what was in their minds.'

David Kelly, in his final television interview, said much the same thing.

'There is no clear delineation between offensive research as opposed to defensive research. It really is a matter of the intent behind it.'

What do you see, when you look into the mind of another person? You see yourself. Your own fears, your own beliefs. When you visit a hostile regime and look into the mind of a man you believe or are told is your enemy, you see a threat. And in the ambiguous world of biological weapons, where baby-milk plants can be bomb factories, there is no way of proving he isn't.

Once the Russian trilaterals tapered off without clear results of any kind, the US and the UK restarted their biological inspections inside Iraq with a vengeance. To the countries with whom it still shared diplomatic relations, America's diplomats explained they would not be subjecting their own country to any biological inspections because they gave foreign governments the opportunity to conduct covert action and generate false results. At the same time, the State Department, the CIA, MI6 and the Foreign Office would subvert UNSCOM to do precisely that.

8

We Need a Crisis by Thursday

Well, I'm a little bit hawkish, having gone through the UNSCOM experience.

DAVID KELLY ON CANADIAN TELEVISION,
23 OCTOBER 2002

After a war sold more crudely than Coca-Cola, the UNSCOM years are almost forgotten now, but they are the story of how, under a UN resolution intended to rid the Middle East of weapons of mass destruction, a single United Nations body came to put out Iraqi scare stories every other month, precipitate unilateral military action, uphold near-genocidal sanctions, and contravene the UN charter itself. It is a story that will probably never be told in full, since some of its component parts lie in the files of at least five different intelligence agencies, but you can trace its outline, and grasp some of its details, if you don't mind putting in the hours. David Kelly certainly didn't. If you add up all the time he spent in-country it totals almost two years. It would have been a few months, had it not been for the workings of democracy, or what passes for it in Washington and Westminster. After all, while he was preoccupied with the Russians, other inspectors had made great strides in the opening chapter of the Special Commission.

Under David Kay, a hard-charging inspector who bypassed UNSCOM's chair Rolf Ekeus and the International Atomic

Energy Agency and reported direct to the American administration, the Commission uncovered what was left of Iraq's nuclear enrichment programme. The Iraqis had been using equipment so outdated, and a method so outmoded, it had been previously overlooked. While Bush the Elder had proclaimed Saddam to be six months away from the bomb, Kay offered it was more like a year or a year and a half, but even this was a gross exaggeration. At a secret international conference in 1992, nuclear weapons designers from Britain, France, Russia and America reckoned it would have taken Iraq at least twice that long, and probably a lot longer.[1] But whatever sounds London or Washington might make, and whatever they got their inspectors to say on or off the record, the nuclear file was closing.

'There is no longer any nuclear activity in Iraq,' said Maurizio Ziffero, an Italian inspector of the International Atomic Energy Agency (IAEA), as early as September 1992. 'They have no facilities where they can carry out this activity.'[2]

On the chemical side, a tremendous amount of work had been done to physically destroy Iraq's declared arsenal of mustard and nerve gas weapons. Neutralising such munitions is a dangerous and arduous task: when the UK decided to eliminate its own stocks in the seventies, the process had taken four years. Working to a ferocious deadline and eschewing the usual safety precautions, the chemical inspectors of UNSCOM had got it done in three, sometimes using jerry-rigged fuel-air explosions.

'The generally accepted figure is that 95 per cent of the chemical capability had been removed,' said Ron Manley, the Old Portonian who helped head up the effort.[3] 'We had accounted for a lot of the dual-purpose equipment, and what hadn't been destroyed was under constant surveillance.'

The matter of Iraq's long-range missiles had also been dealt with. After the sixty-third UNSCOM weapons inspection, Scott Ritter had briefed James Woolsey, the director of the CIA, that 'Iraq had received 819 Scud-B missiles from the Soviet Union, and that all 819 Scud-B missiles had been plausibly accounted for'.

On the biological front, there had been only two inspections after Kelly's, the last led by the German diplomat Volker Beck, which had visited any facility in Iraq with a microbiology connection: universities, medical labs, breweries, fertiliser factories, pesticide manufacturers and castor oil companies. It returned again to the single-cell protein plant at Al Hakum, the animal vaccine plant at Al Kindi and the foot-and-mouth institute at Al Daura. After flying back to GATEWAY in Bahrain, Beck gave an interview to the local press. 'It was a highly successful mission,' he said.[4] 'There are no more gaps to be filled. Iraq's research was basic, at the laboratory level, and there is no suspicion they are hiding any biological warfare programme.'

Things seemed to be drawing to a natural close. Inspections would end, monitoring would begin, and sanctions would terminate, but London and Washington had other ideas.

After Ritter briefed Woolsey that the Iraqi Scuds were accounted for, the CIA put out a line to the media that Saddam had a 'covert missile force' of two hundred more, but they didn't say where they were, or how they knew.[5] Nobody, neither UNSCOM, UNMOVIC, nor its successor the Iraq Survey Group (ISG), ever found any of them. Washington made similar and repeated claims about Iraq's nuclear, biological and chemical weapons, all of which were at odds with what the inspectors were finding on the ground in Iraq.

'Iraq agreed to destroy all of its weapons programs and it's done none of that,' Assistant Secretary of State Richard Clarke told the press.[6] 'We suspect they have weapons hidden away which they have not yet yielded up for destruction. There are between 200 and 300 more missiles still in Iraq, and they are hiding them and they are denying us access to them and they are refusing to destroy them. It's also quite clear they had an offensive biological weapons program, and it's probably still out there.'

Clarke added that Iraq habitually obstructed the UNSCOM inspectors, and relented only under the threat of military action, and even then, only to disclose as little as they could get away with.

'This has been the pattern throughout the work of the Special Commission,' Clarke went on. 'The Iraqis keep testing the limits of the UN's patience, and they expect the UN and the world community to give in ... We just have to keep up the pressure through economic sanctions.'

Clarke gave this interview shortly after Kelly first returned from Iraq, but he could have given it at any point over the next twelve years. Others certainly would. The tripos of hidden weapons, Iraqi obstruction and tested international resolve became a frequent refrain. It was the official line, settled on within weeks of the first inspection, and it never changed. Policy rested on it.

'We have destroyed everything,' an exhausted General Amer Rashid told Scott Ritter when he returned to Iraq in pursuit of the CIA's nonexistent Scud force, 'but there will always be doubts. We will always have enemies. Information will always be sent to UNSCOM. My intelligence people have told me the Iraqis in the north have just sent a letter to the CIA. They say Iraqi authorities are hiding weapons in hotels, factories, schools, farms, Baath party headquarters in city centres, everywhere. They report that documentation on chemical, biological, nuclear and ballistic missiles is hidden in trains or in containers on trucks which are always in movement between cities. The CIA will flood you with this information. I have a special information unit. I could easily set you up, mislead you. You would think you had concrete information. I could mislead the Special Commission with no problem, and so could the enemies of Iraq. They want to corrupt the relationship between the United Nations and Iraq. Who is the loser? The United Nations? No. Iraq. The Iraqi people.'[7]

Rashid made this impromptu speech at the Military Industrial Commission offices in downtown Baghdad in the August of 1992, but as with Clarke's foreboding press briefing, he could have given it at any point over the coming eleven years, and it would still have held equal currency. While the initial biological and chemical inspections had passed without rancour, there was a terrible grid-lock built in to UNSCOM from the beginning. The complete and

utter opposition between American suspicions and Iraqi protestations always had the quality of an unstoppable force meeting an
immovable object. But history shows us now that whatever self-
interest and deviousness existed on either side, the American and
British position was false, and the Iraqi position was correct. Amer
Rashid was speaking true.

Despite its extreme divergence from evidential reality, keeping
UNSCOM in tow with the British and American line was not
difficult. From the outset, it was made clear to chairman Rolf
Ekeus that he would need to retain the confidence of the US government if he was to remain in post. In practice, this meant acting
as an adjunct of the CIA and the State Department: as long as US
and UK intelligence fed doubts into the system, UNSCOM was
obliged to allay them. This was made clear at a New York briefing
that Washington's spooks gave to Ekeus and his commissioners
before a single inspector had ever set foot inside Iraq.

'Well, these guys with their dark glasses and briefcases hand-
cuffed to their wrists come into the room,' said Johan Molander,
a Swedish diplomat serving as Ekeus's first special adviser, 'and they
start lecturing the commissioners on Iraq's programmes like they
were little children who could not really understand nuclear and
chemical weapons. And they show their grainy photographs that
had clearly been so degraded that you could hardly make out anything. Well, being treated like that did not go down well with
some of the experts, like Johan Santesson and Bryan Barras. It was
like being told, "we know best, do as we say".'[8]

Dependency on the British and American governments was
built into UNSCOM from the start. According to the same
Security Council resolution that created it, the operating funds for
the Special Commission were to be supplied by Iraq. These could
easily have been appropriated from the country's oil wealth, which
had been successfully sequestered into UN management, and there
would have been little practical difficulty in this. The costs would
have amounted to a fraction of a percent of Iraq's annual revenue,
and the UN was already administering a number of other funds

that drew on the same source, but it never happened. An independently funded UNSCOM could have delivered independent opinions. Instead, the vast majority of UNSCOM inspectors were, like David Kelly, employees of their home governments, working on secondment.

These individuals were offered and accepted by the 'College of Commissioners', the body that oversaw the UNSCOM chairman, and which was also drawn entirely from the civil service of national governments. Partly because the US and the UK possessed a great deal more knowledge about WMD than, say, Burkina Faso, and partly because they wielded considerably more political influence, UNSCOM's staff invariably came from English-speaking countries (or their NATO allies). America and Britain predominated in both the College and the inspectorate, which was why, after Volker Beck proclaimed the biological inspections effectively complete, he was never allowed to lead another inspection, and his report was buried for the best part of a year.

As an UNSCOM inspector, Kelly was bound only by his employment contract with the Ministry of Defence, or, from 1994 onwards, the Foreign and Commonwealth Office. As with his other British colleagues on the Commission, Whitehall provided his salary, set his terms and conditions, gave him his line to take, and one day, he hoped, would pay him his pension. If he spoke out of turn, if he failed in his duties, if his performance was anything other than expected, it was always Her Majesty's Government that provided the stick or the carrot. What control could Rolf Ekeus, from the thirty-first floor of the UN building in Manhattan, hope to exert over inspectors like David Kelly, working for weeks on end in Baghdad? The same power he could wield when these officials returned to their home countries between inspections: none.

Washington and London wanted ultimate ownership of the inspection process, and UNSCOM was how they claimed it. From its inception it was obliged to report directly to the permanent members of the Security Council, which gave the UN Secretary General, or indeed any part of the UN apparatus, absolutely no say in its composition or conduct. The nuclear inspections of Iraq, for example, should have been handled by the International Atomic Energy Agency, a truly international organisation of established repute, but it was effectively frozen out by American political manoeuvring. The IAEA's role was kept to an absolute minimum. It was allowed into Iraq only on the condition that UNSCOM provided all logistics. In practice this meant that the Special Commission recruited the staff that it used and designated the sites it inspected.

'UNSCOM's "assist and support" mandate was replaced by "insist and control",' said Ekeus's fellow Swede (and rival) Hans Blix, then the IAEA chairman, who complained that the 'Rambo-style' actions of his UNSCOM-appointed teams turned the Agency's activities into military operations.[9]

In the first year of the inspections, Richard Clarke, together with fellow State Department official Bob Gallucci, then Ekeus's deputy, and David Kay, their man in the IAEA, engineered a controversial showdown with the Baathist regime outside the Baghdadi Ministry of Agriculture, which housed something called the Nuclear Design Centre.

'Working through the Special Commission,' Clarke later wrote, 'we and the British overtly planned an inspection on another nearby site, but at the last minute it would turn into a surprise raid on the ministry. U.S. and British Special Forces would be among the inspectors and would smash locks and break into files quickly before the Iraqis could react. The problem with the plan, we knew, was how the inspectors would get out once they discovered the nuclear bomb records. Gallucci and I agreed on a stand-off, the U.N. inspectors would not leave the site or give up the documents. Meanwhile, the U.S. would prepare a renewed bombing campaign.'[10]

The air strikes would give America another chance to topple Saddam, and the targets selected were not WMD facilities but Republican Guard units. Kay's team swept into the Nuclear Design Centre, located the archive, blocked the door and began

picking up all the paperwork they could find. After the Iraqis surrounded them they were eventually escorted out to the ministry
car park, where, still refusing to give up the documents, they settled in for a long wait and began their media campaign. Via
satellite phone Kay and Gallucci gave constant interviews to
American TV and radio stations.

'Bob, this is working,' Clarke told Gallucci. 'You were great on
CNN. The whole world is watching!'

'I had hoped the UNSCOM parking lot incident that I helped
contrive would have blossomed into a renewed round of major
bombing,' Clarke later wrote, but to his dismay the jets stayed in
their hangars.[11] Clarke's superior, Secretary of State James Baker,
a man who had privately displayed limited enthusiasm for the Gulf
War in the first place, prevailed upon the President not to use military force, and after four days the Iraqis relented. Kay's team was
allowed to return with whatever they had found, but none of the
documents were ever commented on in a formal IAEA report,
perhaps because they had been illegally obtained, and it remains
unclear exactly how many of the documents seized by American
soldiers and agents were actually forwarded to Blix to begin with.[12]
Over at UNSCOM an incandescent Ekeus was briefed on the
inspection, not by his own staff but by US government officials,
and only after the fact.[13]

Kay's documents proved there'd been a theoretical military
aspect to Iraq's nuclear research, but then this was never in much
doubt. Exactly how far Iraq had progressed remained vague, but
the programme was ended. In fact after the Gulf War Iraq became
the first and so far the only country to be banned from conducting any nuclear research at all: its nuclear engineers were known
and interviewed, its facilities were mapped and visited (many had
already been bombed), its equipment was confiscated or destroyed,
and its stockpiles of uranium were removed or tagged. What Kay's
inspection achieved was politically useful media attention and the
pretext for possible military action, two things that UNSCOM
could always be counted on to supply.

The second biological inspection that Kelly missed during his trilateral hiatus worked out much the same way. British intelligence visited Scott Ritter in New York while the inspection was in progress and told him they were debriefing an Iraqi defector who had been picked up by the Germans. As Kelly was MI6's paramount biological interrogator he may well have been part of the process, but his possible involvement remains entirely unknown, as does the identity of the source, who claimed that Iraq was still storing a 'treasure trove' of documents in another part of the Ministry of Agriculture.

Germany was to become a regular destination for Iraqi defectors, few of whom ever proved reliable. The most famous and fraudulent of them all the CIA codenamed CURVEBALL, a taxi-driving chemistry graduate who said he had helped Saddam build a fleet of secret mobile biological-warfare labs. Perhaps asylum in Germany offered a calculated obfuscation of the covert American and British inducements that had triggered these defections in the first place; it would certainly have enabled the anti-Iraqi agents of London and Langley (the CIA's HQ) to feed disinformation into the Western intelligence community without soiling their own doorstep.

After MI6 had tipped off Ritter about this new German humint, he jetted off with Mark Silver, a US Air Force lieutenant colonel, to join Major Karen Jansen of the US army, who was then leading a joint biological and chemical inspection in Baghdad. Her team was abruptly commandeered and instructed to re-inspect the Ministry of Agriculture. Ekeus was not informed because the mission was apparently too urgent: it was based on 'time-sensitive intelligence', according to the anonymous British spook who supplied it.[14] This, of course, was a self-serving tautology: all intelligence is time-sensitive.

When UNSCOM appeared outside the Ministry of Agriculture for a second time they were denied access outright. It was Sunday, a working day in Iraq but in the States the third day of a three-day holiday, and the Security Council was unreachable. On their own initiative, the inspectors surrounded the building and demanded to frisk any employee who left, including the women. In response the Iraqi civil servants elected to remain inside. By that evening, a crowd of chanting, banner-waving demonstrators had gathered outside the ministry. The hospitality Iraq accorded UNSCOM in Kelly's early inspections had by now entirely evaporated, and it would never return.

This second stand-off dragged on for an incredible seventeen days. The protests became constant; some days saw crowds of several thousand, one Baghdadi even set himself on fire. Many of the demonstrators were relatives of ministry employees, who understood that if UNSCOM was allowed access to personnel files the information would probably fall into the hands of Mossad, who had never shrunk from assassinating the scientists of enemy countries, or even friendly ones. In all likelihood it was the Israelis who had murdered the Canadian artillery genius Gerald Bull outside his apartment in Belgium two years previously because of his design work for the Iraqi military. Bull wasn't the first of these deaths, and he certainly wasn't the last.[15]

Maintaining their twenty-four-hour vigil in shifts, with downtime spent resting in the nearby former Sheraton, the UNSCOM inspectors dug in their heels and awaited military escalation as media reports began to circulate.

'This is just another example of Iraq's cheat-and-retreat approach,' said James Baker, coining a phrase that American and British politicians would use repeatedly over the next eleven years.

Bush the Elder, as out of the loop as Ekeus had been, cancelled his vacation in Maine for a crisis meeting at Camp David with his Defense Secretary Dick Cheney. In Washington, US officials briefed the media that an extensive aerial campaign would probably begin the following week, and – significantly, given what the future held in store – that additional authorisation from the UN Security Council would not be needed.[16]

'It's going to be bombs away,' said Republican Senate leader Bob Dole.

But to the frustration of the hawks, the fireworks were cancelled yet again. When the UN Security Council convened to issue a Presidential Statement, the US Representative Edward Perkins deliberately toned down the response. Any mention of military action was dropped. Britain's Ambassador to the UN, Sir David Hannay, whose Foreign Office had been instrumental in precipitating the dispute, apparently almost fell off his seat.[17]

In an attempt to de-escalate matters Ekeus flew out to Baghdad himself, where the Iraqi Deputy Prime Minister Tariq Aziz told him he was happy for the ministry to be inspected as long as it was by neutral or non-aligned countries. The UNSCOM chairman promptly returned to New York and reported this back to the Security Council. Wisely, he insisted on removing Scott Ritter and Karen Jansen from the scene and bringing them back with him. But before the Council could respond to Aziz's proposal in a way that might terminally sideline US and UK dominance over the inspection process, Silver withdrew his team from the ministry.

Officially, this was because of fears for their personal safety: an Iraqi civilian had apparently waved a skewer at two inspectors while they sat in a parked car. Exactly how threatening this 'attack' was can only be speculated on. According to Ritter, one of the two inspectors was a member of the Operations Planning Cell of the CIA, and it appears the other was a former Royal Marine. Neither needed any medical attention. Perhaps a more valid reason for the withdrawal was given by the ex-Foreign Office diplomat who was then Ekeus's special adviser, Tim Trevan.

'It was in UNSCOM's interest to have a period without surveillance before access was obtained,' he argued.[18] 'If an inspection team then gained access and found nothing, UNSCOM could easily claim that things could have been removed in the intervening period; this would protect the credibility of the intelligence on which the inspection was based. It would be harder to explain how everything had been spirited away from under the noses of the inspectors watching the three exits if access were obtained without any such gap.'

Only a few days later, after tensions had dissipated and the original hardline inspectors had pulled out, Iraq relented and allowed another team inside. They found no archives relating to WMD whatsoever, and just as Trevan had advised, several of them asserted the building had been duplicitously sanitised before their arrival. Their evidence for this centred on dirt lines on a wall which suggested the removal of 'incriminating shelving'.

Ironically, Ritter's anonymous British spook had been right in one respect. There was a decidedly time-sensitive aspect to these provocative inspections after all, as the *New York Times* found out the following month: they were too soon.

'American officials familiar with administration planning' told Patrick Tyler, the paper's chief correspondent, 'that the US and its allies have decided to provoke a confrontation with Iraq which would give President Bush a boost during the upcoming Republican National Convention.'[19]

Bush the Elder was seeking a second term, and struggling in the polls against a charismatic Bill Clinton and an independent Ross Perot. At home, the economy was nose-diving into recession. Abroad, the man Bush had labelled the worst tyrant since Hitler, and over whom he had wielded an astonishing military advantage, had been bizarrely allowed to remain firmly in power. A brief, justified display of resolve by the US Air Force might galvanise support for his election campaign.

'We are going to stage an incident to help the President get re-elected,' one anonymous staffer complained to Tyler.

After the Ministry of Agriculture and Irrigation, UNSCOM inspectors demanded entry to the Ministry of Military Industrialisation. If they were allowed in, Tyler was told, they would then insist on visiting the Ministry of Defence, the heart of Iraq's national security apparatus. Other sources explained the sites 'were selected not because American intelligence has identified specific documents there, but because those buildings are so important to Saddam's survival that he is certain to refuse access'.

It was a scoop. Journalists from other papers, like the *Chicago*

Tribune, chased the story and found corroboration from their own contacts. 'If Saddam lets us into his Defence Ministry, then we go a step further,' a Bush policy adviser told one journalist. 'Maybe we demand access to his private offices. We will continue to escalate as long as necessary and sometime he will say no or admit total impotence. When he says no, we bomb.'[20]

Only the day before, Bush had given an interview to David Brinkley of ABC News in which he claimed his leadership was going to make America 'a moral inspiration for the world'. When the story broke he responded only once, by calling the accusations 'ugly and uncalled for'. Formally the White House refused to comment (as did the British Foreign Office), except for a single unnamed spokesman who said the UNSCOM inspection teams were organised, implemented and timed entirely by the United Nations, and had nothing to do with the American or British governments. This was a complete untruth, although no one could prove it at the time.

Then the political machinations of an air strike became too obvious to be palatable. Bush's opponents began to round on him. 'Bush said he would do anything to win,' said the Reverend Jesse Jackson. 'I hope it doesn't include a bombing raid to shift attention away from the economy.'[21]

Even those normally loyal to the Republican Party had a hard time swallowing the idea. 'The Persian Gulf calls for a fundamental change of policy,' wrote the right-winger William Safire, 'not a spasm of poll-boosting violence.'[22]

Perhaps most damningly, even the nominal Iraqi opposition, in Kurdistan and the Shiite south, argued against the bombings.[23] They told reporters such strikes would achieve little except damage infrastructure and kill civilians. As an alternative tactic James Baker suggested war crimes trials, but any prosecutions would also incriminate the inner circle from whom Washington hoped to appoint Saddam's successor, and so the notion was dropped. Bush never initiated any further military demonstration against Iraq (though he did green-light Operation Southern Watch).[24]

Conversely, his successor rarely hesitated to drop bombs on the Iraqis. Clinton's first sally came only five months into his presidency, when he ordered a salvo of cruise missile strikes against the headquarters of the Iraqi Intelligence Service. This was prompted by a media furore triggered by Kuwaiti claims to have foiled an Iraqi assassination attempt on the former President Bush during his visit to the Emirate that April. As well as hitting the Mukhabarat HQ the strike also destroyed three houses and killed eight civilians, amongst them Layla Al-Attar, perhaps the foremost female artist of the Arab world.

'We got lucky,' said a security aide, on discovering that only three of the missiles had gone off course. Polls showed that Clinton's approval rating increased by eleven points the following day. Two weeks later, somebody at the CIA leaked a counterterrorism report to the *Boston Globe*.[25] It concluded that Kuwait had 'a clear incentive to play up the Iraqi threat' and had probably fabricated the whole thing. The supposed hit squad were actually whiskey smugglers; most of them retracted their confessions in court and several said they were tortured. At least fourteen were originally arrested, only six were eventually convicted, and the sentences of at least four were later privately commuted.[26]

Meanwhile the CIA began sponsoring their own terrorist bombing campaign inside Iraq. Amongst the Agency's anti-Saddam assets could now be counted Iyad Allawi, leader of his own 'Iraqi National Accord', and long-favoured by MI6 as the opposition leader of choice (Allawi had moved to London in 1971, when he was twenty-six). Years later, former intelligence officers told the *New York Times* that under CIA funding and direction Allawi's exile organisation sent agents into Iraq from Kurdistan to detonate car bombs and other explosive devices.[27]

'I remember somebody blew up a bus,' said Robert Baer, who had been stationed in the country at the time. 'Schoolchildren were killed.'

'No one had any problems with sabotage in Baghdad back then,' said another, anonymous, former officer.

One of Allawi's bombmakers earned notoriety in the mid-nineties when a video tape of him complaining he hadn't been properly paid circulated amongst Iraqi opposition leaders. A copy of Abu Amneh al-Khademi's filmed grumblings found its way to Patrick Cockburn at the *Independent*. 'More than a hundred civilians have been killed by the bombs in Baghdad over the last three or four years,' a senior member of the opposition told the journalist.[28]

This was the deeply murky world that UNSCOM belonged to by the time Kelly rejoined it in the summer of 1994. It worked amongst a hostile people angered by their continued exposure to the most comprehensive economic sanctions in history, against a backdrop of covert activity by a range of foreign governments and non-state actors that extended beyond simple espionage into the realm of disinformation and even terrorism. From its inception it was designed to be an instrument of US and UK foreign policy, and it quickly became a vehicle for US and UK intelligence collection too. Inspectors were routinely expected to share their findings with their own spooks, and sometimes – as was the case with UNSCOM's signals intercepts, some of its seized documents and biological sampling, most of its GPS readings and all of its original high-altitude aerial photography – the information was not so much shared as sent straight to Washington (and occasionally London) without ever gracing an UNSCOM filing cabinet.

During its opening months some of its inspectors had developed, almost as a hallmark signature, a confrontational technique that could justify military intervention on demand. Provocative demands for access to sensitive sites could be raised any time a British or American intelligence agency told them there might be something inside to find, tip-offs that UNSCOM rarely showed any inclination or ability to verify or assess. Other countries, France and Russia specifically, would try to use the Commission for their own national interests too, but they could never steer it the way the US and the UK could. By the time Kelly came back, the organisation had been infiltrated by just about every country that had donated personnel.

'UNSCOM was a spy magnet,' said Charles Duelfer, Ekeus's State Department deputy at the time of Kelly's return. 'In many cases you never knew who was working for who.'[29]

Some days, Kelly himself must have wondered who he was working for. By the time he reappeared in Iraq he had been seconded from the Defence Science Technology Laboratory at Porton Down to the Proliferation and Arms Control Secretariat at the Ministry of Defence, from where he had been seconded again to the Non-Proliferation Department at the Foreign Office, which had seconded (or perhaps 'fourthed' him) yet again to the Special Commission.

The only constant oversight of Britain's UNSCOM inspectors was provided by Operation Rockingham, or as Kelly himself referred to it, the Rockingham cell. It was nominally an offshoot of the Defence Intelligence Staff, but also, and less observably, it was the conduit by which SIS could place their own imprint on the inspection process. An officer of MI6 was present at most Rockingham meetings, although their participation remains an official state secret, just like everything else the Secret Intelligence Service does.

'MI6 were the real thoroughbreds,' revealed Brian Jones, the head of the biological and chemical desk at the DIS, and the man chiefly responsible for Kelly's Cold War conversion to the world of intelligence.[30] 'They acted like the spies in the novels. They knew everyone in Whitehall and were everywhere. They were highly polished in all that they did. They drifted in and out of meetings unidentified or sometimes giving a false affiliation, but they always made sure everyone knew how clever they were. And they were clever.'

After Pasechnik defected, Jones had been something like Kelly's sponsor in the UK intelligence community. In that need-to-know world Kelly had originally read classified reports only at Jones's discretion. Then, after Kelly's involvement with UNSCOM intensified, Jones lost sight of him. Often he would see him in the corridors and offices of the Metropole Building without knowing why he was there. 'At some stage I became aware there was a direct relationship between David Kelly and officers of the SIS,' Jones wrote to Lord Hutton, 'so I ceased to be aware of the full scope of his visibility of intelligence or his involvement with it.'[31]

Unsurprisingly, there is no record of a single meeting between Kelly and MI6 ever having taken place, but Kelly later told the Intelligence and Security Committee that as an UNSCOM inspector he met with officers of the Secret Intelligence Service about every two months. Like every other senior staff member on the Commission, he also had regular contact with the CIA, and after the trilateral inspections were over, some sort of channel to Mossad. 'Every senior weapons inspector had his or her own "unique" contact with the Israelis, which was kept secret from all the others,' Scott Ritter wrote.[32]

So by the time Kelly returned to Iraq, he was being handled by 'friendly' case officers in the intelligence agencies of three different countries, not counting any file opened on him by, for instance, the British Security Service, the Iraqi Mukhabarat, the Russian SVR. His meetings with Mossad, MI6 and the CIA were routine, but they form no part of any official record. When Hutton came to inquire into the circumstances regarding his death, the law lord never showed the slightest interest in asking about them.

Whatever subtle changes might have happened under its surface, Kelly rejoined an UNSCOM that was visibly much enlarged and empowered. Gone was the ad hoc assemblage of experts whose headquarters was a floor in the former Sheraton, and who thought it would all be over by Christmas. The new UNSCOM had its own walled compound in central Baghdad, with its own (three hundred foot high) communications mast, garage, contained laboratory, canteen, bar, medical surgery and high-security surveillance room. The Baghdad Monitoring and Verification Centre was a large four-storey building with its own courtyard in the northeast centre of the city. It had once been known as the Canal Hotel.

A new Security Council resolution had also given the inspectors an unprecedented amount of authority.[33] A member of UNSCOM now had the right to enter or leave Iraq whenever he wanted. He could turn up without notice anywhere in the country on a whim and demand unimpeded access to any building he desired. He could insist on immediate possession of any documents, video or photography he thought relevant; could designate any site he liked for inspection, continuous observation, or demolition; could install whatever monitoring equipment or build whatever support facilities he thought necessary; could take photographs of whatever he liked, samples of anything he wanted, and conduct interviews with anyone he chose. At the same time, Iraq had to guarantee the inspectors' safety and diplomatic immunity at all times. It was a preposterously impractical amount of power, as even the most hardline inspectors knew, and they were careful not to push things too far. They could theoretically have insisted on interviewing Saddam Hussein in his pyjamas, but none of them chose to.

The rather neglected biological desk at UNSCOM had also been considerably expanded. It had previously fallen to a young Frenchwoman called Annick Paul-Henriot, apparently a lawyer by profession, but as the Commission's inspections in other fields approached an acceptable level of verification she found herself suddenly surrounded by a host of new and very senior experts. Perhaps the foremost amongst these was Dick Spertzel, a former deputy commander at Fort Detrick, who had once bulk-produced anthrax in its 'Tower of Doom'. After him came Kelly himself, the former biological chief at Porton Down. They were joined by Hamish Killip of the DIS, who had worked with Kelly on the Russian inspections, and Rod Barton of Australia's Defence Intelligence Organisation. More recently, both Killip and Barton had worked at GATEWAY as the UK component of the CIA's UNSCOM-handling facility. They had now crossed over to join UNSCOM itself.

Spertzel, Kelly, Killip, Barton. These men were the thermal core of UNSCOM's biological inspections, inspections that would become the biggest sticking-point between Iraq and the US–UK alliance. Between them they probably amassed more knowledge on Iraq's BW than could be found anywhere else in the world, except of course amongst the Iraqis themselves. Their colleagues nicknamed them the Gang of Four. They were UNSCOM's first and only full-time bioweapons team.

Sadly, the prickly Spertzel is now at a stage in his old age when he is best left undisturbed by questions from inquisitive authors. The mild-mannered Rod Barton, a keen gardener and currently the co-owner of a wine merchants in Canberra, refused to speak to me. I got the same flat-out knock-back, via an intermediary, from Hamish Killip. The chipper round-faced Manxman who started his military career as an officer in the Royal Engineers has now retired to his native Douglas, where he spends his time on school boards and planning boards and other civic duties. These three men were David's closest colleagues, and Barton, at least, was a personal friend. Spertzel can be excepted, but I was disappointed to discover that neither Barton nor Killip would consent to an interview, either on or off the record. Then I realised that none of them had spoken at the Hutton Inquiry either. Or at Butler, for that matter, or Chilcot, or any of the previous parliamentary committees. Their voices are a curious absence when it comes to the death of David Kelly.

Their first task was substantial, and in the strictest sense it wasn't an inspection at all. UNSCOM's other responsibility was monitoring: implementing a permanent and ongoing surveillance of the factories and laboratories inside Iraq that had the potential to be used for weapons development, if Saddam decided to restart it. Originally this phase was supposed to come after the inspections had declared the country free of WMD, and so Iraq had resisted monitoring until the inspectors had finished and the sanctions were lifted. Ekeus managed to convince them that allowing both simultaneously would speed up the process, and failing to make any headway with the Security Council, Iraq gave in.

The scale of UNSCOM's biological monitoring was immense. BW5 visited thirty-one sites, all of which had already been inspected on BW4, to tag, photograph and inventory equipment, some 330 pieces in all. BW6 visited another thirty-five sites – again, most of them had already been inspected, but eight had not been officially declared, and so UNSCOM promptly put them on its monitoring list as an example of deliberate omission by the Iraqis. Rihab Taha asked if it was really necessary for UNSCOM to visit all these universities, breweries, tanneries and yoghurt factories, and she was told it was essential because they could all be turned into weapons plants. BW8, which Kelly led, was probably the biggest of all UNSCOM's inspections. This mission laid down monitoring protocols at fifty locations, at a rate of two a day. It lasted for six weeks; junior staff were rotated in and out of the country to keep them fresh, although Kelly remained in place and in charge throughout.

'It was one of our best pieces of work,' said Killip. 'A hands-on assessment of Iraq's ability to engage in biological warfare activites.'[34]

These baseline monitoring inspections that Kelly participated in that year took in over two hundred facilities. UNSCOM rated seventy-nine of them worthy of permanent monitoring, and they were all fitted with sampling sensors that would detect the presence of any prohibited microbes, as well as video cameras that provided a live feed to the communications room at the Monitoring and Verification Centre in Baghdad (the BMVC). These were installed by Rick Francona, a US Air Force officer on secondment to the CIA who used them as a cover to set up supplementary surveillance devices that fed back to American, British and Israeli intelligence.[35] Did Kelly know about this? He was the Chief Inspector inside Iraq when they were put in, he was the regular liaison point with the Rockingham cell that received and analysed the data, and he had top-secret security clearance. At the very least, it's inconceivable he didn't have extremely strong suspicions. Like so much else, he never talked about it. Not once.

At the BMVC, the split-screen software in the communications room allowed inspectors to view sixteen sites simultaneously. Some, probably most, of these locations were entirely innocuous: they included dairy processors and several minor colleges, but a few presented more serious prospects, such as Al Hakum, the single-cell-protein plant out in the desert that Kelly had always been convinced was initially intended to bulk-produce pathogens. Fourteen video cameras were installed at Al Hakum alone. The tapes from these cameras also ended up in American possession, when Francona passed them to a US Air Force intelligence unit.[36] Later, somebody set up a live feed to New York, and, one imagines, to a few other places too, so the tapes were dispensed with.[37] None of the footage from these cameras ever revealed BW activity of any kind.

At the same time all this was going on, the Gang of Four conducted an equally huge number of interviews. They talked to everybody, from the bottle-washers to the lab directors. As noted earlier, Kelly often felt the most junior staff made more revealing subjects than their superiors, and he was always keen to talk to the more lowly members of the workforce. It was only a few years back, in Soviet Siberia, that a relatively insignificant lab assistant had told him that Vector was working with smallpox.

Back in America, before these interviews had commenced, Charles Duelfer had arranged for the FBI to teach the inspectors additional questioning techniques.[38] On the inspections themselves, Kelly had also arranged to bring along a criminal psychologist to interpret body language. According to Tim Trevan this man came from police CID, though in reality he may well have been Special Branch or even MI6. Kelly was already an experienced interrogator before this lengthy round of interviews began, and when it was over his expertise can only have increased even further.

Whatever Kelly's proficiency in the interview room, the formal conclusions UNSCOM drew from all this questioning were a different matter. Not once, it seems, did the Commission see any reason to drop its by now institutional level of distrust. When staff gave consistent answers it was assumed they'd been coached in what to say. Conversely, whenever there was any variance in a workforce's answers, it was held to be indicative of dissembling. And when an employee had forgotten something, or he just didn't know, it was assumed he was deliberately withholding the truth. Each of these three perceived responses was held to point towards the cover-up of a hidden weapons programme, and it appears this attitude applied even when questions were trivial or irrelevant.

Rihab Taha was, naturally, amongst the interviewees, and Kelly reduced her to tears.

'Did anyone at Salman Pak ever train abroad?' he asked her.

'No,' Taha answered.

Kelly pointed out that Taha herself had spent five years at the University of East Anglia.

'Did Iraq ever produce significant quantities of biological agents?' Kelly inquired.

'No.'

Kelly archly observed that she had replied without asking what constituted a significant quantity. Taha swallowed and went on to explain she had been recruited to work at Salman Pak on the contamination of foodstuffs, to make sure that high-up Baathists couldn't be poisoned with bacteria. This had segued into microbiological defence generally.

'Originally the work was designed to protect high Iraqi officials,' she explained. 'The Iran–Iraq war was at its apex, and so I thought, why only focus on high-ranking personnel? It should be on protecting all the Iraqi people. For example, in 1986 we had a cholera epidemic, which was attributed to water coming from Iran. So if we received contaminated water or meat, how would we detect this? We must have the basics. So it was decided to have a defence against this and we studied the characteristics of pathogenic organisms. It started simple and kept building up.'[39]

Kelly couldn't swallow it.

'There is a fundamental difference between defending against biological weapons and the situation you describe for the detection of contamination in foodstuffs. Who authorised this change? How did it come about?'

'It wasn't a change,' Taha said, her voice rising, 'just an expansion of what we were already doing.'

'Your accounts have changed over the last four years,' Kelly said.

'I am trying to tell you what happened and you don't believe me!' Taha responded, her voice now shrill. 'This is the way it was! I did it, and others were not needed. It's up to you to accept or not!'

Soon after, according to Barton, her answers grew disjointed and circular and eventually incomprehensible.

'Dr Taha,' said Kelly firmly, once the young woman had become hard to understand, 'please stop.'

Dr Germ picked up a glass of water and her hand shook so much it spilt. She stood up, opened her mouth to speak but then surrendered to racking sobs instead, and quickly ran out of the room.

The Gang of Four considered it a good time to break for lunch. That, at least, is how the story goes. None of the inspectors ever pretended they knew what had triggered Taha's outburst, but there is a flip side to the UNSCOM BW interviews that has never seen much attention. Behind the scenes, a huge amount of pressure was being applied to the Iraqi scientists.

The basic approach, particularly with high-ranking personnel like Taha, was automatically tough. Kelly, as far as I can gather, while firm, was always civil. David Huxsoll believed in an empathetic approach, and David Franz too thought the carrot always better than the stick. If nothing else, they were all scientists, there was a degree of common ground. Others, however, like Terry Taylor, had no hesitation in acting the 'bad cop' if they thought it would work. And some were outright abrasive or threatening, shouting that their interviewee was a liar, or would be prosecuted for war crimes.[40]

There were also occasions when subjects were persuaded to provide information surreptitiously, or invited to defect. John Turner,

Taha's supervisor at the University of East Anglia, told me that
American intelligence asked him to make a defection offer to her
the year before the Gang of Four interviews. There was an Iraqi
meeting scheduled at the UN headquarters, and Turner was flown
over to participate in a staged encounter outside.

'She was really angry about it,' he said. 'She told me that just by
asking her I had endangered her family, all of whom were still in
Iraq, and couldn't be got out. I feel very bad about it now. I have
no idea what happened to her.'

The money US intelligence paid Turner he spent on new windows for his family home. Interestingly, soon afterwards Taha
married General Amer Rashid, who was present on the same trip.

'I was the matchmaker for this dreadful pair,' Ekeus ruefully told
Patrick Cockburn, when he found out about the nuptials.[41]

Did Ekeus know that Taha, squeezed between the advances of
American intelligence on one side and the brutality of the
Baathist regime on the other, may only have been seeking protection for herself and her family? Did he know what his
inspectors were doing? The late Christopher Hitchens attended
a cocktail party where Ekeus related that Tariq Aziz had offered
him a million dollars (or a million and a half, or two million, or
two and a half million dollars – Hitchens's sum varies) to change
his inspection report. I don't doubt the story is essentially true.
Whatever Hitchens's faults he wasn't a fabricator, and to him it
was an outrageous case of Iraqi duplicity. But I think the point
of Aziz's 'bribe' was only to illustrate that similar sums of money
were being offered by UNSCOM staff to Iraqi scientists if they
changed their tune about WMD. In any case, bribing Ekeus was
essentially impossible: the UNSCOM chair couldn't have
declared Iraq WMD-free with simply a flourish of his signature,
not over the heads of his small army of hawkish, hardline
inspectors.

Charles Duelfer, Ekeus's deputy, told me that 'it was understood'
by senior Iraqis that if they 'thought they wanted a change of
scenery' their defection would be warmly received by American

intelligence. Of course, it begs the question of what the CIA or the State Department thought they were buying. After all, these people had no WMD to reveal. Presumably, after any defecting Iraqi had been put through the intelligence machine's spin-cycle, they would have ended up making claims as far-fetched as Curveball's.

'Yeah, well,' Duelfer went on, 'it basically became a kind of unspoken thing. They knew the offer was always there. One of them came back to me once and said would I like a million dollars to go and live in Iraq? You know, wouldn't I like to defect too? I think it shows they have a sense of humour.'

What about his inspectors? Were they making offers of their own?

'We would have really frowned on that sort of thing,' he said. 'That's a bit Rambo. I mean, I had authority.'

But who else did? And who said what? Duelfer admitted to me he had no way of knowing.

'Inspectors sometimes fancied themselves as minor spooks,' Killip once complained to a Senior Fellow at the James Martin Center for Nonproliferation Studies (CNS).[42] Yet it seems to me that minor spooks is more or less what most of them were.

During the long inspections of 1994, a few even attempted to run their own counter-intelligence. Assuming the Mukhabarat had tapped their phones and bugged their rooms, some inspectors tried to inject a little disinformation into the system, talking on open lines about events that had never happened, things people had never said, inspections that were never planned. Pushed too far, this can be a dangerous game, although it's rarely the player who gets hurt.

The interviews conducted by the Gang of Four unearthed very little new information, if any, but in their finer details they dug up the inevitable crop of contradictions and don't-knows, all of which could be used to point towards deception. In December, Kelly revisited Al Hakum, for UNSCOM's fourth or fifth time, and his team took samples from the spray drier and the waste tanks. Tests in US labs would show no traces of pathogens. The facility was still producing single-cell protein, although it had also branched out into biopesticide, which must have reminded Kelly of his Oxford days. The large stock of growth medium was still in its storage bunker, although it was now around or beyond its expiry date. After Kelly showed an interest in it a few workers began hauling the drums out and tossing them onto a bonfire. After Al Hakum, Kelly revisited Salman Pak, but there was nothing to see there. The place was still a bombsite. After that, he went home for debriefing and Christmas.

By the end of this year, UNSCOM's monitoring efforts had accomplished a mammoth amount of work. Iraq, understandably, thought the matter was finished. The Commission had no more sites to visit. It asked Ekeus if he was going to tell the Security Council that the monitoring system had been completed. It was a reasonable enough request, but America's agenda for UNSCOM dictated it should never complete anything. When it looked like Ekeus might announce that monitoring was now in place, Charles Deulfer came very close to resigning in protest.[43] Instead, Ekeus compromised by saying that it was only 'provisionally operational'. The end of sanctions would remain a distant prospect, and Iraq was still ruled to be in non-compliance. It came as a bitter disappointment not just to Iraq itself but also to Russia, France, China and Brazil, who had been arguing since the summer that the blockade should end.

'They have a capability we have not yet put our hands on fully,' Ekeus told American television that Christmas Eve, 'a capability to mass-produce microbiologic items. Viruses and bacteria. For warfare purposes.'

The same, of course, could be said of any halfway developed country. It didn't stop the English-speaking press from running the usual stories: 'Hussein Hides Germ Weapons, Inspectors Say'.[44] Yet none of them had said any such thing, at least not on record.

The next year, the inspections continued, more than ever before, but things were getting very strange.

In January, in an apartment in midtown Manhattan not far from the UN building, Mossad had arranged a meeting with the Gang of Four. How it was arranged remains a little vague, but one source says it was via Annick Paul-Henriot, the Frenchwoman sidelined by the new BW team, and who had been clinging on ever since. The men from Tel Aviv said they had intelligence on Iraq's WMD programmes that they wanted to share.

High above First Avenue and Thirty-Eighth Street, they drank lemon tea and munched biscuits while an Israeli intelligence officer passed them documents that showed Iraq had imported a vast quantity of growth medium from Oxoid in Basingstoke. According to Tom Mangold, who describes this meeting in his book *Plague Wars*, it was thirty-two tonnes. Tim Trevan in *Saddam's Secrets* says it was thirty-nine. Rod Barton, who was present at the meeting and describes it in his own account, *The Weapons Detective*, is deliberately vague, and says only 'several tonnes'. But however much it was, the startling thing about this supposed revelation is that the Gang of Four already knew the transaction had taken place.

Kelly had first seen the Oxoid drums at Al Hakum in 1991, and he had seen them a second time only the previous month. What's more, Iraq had officially named and declared its growth media imports to UNSCOM in 1993. When the coalition finally invaded Iraq ten years later, American forces were able to secure masses of Iraqi records from the ministries across Baghdad, a mountain of intelligence the Pentagon simply didn't have the resources to scale in a suitable time-frame. Instead, in an unparalleled gesture of commendable and astonishing openness, they scanned and published them online for citizens to translate in their spare time. They weren't up for very long; the US military soon reverted to type and pulled them all down again, but not before some of the cache had been mirrored, and a few surviving dossiers are still sliding around the Net. One relates to the UNSCOM biological inspections, and it contains a print-out listing forty-six tonnes of growth media and each of the foreign companies it bought it from. It is hand-signed, 'Received from Dr Taha Rihab [*sic*] 28 September 1993, UN Special Commission, Tim Trevan.'

According to a former Oxoid employee I spoke to (not the sales rep who sold Iraq the growth media, but the man who put me onto him), the British government already knew about these exports in detail. Not only had they been declared at the point of sale, but in 1993 or '94 a team from Porton Down actually visited the Oxoid staff at Basingstoke to go over the matter. As well as clearing up the details, they offered advice and training on what to say and who to inform if foreign governments ever requested such large quantities of growth media in the future. So when David Kelly quietly sat there in the Manhattan apartment that afternoon he was listening to information he had known for years, that UNSCOM itself had known for years, and done nothing about. Seen in this light, it was a bizarre sort of tip-off.

What makes this meeting even odder is that the sales rep himself told me the deal had been a cash transaction. There were very few records of any kind; the sale had been set up to deliberately reduce the paper trail. Yet Rod Barton says the Israelis supplied him with credit notes, while Tim Trevan says they provided contract details, but as far as the man that sold the growth media is aware, neither of these things existed, which is entirely plausible. A subsequent Iraqi chemical declaration, later leaked onto the Internet by someone identifying himself as Michael John Smith, the General Electric engineer entrapped for espionage by MI5 in 1992, shows it wasn't at all unusual for Iraq to pay for imports in cash.[45] Stranger still, when UNSCOM eventually sent someone to Oxoid to verify Israel's information, it sent not Kelly, for whom Basingstoke was only a few hours away by car, or any other British inspector, but Barton, who had to make a round trip of seven thousand miles. Nobody has ever explained why.

On its own terms, given everything we now know, the secret encounter with the Israelis doesn't quite add up. That they might want to assist UNSCOM makes sense, given that the Commission was enforcing disarmament on a regional enemy, but why provide help now? Why not before? And why offer this information through a secret meeting with the inspectors themselves, rather than through the national intelligence channels? If it had become public knowledge that UNSCOM was 'collaborating with Zionists', the political fall-out would not have helped its cause. Similarly, why hadn't UNSCOM acted on this knowledge already? What Mossad had to impart that afternoon was nothing new to them. Was Kelly trying to hide the role that Britain had played? These exports couldn't be hidden for ever, given the range of nationalities who worked for the Special Commission. Iraq's Deputy Prime Minister Tariq Aziz later offered his own explanation of UNSCOM's abruptly renewed interest in Iraq's biological research programme. He believed it was a way of prolonging the sanctions, because all other aspects of Iraq's WMD had been dealt with; a card to play that had been held back till now.[46]

The Gang of Four's January meeting with Mossad was the first strange thing to happen that year. A day after the biologists returned to the Commission's office in the UN building and sat down with Iraq's chief disarmament officer Hossam Amin, who asked them what percentage of the work they felt they still had to do, Kelly leant forward in his seat and looked him in the eye.

'Ninety-five per cent,' he said.

Amin was crestfallen.

'What is the point of UNSCOM if over four years of inspections and interviews and declarations you start from zero now?' he asked.

What answer he received is unknown. Rod Barton says they got 'a buzz out of rattling Amin'.[47] Annick Paul-Henriot, who appears by now to have been entirely marginalised, privately observed it looked like the biological inspections were starting all over again. Most of the other French members of UNSCOM, too, were effectively frozen out by this stage, given their country's opposition to sanctions. Mission information was compartmentalised, often under the simple codename 'NO FRENCH'.[48]

'We never let the French fully in,' said Charles Duelfer.[49]

The following day the inspectors attended a meeting of the UN's Iraq sanctions review committee. The Russians and the French were still arguing that Iraq, which now formally recognised Kuwait and its borders, had demonstrably met its obligation to disarm, and the time had come to lift the blockade. Against the set positions of the US and the UK, and the grim warnings of the Gang of Four, they made little headway.

Sometime this week, or the next, Annick Paul-Henriot died. The inspectors were told it was a heart attack. Annick was in her thirties, didn't smoke, didn't drink heavily, and appeared physically fit. As far as I'm aware she died alone in her flat. Inspectors were subsequently told she had been hiding a heart condition; Ekeus was led to believe she wore a pacemaker. Annick had been on at least one summer biological inspection inside Iraq. Would a person with a pacemaker volunteer for such duties? Would she have been able to conceal her condition from the team's medical officer? I was unable to track down her death certificate, or indeed find any record of her at all, outside the accounts of ex-inspectors.

The death of Annick Paul-Henriot was the second strange thing to happen that year. She was replaced by the German Colonel Gabriele Kraatz-Wadsack, who would become a good friend of Kelly himself, and who some colleagues described as paranoid.[50] Perhaps she had good reason to be.

The biological inspections began again in February. They centred almost exclusively on Iraq's imported growth media. Some of the documents UNSCOM had received it claimed were not the historical originals, which Iraq apparently conceded: the imported media was by now either seven or eight years old, and all of it was past its sell-by date. BW23 'found' eleven tonnes at a warehouse in Al Adile, although it had been seen in previous inspections and ignored. Kraatz-Wadsack inventoried another two and half tonnes at the Al Razi Institute, about a tonne and a half at Al Kindi, another tonne at Al Amiriyah, and six were still left unburnt at Al

Hakum. Including a few other stocks at hospitals and elsewhere, it left seventeen tonnes unaccounted for.

In further interviews with Kelly and his team, the Iraqis said that several tonnes of the material had been destroyed, either by facility staff or by lootings and fires during the postwar Shia uprising. The rest had been used for civilian purposes. The amount ordered, the Iraqis argued, reflected their anxiety that their trade links might be cut off. Kelly didn't believe it, and neither did the rest of his team. Thirty-nine tonnes was by any consideration an absolutely extraordinary amount of growth media to have imported, and the missing seventeen was not much less remarkable in quantity. These were industrial levels of stock.

'This can only coincide with the production of biological weapons,' Ekeus told the press, adding that Iraq no longer had 'militarily significant amounts of chemical weapons', and that he was optimistic that he could declare Iraq in full compliance later that year.[51]

The following month, in Iraq, the Gang of Four (with Ekeus observing) came out with their suspicions. Kelly told Taha he believed the desert facility at Al Hakum had been designed and built to produce biological agents, and that the seventeen tonnes of missing growth media had been used there to make them. Taha stood up and sketched out a few calculations on a whiteboard to show that, given the fermentation capacity at Al Hakum, the plant would need over twenty-six years to use up seventeen tonnes, and had no safety containment for working on dangerous organisms. Privately, Kelly had always asserted the Iraqis could have achieved a workable level of containment by wrapping the fermenters in clingfilm, but the team met Taha's defence with silence. Ekeus was apparently irate. Publicly, he had already put UNSCOM's credibility on the line. But he did not have to wait long for his inspectors to respond.

That night the team met with Abdul Rahman Thamir, Taha's deputy, the young man Kelly had once brought back to Porton Down, and went through the history of Al Hakum with him. He had brought with him no written records and contributed only from memory the installation dates of various bits of equipment and any operational problems they had experienced. The following day Kelly and his crew met again with Taha and laid out their own calculations which, contrary to Taha's, suggested Al Hakum could have used up all the missing media in just nine months. This assumed, amongst other things, that every aspect of the line had worked perfectly and constantly from the moment of its installation, that the line had run non-stop, and that every large tank in the line was actually a fermenter.

When he'd finished these mathematics, he turned around to see Dr Germ sitting there with tears running down her face.

'That's impossible,' she said. 'We couldn't have run it all the time. What about maintenance? What about getting spare parts?'

Her new husband, General Amer Rashid, was sitting next to her, and took up her cause.

'These sums are outrageous,' said the General. 'They are lies. Not every vessel is a fermenter, and you know it. There is a chain, a process, you know this. It is how in-line fermentation works. It scales up, from the small tank to the medium tank to the largest. They are piped together. You have seen this. Some are not fermenters at all, they are mixing tanks. You know this too.'

The Gang of Four looked at each other. Rashid was quite right, and they had anticipated his argument. Kelly passed Barton an inventory that had been taken of Al Hakum's equipment earlier in the year, in which UNSCOM had described every large tank in the line as a fermenter. This was technically accurate, but it wasn't how in-line fermentation works: you take the concentrated product from the end of the production line, not from every vessel in the chain.

'Dr Taha said they were fermenters,' said Barton, sliding the inventory across the table. 'She signed the declaration.'

Rashid's hands were shaking when he picked it up. The Iraqis had been hooked on a monitoring technicality, and one that fundamentally misrepresented the fermentation process.

'I thought it was important not to become too technical,' was how Barton later explained it.[52]

Taha looked at her husband. 'They made me sign it,' was all she said. This time the meeting ended with silence on the Iraqi side. Ekeus, who said Taha's tears had 'not impressed me for a second', recalled that he was 'very pleased'.[53]

In April, the following month, UNSCOM delivered its report to the Security Council.

'The Commission assesses that Iraq obtained or sought to obtain all the items to produce in Iraq biological warfare agents,' it read. 'With Iraq's failure to account for all these items and materials for legitimate purposes, the only conclusion that can be drawn is that there is a high risk that they had been purchased and in part used for proscribed purposes: the production of agents for biological weapons.'

The Gang of Four had finally submitted their knowledge of Iraq's growth media to the public domain, and both public and political opinion began to sway in their favour. Even France, still championing a lifting of sanctions, had to concede the report was 'negative on certain points'.

'Iraq Hides Stockpile of Biological Arms', ran a headline in the *Guardian*, although this stockpile had never once been hidden from UNSCOM since the day it had arrived in the country. The inspectors had photographed and videoed it unhindered from the time of Kelly's second visit.

'Confession is not enough,' Ekeus told the *New York Times*. 'We need to get our hands on it and destroy it.'[54]

And with that, Iraq's fate was sealed, though it would be years before the end finally came. There was nothing in the entire country to lay hands on. It had all been destroyed four years earlier. The US Secretary of State Warren Christopher went one step further than Ekeus, declaring that Iraq was bent on developing biological weapons and Al Hakum was 'an active germ warfare facility'.[55] At the time, Al Hakum was under constant live monitoring from fourteen video cameras and was visited by UNSCOM's Baghdad staff every week.

In response, Iraq invited the world's media to come and see it.

Taha, now described in the American press as 'the world's most dangerous woman', led a group of twenty-five foreign journalists around the premises, showed them the biopesticide the plant was making, and its production line for single-cell protein. The facility couldn't increase its output of animal feed, she complained, because the sanctions prevented them from importing stirrers for their fermenters.

Some of her visitors told her they'd been briefed that Al Hakum had been used to produce quantities of anthrax and botulinum toxin. Taha didn't deny it. 'Well, this is the problem with all biological facilities,' she said. 'Their purposes can be changed, but believe me, this project is for purely civilian use. Our country needs fat chickens and lots of eggs, so we are trying to do just that here.'

At the end of the tour, an Iraqi man stood at the exit with a tray full of eggs from the flock of chickens that Al Hakum was using to test the nutritional value of its manufactured protein.

'These are good Iraqi eggs,' he said, offering them to the departing journalists.

It would be interesting to know if anybody took any. Although none of the subsequent articles that appeared in the press mentioned it, under sanctions the Iraqi price of a tray of thirty eggs had risen five hundredfold to roughly a thousand dinar, the equivalent of half the monthly salary of a university professor.[56] Purchases of animal vaccines, animal feed, pesticide, irrigation equipment and refrigeration units had all been banned by the shadowy UN sanctions committee to which UNSCOM's inspectors gave their expert advice, and Iraq's livestock and poultry had been devastated by drought and disease as a consequence. So too had its harvest of wheat and barley.[57] Eggs themselves had been placed on the 'Red List' of prohibited imports in case Taha or her colleagues used them to grow viruses in, and so too had thousands of other innocuous items with apparent 'dual use' potential, such as lightbulbs, socks, wrist-watches, ovens, sewing machines, mirrors, diskettes, nails, pencils and textbooks; almost everything, in fact, apart from a very narrow range of foodstuffs and medicine. Because of the way the sanctions had been established, no justification for these decisions ever needed to be given.

'To eliminate a nation's capacity to produce biological weapons means eliminating all science education above the secondary school level, eliminating the capacity to produce yoghurt and cheese, eliminating eggs,' Professor Joy Gordon has written.[58] 'Any industrialized nation relies continually on manufacturing processes that could possibly be converted to produce some aspect of a biological or chemical weapon. To eliminate this capacity, as opposed to the weapons themselves, would literally require reducing a nation to the most primitive possible condition and keeping it in those circumstances in perpetuity. This was not at all the policy adopted by the Security Council, which required only that Iraq be subject to partial disarmament and monitoring, but it was the policy of the United States.'

And so, too, of the United Kingdom. David Kelly, and his colleagues at UNSCOM, for all their training and perception and experience, became the tools, the blunt instruments by which this policy was effected. It came at some cost to them, in terms of their personal comfort and their relationships with loved ones back home, but this was nothing compared to what it cost the Iraqi people.

By 1995, Iraq's rationing system could provide only 1100 calories a day.[59] The same year the *Lancet* published the first of innumerable studies on the humanitarian effect of sanctions.[60] It was written by two American scientists working for the Food and Agriculture Organisation of the United Nations who had examined over two thousand children under the age of ten in neighbourhoods all over Baghdad. Almost a third of them were stunted in growth. Over a tenth were 'wasting', or emaciated. Their 'underweight rates', previously the same as Kuwaiti children's, were now comparable to the infants of Ghana and Mali. Child mortality rates had increased fivefold and were still growing. Deaths related to diarrhoeal diseases had tripled. Hospitals were running at under half-capacity, and the general population was still at risk of widespread starvation. The authors subsequently withdrew their calculation of how many Iraqi children the sanctions had killed, but over forty-six other studies were to follow, by various UN offices and academic institutes.[61] All of them reckoned on a total well into six digits; most reckoned several hundred thousand.

In May, Madeleine Albright, then US Ambassador to the UN, gave an interview on CBS television that will be well known to anyone at all familiar with the history of British and American policy towards Iraq.

'We have heard that half a million children have died,' said the *60 Minutes* anchor Lesley Stahl. 'I mean, that's more children than died in Hiroshima. And, you know, is the price worth it?'

'We think the price is worth it,' she replied.

Kelly, as far as I could find out, never spoke about the infanticide his inspections helped inflict upon Iraq. When his colleagues did, or his masters, it was only to decry the suffering as Baathist propaganda, or to lay the blame for it wholly on Saddam Hussein, or, contradicting themselves somewhat, both. But whatever they said or thought, Iraq's plight must by now have been obvious to each and every one of them, just as it was becoming obvious to the world at large. Yet still they ploughed on. None of them seemed able or willing to change course now. None of them ever would.

'Quite simply,' explained Charles Duelfer, 'no one really thought the process would go on this long with Saddam still in power.'[62]

After the stunt the Gang of Four had pulled on their last visit, Iraq refused to meet with UNSCOM's biological inspectors. They very nearly pulled out of meetings with its chemical inspectors too. The Commission had declared its monitoring system officially complete, and its chemical, nuclear and missile verifications were effectively completed. Yet there had been no official recognition of any of this, no formal acceptance of any progress on any front whatsoever. The whole affair had reached an impasse, and Iraq's humanitarian crisis seemed never-ending.

Something had to give. At the end of May 1995, Iraq changed tactics. Ekeus and Tariq Aziz, the most senior Iraqi anyone in UNSCOM would meet, held a summit in Baghdad. Barton and Spertzel came along too. According to official UNSCOM pronouncements thus far, the biggest barrier – the real remaining obstacle – to declaring Iraq in compliance with its disarmament obligations was its biological-warfare programme. So the two men struck a deal. When Ekeus delivered his next Security Council report, it would reflect the progress that been made elsewhere. Then Aziz would instruct Taha and her colleagues to tell the Gang of Four whatever they wanted to hear. The Swede agreed.

When he left the Rashid Hotel where the meeting had taken place, he found that a crowd of protesters, including doctors and nurses, had gathered in the reception area. 'The UN kills babies', their signs read. 'Lies, lies, lies,' they chanted. Outside, there was worse to come: angry Iraqi women awaited them with dead or dying babies in their arms. As they quickly piled into their waiting car, one old lady tapped a dry crust of bread on the windscreen.

'This is all we have to eat,' she said.

It was the first of many such demonstrations Kelly and the Gang of Four would face. Back in New York, Ekeus set about his task. Working under a high level of American dominance and no small amount of British influence, he had a tricky job ahead of him. There was no way either country would accept a judgement that Iraq was meeting its disarmament obligations in any of its four WMD fields, so the report required some rather deft composing. The UNSCOM chairman and his biological inspectors spent days on it, crafting ambiguities that would please both sides, producing a document where 'every word could be interpreted as half-full or half-empty', according to Dick Spertzel.[63]

Amongst his other accomplishments, Ekeus was a proficient jazz pianist, and as Charles Duelfer put it, he began to play the Security Council and Iraq like a piano: 'In the June report, he played the notes of a dirge with the lightness of a lullaby.'[64]

Even so, for the US, some of his melody was decidedly off-key, especially after he had hinted in the press that sanctions might be lifted if Iraq would make further disclosures. Before his next trip to Baghdad Madeleine Albright called him into her office at the US Mission opposite the UN headquarters, and issued him with a stark warning, both verbally and in writing.

'I am concerned about your credibility,' her two-page list of 'talking-points' concluded. 'To put it bluntly, the Council will *not* act soon to lift sanctions (unless Iraq quickly reverses its position on issues not related to WMD). If you continue to lean so far forward on this, you put yourself in the position of seeing your advice *ignored* and rebuffed by the council.'[65]

Ekeus had been telling the Iraqis that if they met UNSCOM's demands, he could finally declare them in compliance, and the sanctions would be lifted. It wasn't true. As had now been made painfully clear to him, just as it had been clear to many others from the start, the sanctions had nothing to do with weapons programmes. Did he inform his Iraqi counterparts about all this? It appears not. On his next visit to Baghdad Tariq Aziz, having read his last report, told him that Iraq was prepared to make a biological disclosure.

At the end of the month Ekeus and the Gang of Four checked into the Holiday Inn in Bahrain, as they still did before every inspection. At the CIA's GATEWAY facility, the night before they left for Iraq, Ekeus informed them that on their first morning in-county General Amer Rashid and Dr Rihab Taha would be making a ninety-minute presentation to the headquarters of the Military Industrial Commission. He gave no clues as to what it might contain. For the first time, the inspectors felt a certain air of suspense.

After the usual pre-dawn flight routine, and the drive from Habbaniyah to Baghdad, the eight-person team were led into the conference room at the MIC. The Iraqi delegation and the inspectors sat opposite each other on either side of a long table. Also present, unusually, was Iraq's Deputy Foreign Minister, Riyadh Al

Qaysi. After the briefest of pleasantries, Taha stood up and read robotically from a speech she had clearly been given. Her voice was a hesitant monotone, but her face was tense and taut.

'To clarify the beginning of the biological programme, we state here that the programme began at the end of 1985 at Al Muthanna State Establishment. At the time Dr Rihab Taha was working on biopesticides in the aforementioned establishement.'

The entire script, it turned out, referred to Taha in the third person, and as she read it, Al Qaysi watched her intently.

'In the first quarter of 1988, and after the success of researches in relation to botulinum toxin and anthrax, a decision was adopted to prepare the requirements for producing biological agents.'

Quietly, her husband corrected her. 'Not biological agents,' he said. 'Biological *warfare* agents.'

Taha, repeating his words, went on to explain that large quantities of toxin and anthrax couldn't be made at Salman Pak because the neighbourhood was partly residential. So, as Kelly had always suspected, the desert site at Al Hakum was selected for development, and construction of a new facility began. She described the growth media and fermenters and other equipment that Iraq had imported, or tried to import, and – astonishingly – how from May 1989 onwards, the programme had produced nine thousand litres of botulinum toxin and six hundred litres of anthrax.

'The total batches of production consumed about fifteen tonnes, plus or minus a tonne, of growth media. Due to the threats of bombing in the autumn of 1990, the authorities gave orders to dispose of the biological agents, the biological warfare agents, to avoid contamination of the environment. We destroyed the agents with chemical inactivation and with heat. It took months. By October 1990 everything was clean and we stopped work.'

Taha collapsed in her seat. Iraq had declared having an offensive weapons programme, and of substantial scale. Nine thousand litres of botulinum required fifty-five batches in eight-day cycles, six hundred litres of anthrax took forty. And it had all been produced in little more than a year. The inspectors had little to say. As was now customary in these exchanges, the meeting ended in silence, and everyone filed uneasily out of the room.

By evening, in their quarters at the BMVC, the inspectors had rallied. Given a few hours on their own, they were able to regain their practised posture of antagonistic suspicion. Why hadn't the Iraqis poured these agents into munitions? And why destroy them all just as you were going to war? There was a case they could make there. They could also argue, Spertzel suggested, that given the types of growth media imported, they should have made more anthrax than botulinum.[66] Minus Ekeus, the biological team met with their Iraqi counterparts the next day, to poke holes in their startling and monumental declaration. They opened with the issue of weaponisation.

'We didn't even think about it,' said Taha. 'The programme didn't run long enough to get to that stage. There wasn't enough time.'

'We couldn't have carried on producing and storing bulk agents after the invasion of Kuwait,' her husband added. 'Not when we were facing air strikes. And all we were trying to do until then was prove that we could make these agents in quantity; we never reached the point of weaponisation.'

The inspectors refused to budge from the lines they had worked out the previous day. If the Iraqis were producing agent, they must have at least planned weaponisation, and again, why disarm yourself precisely at the moment you expected conflict? Back to their strident and dismissive selves, the inspectors told them their story made no sense, and that their declaration was untrue. They had mentioned only BW facilities and agents that UNSCOM had openly suspected, and this in itself they considered suspicious. The Iraqis had declared not just an offensive programme but the production of enormous amounts of agents, and the Gang of Four countered the same way they always had: Iraq was holding back.

'I must say now in the strongest of terms,' Spertzel warned them, 'that unless there is a fundamental shift from the present draft of your declaration, it will not be acceptable to us, nor, we believe, the international community.'

By 'international community', Spertzel meant America and its allies, but his point stood. The Gang of Four deemed the declaration untrustworthy, and that made it worthless.

'There should be a confidence and trust between us,' Taha protested. 'If there is no confidence, why all these meetings? Why all these talks?'

Why indeed? Why, in retrospect, had the Iraqis made this declaration at all? Only because of the deal between Ekeus and Aziz, that promised the lifting of sanctions. The Iraqis had only told them what they believed the inspectors wanted to hear.

'You must understand,' Hossam Amin explained to them, 'this is political. It is all political.'[67]

The inspectors returned to New York, Ekeus delivered a letter to the Security Council, and it leaked to the press within hours. At the same time Madeleine Albright issued a State Department press release that expressed exactly the same suspicions Kelly's team had articulated two days ago in Baghdad.

'After admitting that it had lied for four years about production of biological agents, Iraq now wishes us to believe that it never even thought about weaponizing and storing these agents,' said the American Ambassador to the UN. 'Iraq has a problem not only because of its uninterrupted record of lying for four years, but because it has not yet produced a story that is internally consistent.'[68]

The doubts of UNSCOM's biological inspectors and the accusations of the US State Department had now synchronised. They had become one and the same thing. Spertzel led Kelly and the other biological inspectors back to Iraq less than a fortnight later to review Iraq's drafting of Taha's confession into the formal declaration that UNSCOM's procedures required. The day they arrived back in the country was the same day Iraq celebrated the anniversary of the bloodless coup in which the Baath Party took power. That afternoon, as was customary, Saddam would make his National Liberation Day address to the nation. In his speech he announced that if no progress was made in lifting sanctions, Iraq's cooperation with UNSCOM would cease completely (a few days later, on a visit to Cairo, his Foreign Minister supplied a deadline: the end of August, the following month). Saddam told his country, and the world, there was nothing stopping the inspectors from finally declaring Iraq free of WMD. It was a deft piece of timing.

Back in the States, Ekeus still stuck to the cautious optimism which had underpinned his deal with Iraq, even if he now knew that lifting sanctions was beyond his power. He declared he was satisfied with Iraq's statements on its chemical, nuclear and long-range missile programmes, and that only its biological weaponry remained problematic.[69] The world waited to see if the final piece of Iraq's weapons jigsaw would slot into place. But Taha's confession remained unchanged, and the Gang of Four stuck to their guns. UNSCOM had settled into its usual gridlock. Meanwhile, Saddam's deadline was inching nearer. And Iraq blinked first.

Tariq Aziz personally invited Ekeus and his biological inspectors back to Baghdad in mid-August. Kelly and fourteen other team members touched down yet again in Habbaniyah airport, and made what by now was the dreary commute along the highway into the capital. But what they met with in Baghdad was even more extraordinary than Taha's confession.

Instead of the usual faces, Iraq had brought out the big guns. Dr Ahmed Murtada was there, the former director of the Technical Research Centre, and Taha's old boss. After the TRC had been disbanded he had been appointed Minister for Transport and Telecommunications, but was now making a cameo appearance, in his honorary general's uniform, with a view to burying the biological business once and for all. Also present was the similarly titled Lieutenant General Dr Amer Al Saadi. No one in UNSCOM had met Al Saadi before. He was now the scientific adviser to Saddam Hussein, but had been second-in-command at the Military Industrial Commission under Hussein Kamel, who had fled to Jordan earlier in the month (and from where he hoped the US might install him as the new ruler of Baghdad).

Between finger and thumb, Murtada held up by its corner a copy of Iraq's previous declaration and announced it null and void. He said Iraq understood the inspectors' reservations, and would meet them all. Under his supervision and authority, he vouched, Iraq would deal with them all. A full, final and complete disclosure would finally be made. Taha was rolled out again, and Amer Rashid, and no small number of their old colleagues. Taha's husband, and even Tariq Aziz, made frequent appearances to urge the inspectors to ask whatever they wanted. More than once they demanded their interviewers tell them exactly what they wanted to know.

Each and every one of the suspicions the Gang of Four had raised on their last visit was confirmed and admitted to.

The UNSCOM team had said it made no sense to produce biological agents and not put them into weapons. So Taha said they had filled 157 R-400 bombs and 25 Scud warheads. They had also investigated the possibility of using an Iraqi-designed aerosol disperser, spray tanks, and an unmanned drone.

They had said it made no sense for Iraq to destroy its biological weapons just as the country was commiting itself to another war. So Taha said her staff had destroyed the agents and the munitions not in October 1990, as she had previously read out, but in the summer of 1991.

They had said that, based on the growth-media imports, Iraq should have made more anthrax. So Taha said Iraq had produced not six hundred litres but eight and a half thousand, and she raised the production output of botulinum toxin from nine thousand litres to nineteen.

They had complained because Iraq had declared working only on the agents that UNSCOM already suspected were part of its programme. So Taha said Iraq had also made over two thousand litres of aflatoxin, and researched the potential of using ricin, mycotoxins, *Clostridium perfringens*, various viruses and wheat smut (to use against crops).

Similarly, they were unhappy that Iraq had confirmed BW activity solely at the sites UNSCOM had already flagged. So Taha said they had made botulinum toxin at the foot-and-mouth vaccine plant in Al Daura, which they had converted to peaceful purposes after the fact.

These were the most incredible admissions. They remain, literally, unbelievable.

'I'm sure those people didn't tell us everything because they were scared,' Ekeus later said. 'The whole episode had an atmosphere almost of panic. People have forgotten the systematic and fantastic lying by the top Iraqi leaders.'[70]

Other inspectors would say much the same thing. Even after this tsunami of disclosure, inconsistencies were poked at, the lack of supporting documentary evidence was cited, and the absence of corroborating employee testimony observed. Doubts were understandable. But fixed by policy, and perhaps by their own personalities, in a permanent state of accusation, they could only (and endlessly) maintain that their doubts reflected a hidden threat. None of them has ever publicly considered that, desperate to escape from under the crippling imposition of sanctions, the Iraqis were not holding back, but quite the opposite: they were making things up. Whatever it was they thought Kelly and his colleagues needed to hear, they told them, and then some more.

The R-400 bombs were designed for chemical weapons, not germ warfare. The Iraqis had made no alterations to their design for biological use. Had they filled some with agents? Perhaps. Had they really filled almost two hundred? There has never been any objective evidence to prove it. The Scud warheads were also entirely unchanged from the chemical prototypes. They were crude aluminium buckets that held 150 litres, of extremely debatable effectiveness, and none had ever been used. To employ these warheads as delivery vehicles for bacteria would have been even stupider than filling them with gas. Bacteria are, after all, living things. In explosive munitions, less than 4 per cent of a biological payload survives, and often much less: as little as one-tenth of a percent, according to one report.[71] Pouring anthrax into a metal cone, which you then smash into the ground at something approaching or over the speed of sound and with several tonnes of rocket behind it, is not the most practical way to infect your enemies. You would probably do more damage if you filled the warhead with concrete (which, oddly enough, was exactly what some of the Gulf War Scuds Iraq fired into Israel were carrying).[72]

Iraq's production levels in Taha's weird third-person confession were pretty high, but her new and improved figures were astronomical. Was there ever any corroborating evidence – any at all? UNSCOM, and Kelly himself, later did some minor sampling at a few sites, and traces of anthrax were detected. It seems they *had* made some. But eight and a half thousand litres of ten-times concentrated anthrax in eleven months? The US army had made its anthrax at Pine Bluff Arsenal in Arkansas, the decommissioned site Kelly had visited with the Soviets during the trilateral inspections. It absolutely dwarfed Al Hakum, and at its height, before Nixon dropped BW, its former project engineer Bill Patrick has said, if they managed to turn out a tonne it was a good year.[73] That was the result of a lavishly funded programme of thirty years' maturity. Taha, a plant pathologist from the University of East Anglia, claimed to have thrashed this record in the first production run of a programme started from scratch in a country under considerable import restraints. And nobody at UNSCOM batted an eyelid. It was, after all, exactly what they wanted to hear.

Had Iraq really made five thousand litres of botulinum toxin at the foot-and-mouth vaccine plant? UNSCOM inspectors, Kelly included – some of the most suspicious men and women to have ever visited Iraq – had examined the facility on numerous occasions, and not once had they seen any sign of BW production.

UNMOVIC had never found any definitive proof that botulinum had been made here.[74] This was the facility overseen by Dr Hazem Ali, the biologist who gained his doctorate from Newcastle University, where Professor Geoff Toms still remembers him. 'His PhD was in breastfeeding in guinea-pigs,' he told me. 'Not really the best preparation for a career in biological weapons.'

Some viral research might have been done there, but not very much, and the three viruses Iraq declared working on that August were all non-lethal. Aflatoxin is non-lethal too, unless you wait ten years or so. It's a carcinogen sometimes naturally present in grain dust, and if you sucked in enough of it you might one day develop tumours in your liver and your lung. The Iraqis now said they had made it at the Centre for Agriculture and Water Resources at Al Fudaliyah, in the outer suburbs of Baghdad, another laboratory that had been closely scrutinised by UNSCOM and declared bereft of any BW signature. Did the Iraqi biological warfare programme really brew up nearly two thousand litres there? Maybe. The real question is why they would want to.

'This was weird,' Ekeus's deputy Charles Duelfer later admitted. 'Exposure to aflatoxin may prevent a lieutenant from ever becoming a colonel, but there was no obvious military rationale for this agent.'[75]

Weirder still, and surely strange enough to show where these new Iraqi admissions were coming from, was the disclosure that they had put this aflatoxin into Scud warheads. The Iraqi aflatoxin Scud is probably the most pointless weapon ever conceived in the history of warfare. At great expense it would deliver its carefully created payload to within half a kilometre of target, where it would destroy practically all of it on impact. Anyone unlucky enough to be at the crash site, and unlucky enough, again, to inhale the minuscule portion of payload that arrived intact, would find they had a statistically increased chance of needing cancer treatment in about ten years' time. Rather than firing that missile from a launcher, you would do more damage rolling it down a hill. Some inspectors advanced that it was intended to commit genocide against the Kurds, at which point we finally leave worst-case scenarios behind and enter a mindset that can be explained only as outright propaganda or personal obsession.

On Kelly's next trip, the inspectors quizzed the Iraqis about it.

'Are you sure you filled seven of these warheads with aflatoxin?' one asked. 'It would make more sense to use anthrax or botulinum.'

'Put down whatever you like,' said Rashid. 'It makes no difference to us.'

In the end UNSCOM settled for two, and it did make no difference to the Iraqis. Whatever they admitted to; whatever they made up; whatever they were holding back – in the now unlikely event they were holding back anything at all – was purely historical. Iraq's biological weapons had been destroyed before Kelly or any of his team-mates had first set foot in the country, and the facilities that had made the required agents had all been converted to peaceful use. Not that any of this would matter.

Another oddity was the appearance of General Faiz Al Shahine, the former head of the chemical programme, who brought with him one General Hatham El. El told Kelly about some tests that had been done in the late eighties on a defensive 'dirty bomb', using material irradiated at one of Iraq's test reactors. The tests had been considered unsuccessful (after four days the bomb's radioactivity dropped below harmful levels), and further research had been axed. Properly, this admission should have been made to the IAEA, not to an UNSCOM biological team, and it's impossible to understand it without accepting that these declarations were Iraq's desperate last-ditch attempt to appease the Commission before Saddam's end-of-August deadline.

'We wanted to explain everything,' Shahine told them, 'no matter how small they may be [sic].'[76]

Clearly, Shahine believed there was still a deal of some sort on the table.

Before Ekeus left Iraq, there was one more surprise in store. He had complained about the lack of any supporting documents, and at Habbaniyah airport, as he was about to board the plane back to Bahrain, a breathless Hossam Amin caught up with him.

'Mr Ekeus,' he gasped, 'we have the archives for you. All of them. Everything. You must come with me to see them.'

Ekeus was apparently not too keen to accompany him. He was looking forward to the comforts of Manhattan, but Amin convinced him.

'The mistress of the traitor Hussein Kamel has informed us where he hid the records,' he explained. 'Please come.'

This was itself probably something of a lie. Ever since Kamel had fled to Jordan and declared himself a rival to the regime, Iraq had been keen to vilify him, which they did in part by shifting the blame for their failure to placate UNSCOM onto his shoulders. His name had come up repeatedly over the last week. But ruse or not, there were four trunks of documents awaiting him in the warehouse at a place called Haidar Farm, each of them filled with material relating to Iraq's WMD programmes, and all of it authentic. The documents amounted to roughly a million and a half pages, and they were complemented with videos and photographs. Before the Iraqis might change their minds, UNSCOM staff speeded the cache back to their headquarters in Baghdad, and Ekeus went off to catch his plane.

The documents were later removed from Iraq, and after American intelligence had had a good look at them, deposited at the UNSCOM offices in Manhattan. Iraq took no copies of any of these documents; it was a complete submission. When they discovered the inspections would still drag on, for three more years, they regretted their naivety. They had to answer continued questioning without access to the records, which the Commission cynically refused to provide.[77] The missing paperwork made it almost impossible for the Iraqis to verify or substantiate their answers to some of UNSCOM's questions, and whenever this happened they were accused of non-cooperation. Conversely, in instances where the Iraqis might have been able to refer to written records, they were doubtless dissuaded from doing so by UNSCOM's now frequent assertions that the mere existence of a document – the inspectors turned up a few – constituted part of a hidden programme.

'We just could not get a consistent story,' Kelly later complained.[78] In retrospect, this isn't at all surprising.

Later that month the CIA granted Rolf Ekeus an hour-long interview with Hussein Kamel. The UNSCOM chair arrived in Jordan with Maurizio Ziffero, Hans Blix's deputy at the IAEA, and his chief missile inspector Nikita Smidovich ('that Americanised Russian', as Tariq Aziz privately referred to him), the former Soviet weapons expert who had transplanted himself to the United States.

The discussion they had with Kamel was wide-ranging, but the most central, most important, assertion made by the head of Iraq's WMD programmes was that each of them had been abandoned, and their proscribed arsenal destroyed, by the summer of 1991. He said the same thing to MI6 and the CIA. And, given his position, Kamel was not a man inclined to paint Saddam's rule in a positive light.

'I ordered destruction of all chemical weapons,' he told Ekeus. 'All weapons, biological, chemical, missile, nuclear, were destroyed.'

It was a blunt statement, and Ekeus and UNSCOM buried it deep. The world would not get to hear it for another eight years, until *Newsweek* obtained a transcript of the interview.[79] In the meantime, UNSCOM, George Bush, Tony Blair, Dick Cheney, Donald Rumsfeld, Colin Powell and others with 'privileged access' would all allege Kamel's classified interview proved the opposite: that Iraq was a duplicitous enemy whose programmes and weapons were expertly concealed.

It was the truth that was hidden.

When Ekeus came to deliver his next biannual report to the Security Council, he effectively reset the inspection process back to square one. Everything Iraq had told Kelly that August was considered not the end, but another beginning. After withholding such information for so long, it was assumed there must be

more to come. Its disclosures were considered not confessions but
dishonesty, and behind that lay more weapons, more agents, more
secrets.

The inspectors set about chasing them.

Kelly, it must be said, was not in the vanguard of this. The
inspections he led were largely technical, and none seem particularly confrontational. At a patch of desert north of Al Hakum,
where the Iraqis said they had dumped their deactivated anthrax,
he excavated and sampled the soil for verification. It was a job very
similar to the work he had done on Gruinard, and on exactly the
same strain that was used there. It would have been well within his
capabilities to estimate just how much anthrax had been disposed
of (UNMOVIC would do exactly that[80]), but he seems only to
have checked that it was present. Had the anthrax not been there,
it would have contributed a strong bullet point to the next
Security Council report. Instead, Kelly's survey never appeared in
a report at all, although it confirmed the Iraqis' account. The same
went for the sampling tests he conducted on the equipment at Al
Hakum, the soil at Salman Pak, and the soil underneath Taha's lab
at Al Muthanna, all of which proved pathogen-negative. This
seems to have been the rule for Kelly's biological sampling, and for
the Gang of Four as a whole: when it proved the Iraqis right, you
never mentioned it, and when you thought it *might* prove them
right, you didn't do it in the first place.

When Kelly and Killip were taken to a range where the Iraqis
had done static testing on botulinum-filled bombs they declined
to take samples, apparently because Killip said he didn't think it
looked like a test site. When Kelly was shown where animal test
subjects were buried at Salman Pak, the sheep and donkeys that
Taha had used in her experiments, he called off the dig, supposedly because he thought it would be too difficult to find them.
When UNSCOM began inspecting 'presidential sites', where
nuclear and chemical sampling were both carried out, the Gang of
Four refused to run tests. Dick Spertzel privately told the inspector
in charge he didn't think biological weapons had been anywhere

near them, and he didn't want to give the Iraqis the benefit of a negative reading.[81]

Although he still carried the same knowledge and used the same tools, it all reveals a Kelly who had ceased to be a scientist entirely. His days in Leeds and Birmingham and Warwick and Oxford were a long, long way behind him.

Other inspectors eschewed such selectivity and took the straight line to goal. With Ekeus's permission Scott Ritter began 'Operation Shake the Tree', a deliberately provocative series of inspections that dealt with Iraq's 'concealment mechanism'. Now that Iraq had officially declared everything but the kitchen sink, Ritter abandoned the search for hidden weapons and secret programmes and merely strove to prove Iraq was hiding things. Anything. Which wasn't hard: American, British and Australian inspectors could simply turn up at presidential offices and sensitive ministries and would, inevitably, be turned away. Each time this happened it was counted as a kind of victory. The Commission's reports could make continued complaints about Iraq's lack of cooperation.

'I am the alpha dog' was how Ritter explained Shake the Tree to his team.[82] 'I'm going in tail held high. If they growl at me, I'm going to jump on them, I'm going to let them know who the boss is here. I'm in charge. They report to me, they do what I say. You work for me, so every one of you are alpha dogs. When you go to a site, they're going to know we're there, we're going to raise our tails and we're going to spray urine all over their walls, that's the equivalent of what we're doing. So when we leave a site they know they've been inspected.'

Doubtless Kelly was grateful not to be involved, but hundreds were. The country was now flooded with inspectors, and every year saw more inspections than the year before. The next February, Hussein Kamel, apparently despondent at the lack of American support for his cause, returned to Baghdad.

'He was just an idiot,' said one of his CIA handlers. 'His plan was that he would return to Baghdad behind the US Army and Air Force. End of subject.'[83]

Instead he drove back in his own Mercedes, was divorced by his wife, then shot by his cousins in his own home to avenge the shame he had brought on his clan.

Gabriele Kraatz–Wadsack revisited Al Hakum and the foot-and-mouth vaccine plant at Al Daura and sealed them off with tamper-proof tape. At UNSCOM's request, Iraq ceased all activity at both. What next? The biological inspectors were split. Ekeus spoke to the UNSCOM lawyer, a Briton called John Scott, who said that as Iraq had not initially disclosed Al Hakum as a bioweapons facility, they could demolish it. The Iraqis protested, but the Commission's authority was absolute. When they discovered the building could not be saved they asked if they could transfer some of the equipment to other sites, but that too was denied them.

Under the terms of the binding UN resolution, Iraq had to provide the explosives and the labourers needed to perform the task, and that summer Terry Taylor, the former British infantry colonel, arrived at Al Hakum to supervise the demolition. He was continually pestered by sanctions-starved Iraqis desperate to reclaim anything of value. The toilet bowls were particularly sought after, but they were the toilet bowls of a former germ warfare factory, and so they had to go. Everything went. Taylor started with Al Hakum's animal house, which had always been totally unrelated to agent production, just to make clear the destruction would be total.

In creaking post-Soviet Russia, the Biopreparat labs that Kelly had spent months studying were now receiving American subsidy. Under the Nunn–Lugar Act, the very facilities he had inspected and fretted over were being paid millions of dollars to ensure their conversion to purely peaceful work (and to make sure the scientists who worked inside them wouldn't crop up in places like Iran, with heads full of dark knowledge and suitcases full of schematics). Almost fifty of Russia's former BW laboratories received this money, and the sites that it refused to release from military activity were offered funds to improve their security.[84] So as to increase the size of their handouts, some lab directors would play up the possibility that their staff might elope, and there were rumours that the generals at the top were skimming off funds for themselves. But overall, the policy was considered a great success.

Sam Nunn, the Georgia Senator who was the Act's co-author, called it the agreement of the century. At Al Hakum, south of the Euphrates, Iraq had dedicated its sole bioweapons plant to peaceful purposes over five years earlier, entirely unaided, and before the Special Commission had even turned up. The site had been the subject of constant monitoring and countless inspections ever since, it was unsuited to weapons production in the future, and there was never the slightest doubt it had ever done anything other than what the Iraqis had said it was doing since their initial declaration: manufacturing biopesticide and animal feed to help provide for a blockaded people. And with the blessing of his masters, Kelly's British UNSCOM colleague razed it to the ground, and left it as a patch of sand.

'Mister Duelfer,' Amer Rashid later asked, 'why do you always blow up buildings?'

'It's in our genes,' he explained. 'We're Americans, that's what we do. We blow up buildings.'

Duelfer said he was being facetious, but later conceded that 'it was a fascinating question'.[85]

In truth, the demolition of Al Hakum gives a glimpse of the madness that had become the Commission's institutional mindset, an attitude that reflected only the British and American governments from which it drew its staff and its support. If their outlook can be explained at all, it is a symptom of a suppressed and frustrated desire for war. America had already bombed Iraq again that January, again with no clear authorisation from the Security Council, for taking sides in the Kurdish civil war. Tellingly, none of America's allies in the Gulf, except for Kuwait, had been willing to let the US Air Force use their territory for the mission.[86] It's stated purpose was to destroy Saddam's capability to threaten his neighbours and his own people, as Clinton described it, but it targeted only air defence systems in southern Iraq. None had fired at a plane since Schwarzkopf's Safwan ceasefire in 1991. When Turkey invaded Kurdistan, which it did three times that decade, America and Britain offered no response.[87]

The same summer that Taylor demolished Al Hakum, the CIA launched the Baghdad coup attempt it had been planning ever since the leadership of its Near East Division had passed from Frank Anderson, who had always been pessimistic about toppling Saddam, to Steve Richter. An intimidating and turfish officer, Richter had already courted Agency controversy earlier in his career, when his thirty-strong Iranian spy network got rounded up by Tehran.[88] His 'silver bullet' plans for Baghdad ended even more dismally.

DBACHILLES, as it was codenamed, hoped to turn the leadership of the Iraqi military against Saddam. It relied partly on MI6's Great White Hope, Iyad Allawi, and his Iraqi National Accord, together with a defected Iraqi general called Mohammed Abdullah al-Shawani, who had commanded the Iraqi Special Forces helicopter unit. As a younger man, he had received training from the US Army Ranger School. Crucially, Shawani had three sons still serving as officers in the Iraqi Republican Guard in Baghdad, and who could move freely around the capital.

In February, Allawi opened the INA headquarters in Amman, and practically outlined the coup's concept in a press conference.

'We think that any uprising should have at least at its very centre the armed forces,' he said.[89] 'We don't preach civil war. On the contrary, we preach controlled, coordinated military uprising, supported by the people, that would not allow itself to go into acts of revenge or chaos.'

It was the Western spook's age-old dream. Hussein Kamel made his suicidal return to Iraq a few days later. Whether he was really frozen out of the coup, or lured deep inside it, remains unknown.

The week before the coup was scheduled to take place UNSCOM inspected Special Republican Guard barracks around Baghdad. The team included nine CIA paramilitaries and a number of British SAS, and they were refused entry at almost every site they visited. It's impossible to say what WMD intelligence they thought they were after, or what their true purpose was, but it was undoubtedly related in some way to the scheme hatched in Amman.

How badly the coup failed remains unknown, but Richter's silver bullet certainly missed its target. The third battalion of the Special Republican Guard got into a firefight somewhere, and the outfit was later disbanded: Ritter recounts how on CIA advice its barracks was taken off the first inspection list. When he visited on subsequent inspection, he discovered their armoured Mercedes were riddled with bullet holes. Photos of the cars were later leaked to the press. I can remember poring over them, and even as an uninformed teenager it struck me that the papers were reporting on events they had no idea about, using sources they knew were not telling the truth. In the meantime, hundreds of officers had been arrested, and over eighty were executed, including Shawani's three sons.

In the aftermath, recriminations were rife. Some in the CIA blamed UNSCOM, others blamed Allawi's rival, Ahmed Chalabi, claiming that he had tipped off Baghdad. Chalabi, another Langley favourite, had established a power base in northern Iraq, where he was assisted by officers like Rick Francona, who had dropped his UNSCOM inspector persona to provide full-time insurrectionary assistance.[90] He had led his own doomed uprising earlier in the year, but unable to overcome Kurdish factionalism, or win American air support, it too had come to a bloody end. Washington had fired up and then let down the Kurds for the third time since the mid-seventies.

'Covert action should not be confused with missionary work,' Kissinger later explained. The Agency's covert action in Iraq had now achieved two Bay of Pigs-scale disasters in the same year.

This was the nature of the Special Commission that Kelly now worked for. SAS troops and CIA officers would regularly appear on the duty roster, and no one asked who they were, why they were there, or what they were doing. Nobody peered too closely at their luggage, or the equipment they installed. Kelly never spoke once about Richter's coup, as far as I'm aware, although he was in Iraq the same month, just as he was the month before, and the month after.

The biological inspections, another forty of them, continued, finding little but making loud noises.

The next year Terry Taylor led an inspection that called on the University of Baghdad. There, in a lecturer's office, he found a folder of papers, seven years old at least, about some studies on ricin. These belonged to Professor Shakir Al Akidy, who had once worked in the Public Health Laboratory Service at Porton Down. 'UN Discovers Banned Arms in Baghdad', ran a typical headline. 'Terry Taylor said his team uncovered an advanced biological weapons programme which the Iraqis had previously only hinted at.'[91]

When UNMOVIC came to investigate, they found nothing to suggest that Taha's original ricin declaration was anything other than complete.[92] The Iraqis had made ten litres of it at Salman Pak, tried it out in static tests with four artillery shells, and given up, because the agent was useless. The documents UNSCOM had been given at Haidar Farm corroborated the fact.[93] Whatever UNSCOM claimed to have uncovered at the University of Baghdad, it was discounted by UNMOVIC, the organisation that came after it. It's not clear whether Akidy's papers were even passed on to them. And it is probably no accident that Taylor's press briefing coincided with UNSCOM's biannual report to the Security Council, where France, China and Russia were still arguing for a lifting of sanctions.

Taylor's ricin story is a typical example, one of many, of what the Commission's relationship with the media had become. There was a dubious VX-gas analysis that was leaked to the press (an American lab found traces of it on a missile fragment, French and Swiss laboratories found none).[94] There were bomb-damaged mustard-gas shells that had been tagged by UNSCOM in its first year and then 'rediscovered' as a 'material breach' in its last.[95] A food-testing kit was found in a security office and held as evidence of a hidden biological programme simply because it was designed to detect pathogens.[96] And on top of all this were the stories from a string of dubious defectors, most of which came through Ahmed Chalabi, who had received tens of millions of dollars from the CIA to invest in anti-Saddam propaganda.[97] The Chalabi material was too flaky for UNSCOM to report, but they happily justified inspections off the back of it, and the claims found their way into the press anyway, through other channels.

Inspectors sometimes complained of an 'anti-UNSCOM industry' inside Iraq, but this was dwarfed by the scale of the anti-Iraq industry outside it. The Commission played its part in this, as did a cast of thousands, a credulous news-hungry media included, and to check and cross-reference all they said is to swim against the pull of a mighty tide, one that has held sway for years. The days and nights I spent ploughing through all this bred something like resentment, and in the early hours of the morning, bitterness. Public opinion feeds not on accuracy but on volume, on quantity over quality, and these are bad odds for any author.

Rolf Ekeus quit his post as UNSCOM chairman a few weeks after Taylor's ricin interviews. On his visits to Baghdad he was now encountering not just Iraqi protesters but American ones as well. At the BMVC building, space was also given to the various UN aid agencies which were trying to relieve the effects of the sanctions that his inspectorate was helping Britain and America to sustain, and the atmosphere there had become one of animosity too. The UNSCOM inspectors had their own gym, sealed off the bar whenever they drank there, and generally strutted around with an air of belligerent machismo (although not Kelly, one imagines). The relief workers had their own nickname for the Special Commission: UNSCUM. Denis Halliday, the first UN Humanitarian Coordinator in Iraq, resigned in despair.

'I often have to explain why I resigned from the United Nations after a thirty-year career,' he said some years afterwards. 'In reality there was no choice. You all would have done the same had you been occupying my seat as head of the UN Humanitarian Programme in Iraq.

'I was driven to resignation because I refused to continue to take Security Council orders, the same Security Council that had imposed and sustained genocidal sanctions on the innocent of Iraq. I did not want to be complicit. I wanted to be free to speak out publicly about this crime. And above all, my innate sense of justice was and still is outraged by the violence that UN sanctions have brought upon the lives of children, families, the extended families, the loved ones of Iraq.

'There is no justification for killing the young people of Iraq, not the aged, not the sick, not the rich, not the poor. Some will tell you that the leadership is punishing the Iraqi people. That is not my perception, or experience from living in Baghdad. And were that to be the case, how can that possibly justify further punishment, in fact collective punishment by the United Nations? I don't think so. And international law has no provision for the disproportionate and murderous consequences of the ongoing UN embargo.'[98]

In his own resignation speech, Ekeus did comment briefly on the iniquity of sanctions, but afterwards he continued to issue on-message warnings about Iraqi WMDs. 'Saddam will get a bomb, because these materials are floating in,' he told the investigative journalist Seymour Hersh. 'Every day, they are more advanced.'[99]

That was after six years as chairman of UNSCOM, during which he found no weapons, no programmes, and no imported weapon materials. For his services to UNSCOM and America, Rolf Ekeus, until then only a Swedish disarmament official, was appointed as Sweden's Ambassador to the United States, the most prestigious posting a diplomat could hope for.

He was replaced by the Australian Richard Butler, appointed at American insistence and largely against the wishes of his own government.[100] He would prove one of the least diplomatic diplomats of modern times, although he began neutrally enough. In his first meetings with Tariq Aziz, the inspectors were dismayed at his lack of hostility. So his American deputy slipped him 'a pointed note' – 'the guys on the other side of the table have directly or indirectly killed lots of people'.

'You have to grab them by the throat and feel the pulse of the carotid artery under your thumb. Apply pressure and don't let go,' Duelfer advised him.[101] He commented later: 'Whatever he may have first thought, it did not take him long to become very antagonistic.'

Other, more senior Americans privately gave him similar briefings when he returned to New York. From then on, Butler sang in tune, and never ceased to describe the Iraqis he dealt with as vile, murderous liars bent on death and destruction. He was rebuked by Kofi Annan for his language, but the Secretary General was powerless when it came to the Special Commission.

'I know what these bastards are like,' went a typical Butler interview.[102] 'We've got to win.'

The press ate him up, but it was never clear what winning looked like to Richard Butler, unless of course it was regime change in Baghdad. By the time he delivered his first Security Council report, he was unequivocal. It was as if Ekeus's six years had never happened.

'The Commission is convinced of the need for the Council to insist that Iraq meet its obligation to disclose fully all of its prohibited weapons systems and associated programmes,' it read.[103] In particular, Butler complained that Iraq had failed to 'give a remotely credible account' of its biological weapons. He then, again at American instigation, and based on what intelligence God only knows, demanded access to what Iraq called its 'presidential sites'. These have been misreported in the press as a series of opulent palaces that Saddam had built to indulge himself at the expense of his people, but in fact they were the administrative centres of the Baathist regime, where officials met, policy was thrashed out, and personnel files were kept. Some of the buildings inside them were grandiose, but as a matter of course they were also well guarded and deeply sensitive. Butler insisted that his inspection teams, with their usual cobweb of hidden agendas, fake identities and mysterious equipment, be allowed inside each one.

'Sanctions will be there until the end of time,' said Bill Clinton, as if there was any doubt, 'or as long as Saddam lasts.'[104]

If it was not obvious enough already, to Kelly and the world, it was further and final proof that the sanctions were not about disarmament. And by now, neither was UNSCOM.

'UNSCOM never wanted to inspect these Presidential sites,' said inspector Chris Cobb-Smith, a former Royal Marine. 'I don't believe anyone in UNSCOM actually believed there were going to be weapons of mass destruction hidden in any of these compounds, but UNSCOM were driven to exercise their right to go anywhere and inspect anything and therefore the decision was made.'[105]

This tactic might have kept Iraq in non-compliance for as long as the regime endured, despite the personal intervention of Kofi Annan. As policies go it could have rolled along for years, had external events not spun the political compass off course.

Bill Clinton fucked a 22-year-old White House intern from Southern California in the Oval Office. Scenting an enemy with extramarital predilections, Republicans and journalists had long been searching for scandal, and when Monica Lewinsky confided about the relationship to Linda Tripp (a former army intelligence secretary, as it happens), her friend taped the phone call and forwarded it to Special Prosecutor Kenneth Starr. Starr was already conducting a lawsuit for Paula Jones, an Arkansas state employee who may or may not have had sex with Clinton six years previously, and was suing him for sexual harassment. Paula Jones's case was settled out of court, but not before Clinton had submitted a written deposition in which he denied having sex with Lewinsky, which meant Starr could go after him for perjury. The Senate refused to convict, but a judge later found the President in contempt of court, and the Republicans began making moves to impeach. After Clinton was subpoenaed to appear before a grand jury, Butler's inspections began to get even more aggressive.

Scott Ritter, the most hardline inspector of all, was chosen to lead an inspection of the Iraqi Ministry of Defence. Butler told him that under instruction from Clinton's National Security Advisor, Sandy Berger, the timetable had been 'accelerated'.

'Using a marker on the easel,' Ritter wrote, 'Butler drew a chart on the whiteboard listing two timelines. One he labelled "inspection", the other "military action".' Down the side of the board he wrote out the dates in March from the 1st to the 15th. Butler circled the number 8. 'We have to have a crisis by this date,' he said, tapping the board with his pen, 'so that the US can complete its bombing campaign by this date', his pen moving to the number 15. 'I have been told that the US has a bombing campaign which needs to be completed in time for the Muslim religious holiday that begins on the 15th of March.'[106] Ritter was told the same thing by Jim Steinberg, Berger's deputy.

When his team arrived in Baghdad, they found it full of Australian SAS and a US Delta Force commando wearing a secret homing beacon. In Kuwait, a helicopter rescue team was put on standby. In Bahrain, the US Fifth Fleet waited for action. And then something unexpected happened. The Iraqis let them in. The inspectors found nothing, and the cruise missiles of Admiral Fargo's Fifth Fleet remained in their launch tubes.

Four days later, Clinton escaped testifying before Starr's grand jury by invoking executive privilege, without the distraction of military action in the Middle East. Ritter's security clearance was revoked, the CIA ceased cooperating with him, asked other intelligence agencies to do the same, and Butler took him off chief-inspector duties. His bids for further inspections of Iraq's 'concealment strategy' fell on stony ears. He resigned later that year, citing lack of support in the Security Council in forcing Iraq to comply with its obligations to prove it had disarmed. Almost immediately he began telling journalists that UNSCOM had been 'captured' by American intelligence.

Britain had clearly been expecting a crisis too. Before Ritter had returned from Baghdad, the Home Office put out an all-ports alert to Customs, Special Branch and the Ministry of Defence, warning that Iraqi agents might try to smuggle anthrax into the country by disguising it as harmless liquids. It was the first time any country in the world had been put under nationwide alert of biological attack, and inevitably, it leaked to the media.

'Saddam's anthrax in our duty frees!' screamed the *Sun*, which broke the story, promptly doing the job expected of it. 'One sniff and you're dead in four days. Saddam could kill the world! Before long, the boil on the world's backside must be lanced. Before its poison spreads too far.'[107]

The story was published by every other major British paper the same day. Jack Straw told the Commons his Home Office had acted on 'specific intelligence', shamefully leaving his junior minister to backtrack for him.

'It is important that we should not take this threat lightly,' said Michael O'Brien QC on BBC Radio. 'But at the same time, it is important to avoid scaremongering. And I do not think there is any likelihood that Saddam or Saddam's agents would put the anthrax in duty-frees in the vague hope some tourist would pick it up. I do not think that is practical.'

Had Ritter done what his masters asked of him, the story could probably have been left to stand, but duty-free was not the only focus of Britain's propaganda drive. In the weeks before he left for Iraq, lobby correspondents in Westminster received a briefing paper put together by the Joint Intelligence Committee and MI6 describing the brutality and corruption of the Baathist leadership. And not content to leave propaganda solely to the spooks, Downing Street had put out its own line too. A media press release issued by Alastair Campbell's office ranted: 'UNSCOM has found a HUGE arsenal, including a factory to produce 50,000 litres of anthrax and botulinum. UNSCOM has so far not been able to account for seventeen tonnes of media for biological weapons agents, enough to produce more than THREE TIMES the amount of anthrax Iraq ADMITS it had.'[108]

The figures were meaningless and the intention was clear. It was all a portent of what would come, five years hence.

Although Ritter had dropped the ball in Baghdad, inspections of the same tenor continued throughout the year. At the same time, the US military began Operation Desert Thunder, a build-up of air, land and sea forces in the Persian Gulf. Under its new Prime Minister Tony Blair, Britain's contribution included its light-aircraft carriers HMS *Invincible* and HMS *Illustrious*. It became clear to many diplomats that military action was all but inevitable.

The first flare-up came in November 1998, after the US Congress passed the Iraqi Liberation Act, which turned America's seven-year covert campaign against Saddam into an acknowledged legal obligation. Without informing the Security Council, Butler withdrew his inspectors, citing non-cooperation. Iraq's tolerance of UNSCOM had been diminishing since August, but when the Act became law it banned no-notice inspections. Earlier that same day the British Foreign Office had already proposed to the Security Council that sanctions could continue regardless of Iraqi disarmament.

With Kelly and all of his colleagues out of Iraq, Kofi Annan visited Baghdad in his second attempt to diffuse the mounting tension. At his encouragement, the government yielded, and said it would revert to the 'Sensitive Site Modalities', an agreement that had been struck at Annan's instigation earlier in the year to escape bombing over the presidential sites. It stipulated that Iraq would let inspectors visit government buildings if they gave notice and brought a team of international observers with them. That UNSCOM now needed a team of international observers gives some idea how far detached from the international community it had become (the IAEA, in contrast, was conducting its inspections without difficulty).

So Kelly and the other inspectors went back in. But at Butler's instructions, chief inspector Roger Hill told the Iraqis that the Sensitive Site Modalities agreement no longer applied, and would not be honoured. The Security Council was not informed of this, although America almost certainly knew, and had probably encouraged it. Hill now insisted on immediate, unconditional, unrestricted access to anywhere he wanted to go. 'And on that basis,' he said, 'I started my inspection programme.'[109]

Hill's team then appeared outside the Baath Party headquarters, was denied access for two hours, and went back to the BMVC, at which point every UNSCOM member in Iraq abruptly pulled out of the country.

'There was no contact between UNSCOM and the rest of the UN community,' said Hans von Sponeck, Halliday's replacement as Humanitarian Coordinator. 'One can only wonder why UNSCOM staff were singled out by the US government for "early" protection. Only in a later "advisory" were Secretary-General Kofi Annan's office and the UN Security Coordinator in New York encouraged by US authorities to evacuate the "other" staff.'[110]

When the Secretary General was informed that the Special Commission had withdrawn, he ordered a partial evacuation of the other agencies; while the inspectors were flown out to the CIA station in Bahrain on a military transport, everyone else had to get on coaches to Amman.

That afternoon, Butler gave his report to the Security Council, having already discussed its content in substance with Sandy Berger, the US National Security Advisor, and with Peter Burleigh, the new US Ambassador to the United Nations.[111] As the Australian began to regale the Council with his all-too-familiar tale of Iraqi intransigence, mobile phones started going off: the bombers were leaving their bases. Operation Desert Fox had begun. The meeting was cancelled.

The House of Representatives was scheduled to begin its vote on Clinton's impeachment the following day.

In the BMVC at Baghdad, abandoned by Richard Butler and Roger Hill and David Kelly and every other member of the Special Commission, four hundred and fifty UN employees lay prone on foam mats as the air campaign commenced. It lasted for three wall-shaking, window-shattering days.

And in the media, the spin-machine went into top gear. 'UN

weapons inspectors have concluded that Iraq could be hiding two to five times more deadly germ agents than it had admitted to making, as well as warheads to deliver them,' reported Judith Miller.[112] Such a conclusion was never formally stated, was entirely unjustified, and utterly untrue. Which of UNSCOM's biological inspectors spoke to her is unknown, but Kelly was one of Miller's contacts.

And he was the sole named source in a piece by Nick Rufford for the *Sunday Times*, which proclaimed, outrageously, that 'Saddam Hussein built and tested a doomsday weapon designed to mimic the effects of the Chernobyl disaster.' At first glance this seems like blatant disinformation, but the journalistic compulsion to puff up your own story should not be discounted, and anyway, Kelly was subtler than that. He had by then conducted hundreds of intelligence interviews, had received training from MI6, the DIS, the FBI and CID. Everything within Rufford's article's quotation marks was probably true – everything else, I suspect, was an impression Kelly managed to give without lying once.

When Kelly was up before the Foreign Affairs Select Committee during the Hutton Inquiry, the day before his death, the Tory MP John Maples called him out on this story, in which Rufford had reported that the Iraqi Supergun was designed to fire 'radiation bombs that could spread a cloud of lethal zirconium dust over Middle Eastern cities'. Most of Iraq's zirconium had already been removed, Rufford wrote, but 'some may have been stolen from the Chernobyl reactor'. Evidence for this is nonexistent. The Supergun was designed to launch satellites, and its construction had been stopped in its very early stages by the assassination of its inventor.

'Is it true, that they invented a radiological weapon?' Maples asked him.

'Undoubtedly it is true.'

Kelly was a percentages man, someone who stated things as probabilities. Nothing was ever absolutely certain. The only time he ever seems to have vouched for something entirely was when Maples cornered him on it, with the clear implication Kelly had himself been exaggerating Iraqi WMD. Facing a phalanx of tele-vision cameras, the soft-spoken Kelly bridled. It was the only time he did so; an apparently insignificant, but revealing, episode. He went on to say he had subsequently visited the site, which may be true, but he didn't see the supposed test range, ten or twenty miles out in the desert. No one at UNSCOM did, and no samples were taken: there was never any need to verify facts when they stood in your political favour.

Before the Committee chairman could move things on, Maples asked him why this 'Chernobyl weapon' wasn't included in Blair's infamous dossier.

'Essentially it had to be a concise account and you cannot include everything,' Kelly said. He could have said Rufford had got his facts egregiously wrong, just as he or any of his many myste-rious masters could have offered a correction to the paper at the time, but nobody did. His interview had served its purpose.

Kelly was 'in international demand as an accomplished media performer,' Patrick Lamb, the deputy head of the Ministry of Defence's Non-Proliferation Department, wrote in his staff review. One can see why.

Kelly's Chernobyl Supergun story was probably the most ridicu-lous piece of Desert Fox propaganda anyone put out, but there were some very close ties for second place.

In a stumbling presentation on ABC News, Secretary of Defense William Cohen held up a bag of sugar and maintained that 'this amount of anthrax could be spread over a city. Let's say the size of Washington. It would destroy at least half the popula-tion of that city. If you had even more amounts . . . one of the things we found with anthrax is that one breath and you are likely to face death within five days . . . Now I want to point out, I will spill it on the table, point out that [Saddam] had enormous amounts. And I'd like to go into some of the details of the lies that have been told about this . . . We found 2,100 gallons of anthrax. That little bag of sugar I showed you, he had 2,100 gallons of that. He said he had only 49 combat-ready missiles. We found at least triple that number ... Saddam Hussein's son-in-law, Hussein Kamel, defected, it was a very prudent thing for him to do, revealing that they were successful in hiding the facilities that were producing ... the anthrax and the VX gas.'[113]

This was a blanket of falsehoods from beginning to end. Where Cohen got his numbers from remains unknown. In the *Independent*, the Prime Minister was reported as going a step further. 'Mr Blair, citing figures from Porton Down, the government scientific establishment that tests biological and chemical weapons, said that a teaspoon of botulinum toxin could cause seven million deaths, and the same amount of anthrax 100 million.'[114]

It was the same sort of line that Colin Powell would use in front of the United Nations, in the build-up to the British and American invasion, when he held aloft a four-inch vial of powder. Fearmongers had always talked about biological weapons in such terms, and probably always will. The first person it seems to have annoyed was Major Leon Fox, of the US Army Medical Corps, a great debunker of biological weapons. 'There were over one hundred billion bullets manufactured during the World War,' he wrote, 'enough to kill the entire world fifty times, but a few of us are still alive. Bacterial warfare is one of the recent scare-heads that we are being served by the pseudo-scientists who contribute to the flaming pages of the Sunday annexes syndicated to the nation's press.'[115]

That was in the first year of Franklin Roosevelt's presidency. Not much has changed since. Two hundred inhaled microscopic spores might very well kill a person, but evenly distributing billions of them amongst thousands would be insanely difficult.

'To say that the UN inspectors have found "enough biological weapons to have killed the world's population several times over" is equivalent to the statement that a man in his prime can produce a million sperm a day, therefore he can produce a million babies a day,' the Cambridge Professor Robert Neild succinctly summarised. 'The problem in both cases is that of delivery systems.'[116]

It's an argument that had some resonance with the US Embassy in Kuwait, which in 1998 issued a memo to visiting businessmen that was far more level-headed than anything that was coming out of Washington or London or UNSCOM. 'Gas masks are not required,' it read.[117] 'No one at the American embassy has gas masks and the American embassy does not recommend any. They are not even interested in finding out a source for gas masks. The main reasons for this decision are the new interceptor missiles in place in Kuwait and the fact that the biological and chemical warheads are very ineffective. Chemical and biological attack is an extremely remote possibility.'

The target list for Desert Fox is still classified, but it seems the only biological target to be hit was the Biology Department at the University of Baghdad. As far as I could find out, the only other target with even a tentative WMD connection was a missile research and development centre in northern Baghdad. Everything else, all seventy or so sites, was related to regime security – like intelligence offices, radio and television centres, and Republican Guard headquarters.

'Our objectives have been achieved,' said Blair.[118] 'We can be satisfied with a job well done.'

Hans von Sponeck later resigned his role as UN Humanitarian Coordinator, just as Halliday had. He met with Robin Cook sometime after Blair had sacked him as Foreign Secretary. Cook told Sponeck he had repeatedly pressed the Ministry of Defence for an explanation of how Desert Fox had damaged Saddam's WMD capability. 'I never received a satisfactory answer,' he said.[119]

Perhaps it was because there had been no capability there to begin with.

Having reduced UNSCOM to a transparent arm of American foreign policy over Desert Fox, Richard Butler was roundly criticised for letting Clinton 'wag the dog' over his impeachment vote. The Special Commission didn't survive, and his tenure as chairman ended the following summer. Defending himself in his 2001 UNSCOM book *Saddam Defiant*, Butler argued that his actions were justified by the staunch support of Tony Blair. 'It is not credible to think he would allow his government and armed forces to participate in a mere distraction,' he wrote.[120]

Operation Desert Fox was Operation Iraq Freedom in miniature. Kelly never once voiced any objection to the conduct of UNSCOM over the seven years of its existence, or to the military strikes that it triggered, or to the coverage either operation had ever received in the press, even when he seemed badly misquoted. His only unhappiness was that his career as a weapons inspector was over.

'It was us against the world,' an ex-Commission colleague of his once said to me, the misty-eyed memory of former battles in his voice. But I had digested the reports, and the reports of the organisation that succeeded UNSCOM, and the one that came after that. I had ploughed through the headlines and read some of the cables, and thumbed every self-serving autobiography that ever came out of it. You have to peer closely to see Kelly through all of that, but he is there, in the background, which was where he preferred to be. And when your eyes finally catch him, you realise, as all adults must accept of everyone, when they put away their illusions, that you have glimpsed a man who is something less than a hero.

9

Appointment in Samarra

There was a merchant in Baghdad who sent his servant to market to buy provisions and in a little while the servant came back, white and trembling, and said, Master, just now when I was in the marketplace I was jostled by a woman in the crowd and when I turned I saw it was Death that jostled me. She looked at me and made a threatening gesture, now, lend me your horse, and I will ride away from this city and avoid my fate. I will go to Samarra and there Death will not find me. The merchant lent him his horse, and the servant mounted it, and he dug his spurs in its flanks and as fast as the horse could gallop he went. Then the merchant went down to the marketplace and he saw me standing in the crowd and he came to me and said, Why did you make a threatening gesture to my servant when you saw him this morning? That was not a threatening gesture, I said, it was only a start of surprise. I was astonished to see him in Baghdad, for I had an appointment with him tonight in Samarra.

TRADITIONAL IRAQI TALE AS TOLD
BY SOMERSET MAUGHAM

Something terrible would happen to the weapons inspectors after UNSCOM was disbanded. They would get what they wanted. A war.

It was some years distant, and just as Desert Fox had been, it would be triggered by events that had nothing to do with Iraq, but war would come. The ex-inspectors would help pave the way. With the exception of Scott Ritter, they never once dropped their governments' line: that Saddam Hussein's Iraq had weapons of mass destruction, was developing more, and was intent on using them.

After Operation Desert Fox, the Special Commission rushed out a nakedly self-justifying *Comprehensive Review* that was an encyclopaedia of every reason they could construe to cast doubt on the Iraqi position, while proving nothing. Things that had never been mentioned in eight years of inspections were now thrown at the wall in an attempt to create a convincing collage of what-ifs. Richard Butler also outlined plans for doubling the size of the BMVC in Baghdad (which was 'barely meeting the Commission's requirements'), building new UNSCOM substations in Basra and Mosul, and increasing the staff roster. It was fantasy, or politics, which looks much the same when it fails badly. After Desert Fox, the Commission was dead in the water. Its reputation as a multinational disarmament body had been shredded beyond saving. The media reports that it had been infiltrated by American agents, which soon followed, were only the scattering of dirt over its coffin. They surprised nobody. Iraq had been making the charges for years, although no one had listened.

The mammoth network of monitoring cameras and samplers Kelly had helped install over months of inspections, the biggest WMD surveillance system a single country has ever seen, was sacrificed for four days of bombing that knocked out nothing of any biological significance but a university department. In New York, for some time afterwards, it was still possible for inspectors to watch the live feed; an eerie monochrome glimpse into the labs and offices of a far-off country now closed to them, until, unmaintained, the cameras blinked out one by one.[1]

UNSCOM's BMVC headquarters remained locked up and empty, although other UN agencies continued their residence in other parts of the building. When the bombing stopped they walked out to discover the inspectors had left a petrol dump and a trailer full of fuel under their office. The UN staff in Baghdad already had misgivings about Butler's inspectors, and after this, worried rumours began to spread about what the Commission might have left in its labs. Hans von Sponeck, the Humanitarian Coordinator, began a protracted correspondence with the UNSCOM chairman about how the BMVC quarters could be safely secured. This went on for months, dragged in the foreign ministries of Iraq, Russia, China and France, and reached a denouement when Butler admitted there was over a kilo of mustard gas up there. Apparently, this was for testing the Commission's sampling equipment.

When Sponeck was finally granted permission to enter, he did so with a team of international observers, all wearing NBC suits, and they discovered two things. First, there were meticulously organised evacuation print-outs, all dated for UNSCOM's supposedly spontaneous withdrawal the day Desert Fox began.[2] Second, as well as the mustard, there were vials containing quantities of tabun, sarin and VX nerve gas, the last of which the Iraqis had always maintained they had never successfully stabilised. The only BW agents, and the only VX, found in Iraq in eight years of inspections were what UNSCOM had covertly brought into the country itself. And every missile, bomb and shell fragment the inspectors ever sent back for testing had passed through the same lab where these agents were stored.

Hossam Amin and Amer Rashid were both present at the BMVC that day. They both asked that the agents be analysed, in particular the VX, to see if it matched the VX that a US lab claimed to have found on an Iraqi warhead. They were told that identifying the origin of these samples was beyond the UN mandate. Russia, France, and China took the matter to the Security Council, but made little headway.[3] They were told, incorrectly, that such analysis was impossible, although this was far from the truth. The Los Alamos National Laboratory had secretly been

DNA-fingerprinting foreign microorganisms for years, including the biopesticide manufactured at Al Hakum, which the CIA had somehow procured from its sources inside UNSCOM.[4]

So the full truth of what was in UNSCOM's Baghdad laboratory, and why, will never be known. It was another example of the Gang of Four's unscientific sampling tactic in action: don't run tests if the results won't advance your agenda.

Butler's last hurrah, the UNSCOM Compendium that the Gang of Four helped draft, included a single sentence complaining that Iraq's final declaration had not mentioned the 'mobile production facilities once considered' by General Amer Al Saadi. In fairness, no previous UNSCOM report had mentioned them either. Inspectors had been kicking the idea of mobile biolabs around since the early nineties, as a way Iraq might continue its BW programme without detection. Or rather, I suspect, as a way they could continue to allege a BW programme without having to find one, after every single biological facility in the country had proved to be totally devoid of WMD activity.

In the summer of 1995, when Iraq was exhaustively listing all the WMD work it had ever carried out, and possibly more besides, Kelly had asked Al Saadi if Iraq had ever considered using mobile labs. Apparently the Doctor General volunteered that the idea had occurred to him chiefly as a way of reducing the supply chain to the front line, but his scientists had dismissed it out of hand as impractical and so nothing was done. This was entirely sound advice. Neither the US programme nor the Soviets' had ever featured mobile production labs, despite what some defectors later claimed. The technical challenges were too difficult, the production output was too small, the safety risks were astronomic, and the military benefit was negligible. The state of Iraq's woeful road network wouldn't have helped the transport of bulk BW agents and precisely calibrated equipment either. Its mobile biolabs had never been anything more than a swiftly dismissed off-hand suggestion, which was why Iraq hadn't thought of mentioning it in its final declaration, despite Al Saadi's admission to David Kelly.

The Special Commission never found any evidence to suggest such mobile labs existed, nor that they had even been researched, which is why it had never mentioned them at all until the embarrassment of Desert Fox prompted it to throw as much mud as it could onto the wall. In truth, the first written reference to Iraqi mobile biolabs comes not from UNSCOM but from a bestselling airport thriller written by Richard Preston.

Preston was (and is) a gifted writer, a regular contributor to the *New Yorker*, and the author of an earlier non-fiction book called *The Hot Zone*, about terrifying outbreaks of viruses like Ebola. That too sold by the bucketload. Stephen King said it was one of the most horrifying things he had ever read. After its publication, Preston was invited to a Washington lunch with Richard Danzig, Under Secretary of the Navy. Danzig was a germ warfare buff who wanted increased funding for biological defence, and he saw in Preston an ally for his cause. He helped hook the author up with various personnel at Fort Detrick and the Special Commission, and the result was *The Cobra Event*, which features three UNSCOM inspectors heroically chasing down an Iraqi mobile biolab in one of its opening chapters. On board is a highly transmissible genetically engineered pathogen, designed with Russian assistance, that uses the insect virus NPV as its base (the same NPV that Kelly had studied at Oxford). A little while later, the first human cases appear in New York City. The premise is a rare glimpse into the sinister fantasies of the UNSCOM psyche.

Clinton had already expressed concern about biological attack, and tasked his counterterrorism chairman Richard Clarke with convincing his cabinet of the threat. Only the Department of Defense seemed to be taking it seriously.

'What you have to do, Dick, is scare the shit out of them,' Sandy Berger advised.[5]

In the politics of fear, the mysterious and misunderstood world of biowarfare was a potent tool. Danzig's ploy worked. Clinton himself read *The Cobra Event*, and afterwards summoned forty experts from a dozen federal agencies to the White House for a

summit on America's ability to withstand germ warfare.[6] In that
year's budget, funding for biological defence increased fourfold to
200 million dollars, and it would keep increasing, almost expo-
nentially, every year.[7] It became a billion-dollar industry, and its
lobbyists would never hesitate to add their own adamant shriek-
ing chorus to the fray whenever the question of Iraqi WMD came
up. Except to them, of course, as to the inspectors of UNSCOM,
it was never a question at all. But the mobile Iraqi biolabs were fiction to begin with. They were the product of a conversation
America was having entirely with itself.

They took a step nearer to reality later that year, when in
November a young Iraqi whose passport identified him as Ahmed
Hassan Mohammed landed at Franz Josef Airport In Munich. He
had flown in from somewhere in North Africa, but the stamps in
his passport showed he had spent the last six months in Turkey,
Jordan, Cyprus, Morocco and Spain, although this detail is of little
consequence: the passport was fake, as he freely admitted to the
Grepo, the border-control police, the moment he took it out of his
pocket.

'Please, I am from Baghdad, and I want political asylum,' he said,
in very passable English.

For Iraqis to turn up at Franz Josef was not that unusual.
Germany has the highest Iraqi population in Europe, although
there are few of them in Munich. 'Ahmed Hassan Mohammed'
was shuttled off to a refugee centre in the nearby town of Zirndorf,
where like every other exile from a politically interesting country,
he was sectioned off to await an interview with the
Bundesnachrichtendienst, or BND, the German intelligence service.
When his turn came up he told them he was a chemical engineer
who worked for the Military Industrialisation Commission, the
organisation run by Hussein Kamel, at the Chemical Engineering
and Design Centre, later named the Al Zahrawi Centre, in the
Karadat Mariam district of west Baghdad. There he had been part
of a team designing agricultural spraying equipment to help aid the
country's ailing arable farms. That was until May 1995, he said,

when Kamel, three months before his defection, had instructed the Centre to come up with a new, secure system of BW-agent production. The crop work would remain as a cover. The solution hit upon was mobile labs, 'Ahmed' became one of the project managers, and he routinely liaised with Rihab Taha at a seed purification plant called Djerf al Nadaf, which appeared to be a warehouse complex ten miles southeast of the city.

And so 'Curveball' was born. That was the codename the CIA gave him when they got the information second-hand from the Defence Intelligence Agency, or DIA, to whom the Germans passed their reports (recent acrimony between Langley and the BND meant direct contact was minimal). The CIA routinely codenamed their defectors with the suffix 'ball'; 'Curveball', baseball's equivalent of a googly in cricket, apparently just happened to be the next one on the list. He was born, probably, as Rafid Ahmed Alwan al-Janabi, but what name he goes by these days is unknown.

Curveball is the most enigmatic of all the Iraqi defectors. According to Tyler Drumheller, the former chief of the CIA's European division, he was 'a guy trying to get his green card, essentially, in Germany, and playing the system for what it was worth'.[8] The idea of Curveball as some sort of off-the-cuff, enterprising amateur has persisted ever since. Nothing could be further from the truth. After they first heard his claims the BND put together their usual team of handlers for a specialist defector, the same assortment of scientists, psychologists, interrogators and intelligence men that MI6 put together for Vladimir Pasechnik, and they kept him in a monitored safe house. Rafid Alwan fooled them all for over a year, before pressure got the better of him, and the cracks began to show.

He knew the names of at least thirteen senior officials at the Military Industrial Commission. He was able to sketch out a plausible diagram of an interjoined three-truck production facility. He could talk with some authority about fermentation temperatures, pipe diameters, pressure gauges and other technical details. He described how a spray dryer was used to turn anthrax into a fine powder, a technique the Iraqis themselves had not perfected (their anthrax agent was a wet slurry; it germinated in about three years, then its virulence nose-dived). He knew the locations and appearances of other facilities that were suspected of being WMD-related. By the time he had finished talking, the BND's debriefings had produced over a hundred reports.[9] Later, when they eased off him a tad, or pretended to, Curveball would disappear, sometimes for weeks on end. The BND have said they have no idea where he went, which might be true or it might not. But the only reasonable assessment is that someone was handling him. He was coached. He was somebody's boy. David Kay thought so, because when he came to head the Iraq Survey Group he tried to find out, but he pulled the investigation.

There were rumours that Curveball was somehow connected to Ahmed Chalabi and the Iraqi National Congress (INC), which had long been a conveyor-belt of anti-Saddam fabricators. Reports surfaced that Curveball's brother was a senior aide to Chalabi himself, but they were never confirmed, and both Curveball and Chalabi deny the link.[10] This is perhaps one of those occasions when Chalabi might be telling the truth: the Iraqi National Congress made a point of hand-delivering dozens of fabricators unto the CIA, sometimes even providing their own translator. All of these Chalabi readily admits; it was perhaps a way of illustrating he was doing something with the tens of millions of dollars the State Department was giving his organisation.

After the war, Curveball (and by association, the BND) was scapegoated as 'the man who caused a war'. According to the Iraq Intelligence Commission, he supplied 'virtually all of the intelligence community's information on Iraq's alleged mobile bioweapons'.[11] Yet as the same report later concedes, the CIA subsequently developed two other INC sources with mobile-biolabs stories, and the product of both was inserted into the policy-making process even though one had been classified a fabricator after his first interview. The Agency also passed on mobile-lab testimony from the flakiest source of all, an MI6 agent codenamed RED RIVER whose evidence was based on what he had heard second-hand from the INC itself.[12] Chalabi appears to deny none of this. Why would he deny Curveball? Why would Curveball deny it?

What's more, all the INC sources crumbled very quickly, some almost instantly. The guy who turned up in Munich, although he could have walked into any embassy in the world, held on for years, even until well after the war.

'Do you think a twenty-something guy makes a plan like this?' said Hans Pieper, the BND officer who supervised the Curveball debriefings. 'I will go to Germany. I don't speak the language. I know nothing about the country. But I will make up a story and even though I am a chemical engineer, I will make up a story about biological weapons. And I will trick them all. Is this logical? No.'[13]

So who was running him?

'Yeah, Curveball,' Charles Duelfer sighed. 'Look, I think he got all that stuff from UNSCOM. I mean the files and reports that UNSCOM had on the Iraqi programme, all the Iraqi programmes, that was the repository for it all. It was the definitive archive. If you wanted to come up with a story like his, something that would convince an intelligence agency, that's what you would want to read. That's what you'd want access to. You should ask Gabriele about it.'[14]

Gabriele Kraatz-Wadsack, a lieutenant colonel in the Bundeswehr Joint Medical Service and Annick Paul-Henriot's successor on the UNCOM biological desk, now works at the United Nations Office of Disarmament Affairs, but she never replied to any of my emails.

'I understand why she can't,' said a colleague of hers, an inspector who had been in UNSCOM and UNMOVIC and the Iraq Survey Group, but she didn't elaborate.

If you consider Curveball not a fantasist but a managed agent, the most revealing thing about him was his consistent refusal to meet with any Americans at all, a deal-breaker he established from the outset. Even when he knew the reports from his debriefings were being supplied to US intelligence, he continued to insist on not speaking to Americans, and when the BND finally allowed some limited US access, it was only to officers who could feign German nationality. His stated reason was a visceral hatred of the country and its people, but there is an alternative explanation. As a matter of statute neither the CIA nor the Department of Defense is allowed to deceive the American people, and with the sole exception of counter-intelligence, in no field of activity is one branch of US intelligence allowed to disinform another.[15] An American handler would have had to keep him compartmentalised. Sending his agent to a friendly anti-Saddam country with its own intelligence agency, one that was naturally wary of the CIA, would have been a perfect solution.

To this day, Curveball has never publicly elaborated on where he was or what he was doing in the months between leaving Iraq and turning up at Franz Josef, and despite openly admitting to spectacularly deceiving the BND, technically a criminal act, he still continues to live under the protection and sponsorship of German intelligence. There is a secret to Curveball beyond his disproven claims of Iraqi WMD.

Forbidden to return to Iraq, David Kelly and the rest of the Gang of Four spent most of 1999 kicking their heels in New York. For the entire duration of this defector's mysterious wanderings before arriving in Germany, they were the chief custodians of the UNSCOM biological archive. They decided who accessed it, how, and when. Indirectly or otherwise, Curveball's coached testimony may have been their parting shot. Whether they heard the echoes of their own suspicions in the reports that would soon reach them, who knows? Ironically, or not, they knew at least that he'd arrived. One of the few forward steps the Commission had taken that year was to ask European immigration authorities to update it on the identities of all Iraqi asylum seekers.[16] Ahmed Hassan Mohammed would have flashed up on their database not long after he talked to the Bavarian *Grepo*.

Ostensibly, the Gang of Four's final year was spent writing biological guides for the inspectors who would succeed them, but precisely what these guides constituted, and how long it really took to write them, remains unknown.[17] In effect, it was little more than an attempt to steer those who would come after them into accepting their own worst-case conclusions. At the same time Kelly and his team were compiling these volumes of advice, they were also pulling information out.

Draft proposals for a replacement organisation had begun to circulate by the spring, and it was clear from these that Washington and London would be unable to dominate it the way they had UNSCOM. As a consequence, the Gang of Four quietly began purging the archive of any sensitive material that America or Britain might wish to withhold.[18] This was done under the guise of national security, but it also provided them the opportunity to excise anything that didn't support the official position. Material that the CIA or MI6 wanted to bring to the table they could always drip-feed in later, if the timing and reception were conducive, and so they did, keeping UNMOVIC busy with an endless string of fruitless tip-offs, just as they had the Special Commission.

The Gang of Four, like all of the UNSCOM hardliners, seem to have had a reflex contempt for this new organisation even before the Security Council had decided what it was going to be. When Richard Butler quit as chair that summer, within days of leaving office he haughtily dismissed the need for a replacement entity. 'It's pathetic,' he told one press editor. 'I want that on record. Pathetic. It flies in the face of the practical reality of what UNSCOM achieved. It focuses on the mechanism, not the problem. The problem is what it always has been, which is the refusal of Saddam Hussein to stop making or secretly acquiring illegal weapons of mass destruction.'[19]

But that, of course, was never the problem at all.

Kelly spent a long time away from home that year. His absence from Southmoor was more prolonged by the business of tying up

UNSCOM than it had ever been by the Russian or Iraqi inspections. It was around this time that he struck up a relationship of
sorts with Mai Pedersen, a master sergeant in the US Air Force,
some twenty years his junior. In the wake of Hutton this is the
woman the British press would describe, in their own indomitable
fashion, as 'a shadowy Mata Hari figure', a twice-divorced
Kuwaiti-born 'American spy with eyes that could bewitch any
man'.[20]

Pedersen had worked at the Defense Language Institute in
Monterey, where enlisted instructors educated servicemen and
women in everything from Portuguese to Pashto. She was a
teacher, just as Janice had been, and Kelly's own tormented
mother. Her origins were exotic, and she was undoubtedly fluent
in Arabic, but Pedersen was not a spy – or if she was, then not for
long. She was reportedly attached as a translator to some of the
very last UNSCOM inspections, which would have necessitated
a transfer or secondment to intelligence, but I have no access to the
Commission's staff rosters and no inspector I spoke to has any
memory of her. Still, it seems entirely plausible.

Some of Kelly and Pedersen's time together that year was spent
not just in New York but in Monterey itself, where Pedersen still
owned a home, on the other side of the country. It's a small town
on the Californian coast which began life as a Spanish port, the
sort of place guidebooks happily describe as 'picturesque': the calm
blue waters of a sheltered bay, a fishermen's wharf, orderly streets,
old buildings, pine-covered hills, West Coast weather. John
Steinbeck grew up down the road and used it as the setting for his
earlier novels. And during this time, it appears, Kelly had something of a spiritual awakening.

For over twenty years or more, Pedersen had been a follower of
the Baha'i faith, an obscure religion, and one that in Britain will
probably always now be associated with the death of her friend. It
was founded by a nineteenth-century Iranian visionary, and despite
its small following and short history Baha'i has not escaped per-
secution. Its followers are considered apostates in many Muslim

countries, and Iran has always been especially hostile. After some study, and discussion with a Californian Baha'i, the values of the faith remain a little unclear to me, but then I'm an unapologetic agnostic who has never seen a convincing framework of values at work in any religion. Rules are far easier to determine. Baha'i scripture decrees (among other less sensible things) that religion must conform to science, that truth can only be arrived at through independent investigation, and that peace is always better than war. There was some resonance in all these beliefs, perhaps, for a jaded weapons inspector, although there is no reason to think Kelly would ever have adopted them had he never met Mai Pedersen.

During his time in California, she began to expand on her adopted religion, read to him from texts, and lend him books. Marilyn Von Berg, secretary of the Monterey Baha'i assembly at the time, remembers them attending religious gatherings at her home.[21] 'They were devoted friends,' another local follower told *The Times*.[22]

He converted, or registered, as the Baha'is formally call it, in September 1999. Not for the first time in his life, the inspector thought he had found something. He would continue to attend Baha'i meetings back in Oxfordshire, where he was elected onto the local Spiritual Assembly, and served briefly as treasurer until boundary changes left him an isolated believer.

As the Security Council was getting ready to vote on the powers and structure of UNSCOM's successor, the Gang of Four sat around a table in the UN canteen and talked about the future. Each of them was about to go home for the winter, and they might never work with each other again. Rod Barton asked if anyone amongst them would want to be involved with 'the watered-down version of UNSCOM' that was coming.[23]

Nobody was keen on the idea. Spertzel, always the most ornery member of the quartet, said the whole thing would be a politicised sham from the start, and he wanted nothing to do with it. A true believer from the get-go, apparently it never occurred to him that much the same thing could have been said of the Special Commission. Killip and Barton both agreed that they would wait and see. The sole member of the Gang to offer unconditional acceptance was the only one who was still a government employee.

'If the British government back the new organisation, of course I'll work with it,' said Kelly. In truth, he had little choice.

After that came goodbyes, the yellow cabs to JFK airport and the long haul home.

The United Nations Monitoring, Verification and Inspection Commission, or UNMOVIC, was formed by UN resolution shortly before Christmas that year. It enjoyed exactly the same powers its predecessor had, but the resolution stipulated its inspectors should be 'international civil servants' rather than government employees, 'drawn from the broadest possible geographical base'.[24] Otherwise it was almost exactly the same. Ever sceptical, UNSCOM's longer-serving British and American inspectors took to giving it a cod Russian pronunciation, which made it half rhyme with Milošević.

Hans Blix was appointed chairman, drafted in from retirement after his time at the IAEA, although Washington and London had both argued for the return of Rolf Ekeus. Eager to establish the new Commission as a clean break, Blix drafted a set of rules designed to protect it from the undue influence that had corrupted the old one. The post of Deputy Chairman, 'which had always been a direct channel to authorities in Washington', as Blix later put it, was abolished.[25] All its staff would be on UN contracts and remunerated by UNMOVIC itself. Cooperation with the CIA's GATEWAY station in Bahrain would cease. Electronic eavesdropping was prohibited, and only a special designated officer and Blix himself would be entitled to receive intelligence from national governments.

And then nothing happened. The Security Council never decided exactly what to do with the organisation, and in Iraq, where the sanctions regime was now crumbling of its own accord,

Baghdad saw no reason to accept another horde of intrusive inspectors.

Back in Britain, Kelly became a spare wheel, spinning loosely in the labyrinth of Whitehall. He was almost a stranger there these days. He had spent most of the decade abroad, and the people he had worked with during the Cold War were almost all gone now. Few of his managers knew exactly what to make of him. He retained top-secret security clearance, which often exceeded their own, and he had some vague and undefined relationship with the Secret Intelligence Service. He continued to divide his working hours between the Ministry of Defence and the Foreign Office, but he belonged in neither of them. The secretive Rockingham cell, the intelligence group that had provided his only real continuity within the Whitehall world, had effectively gone dormant, and it seems he was left to wander its corridors without clear purpose.

In the world of politics, Iraq was no longer top priority. Kosovo, briefly, became the big thing. In 2000, the final year of Clinton's second term, Saddam was hardly talked about. Discontent over sanctions had now reached a stage where Madeleine Albright was routinely confronted by protesters at public-speaking engagements. Iraq formed no major part of Bush or Gore's campaign, and the presidential election itself, the most controversial in American history, would preoccupy Washington and the media for months. At the same time, the US remained opposed to biological inspections of any kind on its own soil, while the funding for its defensive germ warfare programme had become so excessive that some of the experts working within it considered it a breach of the Biological Weapons Convention.[26]

Under Tony Blair, Britain became involved not just in the Kosovo intervention but in the Sierra Leone civil war, and Iraq edged further away from the forefront of debate here too. Around this time the Middle East section of the Foreign Office, where Kelly's advice was sometimes sought, published a classified paper called *Iraq: Future Strategy*, which argued it was time to ease off Baghdad.

'The status quo is not sustainable,' it argued.[27] 'Support for the UK/US approach is diminishing. Our position in the Security Council is weakening over time. Containment, but a looser version, remains the best policy for achieving our objectives in Iraq. Regime change would command no useful international support. An overt attempt would require a massive military effort, probably including a land invasion. It would also be illegal.'

In London it was as if Kelly no longer existed. He remained in contact with a few journalists, such as Tom Mangold and Judith Miller, but he gave few interviews. He continued to attend, and sometimes formally speak at, academic conferences, but not too many. Each time he clung to the old UNSCOM line. His old friend from Warwick, Roger Avery, now at the Virginia–Maryland Veterinary College, invited him to lecture to the students on the dangers of Iraqi WMD, and Kelly delivered his usual grim news. The local paper gave him some coverage.[28] Possibly the visit may have coincided with business at the Pentagon or at the CIA HQ at Langley, both of which were near by, but after his year in New York he seems to have been released from intelligence duties (at least in Britain). So too had Mai Pedersen, now working in Enlisted Skills Management at the US Air Force headquarters in the Pentagon itself.[29]

In April 2000, Kelly gave a briefing on UNMOVIC to Paul Taylor, the director of what was now called the Defence Evaluation and Research Agency, in the old Chemical and Biological Defence buildings at Porton Down, which was now his nominal employer. He hadn't been back there for years. 'There is the distinct possibility,' Kelly told him, 'that for political reasons, outside the UK and the US, associated with my profile as an inspector, it would be inappropriate for me to support UNMOVIC.'[30]

What these reasons were Kelly didn't expand on, but as a civil servant, the situation left him hanging in the wind. His relationship with Porton, and also with the Ministry of Defence, had been precarious ever since his arrival in the Foreign Office, when his relationship with MI6 deepened. In 1992 Porton Down had awarded him a merit promotion to Grade Five, which meant he had finally entered the Senior Civil Service. After UNSCOM, he returned to find that Porton Down's latest incarnation had downgraded him out of the senior civil service during his absence, and no one had told him. His pay slips still listed him as Grade Five.

Nearing sixty, and now bereft of the carpe diems and expenses he enjoyed as an inspector, Kelly's grading and salary seemed starkly inadequate. He hadn't had any kind of merit pay or promotion for four years, and even the cost-of-living increases had taken three years to negotiate. In preparation for a negotiated early retirement, it appears, Kelly set about tackling the monolithic bureaucracy that stood between him and a decent pension. It was a fight he carried out with his usual quiet determination. He was still typing out very long letters to the relevant officials when the World Trade Center came down, and the century as we know it began.

Less than five hours later, in the secure National Military Command Center at the Pentagon, the Secretary of Defense Donald Rumsfeld was already thrashing out America's response with his aides. Department staffer Stephen Cambone took hurried notes. 'We need the best info fast,' Rumsfeld said. 'We need to judge whether it's good enough to hit Saddam at the same time as Osama Bin Laden. It will be hard to put a good case, but we need to move swiftly. We should go massive. Sweep it all up. Things related and not.'[31]

The debate over why we invaded and occupied Iraq has rumbled on for over ten years. Unless Tony Blair can deliver a plausible answer, which would require him to experience an actual spiritual journey, unlike the pathological levels of self-justification that comprise his autobiography, it will be argued over for the rest of my life. The possible reasons will bounce around until they exist nowhere but in history departments, and settle into an academic consensus. Until then:

Oil. Freedom. Humanity.

The 'special relationship'.

The balance of power.

The balance of risk.

The Iraqi people.

Righteousness.

Security.

Peace.

Take your pick. But the war that appeared on the tables of Pentagon planners had nothing to do with the events that preceded it, and it was sold both at home and abroad as an intervention to disarm Saddam of weapons and programmes he had somehow hidden from the world for over ten years. It was the same line Kelly had spent the last decade meticulously preserving.

The following summer the head of MI6 returned from talks in Washington and reported that 'military action was now seen as inevitable'. It would be 'justified by the conjunction of terrorism and WMD' and 'the intelligence and the facts were being fixed around the policy'.[32] But it was too late to change any of that now. Blair and Bush had met at the President's Prairie Chapel Ranch that April, and the Prime Minister had already promised his support.[33]

In the depths of Whitehall, the Rockingham cell was reborn, and suddenly David Kelly, his pay and pension problems swiftly resolved, found himself back in the game.

At the United Nations, the disarmament issue was inevitably re-energised too. It had to be, if Iraqi WMD were to carry any political credibility at all. That November, after eight weeks of negotiations, a Security Council resolution finally gave UNMOVIC its mandate, and Iraq announced it would comply. New inspectors were soon recruited, but Kelly wasn't one of them.

In June he had participated in a round-table talk at the Wisconsin Institute in Washington, where alongside the former deputy UNSCOM chairman Bob Gallucci and IAEA inspector David Kay, he debated whether the new Commission would be more likely to 'defeat Iraqi concealment efforts'.[34] The panel was composed entirely of old UNSCOM inspectors, and their verdict was a unanimous no. The reasons were multifold. UNMOVIC couldn't handle sensitive intelligence, it wouldn't be able to conduct surprise inspections, it lacked the right personnel, and it would lack the nerve and the will to accuse Iraq. It would be hindered by two external factors, the panel argued. Iraq's vast presidential sites would be off limits, and it had rendered much of its BW work mobile, which would prevent detection.

It is tempting to attribute Kelly's views as expressed at the Wisconsin Institute to something like professional rivalry, but there is far more to his lambasting of UNMOVIC than that. It was, like everything else he ever said on record, an official line. In reality, he had no way of justifying anything his panel concluded that evening. The personnel hadn't yet been recruited, its intelligence security was unknown, and UNMOVIC's nerve and will were a matter of pure conjecture. The Commission hadn't even got its mandate at that point. Access to Iraq's presidential sites had yet to be negotiated, but it had let inspectors visit them before, and there was no reason to think it wouldn't do so again.

So where does this line come from? The answer lay only a few miles from where the meeting was held, in the office of the Secretary of Defense at the Pentagon. The month before, when Rumsfeld toured the US Joint Forces Command in Norfolk, Virginia, he had told the assembled reporters that sending UN weapons inspectors into Iraq would be a waste of time. 'I just cannot quite picture how intrusive something would have to be,' he said, 'that it could offset the ease with which they have previously been able to deny and deceive, and at which today one would think they would be vastly more skilful, having had all this time without inspectors there.'[35]

He was half right, or, rather, perhaps what he said was half true: if UNMOVIC did end up in Iraq it would find nothing, but only because there was nothing to find. Yet the war had been timetabled, and an absence of 'material breach' could not be allowed to stand in its way. Therefore UNMOVIC, and its mission, had to be rubbished before either had even begun. Kelly played his part in this.

While in Norfolk Rumsfeld also mentioned that Iraq's biological labs could, theoretically, be inside mobile trailers. This was the first time anyone in the Bush administration had officially hinted at the existence of Iraqi mobile labs. Within less than a month, Kelly was not hinting but asserting. The intelligence to support his argument came only from the now known to be dubious Curveball and three discredited INC fabricators. Their debriefings were still highly classified. His disclosures in Washington were public, but they never met with any disciplinary action from the Foreign Office or the Ministry of Defence. Kelly was back in the loop, and the Rockingham cell was in action again.

The only member of the Gang of Four to end up inside UNMOVIC was Rod Barton, but he too would be used to traduce his new employer. He flew to New York for a preliminary interview with Hans Blix, but he spoke to the CIA, Judith Miller and David Kelly before he accepted the job.[36]

According to Barton's account, while he was in New York waiting to see Blix, Miller had passed him declassified human intelligence suggesting that sometime in June 1991 Iraq had stored seven thousand litres of anthrax at 'Electronic Warfare Unit 114', a site entirely unknown to the inspectors of UNSCOM. Miller apparently said she found it on the Internet, but there's no sign of it ever having been online, and if it was declassified at all it was reclassified very soon afterwards. If the anthrax at 114 had never formed part of the Iraqi declaration, which seemed likely, it was a clear case of material breach.

Barton jumped on a flight to Washington and met with a CIA officer he calls 'Henry', who had been attached to UNSCOM during the inspections. They agreed that the intelligence looked reliable and the implications were damning. Miller's 'Document 62856', it appears, dated back to August 1991.[37] It would have been interesting to know why in seven years of inspections the Agency had never passed it on, considering how important Barton and 'Henry' considered it to be, but no convincing explanation has ever been given.

Barton's next stop was Southmoor, Oxfordshire. He stayed at Westfield, the Kellys' home, for a day and a half. Kelly told him he would be staying on the outside, and sticking to the position outlined at the Wisconsin Institute, but he encouraged Barton to take up the job. The pair presumably discussed Unit 114, but Barton's descriptions of these conversations are not expansive. On joining UNMOVIC he then tried to get Miller's tip-off into a formal report, but it broke the Commission's rule on the receipt of intelligence from national governments: if the CIA wanted to try and steer UNMOVIC, they could talk to Hans Blix. Barton's attempt to open a channel of American influence inside the new Commission had failed, but it was not a complete loss: months later, when inspections were about to begin and Washington's media campaign against Blix was at its height, UNMOVIC's possession of Document 62856 could be helpfully leaked to the press.

'The failure to inform the council [about Miller's mysterious information] has raised questions about whether Mr. Blix will report accurately on anticipated Iraqi obstruction of weapons inspections,' wrote the *Washington Times*, having listened to 'administration officials who spoke on the condition of anonymity'.[38]

Meanwhile, despite his scepticism, or perhaps because of it, Kelly had found a role with UNMOVIC after all.

'Dr Kelly was like an Adviser,' said Kay Mereish, a former UNSCOM colleague of his, who Blix appointed chief of biological operations. 'He gave lectures at every training course for biological inspections that we organised. His contributions were in presenting Iraq's past BW programme: the agents, equipment, material, locations, the quantities, and so on; and he also used to introduce and describe the personalities that were involved.'

Mereish told me she would be happy to tell me more, but that she needed permission from the US government before she did. That permission never came, but even without it, it's not hard to see how Kelly would be an excellent choice for the role. He knew more about the subject than anybody in UNMOVIC, and he was a former academic who had lectured at Oxford. I suspect he might have enjoyed it, and the travel might have come as a welcome break from the London departments: these courses were held not just in the UK but in New York, Vienna, Paris and Ottawa. His contributions here were undoubtedly outstanding, but there was more to this role than that. As outsiders go, he would have been as close to the centre as it got. It would have given him the opportunity to influence, to gauge moods, to foresee problems, and monitor candidates. Undoubtedly, Rockingham wanted to hear about it whenever he returned.

Throughout this time, Kelly's contact with the media was increasing. In November he appeared as the sole named source in a Judith Miller article claiming the Iraqi BW programme had obtained a 'particularly virulent strain of smallpox from a Russian scientist who worked in a smallpox lab in Moscow during Soviet times'.[39] It was an UNSCOM inspector's wet dream. But Nelja Maltseva, or Madame Smallpox as Miller christened her, worked for the World Health Organisation, and she had been in Iraq on WHO business, way back in 1972, not to weaponise smallpox but as part of the global campaign to eradicate it. Maltseva had never returned since. Her last trip outside Russia was to Finland, in 1982, and she died in 2000.[40]

Publicly at least, Kelly never gave up on the idea of Iraqi smallpox, just as he never gave up on the idea of Iraqi plague. He told Mai Pedersen that on one inspection he had seen a drying machine with Arabic script on it, which his translator told him included the word for smallpox. Perhaps there was something to that: one of the samples UNSCOM had left behind in the BMVC, amongst the mustard gas and the VX, was a test tube labelled 'smallpox vaccine'. But that was as far as it went. If Iraq had an interest in the disease at all, it was an entirely medical one, and probably historical. Nothing more was ever proven, and given the lack of high-containment laboratories in Iraq, it's extremely doubtful they would have wanted to work on live smallpox at all, for any reason – assuming they could get their hands on any, which would have been well-nigh impossible. Even with the Soviet programme, perhaps the most apocalyptic in the world, the evidence to suggest weaponisation of smallpox is extremely ambiguous.

None of this implausibility stopped Kelly from offering the BBC journalist Susan Watts the Iraqi smallpox story too, just as he informed her, on the day President Bush announced that mobile labs had been found, that he was '90 per cent confident these claims are correct'.[41]

The only sign of any discomfort on Kelly's part in the run-up to the war comes in a conversation he had with David Broucher, the Foreign Office's Permanent Representative to the Conference on Disarmament in Geneva. Broucher had been meaning to speak to Kelly about biological weapons for months, and then the month before the war, with only a few hours' notice, he turned up at Broucher's office, having cancelled a talk in Baltimore and flown over last-minute from the United States.

'As far as I recall,' Broucher would tell Hutton, 'he felt that if the Iraqis had any biological weapons left it would not be very much. He also said that the – I believe it is called the fill – for the weapons would be kept separately from the munitions and this meant the weapons could not be used quickly ... I said to Dr Kelly that I could not understand why the Iraqis were courting disaster and why they did not cooperate with the weapons inspectors and give up whatever weapons might remain in their arsenal. He said that he had personally urged, he was still in contact with senior Iraqis and he had urged this point on them ...

'He said that he had tried to reassure them that if they cooperated with the weapons inspectors then they had nothing to fear ... My impression was that he felt that he was in some personal difficulty or embarrassment over this, because he believed that the invasion might go ahead anyway and that somehow this put him in a morally ambiguous position. I drew the inference that he might be concerned that he would be thought to have lied to some of his contacts in Iraq.

'As Dr Kelly was leaving I said to him: what will happen if Iraq is invaded? And his reply was, which I took at the time to be a throw-away remark, he said: I will probably be found dead in the woods.'

It was the only intimation of his future suicide in five weeks of hearings, but Broucher's testimony was not wholly accepted by the Hutton Inquiry. The QC who pretended to be cross-examining him, in that pseudo-courtroom fashion that government inquiries are prone to adopt, cast doubt on the accuracy of his memory. Lord Hutton's final report ignored Broucher's contribution completely, and Sarah Pape found it difficult to accept, given that the dates in her stepbrother's diary put him on the other side of the world.

What Broucher said to Hutton cannot be so easily discounted. The omission of an entry in Kelly's scrupulously kept diary reflects one thing: he was in Geneva on intelligence work. He was still in contact with senior Iraqis, and that channel could only have been managed by MI6, almost certainly with the cooperation of the CIA. It is inconceivable that this line of communication would have existed without their authority. And at the same time Kelly was in Geneva, so were the Iraqis. It was their turn, by alphabetical rotation, to chair the conference, something which incidentally the Foreign Office and the State Department managed to successfully prevent.

Kelly would have been a logical choice for a liaison. He had known each of the senior personnel on the Iraqi programme for over ten years. At some pre-arranged rendezvous, a discreet meeting was contrived. By his own admission, Charles Duelfer was doing the same thing at the OPEC summits in Vienna; the two cities were perhaps the only places where Iraqis could turn up under diplomatic cover.[42] It reveals a glimpse of the real Kelly – a man run by, and working for, the Secret Intelligence Service.

Broucher was one of only two government insiders to appear at the Inquiry uninvited and wholly of their own volition. Both shed more light on the mystery of David Kelly than any other witness outside his family. The other was Brian Jones, the man responsible for recruiting him into the intelligence community in the first place.

When the September Dossier, Downing Street's wholly and wilfully false prospectus for war, was being drafted, Jones's section at the Defence Intelligence Staff had huge reservations about the forty-five-minute claim. It made no sense, even on its own terms, and related to no known weapons system that they could think of. When they asked MI6 about it, the answers were deliberately vague and unhelpful. Jones's boss instructed him to keep his section 'pliant', but there was a groundswell of dissatisfaction that would build up to something tantamount to open rebellion in the usually obedient cloisters of the DIS: a minute of discontent, for the permanent record, emailed to the Deputy Chief.[43]

Before Jones took this step, he caught Kelly in an office down the corridor, and asked him what he thought of the Dossier. If Kelly had any serious reservations, he could have expressed them then, at a time when he could have helped change things. But he offered no dissent.

'I think it's pretty good,' he told Jones.[44]

Just as he did over Colin Powell's presentation to the UN, or Bush's State of the Union address, or Blair's speeches in Parliament, or any of the innumerable falsehoods that fell on us like rain in the run-up to the invasion, Kelly offered no correction and only silent assent. He never once said anything that would derail the case for war. Not once. Kelly stuck to the line.

In private, with his family, he was a little different.

'He was absolutely and utterly convinced that there was almost certainly no solution other than regime change,' his stepsister told Hutton. 'He explained it in great detail that I probably did not understand at the time, in a very convincing way, and made me realise that the war was not only inevitable but that it was entirely justified in the light of what the Iraqi regime could produce in the future.'

It was the dilemma that has haunted all the central characters in this book, that has touched each and every one of us at some time or another, and runs through the political arena and the secret world of intelligence like words through a stick of rock: truth or consequences? In the end, Kelly sided with the politicians and the spooks, perhaps even with most of us. Consequences won out. You prevented Iraq from getting weapons of mass destruction in the future by pretending it had weapons of mass destruction in the present.

Dark actors, playing games.

Blair lined up the entire British military presence on the Iraqi front line before he asked the Commons to decide on the war. Kenneth Clarke said later that he had taken forty-five thousand troops hostage. A man who could always play Parliament like a violin, Blair got his vote. Baghdad fell three weeks in, and a fortnight after that Bush landed at an aircraft carrier off the Californian coast to declare Mission Accomplished. The next month, after five years' absence, Kelly flew out to join the new Iraq Survey Group in the quest to unearth whatever was left of Saddam's WMD. Some were expecting him to serve as the senior British civilian inspector, alongside David Kay.[45]

In an episode that has always puzzled me, he never made it. He flew back the day after he landed. Lord Hutton was told he had caught a flight out to Bahrain with Brigadier John Deverell, the ISG's British deputy commander, but his visa wasn't in order, so he came home. Yet Lord Hutton was also told, by Kelly's daughter Sarah, that he was deported from Kuwait. His wife Janice told Hutton he was physically restrained, had his phone taken from him, and was held overnight in a hotel. These incongruities never bothered Brian Hutton. As a general rule, none ever did.

I emailed Brigadier John Deverell, now retired, and asked him. No, he said, he wasn't with David Kelly; and no, Kelly never reached Bahrain.

I racked my brain about it for a while; then gave up, and rang a guy who knew a guy, an officer in naval intelligence who had served with the Iraq Survey Group. I told him about my book and after a while, some sort of trust developed, enough for a degree of disclosure. I guess all military men, as long they don't rise too high in the hierarchy, develop something like a love for their branch of service over time. When that bond gets bent or broken by politics, this love will overcome the code of silence, and servicemen will sometimes start to speak.

'Iraqi WMD?' he said, and took something like a deep breath. 'Have you ever seen the movie *Green Zone*? It was like that. They sent us out to inspect a list of sites, a long list, and half of them had already been bombed. Some of them had been bombed multiple times. I mean over years. And there was never anything in any of them apart from birdshit and sand.'

Green Zone is a 2010 action movie where Matt Damon plays Chief Warrant Officer Roy Miller, a US soldier tasked with finding WMD in the aftermath of the American invasion. I hate Matt Damon.

'Yeah,' I said, 'I've been meaning to see that one.'

'Yeah? It's not bad. But I mean, I could tell you stories. We had a call once from a defence attaché in the British Embassy in Kuwait. Have you ever met a defence attaché? You know the sort, right?'

I had spent an evening once sat three stools down from one in a hotel bar in New Delhi.

'Well,' I said, 'I suppose so.'

'I mean there's a type. Officers that hit a certain rank and just get stuck there, clubbable, posh, drink a lot of gin, help sell British arms exports, you know? I don't know what else they do.'

'Right.'

'So this guy calls us up: the Kuwait police say they've found some WMD. Great. The lads are flat out to Basra and the border, this is an overnight drive. They arrive at the Embassy. Where's the WMD? In the police station. Really? OK. So it's round to the police station, standard neighbourhood nick, and the cops there hand them a shoebox. A shoebox. And they take the lid off and there's a stoppered test tube inside and a little green bottle with a red cap. Some sort of fluid in each. Well OK. Thanks very much. Then everybody's back off to the British base in Basra to get a flight ordered to take this – this whatever it is – up to HQ in Baghdad, for exploitation, as they call it.

'The NCO in the tent says right you are, one plane. What's it for? WMD, they say. Sharp intake of breath. That's not going on an RAF Hercules. The shoebox is duly proffered, but rules are rules. So the team radio up to HQ, and the Americans send down an unmarked transport. Bloody Air America arrives to take this lot back, and they analyse it, and it turns out to be a bottle of Tabasco and a sample of petrol.'

I laughed. The delivery felt like a joke. Maybe it was. I laughed, but he didn't.

'Did you find anything at all?' I asked.

'I didn't. I suppose the Danes did. They were up on the Iranian border and they dug up a cache of artillery shells. Very old stuff, Iran–Iraq War vintage. They must have got left there when the front moved on. The unit suited up and drilled in and they tested positive for phosgene. But you know what? They had American serial numbers on. These were US exports. The commanding officer had them sent back to the ISG in Baghdad and he never heard back. I think he chased up on it after a while and somebody told him there's nothing in this for us. We pretty much gave up after that. Most of the Yanks, the rank and file, National Guardsmen and the like, spent their time looking for this pilot downed in the Gulf War. Speicher. My lot started going after, well, we started taking an interest in finding certain individuals, but I can't tell you about that. Same with Libya. If I tell you about that I'm not going to work again, at least not in intelligence. Have you heard that story about Habbush?'

Tahir Jalil Habbush Al Tikriti had been the head of the Iraqi intelligence service. The American author Ron Suskind claimed that an MI6 agent called Michael Shipster coaxed him into Jordan for a secret meeting months before the war, and Habbush swore that Iraq had no WMD.[46] The report was shelved. Habbush slipped out sometime just before the war started, and no one has heard from him since.

'I met Michael. Although I could have sworn his surname was Savage. Tall, debonair, well educated. Speaks Arabic with a Lebanese accent. I'm pretty sure that Habbush story is true. At the very least, they knew Iraq had no WMD when they sent us in.'

For a second or too we didn't speak. I suppose he had got it off his chest, the futile and deadly quest for nonexistent weapons in a ruined country that was trying to kill you.

'Did you ever hear about David Kelly in Kuwait?' I asked him, and I told him about the handcuffs, the night in the hotel, the seized phone, and the prompt flight back.

'That was a visa problem? That makes absolutely no sense to me. I must have been over that border three dozen times, and I don't think I ever saw a border guard once. There was a war on, and they were on our side. That's not a visa problem. I mean, there's an overall Status of Forces Agreement that covered everyone fighting that war. That guarantees free movement. Even then, if there's any kind of confusion, someone's only got to contact the Embassy. Or the military.'

'So?'

He scratched his chin.

'That guy was on a list. He was on a list, for whatever reason, and Kuwaiti intelligence picked him up as soon as he arrived. Either that or he was on an operation, and something went wrong.'

'That's what I thought. It's the Ministry of Defence who say it was a visa problem.'

Finally, he laughed.

'The Ministry of Defence? They're the biggest bunch of lying bastards I know. They're worse than the Iraqis. But I didn't say that.'

We said goodbye, but not before he gave me the email address of somebody else he thought might be worth dropping a line to. I put 'Kuwait 19th May 2003' in the subject line, and in the message itself I said only that I was writing a book about David Kelly, if he wanted to help. I never expected to hear back from him.

Officer number two was ex-Iraq Survey Group and ex-SAS, and a former defence attaché himself, but not the guy who called out an exploitation squad for a bottle of Tabasco. He worked for a small firm in the city that made absolutely no money as far as I could see, and while I don't think he was an out-and-out spook, I think he talked to them an awful lot.

He asked me to meet him in a backstreet hotel in Moorgate, and I arrived early in the afternoon and sat at a quiet corner table in a deserted bar. A flatscreen on the far wall displayed Fox Business News on mute. Underneath it, four people in business suits talked in hushed tones about whatever print-outs they were handing each other. I couldn't make out the language, but they were Mediterranean types. My guy arrived a little while after, in a suit but no tie, slightly crumpled but exuding a certain gentility nonetheless. Perhaps I allowed my prejudice about defence attachés to overcome me, but I could have sworn he was extremely hung over.

He clocked everyone in the room, sat down, kept clocking everyone in the room, and then, before we even got started, he tried to get me to list every weapons inspector I had spoken to. I answered him as vaguely and noncommittally as I could. When he did begin talking, it was to make one thing perfectly clear.

'There was absolutely no pressure on any of us to manufacture any sort of discovery of WMD. None. In fact we received a video message from President Bush himself, he said we were the seekers of truth. There was no political pressure of any kind.'

Only after I paid for lunch did we get onto the subject of Kelly in Kuwait. He smiled very awkwardly and his hand shook ever so slightly.

'Look, I can't possibly be associated with this, but I heard that he was drunk. I wasn't with him at the time, of course. But he was drunk, and they're not too keen on that out there.'

'His wife says he was restrained, held overnight, searched, his phone was taken away, and he was deported. The following day.'

'Well that's all par for the course out there.'

Perhaps it was true, but I didn't believe a word of it, and I was sitting next to him looking at him as he said it.

'Well, I did wonder about it,' I concluded.

If you think someone is deliberately lying to you there is nothing you can do about it. I looked up, and the Mediterranean business people had gone. We were completely alone. And we walked out onto the pavement and said our goodbyes.

Afterwards, I checked the flights. According to the details Kelly retrospectively entered in his diary, his outbound journey was on Kuwait Airways Flight 104 from London Heathrow.[47] It hit the tarmac outside Kuwait City at seven thirty-five at night. The following day, he is checked in and on board Kuwait Airways Flight 671, which takes off from Dubai, a thirteen-hour drive away, at nine thirty-five in the morning. Kuwait Airways doesn't serve alcohol, and Kelly, both for medical and religious reasons, didn't drink.

What I was told in the hotel was precisely what I thought it was. A lie. Maybe the Kuwaitis didn't like the idea of Kelly's eight-year relationship with Mossad. Or perhaps he really was on operations, perhaps he was trying to get one of the Iraqi scientists out before the Americans put them all in orange jumpsuits. But it was only when Kelly got back from Kuwait that he really started talking to the press.

After his second, successful, visit to Baghdad, he told Susan Watts that the mobile biolabs weren't biolabs after all, but trailers for making hydrogen. In Baghdad, in Langley and on the Thames riverbank this was already common knowledge, but Kelly was the first to break it to the British media. He also tells Watts that Alastair Campbell was probably responsible for the forty-five-minute claim being included in the Dossier's final draft. He also, fatefully, meets Andrew Gilligan at the Charing Cross Hotel, and over a glass of Coke and a bottle of Appletise tells him much the same thing.

'They probably knew it was wrong when they put it in.'

On the other hand, Kuwait may have had nothing to do with it. It's certainly a secret, but it's not necessarily relevant. Brian Jones always thought that even in his final interviews, Kelly was sticking to a prescribed line, just as he had throughout his entire working life.

'MI6 is an organisation that excelled at giving off-the-record briefings to selected journalists to ensure it was always seen in the best possible light,' he later wrote. As Jones has it, Kelly's 'unauthorised' interviews with journalists were about managing media expectations in the aftermath of the invasion. They were designed to be defensive briefings that protected the Secret Intelligence Service. The only problem was, they were reported in such a way that they placed too much blame on the unelected Downing Street communications team, and the exercise exploded. Intelligence agencies might be able to plant the odd story in the press, but MI6 was no match for Alastair Campbell.

Jones may well be right. Everything Kelly does after Gilligan's piece on the *Today* programme made the government's murderous duplicity front page news has the awkward look of a man following orders.

For starters he comes forward to the Ministry of Defence and identifies himself as a possible source for Gilligan's story, although he says he was misquoted. I asked four journalism professors about this. Has there ever been an instance in the history of print or broadcast media where an individual has come forward, declared themselves to be the anonymous source of a story, and complain they were misreported? David Kelly was the only example anyone could think of.

At the Intelligence and Security Committee meeting, not knowing a transcript might one day be released to the press, Kelly told the MPs the opposite of what he had told Gilligan, Watts, and Gavin Hewitt. 'I think [the Dossier] is an accurate document,' he said. 'I think it is a fair reflection of the intelligence that was available and it's presented in a very sober and factual way.'

In his televised appearance before the Foreign Affairs Select Committee, we finally got to see what he looked like. A very softly spoken, sometimes hesitant man; a bearded, bespectacled boffin; an anonymous middle-ranking civil servant. He sat there with no colleague or adviser at his side, taking the full brunt of these angry politicians without the slightest support from anyone. You felt sorry for him

Well, he had us all fooled. He was one of the most experienced interrogators in British intelligence, talking to a load of bumbling parliamentarians from the shires. It was water off a duck's back.

'While a gentle man, he had a core of steel in him,' Scott Ritter said, after his death. 'I've seen him interact with Iraq governmental officials. There was no give in this man.'[48]

Two days later, he was back at home and life was almost back to normal.

The night after that, he was bleeding to death in a wood.

10

Harrowdown

We dance round in a ring and suppose
but the secret sits in the middle and knows.
'THE SECRET SITS', ROBERT FROST

On the ninth anniversary of David Kelly's death, I took my place at the five-bar gate in the old redbrick wall that runs along the top of Westfield's short driveway, and loitered on the same stretch of pavement where countless journalists and photographers had all once waited, unwanted, for news that wouldn't come. Under instruction from the Ministry of Defence press office, Kelly had already gone into hiding, taking his wife with him. They spent their first night, according to Janice's testimony at Hutton, at a hotel in Weston-super-Mare, yet the following morning when, Janice maintains, they were driving on to a friend's house in Mevagissey in Cornwall, Kelly was somehow able to turn up at a fellow inspector's house outside Swindon at half an hour's notice.

'I myself did not understand how the whole Weston-super-Mare/Cornwall trip works in the chronology,' 'Mr A' told the Inquiry, which showed no sign of understanding either, or of wanting to.[1]

In all probability, the Kellys spent their first night away from home in a government safe house, in which case, Janice's testimony begins to look less than completely reliable. It was delivered, for reasons unknown, via video link, and like all the other evidence given, it was not under oath. Perhaps there were people around this tragically and violently bereaved mother of three who were advising – only advising, you understand, in an expert and subtle way – that there were trivial details, issues of no vital legal consequence, oh most assuredly, that could ideally be elided for the sake of national security. If so, I doubt these people have really left her alone ever since.

The night David and Janice cleared out of Southmoor, every landline in the village went down for several hours. By the time they came home, Kelly's Committee appearance had graced every television set and front page in the country, but the village was devoid of journalists. They had laid off.

'I am pursued by the press and I do not have access to my home,' Kelly had told Andrew MacKinlay, and it was his contact with journalists that had got him into trouble in the first place, so the Fleet Street stake-out had ended. Kelly didn't look like a lead worth chasing. Maybe some in the media even thought he was due a little privacy.

Ironically, if the press had stuck with him, if they had reassembled outside Westfield with their chequebooks and flashbulbs and Dictaphones, he might still be alive.

I stood on the pavement and wondered, not for the first time, what I was doing, and why I had come. The family that lived at Westfield left a long time ago. The girls had moved out; the twins were married, Rachel was about to be. All the members of the household have gone their disparate ways, as modern families generally must, if they are to live the life that is due to them.

Janice put it on the market the first December after his death, 'a most handsome and charming detached country house set in its own extensive grounds in this popular and conveniently situated village'. Eighteenth-century, five bedrooms, 'splendid fireplaces', flagstone floors, beamed ceilings, and almost two acres of garden including a railed paddock. The asking price was three quarters of a million, and it was sold the next summer for something just a smidgen under. She moved to somewhere smaller, but not too far away, kept herself busy with clubs and associations. Local history was always her thing. The village drew around her protectively, and still does.

I was not a wanted presence.

I wondered about the family that lived in Westfield now. What did they make of it all? Had they been bothered by the professionally or personally curious? It must have come up at dinner parties. I could have strolled up to the door and pressed the bell, but privacy is a very British thing. We live in a country of twitching curtains, where homes, for those who can afford them, are always castles, inhabited by a people who are proud and defensive and distrustful of most things, except perhaps authority. David Kelly himself was not that different.

In the end, I left the residents of Westfield undisturbed.

The flip side to all that privacy, of course, is secrecy; huge, cloaking secrecy. We are the most monitored people in the world, and home to the largest intelligence community in Europe. We have an Official Secrets Act with no public-interest defence. In the offices of the Ministry of Defence, of the Security Service, of the Foreign Office, of the Secret Intelligence Service, even in the police, there are people we pay to lie to us. None of this occurs under the least parliamentary scrutiny, and nobody seems to mind too much. It's how the shop is run.

I had tried repeatedly to contact Janice, in the least intrusive way I could manage, without much hope of hearing back. It was important to me that she knew, at least, who I was, and what I was doing. I would have been happy with a refusal. I tried a few local people, and the firm of solicitors she has used to keep out of the public eye since Hutton. All of them said they could send a message on, so I sent them one. I never heard back from any of them ever again. A few weeks after Kelly's death, a letter was sent out to a large number of people, including relatives in Pontypridd who hadn't seen him since the fifties, asking them not to talk to anyone about David ever again. I wonder sometimes if Janice really wrote that letter, or whose idea it was, and who put the mailing list together.

So far the only person we know she has spoken to about her husband's death is Geoff Hoon, then the Minister of Defence, who came to Westfield to see her. Afterwards, to Blair's immense relief, he found out from Hoon that Janice didn't blame him for the suicide.[2] A little after that, when Blair sacked him as Leader of the House, Hoon told friends he would 'make a speech about the Kelly affair that would trigger the instant downfall of the Prime Minister', but his oratorical revenge never materialised.[3] And, incidentally, Janice's solicitors are Bircham Dyson Bell, whose most notable client is Tony Blair himself, for whom they have set up a number of off-shore tax structures and provided a trustee for his Africa Governance Initiative.[4]

Taken far enough, the line between privacy and secrecy blurs beyond distinguishing.

'It's not surprising that the family don't talk about it,' a professor of psychology told me. 'The families of suicides generally don't. It is an incredibly painful memory for them. It's an act which is perceived as the ultimate form of rejection. But I studied the case. I followed Hutton. I heard the way Rachel cared for her own father, that was a nourishing relationship. They'd arranged to go out for a walk together that evening. It's heartbreaking, really it is.'

To Blair, their heartbroken silence was a gift, a canvas he could scrawl his own message over.

I crossed the road outside Kelly's old house and trudged down the lane by the side of the Waggon and Horses pub opposite, past a row of bungalows, through a muddy field and onto the footbridge over the dual carriageway, and then the length of Harris Lane, until I reached the spot where Kelly met Ruth Absalom walking her dog.

'He said, "Hello, Ruth", and I said "Oh, hello, David, how are things?" He said, "Not too bad". We stood there for a few minutes and then Buster, my dog, was pulling on the lead, he wanted to get going. I said, "I will have to go, David." He said, "See you again then, Ruth," and that was it, we parted. He was just his normal self, no different to any other time when I have met him.'

Were those the last words of David Kelly?

'See you again then, Ruth.'

Professor Keith Hawton, of Oxford University's Centre for Suicide Research, was appointed by the Inquiry's solicitors to construct a psychological profile of Kelly that would fit with Hutton's finding of suicide. 'I think it is consistent with the notion that he had made a decision before that to end his life,' Hawton argued. 'Certainly it is not an unusual experience in people who have died by suicide, for people who knew them or came into contact with them shortly beforehand to say that they seemed actually better than they had been shortly before the suicide [*sic*]. And I think it is this, it is having, in a sense, decided on how to deal with the problem that leads to a sort of sense of peace and calm.'

By that point, Keith Hawton had been studying suicide for almost thirty years. As a general observation, there is no reason to doubt the validity of his assessment. As a general observation. I have been very close to the edge when life threw me a fast ball once, and peace and calm seemed a long way distant.

Absalom, the only other witness to give testimony via video link, said Kelly walked off east towards Kingston Bagpuize, although his body would be found due north; and there may be nothing to this at all, except that when you meet intelligence officers it is rarely in your home. They don't stand in your doorway and ring your buzzer. They don't conduct their business in your lounge or kitchen, where they might be overheard or interrupted or recorded. When Kanatjan Alibekov finally defected from the Russian biological programme, not long after his American visit on the trilaterals, the CIA pulled Bill Patrick out of his nine-year retirement for the debriefing. Patrick had been the US anthrax expert at Fort Detrick and Dugway, his security record was spotless, and even then the visiting officers insisted on walking him to the bottom of his yard in rural Maryland, as far as possible from the house.[5] Similar precautions were taken when they asked John Turner to coax Rihab Taha into coming over. I have often wondered if Kelly met anyone else that day apart from Ruth Absalom, and if so, where it was. He had turned his mobile phone off on leaving Westfield, but it was back on again by six.[6] If he was hoping for a call that could save him, it never came.

Five minutes more and I was in Longworth itself, the neighbouring village, smaller, older, and more upmarket by any yardstick, a place of Cotswold stone and thatched roofs and expensive cars. A winding, hedgerowed lane rolled down to the flat fields on the bank of the Thames, and as I descended it rose up on the horizon before me. Harrowdown Hill.

A harrow is a set of spikes or chains or rolling discs used to break up hard soil. The plough cuts deep; the harrow only scratches the surface. For centuries the farmers here have backed their horses against this hill before leading them down towards the flood plain, until the tractor came, and they started wherever they liked. It is not a tall hill at all, merely a tump by Welsh standards, but in this part of Oxfordshire it is prominent, its crown of trees a stark break on a gentle skyline.

When Keith Hawton insisted that 'all the information we have about his death and the circumstances of his death strongly point towards his death having been by suicide', the first reason he gave was Harrowdown Hill. It was quiet, he said, isolated from the view of others, very peaceful and rather beautiful, and whether this really supports his argument or not, it is all true. Harrowdown is all those things, and more.

The word 'Harrow', in English place names, comes not from the farmer's tool but from the Old English *hearg*, meaning temple. The ancient Britons worshipped their forgotten gods at altars that were little more than heaps of stones, but their ecclesiastical architecture came from nature, and that landscape is still with us. If Harrowdown holds true to its name, it has always been a place of offerings. I can believe it was a calculated choice by a deliberate man, having climbed the gate, stepped over the furrowed earth, and waded through the brambles into its wooded clearing. There was something very Welsh, in the old way, about it all, something druidic, a sorcery in blood.

If the ritual sacrifices of the *hearg* on Harrowdown Hill are lost to history, it has a new mythology now, a set of rites that revolve around ulnar arteries and co-proxamol, enacted to keep a crusading liar-king upon the green leather of his Westminster throne, and save us from the foul pestilences and burning vapours of an angry devil in a far-off land, hungry to wreak vengeance upon the world. Its stations are incanted by a church of humming priests in letters pages and Internet forums and online radio, a new hymn for a new age; one of many, since the towers fell. The age of conspiracy, both in theory and in practice.

I had always been a devoted believer myself, from the very moment of my awakening, which happened the instant news broke that Kelly was missing. It was like a divine revelation. Back then the whole country became conspiracy theorists. Blair himself had no way of knowing whether it was an assassination or not, when three days in he sidelined the inquest and put Brian Hutton up in its place. Most people moved on, but others got stuck, hooked on an unquestioning faith that seemed to offer meaning where it was needed. Meaning, after all, has been thin on the ground of late, as far as the Iraq War, international law and British democracy are concerned.

I clung to my faith for years, and I still have respect for its church. Like all religions, it cannot be judged on its clergy alone. Some, a few, are half-crazed demagogues, but others are sensible, intelligent, industrious people, working to relieve what they see as a terrible injustice in an age beset by falsehood and confusion. But if you care about the truth, which all people should and every writer must, you have to confront your illusions.

I stood amongst the trees on Harrowdown Hill on a typically dismal summer afternoon and watched grey clouds drift across the sky. Rabbits skitted in and out of the undergrowth at the edge of the clearing. Crows cawed from the fields below. A single red shotgun cartridge lay amongst the grass, and the remains of a dead pheasant, its bright dewy feathers undiminished. I touched the trunks of the trees, wondering which one was his. From the nearby lane I heard the voices of ramblers, glimpsed bright cagoules through the branches. The world of others was not so far away.

I remembered all the scripture I had read, and all the prayers I had heard. The first that came to mind was the sermon of Michael Shrimpton, a pin-striped London barrister who appeared on a BBC documentary called *The Conspiracy Files*.

'You could hide a platoon or a company of men over the brow of that hill and you wouldn't know, if they kept quiet, until you were right on top of them,' he told his interviewer. 'As a place for an ambush it's just frankly ideal. He was clearly assassinated to keep him quiet – there was no other motive.'

I doubt Michael Shrimpton has ever been to Harrowdown Hill, and I don't know why he thinks it would take twenty-eight infantrymen to 'ambush' David Kelly. If they waited over the brow of the hill they wouldn't even be able to see the lane, unless they were hoping somehow to lure him onto Harrowdown itself. As a place for an ambush it's just frankly ludicrous. It's not even a practical spot for a rendezvous. I'd be surprised if teenagers even went there to have sex, something they will do practically anywhere secluded, and I didn't see a single beer can or vodka bottle anywhere, not even a single smoked cigarette. I can forgive Shrimpton his doubts, though, if not his assumptions. After all, intelligence agencies routinely cover up the truth whenever their agents or officers meet unexpected ends.

Britain's most famous example in recent years is Gareth Williams, a mathematical prodigy from Anglesey who was seconded to MI6 from his job at GCHQ, although there are conflicting accounts of what he actually did there. In 2010, his severely decomposed body was found by the Metropolitan Police in a zipped holdall in the bathtub of a flat in an MI6 safe house in Pimlico. Before MI6 called in the police to investigate, Williams had been missing from work for seven days, during which the flat had been thoroughly and forensically cleaned of evidence, including any traces of foreign DNA. Even the locks and door handles had been removed. In the absence of evidence, there came instead leaks about cross-dressing and bondage fetishism, and the theory that Williams had, impossibly, zipped himself into the bag out of sexual predilection or personal curiosity. The coroner, quite rightly, dismissed it all as media manipulation, but given the scale of the clean-up job she could only deliver a narrative verdict that the spy's death was 'unnatural and likely to have been criminally motivated'. Williams is not the only example. Jonathan Moyle, Saad Al Hilli and Steven Lanham present three other clear cases of deliberate obfuscation. That Kelly's long-established links with intelligence agencies both at home and abroad were never raised by Hutton can be nothing but a deliberate omission.

I spent one hour alone on Harrowdown Hill. It felt long enough. Kelly, Hutton maintains, was there for nine, which I doubt. I am sure there are people who would have wanted to speak to him, somewhere discrete and unobserved. It had, after all, been a very busy few weeks. After an hour, Harrowdown became a hill just like any other. The trees were just trees. The grass held no secrets. The sense of mystery evaporated, and it became just the high corner of a field. There was nothing more that it could tell me.

On my walk back I stopped at St Mary's Church in Longworth to see his grave. He was buried here not three weeks after his extraordinary suicide, without an inquest, and before the conclusion of the government inquiry that replaced it. There wasn't even a death certificate. The Union Jack flew at half-mast from the clock-tower, and a lone bell tolled as a hundred and sixty mourners filed solemnly inside. Church bells tolled all over England. The family had wanted to keep the media out, but they had to make some concession, so they permitted filming, from outside the church, by a single television crew: Sky News. The BBC were not invited. The Press Association was allowed to send a reporter, and everyone else was banned. Thames Valley Police threw a security cordon around the whole area, around Longworth and Southmoor both.

Lord Hutton was there. Brigadier John Deverell, the British head of the Iraq Survey Group, was invited but did not go. He was in Baghdad, busy finding weapons that didn't exist, the ones David Kelly, like hundreds of others, had maintained were there waiting for them. Tom Mangold was apparently present, and so too was Deputy Prime Minister John Prescott, who admits now the war 'cannot be justified'. Geoff Hoon, meanwhile, was on holiday in America, under strong advice to keep a low profile. Blair was in Cliff Richard's mansion in Barbados doing much the same.

They sang 'Cwm Rhondda' for the opening hymn, that time-honoured terrace favourite of the Welsh Rugby Union: 'Guide me, oh thou great redeemer, pilgrim through this barren land; I am weak but though art mighty, hold me with thy powerful hand.'

Father, I have been a good boy.

There was a reading from Wilfrid Howe-Nurse, the local poet who had lived in Westfield himself back in the twenties, and then a Baha'i prayer.[7]

'We are here because of the tragedy that has taken place,' Reverend Roy Woodhams explained to the assembled. 'We are not here for the media or to make a political statement or to apportion blame.'

Hutton would do all that in due course: Kelly was in breach of the Civil Service code simply by meeting Andrew Gilligan, who together with the BBC had then made 'false accusations of fact impugning the integrity of others', namely Downing Street. The Corporation's management was also at fault for 'failing to investigate properly the government's complaints'. The government would get a clean sheet. The smallest part of his conclusion, the reason Kelly killed himself, Hutton delegated entirely to Keith Hawton by simply copying and pasting in his evidence: severe loss of self-esteem resulting from the feeling that people had lost trust in him and from his dismay at being exposed to the media. It made no sense at all. Of the hundreds of emails Kelly had received in the days before his death none had expressed anything like distrust, and he was well used to media exposure, and far more trying things than that.

He was a Walter Mitty character, the Prime Minister's official spokesman, Tom Kelly, briefed journalists before the funeral. Sir Kevin Tebbit, a former director of GCHQ, and then the Under Secretary of State for the Ministry of Defence, sought out the BBC's Diplomatic Correspondent James Robbins to tell him David Kelly was unreliable and eccentric, while circling his finger around his temple.

Neither the Prime Minister's official spokesman nor the Under Secretary of State for Defence had ever debriefed a living soul. They had never stepped into a high-containment laboratory. They had never worked with lethal, highly contagious pathogens. They had never hammered vaccines into their arms. They had never stood at the threshold of a Soviet bioweapons lab in a leaking Russian suit. They had never trodden around unexploded munitions in the baking Iraqi sun. They had never spent months on end in a hostile country where a minder followed you everywhere you went, where your phone and hotel room were bugged, where angry women shoved dead babies in your face. They had never made a single defection approach. Their training in interrogation and counter-interrogation was nil. And everyone in David Kelly's world knew all that only too well. The opinions of mandarins and politicians were as worthless to them as they are to us.

The graveyard of St Mary's is full of military headstones. A few too are graced with the initials of the honours system. Kelly's marker says simply his name, the dates of his birth and death, and a line from Matthew chapter 5. There were no flowers. There was hardly anyone around at all.

'Found what you were looking for, did you?' a retired officer type barked angrily at me as I left.

Maybe I had, somewhere along the line.

I had spoken on the phone to a former Kelly colleague who had

worked alongside him in Russia, an Old Portonian now transplanted to the United States.

'Do you really want to know why David Kelly killed himself?'
he asked me. 'There will be more bodies. I mean, there will be
casualties. And I am talking of his family. To be honest, I wonder
about my own motivation simply in wanting to help you. A
couple of journalists came over to the States not long after he died,
you know. They did an awful lot of work. They really made some
headway. Fly over and we can talk. The phone won't do, and certainly not email.'

I never did visit him, in the end. I knew what he was referring
to. I had heard the same rumour from half a dozen sources, and a
well-known Ministry of Defence psychologist told me the Porton
Down canteen has practically a consensus view on the matter.

'It's *cherchez la femme*,' he said. 'They all think it's to do with Mai
Pedersen.'

But that itself is only half the story, unless we're supposed
to believe our lovestruck inspector ended his life like an angst-
ridden adolescent. None of it made sense until I spoke to Gisli
Gudjonsson, Professor of Forensic Psychology at King's College
London, the man whose expert testimony helped overturn the
convictions of the Birmingham Six and the Guildford Four.
Gudjonsson acted as a security-vetted psychologist for Thames
Valley Police when it investigated Kelly's death, although his
involvement only became known when the new Attorney General
released a swathe of documents in an attempt to head off the legal
campaign for an inquest.

'I suppose I can talk a bit about it now,' Gudjonsson said to
me. 'Did he commit suicide? Yes, I believe so. His family were
very cooperative with me. They were extremely helpful and open.'

'Well, why then?' I asked. 'Why did he do it?'

'I'm not sure I can really go into details, but he lost his security
clearance. It was, definitively, the end of his career. And there were
repercussions beyond that.'

At the time, the full extent of those repercussions did not occur to me. The most obvious effects were bad enough. Kelly was a year off early retirement. He had a top-security clearance that wouldn't expire until three years later, long enough for him to bag a spot of lucrative freelance work in Britain or America, should he wish. In an instant, all that disappeared. He would never work in intelligence again. Even if the Ministry of Defence or the Foreign Office suddenly decided to put him back on the books, he would be out to pasture before his developed vetting could finish. And once he was pensioned off, there was no way he was getting back in. The door was slammed shut. The career he had carved out for himself since leaving Porton had collapsed.

Was this the news that drove him up Harrowdown Hill? I doubt it. There would be anger, and bitterness, and perhaps even depression, but these would be worst-case mid-term consequences. His salary and pension were still secure. They couldn't sack him – not without huge legal difficulties, to say nothing of the political implications – and Kelly would fight for his job just as he had fought for two years for his promotion after coming back from UNSCOM. The public would be on his side. Some of his friends were already getting a 'fighting fund' together as a precaution.

Tom Mangold, who knew Kelly as well as any other journalist, has his own theory about why the scientist killed himself. It is a mark of how much has been concealed that even those of us who believe he committed suicide are compelled to speculation. The one thing that everyone is agreed on is that Hutton never gave us the full truth.

Mangold thinks Kelly was driven to his death by shame at having glossed over his interview with the BBC's Susan Watts before the Foreign Affairs Select Committee. Yet witnesses before parliamentary committees are customarily given forty-eight hours in which to supply written corrections to their testimony, and Kelly had named Watts on the list of journalist contacts he had faxed off to the ministry that morning. Neither was what he told her at all critical of the government, unlike what Gilligan would later report. If Mangold's theory is true, where is the warning? Where is the phone call or email that flagged it up as a problem? It exists nowhere in Hutton, and there would be no reason to hide it.

What killed David Kelly was counter-intelligence. Access to classified information is not a privilege. It is not simply withdrawn as a formality or a punishment, like an executive parking space. You do not lose thirteen years of top-secret security clearance overnight without becoming a security risk, and you will be investigated. Whether it was MI5 or, more likely, the counter-intelligence wing of MI6 itself, David Kelly was being carefully scrutinised the day he took his final walk. It explains the missing dental records, and the bugs in his house, which were probably installed when he was away in Cornwall, if not years before, just as they were in the offices of Richard Butler and Rolf Ekeus.[8] Every one of his emails was being pored over, every bank trans-action, every airline ticket, every phone call. They would have led, inevitably, to a secret that the spooks probably already knew: those three happy weeks in sunny Monterey; that year in New York.

Mai Pedersen was twenty years younger, and attractive. Perhaps their relationship had some sexual element, although she has always denied it and she may very well be telling the truth. Kelly had a family that loved him, and the sanctity of marriage is one of the few things the Baha'i faith is specifically strict about. But it doesn't matter, either way. They would make him deny it. They would make Janice deny it too, and maybe even Rachel, Ellen and Sian. They would go over every visit, including the nights Pedersen spent at Westfield itself. And when they were finished, they would leak it to the press.

It wouldn't matter if they had never even kissed. It was a ques-tion of what it looked like. The Kuwaiti-born Pedersen was a US Air Force NCO, temporarily attached to a foreign intelligence agency. Any extended personal relationship with her, extramari-tal or not, was grounds for concern. Underlying that would have been the potential for blackmail from third parties, should Kelly really have had something to hide, and that threat is often coun-tered simply by striking first.

Julia Sinclair was, and possibly still is, the security-vetted secretary to Rear Admiral Stephen Lloyd, the man in charge of managing Britain's nuclear deterrent. His papers passed her desk. She was also a married mother of two who happened to pick men up on the Internet for group sex. After British counter-intelligence found out, the story appeared in the *Sun* soon afterwards.

'Secret swinger at nuclear weapon HQ!', it blared.[9]

Nobody was blackmailing Julia Sinclair after that.

Dr Philip Davies was a vetted Cabinet-level adviser who trained military officers, counterterrorism police and Ministry of Defence personnel in intelligence and security matters. He is also, still, the director of Brunel University's prosaically named Centre for Intelligence and Security Studies.[10] Davies, it seems, had a soft spot for choking, spanking, and maybe a little light bondage, and he visited websites where women of similar interests hung out. At least one meeting was arranged off the back of it. The Security Service tends to frown on that kind of thing too.

'MoD spy expert is net sex perv!' duly screamed the *Sun*, and counter-intelligence could lay their worries to rest.[11]

Kelly, according to everybody I've ever spoken to, was a very private man, and he knew how counter-intelligence worked. At UNSCOM, Charles Duelfer had tried to run the Commission's own operational security wing, a one-man counter-intelligence division helped along with a little discreet assistance from Langley.

'I learned things about my colleagues that I neither wanted to know nor cared about knowing,' he said.[12]

'Did you ever open a file on David Kelly?' I asked him.

'What, the Gang of Four? Those guys? Come on! I knew those guys. No, I didn't open files on them. Hey, maybe somebody somewhere did, but not me. No one at UNSCOM.'

Sometime that morning, Kelly began to sense what direction all this scrutiny would finally take. Intuition maybe, or a censored communication, or a secret meeting. This system he belonged to was turning on him, impersonally, bureaucratically, mindlessly. The real questions would be starting soon. To save himself, and his family, from the shame and indignity of it all he walked up Harrowdown Hill and rendered his level of security risk to precisely zero.

Given the brutal nature of his suicide, and the secrets surrounding it, there would always have been doubts, but a man can die from a severed ulnar artery and twenty-nine tablets of co-proxamol, just as it's possible to get off three shots from a scoped Mannlicher-Carcano inside eight seconds. Unlikely, but possible. Stranger things have happened, even in Southmoor. There was a murder investigation under way there when I came back into the village: a mathematician was suspected of strangling an astrophysicist.[13] A patrol car was parked in the empty cul-de-sac outside the house, its blue lights silently flashing in the wake of another dead scientist.

In Iraq, the dead scientists number over a thousand. In the chaos of the insurgency, academics of all departments were shot dead, threatened or kidnapped. The nationwide assassinations were non-partisan, non-sectarian, and indiscriminate of both gender and discipline. The BRussells Tribunal said university staff suspected it was a campaign 'to complete the destruction of Iraq's cultural identity which began when the American army entered Baghdad'.[14]

Ironically, by being detained at Camp Cropper and Camp Nama, the scientists who had once worked on Iraq's WMD became the safest in the country. A chemical specialist was killed at Abu Ghraib, apparently in a mortar attack, but everyone else made it out in one piece. Rihab Taha was released first, in 2005, along with Huda Salih Mahdi Ammash, known to the American media as Mrs Anthrax, or Chemical Sally. There was never anything to suggest Ammash had ever been remotely connected with biological or chemical weapons, but she was a prominent Baathist with a doctorate in microbiology, which was close enough. Most of the men came out a few months later. The last prisoner to be released was Dr Mahmud Faraj Bilal, who had overseen the complete destruction of Iraq's chemical and biological weapons in 1991, a process that he had described numerous times to UN inspectors like David Kelly. He had given himself up to the CIA almost three weeks before the war started, perhaps in an attempt to avert it, and instead he was held for nine years.[15]

All the Iraqi WMD scientists were given about a million dollars a head in resettlement money by the CIA. As a condition of their release, they were made to sign agreements that they would never talk to the media, and desist from making political comments of any kind for eighteen months. Then they were taken to Jordan, and after that, they just disappeared. Residency had been arranged for each of them in a range of Arab countries, but only a few people know who ended up where. The true story of Iraqi WMD, and thus the true story of the inspections too, and of the war itself, was thereby bought off, hushed up, and hidden from history. Charles Duelfer manages the channels, he keeps in touch with them occasionally. Rihab Taha lives in Sana'a in Yemen, where she has been trying without success to find a teaching job. Her daughter is almost eighteen now.

I walked on down to the Hind's Head at the other end of the village, where Kelly played cribbage, and got a pint of orange juice and lemonade. It wasn't my usual tipple but then Kelly didn't drink either. The barmaid flicked idly through a magazine. Two locals talked inaudibly across a small table in the corner. The team list for that year's cribbage league was pinned to a noticeboard by the back door. There were a lot of new names on it since it had turned up as submitted evidence at the Hutton Inquiry. Life goes on. Unbearably, mysteriously, mundanely, but it goes on. I drained my glass and said a silent farewell.

I had reached an ending I could understand. I pointed the bonnet of my car towards the Severn Bridge, for another evening drive across western England, and at the booth I paid my toll to get back home. Back from a decade haunted by doubt and conspiracy theory.

The world felt a little lighter, even if the same old lies were still around.

There is a war coming. Syria, Iran, wherever. It may take years to arrive, but it is on its way.

Many generations back, you could tell the approach of an army by its skirmishers, its scouts and saboteurs. Now you can watch the advance party on your television; observers outlining the horrendous abuse of human rights, and experts divining the hidden presence of grim arsenals, illegal programmes and malicious intent. It will all be too important not to stretch the facts. But as long as truth exists, then just as with the outriders of old, casualties can be expected, among the dark actors holding their line.

'A single death is a tragedy. A million deaths is a statistic.'

Often attributed to Joseph Stalin, this quote first appeared in
a 1925 newspaper article by the German-Jewish journalist
Kurt Tucholsky, who described it as a French witticism.

The most conservative estimate, by far, for military- or sanctions-
related civilian deaths in Iraq between the invasion of Kuwait and
the end of the occupation is over 200,000 people.

*'Have you got blood on your hands, Prime Minister? Are you
going to resign over this?'*

The question asked of Tony Blair by *Mail on Sunday*
journalist Jonathan Oliver, at a Tokyo press conference after
David Kelly's body was found.

To this date, biological weapons have not been used by any terrorist group or power, with the exception of the Imperial Japanese army in China, where their tactical and strategic effect was negligible. No ongoing offensive military research is currently known.

Since President Bill Clinton first read Richard Preston's thriller *The Cobra Event*, America has spent and allocated nearly a hundred billion dollars in biological defence. The only American deaths from biological weapons have occurred from agents accidentally (or in the case of the 2003 anthrax letters, deliberately) released from the US labs. The same can be said for the UK. The military vaccination programmes of both countries remain deeply controversial.

NOTES

1 AN INSPECTOR FALLS

1 If true, this was almost certainly the *Daily Telegraph*.
2 Since DC Graham Coe and DC Colin Shields were Special Branch officers, they would have been working in plainclothes as a matter of course. That they were described by other police officers as being uniformed is puzzling. Why would uniformed police officers need to show Thames Valley Police identification to Paul Chapman?
3 The fingertip search found nothing. There were no strange footprints, for example, but then the police were unable to find Kelly's footprints either. In terms of his movements it may be significant that no discarded foil from the co-proxamol blister packs was discovered, which suggests Kelly took the tablets elsewhere.
4 'Lethal versus Non-lethal Suicide Attempts in Jail 1985–1994', Geoffrey McKee, *Psychological Reports*, vol. 82 (1998), pp. 611–14.
5 As confirmed in a letter from the then National Statistician and Registrar Karen Dunnell to Norman Baker MP.
6 Because of the Iraq War repatriations, the backlog of inquests at the Oxfordshire coroner's office was the worst in the country by 2009. It was finally cleared later that year. Some families had waited four years to discover the truth about how their loved ones had died. 'I had the same problem in the Falklands War and the Gulf War,' Gardiner told the *Oxford Mail*. 'But this time it has been a lot worse and we have had many, many more men.'
7 See 'Forensic Science in the Dock', Drummer, Forrest, Goldberger and Karch, *British Medical Journal*, 16 September 2004.
8 'David Kelly: the bellydancing spy whose secrets they just ignored', Norman Baker, *Daily Mail*, 23 October 2007.
9 Clinical pharmacologist Dr Andew Watt experimented with the expulsion of water from a lax mouth in a variety of different bodily positions and found that expelled liquid could only run to the earlobe when the subject was lying flat.

2 DAI

1 'The Loneliness of the Long-Distance Runner' by Alan Sillitoe was published as part of a short-story collection of the same name in 1959. It was adapted for film three years later, and has been adapted for theatre several times since.
2 2002 interview with James Stewart, journalism lecturer at the University of Glamorgan, for Stewart's 'Smallpox 1962' project.

3 This description is based both on the memories of contemporaneous Leeds undergraduates and declassified Foreign Office records. See 'Young Jack Straw blamed for endangering Anglo-Chile relations', Alan Travis, *Guardian*, 7 March 2003.

3 VECTORS

1 Lieutenant Colonel A. E. Kent was commissioned to write an official history of Porton Down on his retirement as Senior Experimental Officer in 1956. When he delivered it in 1961, the director of the Chemical Defence Experimental Establishment (as Porton Down was then called) edited the book down into a 44-page pamphlet that itself remained classified until 1987. The pamphlet is entitled *A Brief History of the Chemical Defence Experimental Establishment, Porton*; Kent's book has never been published. There is, however, a typescript in the National Archives at Kew.

2 Between 1939 and 1989, Porton Down tested agents like mustard gas, sarin nerve gas, LSD and Lewisite on over 20,000 servicemen. Very few, it appears, were told about what they were being subjected to, and more than a few claimed to have experienced lifelong debilitation and illness as a result. A 1999 police investigation examined twenty-five deaths and forwarded eight cases to the Crown Prosecution Service. Ten days before Kelly's death, while the media were distracted by the controversy that had embroiled him, the CPS announced that none of them would be brought to court. A group litigation by the test subjects, initiated in 1994, eventually won £3m in compensation and an apology in the House of Commons following a mediation in 2008. One ex-Porton Down scientist I spoke to actually opined this was all the result of a 'no win, no fee' compensation culture rather than unethical scientific practice.

3 'Essay: Iraq's Ton of Germs', William Safire, *New York Times*, 13 April 1995.

4 US National Archives, Nixon Presidential Materials, White House Tapes, 11 April 1972, 3:06–5:05 p.m., Conversation No. 705–6.

5 US National Archives, Nixon Presidential Materials, White House Tapes, 10 April 1972, 12:44–1:06 p.m., Conversation No. 705–13.

6 *The Fall of the House of Bush*, Craig Unger, p. 54, New York 2007.

7 William Colby, letter to President Ford, 21 November 1975, revealed through FOAI by Anne Cahn.

8 *Secrecy and Democracy*, Stansfield Turner, p. 251, Boston 1985.

9 *America's Strategic Blunders*, Willard C. Matthias, pp. 305–6, Pennsylvania 2001.

10 *Killing Détente*, Anne Cahn, p. 158, Pennsylvania 1998.

11 Unger, pp. 53–5.

12 'Soviet Strategic Objectives: An Alternative View', Team B, CIA classified document, December 1976; declassified 1992.

13 Hansard, Written Answers, 18 January 1982, vol. 16 cc 38–9W.

14 'Soviets Feared Violating Weapons Ban', William Beecher, *Boston Globe*, 28 September 1975.

15 'New war germs "bred in Russia"', *The Times*, 31 January 1978.

16 'Germ Warfare Gap', Jack Anderson, 10 April 1977, Associated Press, Washington.

17 Gary Powers, the pilot of the downed U2 spy plane, was shot down attempting a reconnaissance of Sverdlovsk.

18 'Yellow Rain: is it really a weapon?', Lee Torrey, *New Scientist*, 4 August 1983.

19 Hearing before the Subcommittee to Investigate Problems Connected with Refugees and Escapees of the Committee on the Judiciary, United States Senate, 92nd Congress, 22 July 1971.

20 *The Yellow Rainmakers*, Grant Evans, pp. 109–10, London 1983.

21 'Porton Down and Out', *New Scientist*, 29 March 1979.

22 Professor Jeff Cole, School of Biosciences, University of Birmingham, interview with author.

23 'Hybrids derived from the viruses of variola and cowpox', H. S. Bedson and K. R. Dumbell, *Journal of Hygiene*, vol. 62 (1964), Cambridge.

24 For the sake of context, in 1983 the average wage was £7,700. An MP in the House of Commons earned £14,510. The average property cost £30,898. The past is indeed a foreign country.

25 See *Six-Legged Soldiers*, Jeffrey A. Lockwood, ch. 10, Oxford 2009. Lockwood, Professor of Natural Sciences at the University of Wyoming, calculates that Ishii's insect weapons killed 250,000 Chinese civilians, which is a fairly conservative reckoning. One international symposium estimated a figure twice that.

26 Between 1950 and 1953, the US Department of Defense increased funding for biological weapons development from $5.3m to $345m. See Stephen Endicott and Edward Hagerman, *The United States and Biological Warfare*, chs 4 and 5, Indiana 1999.

27 *Summary of Major Events and Problems 1959*, US Army Chemical Corps, January 1960.

28 Details of Project Screw-Worm, 'redesign concepts for the rearing of 50 million flies per week', can now be found in Box 8, Folder 286, of the Southeastern Special Collection of the US Department of Agriculture Library.

29 The report was written in 1981 but used 1976 dollars in its calculations, which suggests it was referencing earlier research conducted during the Team B period.

30 Dr Gordon Smith's time at Porton Down is perhaps best known for his experiments at St Thomas' Hospital, London, where he deliberately infected thirty-three terminal cancer patients with the lethal Langat virus, apparently to see if it would make them better. It didn't. All of them died, two from Langat-induced brain swelling. The study was written up in the *British Medical Journal*, 26 January 1966. 'You have to remember that in those days everyone with leukaemia died anyway,' the participating microbiologist Dolores McMahon told the *Daily Express* in 2000.

31 Arbovirus is coined from 'arthropod' and 'virus'.

32 Interview with the author.

33 Chapter 5, *ibid*.

34 'Scientist at Chemical War Station missing', *The Times*, 23 February 1974.

35 'Clifftop body believed to be missing scientist', *The Times*, 6 June 1974.

36 When RAF engineer Ronald Maddison was not yet twenty he volunteered to become a test subject at Porton Down. Participation came with a fifteen-shilling bonus and three days' leave. Maddison planned to put the money towards an engagement ring for his girlfriend but he was exposed to sarin nerve gas on 6 May 1953 and died the same day. The Ministry of Defence gave his father £40 for funeral expenses and told him never to discuss his son's death. Details of the inquest were not made public. Papers later released show that some scientists at Porton considered the experiment that killed him to have been pointless, but it was frequently repeated over the next thirty years.

37 *Tribune*, 30 January 1959.

4 SUPERINTENDENT

1 Diplomatic cable from William L. Eagleton Jnr, US Interests Section in Iraq, to State Department, 7 March 1984, declassified in 2003; Document 45, National Security Archive, George Washington University.

2 Diplomatic cable from William L. Eagleton Jnr, US Interests Section in Iraq, to State Department, 20 September 1982, declassified in 2003; Document 15, National Security Archive, George Washington University.

3 Diplomatic cable from William L. Eagleton Jnr, US Interests Section in Iraq, to State Department, 22 February 1984, declassified in 2003; Document 41, National Security Archive, George Washington University.

4 'Clouds of Desperation', William E. Smith, Barry Hillenbrand, Raji Samghabadi, *TIME*, 19 March 1984.

5 These remarks were made by Ali Hassan al-Majid in conversation with unidentified senior Baath officials in 1988 or 1989. The dialogue was recorded onto tapes that were apparently recovered from Iraqi government offices and from al-Majid's home in Kirkuk during the Kurdish uprising of 1991. They were played by the prosecution during al-Majid's trial in Baghdad in 2006. Al-Majid questioned their authenticity.

6 Memorandum from Jonathan T. Howe, Politico-Military Affairs, to Secretary of State George P. Shultz, 1 November 1983, declassified in 2003; Document 24, National Security Archive, George Washington University.

7 Diplomatic cable from Near Eastern Affairs, US State Department, to all NATO capitals, 3 April 1984, declassified in 2003; Document 54, National Security Archive 82, George Washington University.

8 Internal US State Department summary by Allen Overmyer, Near Eastern Affairs, 30 March 1984, declassified in 2003; Document 51, National Security Archive 82, George Washington University.

9 'New Yellow Rain Victims', *Wall Street Journal*, 12 March 1984.

10 'Yellow Rain still stirs debate', *Times Daily*, 3 June 1984.

11 'Chemical warfare threat increasing, experts say', *Sydney Morning Herald*, 28 May 1984.

12 Sound recordist Cyril Bedford was one of them. He was exposed to mustard gas when the team opened a shell on the Iran–Iraq border, and again

when they carried a sample back in the cabin of an internal flight. An Iranian guard used a glass jar stopped only with cotton wool as a container. Bedford suffered lifelong illness as a result and a coroner ruled his death twenty-seven years later as death by industrial disease.

13 'Cuba using poison gas in Angola', *Lewiston Journal*, 26 August 1988.

14 At the Truth and Reconciliation Commission hearings on 9 June 1998. That we know so much about Project Coast is entirely down to the TRC process. Frightened they might face criminal proceedings in South Africa's new democracy if Project Coast ever came to light, many of its scientists (foremost among them Jan Lourens) took the opportunity to offer testimony in exchange for a possible amnesty. Most of what is written about Coast in this chapter draws heavily on the TRC hearings, and also the subsequent criminal trial of Wouter Basson. Both offer a unique glimpse into the world of offensive biological warfare research.

15 The US Senate Select Committee to Study Governmental Operations with Respect to Intelligence Activities (or Church Committee, after its Democratic Chairman Senator Frank Church) was established in the aftermath of Watergate. It triggered a level of disclosure not seen before or since. The testimony of CIA Director William Colby was a series of shocking revelations dubbed the 'Family Jewels' by his colleagues. Colby, the last of the Directors to rise through the ranks, was a religious and deeply haunted man who saw co-operation and openness as the only way to save the Agency he had worked in since its creation from Congressional destruction. He later died alone, in a boating accident near his home.

16 *Secrets of the CIA*, Turner Productions, 1998. Video documentary.

17 Testimony of Dr André Immelman at the criminal trial of Dr Wouter Basson, 29 May 2000. Immelman, Project Coast's laboratory director, testified that two consultants from Porton Down had been appointed to provide final advice on Coast's new P4 laboratory in 1987–8.

17 'Apartheid's master of poison unmasked', Ruaridh Nicoll, *Observer*, 2 February 1997.

18 Steyn Report.

19 'Briefing to President Mandela on the Defensive Chemical and Biological Warfare Programme of the SADF and the RSA's position with regards to the CWC and BWC', D. P. Knobel, SADF document GG/UG/302/6/J1282/5, 18 August 1994.

20 'Special Investigation into Project Coast, Truth and Reconciliation Commission Final Report', presented to President Nelson Mandela, 29 October 1998.

21 *Ibid*.

22 *Chemical and Biological Defence at Porton Down 1916–2000*, G. B. Carter, p. 98, Stationery Office, 2000.

23 Raymond Zilinskas, former UNSCOM inspector, interview with author; John Turner, Professor of Plant Science, University of East Anglia, former tutor of Rihab Taha, interview with author.

24 Former employee of the Centre for Applied Microbiology Research, Porton Down, interview with author.

25 Personal communication, 2012.

26 'Proceedings of the International Workshop on Anthrax', *Salisbury Medical Bulletin* 68 (11–13 April 1989), Special Supplement.

27 John Turner (see note 23 above), interview with author.

28 *Saddam's Secrets*, Tim Trevan, p. 353, London 1999.

29 *File on 4*, BBC Radio 4, 19 November 2000.

30 It's possible that one or two were recruited as agents, as very occasionally happens to foreign students studying certain subjects. Historically, MI6 had enjoyed excellent intelligence links with the Iraqi student community. Ayad Allawi, later installed by the Americans as Prime Minister of Iraq, was first approached by British intelligence when he was a Baathist student representative in London.

31 Joe Selkon, interview with author.

32 ANC gun-runner Conny Braam had her underwear contaminated with parathion while her luggage was left unattended in a Harare hotel room in September 1987. She survived, with lifelong after-effects. Reverend Frank Chikane had the same thing happen to him in Namibia in April 1989.

33 The bestselling US thriller writer Richard Preston used an engineered NPV–smallpox hybrid as the bioweapon of choice for his novel *The Cobra Event*, published in 1997. Preston, who had been a regular contributor to the *New Yorker*, enjoyed terrific contacts with the US BW/intelligence community, who believed the attention and the attendant fear he brought to the BW field was of political benefit. These sponsors included Bill Patrick, Josh Lederberg, James Burans, Richard Danzig and many, many others.

34 In an example of scientific synchronicity, or possibly covert collaboration, Project Coast scientists were doing similar work at the same time. The Roodeplaat veterinarian Dana Goosen tried to strike a resettlement deal with the CIA by sending them a sample of E. coli spliced with the toxin-producing gene from *Clostridium perfringens*. Retired CIA officer Robert Zlockie flew it back to the US hidden in a tube of toothpaste. *Washington Post*.

35 Pronounced 'Grin-yard'.

36 Orders which apparently didn't prevent the drivers from spending a night pissed in Leeds.

37 Photographs also reveal tests were performed using T-shaped sprays about twelve feet high, with nozzles on the cross-bars, probably for aerosol release from aircraft, but this has never been confirmed.

38 *Clouds of Secrecy*, Leonard A. Cole, p. 28, Maryland 1988.

39 *A Higher Form of Killing*, Robert Harris and Jeremy Paxman, p. 73, London 1982.

40 *Central Government Supply Estimates, 2011–12*, 26 April 2011, p. 331. The liability is listed as 'unquantifiable'.

41 'Secret stash of deadly soil', David Leslie, *News of the World*, 21 October

2001. Leslie has made several rather bold claims about Scottish Nationalist terrorists throughout his career. Had he been making these claims about terrorists in Northern Ireland, his status as some sort of government agent would probably have been widely assumed as a matter of course long ago.

42 See the February 2001 letter from the then EU President Romano Prodi to Chris Patten. 'Mr Heyndrickx on his own initiative sent several letters to the President of the Commission. The Commission has not charged Mr Heyndrickx to undertake any studies mentioned in the Honourable Member's question nor is it aware of any other activities of his.'

43 US Department of Defense Intelligence Collection, ITNTREP 91–326, dated June 1991, declassified 25 May 1996.

44 Evelyn le Chêne was the subject of an exposé by the *Sunday Times* Insight team in September 2003.

45 Cuba's Pursuit of Biological Weapons: Fact or Fiction?, Hearing Before the Sub-Committee on Western Hemisphere, Peace Corps and Narcotic Affairs of the Committee on Foreign Relations of the US Senate, 5 June 2002.

5 VLADIMIR TAKES A WALK

1 *The New Spies*, James Adams, p. 275, London 1994. Adams was one of two journalists allowed to interview Vladimir Pasechnik when his defection was officially admitted to the public.

2 *Biohazard*, Ken Alibek, p. 139, London 1999.

3 Pasechnik was allowed to speak to Mark Urban for the BBC and James Adams (see note 1 above), a defence correspondent for *The Times*. Both journalists enjoyed very good links with the intelligence community and the Ministry of Defence.

4 'What to do with Defectors', John Ankerbrand, p. 35, writing for the CIA's secret internal *Studies in Intelligence* series, vol. 5 (1961), approved for release as part of the CIA historical review programme in 1994.

5 'Spy, boffin, disgruntled civil servant: this was the David Kelly I knew', Nicholas Rufford, *The Times*, 25 January 2004.

6 Adams, p. 276.

7 Alibek, p. 144.

8 'The Interrogation of Defectors', Stanley B. Farndon, *Studies in Intelligence*, vol. 4 (1960), p. 18, declassified 1995.

9 Ankerbrand, p. 37.

10 The Black Death's arrival in Europe has itself been blamed on biological warfare. The Genoese chronicler Gabriele de Mussi wrote that the Venetian-supported Tartars besieging the Crimean city of Kaffa, then under Genoese control, had catapulted the bodies of plague victims over the city walls to force its surrender. When it finally fell, and the fleeing Genoese arrived on the Italian peninsula, they brought the plague with them. But it would certainly have spread anyway without this tactic, and despite de Mussi's 'eyewitness' account, historians are now certain he was never at Kaffa but remained in Piacenza throughout the siege. The Venetians represented the

biggest rival power bloc to the Genoese, and de Mussi's unsubstantiated catapult claims served to vilify his country's enemy. Propagandistic or sensational BW accusations against foreign states, then, have been with us for at least 660 years, perhaps far longer than BW itself. This observation may be instructive.

11 *Failing Intelligence*, Brian Jones, p. xxvii, London 2010.

12 Jones, p. 20.

13 Certificate of Developed Vetting Clearance, MOD/3/0061, Hutton Inquiry.

14 Ankerbrand, p. 42.

15 Ankerbrand, p. 38.

16 Sarah Pape at the Hutton Inquiry.

17 *Ibid.*, p. 39.

18 Foremost amongst these, without doubt, are Milton Leitenberg and Raymond Zilinskas. See *The Soviet Biological Weapons Program: A History*, M. Leitenberg and R. Zilinskas, Harvard 2012.

19 *Leningrad*, Anna Reid, p. 288, London 2011. The number is derived from reports written by Leningrad NKVD chief Petr Nikolaevich Kubatkin and sent to Lavrentiy Beria.

20 *The Siege of Leningrad 1941–44*, David Glantz, p. 179, Wisconsin 2001.

21 *Biowarrior*, Igor V. Domaradskij, p. 144, New York 2003.

22 Adams, p. 271.

23 The book Zilinskas co-authored with Milton Leitenberg is dedicated to Vladimir Pasechnik, who received Zilinskas at his home. The dedication describes him 'a highly moral person'. Even so, it also observes (without stating what they are) that 'the reasons for Pasechnik's defection were multiple, complex, and conflicted'.

24 Adams, p. 276.

25 *The Dead Hand*, David E. Hoffman, p. 333, New York 2009.

26 Domaradskij, p. 202.

27 *UK Eyes Alpha*, Mark Urban, p. 131, London 1996.

28 *Ibid.*, p. 132.

29 Domaradskij, p. 247.

30 Leitenberg and Zilinskas, p. 223.

31 Jones, p. 21.

32 *Across the Moscow River*, Rodric Braithwaite, p. 141, Yale 2002.

33 *Plague Wars*, Tom Mangold and Jeff Goldberg, p. 100, London 1999.

34 Hoffman, p. 350.

35 'Protective Efficacy of Anthrax Vaccines against Aerosol Challenge', M. G. Broster and S. E. Hibbs, *Salisbury Medical Bulletin*, 68 (January 1990), Special Supplement.

36 *Gulf War One*, Hugh McManners, p. 170, London 2010.

37 *Ibid.*, p. 113.

38 *Ibid.*, p. 173.

39 *Ibid.*, p. 341.

40 'Two decades on, battles goes on over "Gulf War Syndrome"', BBC website, 16 January 2011.

41 'In Memoriam David Kelly', Terence Taylor, *Biosecurity and Bioterrorism*, vol. 1(2003), no. 3.

42 US Journalist and author David Hoffman both heard and wrote about this before it got to me, second or third hand. I think his source probably got the dates wrong.

43 Communication with retired Intelligence Corps officer, 1998.

44 *Stalin and Architecture*, Dmitry Khmelnizky, ch. 11, Russia 2004. Although, the quotation is taken from Khmelnizky's reading of Khrushchev's memoirs.

45 Years later Kelly claimed that, technically, the first BW inspections were conducted by the Western European Union on West Germany in the forties and fifties. Perhaps he's right, although whether these technical visits really counted as inspections is an arguable point. I'm inclined to think he was just being modest.

46 Alibek, p. 197.

47 This was in Kelly's last television interview with the Australian Broadcasting Corporation, given in the month before his death. After his suicide catapulted him into the headlines, the footage was bought and re-edited by a UK production company and shown in the UK as *David Kelly's Last Interview*.

48 Interview with author, 2012.

49 Zaviyalov visited Paris in 1980, and Edinburgh the year after. Leitenberg and Zilinskas, p. 265.

50 Alibek, p. 196.

51 Leitenberg and Zilinskas, p. 294. In their footnote, the authors disclose that they 'consider it judicious not to reproduce the precise identification of this document', which is probably sensible. Unsourced BW claims are always tricky, but I believe this one is reliable. Rex Kiziah wrote an article about cruise-missile dissemination for the USAF's Air War College at Maxwell, Alabama, and cited what appears to be the same paper.

52 *Ibid.*, p. 181.

53 *Ibid.*, p. 240.

54 Mangold and Goldberg, p. 130.

55 *The Demon in the Freezer*, Richard Preston, p. 113, New York 2002.

56 *David Kelly's Last Interview*, screened on Five on 13 February 2004. This used footage taken from an interview conducted in Westfield by Susan Lambert for the Australian Broadcasting Corporation on 14 June 2003.

6 INSPECTION AS ARCHAEOLOGY

1 *Out of the Ashes*, Andrew Cockburn and Patrick Cockburn, p. 265, London 1999.

2 However keenly Churchill felt about gassing the Iraqis, there is no documentary evidence to suggest gas was ever used. In practice, the RAF in Iraq found conventional bombing to be sufficient, although phosphorus and time-delay munitions were also used. Emboldened by Churchill's stance,

Charles Foulkes, Porton Down's first director, even argued for the use of mustard gas on India's North West Frontier, but it was blocked by Lord Sinha, one of the few native-born Indians to rise to power in the British Raj.

3 According to Maggie O'Kane in the *Guardian* on 5 February 2003, Fitz-Pegado said this in an interview with John MacArthur, author of *Second Front*, a book on censorship and propaganda in the 1991 Gulf War. Fitz-Pegado remained a part-time peddler of Iraqi misinformation: in 2003, she helped promote a book about the 'rescue' of GI Jessica Lynch, itself a propagandistic invention of the US Department of Defense.

4 'Lagging behind in the propaganda war', Jack Germond and Jules Witcover, *Washington Post*, 15 February 1991.

5 After the Gulf War, the UN established a compensation fund for 'individuals who had suffered serious personal injury or whose spouse, child or parent died as a result of Iraq's invasion and occupation of Kuwait'. The money came from Iraqi oil sales, and the fund eventually approved a total of 3,945 claims in 1995. It gave up trying to establish an accurate figure for Kuwaiti civilians, and with the Kuwaiti government settled on an arbitrary number of three thousand affected parties. The fund rejected over a third of applications but even so, compensation criteria seem to have been pretty lax. It awarded compensation to 239 UK individuals, and it is impossible to say who they are. There are no media reports of any UK civilian dying or suffering serious injury during the occupation of Kuwait.

6 According to the UK's National Army Museum, Operation Granby's air campaign (see note 27 below) caused at least ten thousand Iraqi civilian deaths. Nobody was compensated.

7 *Independent Diplomat*, Carne Ross, p. 135, London 2007.

8 Encouraged by the words of Bush One (the Iraqis 'should take matters into their own hands and force Saddam Hussein, the dictator, to stand aside'), both Shia in the south and Kurds in the north mounted uprisings after Desert Storm. But Washington didn't want to see the Shia in power, or a breakaway Kurdistan: what the White House wanted was another Sunni strongman. 'Our policy is to get rid of Saddam, not his regime,' Richard Haass of the US National Security Council told journalist Andrew Cockburn. The Kurds and the Shia who rose up were abandoned, just as the CIA had stoked up and then sold out the Kurds in the seventies, and not unlike Britain had betrayed the Arabs after the Great War. At Nasiriyah, US troops even stood guard over deserted Iraqi army barracks so that rebellious Shia could not arm themselves with the contents.

9 David Kelly speaking to Dr Amy Smithson of the Center for Non-proliferation Studies in Washington, DC, 17 December 2002.

10 Interview with *Frontline*, PBS Broadcasting.

11 'Britain admits bomb missed target and hit town', *Financial Times*, 18 February 1991.

12 *The World Embargo on Food Exports to Iraq*, Susan B. Epstein, Congressional Research Service, 25 September 1990.

13 Senator Paul Wellstone, 10 January 1991, 102nd Congress, 1st Session.

14 'The House of Hashem', Milton Viorst, *New Yorker*, 7 January 1991.

15 Quote from Senator Paul Sarbanes, 10 January 1991, 102nd Congress, 1st Session.

16 *Report to the Secretary-General on humanitarian needs in Kuwait and Iraq in the immediate post-crisis environment by a mission to the area*, S/22366, 20 March 1991.

17 In the formal text of the resolution: 'Iraq shall unconditionally accept the destruction, removal or rendering harmless, under international supervision, of . . . all chemical biological weapons and all stocks of agents and related sub-systems and components and all research, development, support and manufacturing facilities.'

18 'Bush Favours Keeping Most Sanctions on Iraq; President Links Removal to Saddam Departure', David Hoffman, *Washington Post*, 21 May 1991.

19 'Bush Holds to Sanctions against Iraq', Lawrence M. O'Rourke, *St Louis Dispatch*, 21 May 1991.

20 'US Sanctions Threat Takes UN by Surprise: Official's insistence on Hussein's removal may set a collision course with the Security Council', Stanley Meisler, *Los Angeles Times*, 9 May 1991. Gates made the surprise announcement at a meeting of the American Newspaper Publishers Association. It was speculated he was angling for a job as Director of the CIA. Bush had already nominated him for the post once, but the Senate threatened rejection over Gates's role in the Iran–Contra affair (which saw Colonel Oliver North tell the Iranians in 1985 that the US would 'take care' of Saddam Hussein) and Gates withdrew. Bush nominated him again the week after this announcement, and he was finally sworn in as DCI that November.

21 Major's speech to the 1991 Scottish Conservative Party Conference, 10 May 1991, Perth.

22 Cockburn and Cockburn, p. 116.

23 Letter from Abdul Amir A. Al Anbari to Rolf Ekeus, letter no. 117, New York, Permanent Mission of Iraq to the UN, dated 22 May 1991, stamped received, UN Office of the Special Commission, 24 May 1991.

24 'CNN Report from Baghdad causes high-level dispute', Jay Sharbutt, *Associated Press*, 23 January 1991.

25 'U.S. insists that Iraqi baby formula plant made biological weapons', *Baltimore Sun*, 24 January 1991.

26 *Germ Gambits*, Amy Smithson, p. 15, Stanford 2011.

27 The Ministry of Defence had codenamed the Gulf War GRANBY. From 1759, the Marquess of Granby had served in the Whig Cabinet of the Marquess of Rockingham as Master of the Ordnance. Given that the relationship between these names, ROCKINGHAM and GRANBY, is probably no coincidence, and the fact that the Ministry of Defence has always chosen its codenames entirely arbitrarily, it would appear that Rockingham was named by MI6, further suggesting it was predominantly an MI6 operation from its inception.

28   Mangold, p. 308. The quote in full runs: 'Iraq denies working on Plague, but I find its absence conspicuous. There's some intelligence evidence showing that they imported the correct growth medium to grow the Plague bacteria. We came across some of the medium at their Al Hakam [Hakum] facility, and as usual, the Iraqis couldn't account for it. At first they said they had imported it (together with Plague vaccine, in the late 1980s) as a contingency in case the Iranians used bacteria on them. But if that had been true, the growth medium should have been stored at their Food Examination and Analysis Laboratory in Baghdad, and not at their weapons plant in the desert. I remain deeply suspicious.' If this is true, the growth medium (probably MacConkey's agar) came from Oxoid in Basingstoke, the vaccines came from either Porton Down or Fort Detrick, and all sales occurred with the cognisance of the British government. Kelly's point about the location of the agar, and its purpose, makes no sense. A single identification test at the Baghdad laboratory for *Yersinia pestis* would have required only about fifty grams of agar. MacConkey's agar can also be used for *Bacillus cereus* and *Bacillus subtilis*, two harmless bacteria the Iraqis freely admitted to growing at Al Hakum.

29   Smithson, p. 39.

30   Interview with *Frontline*, PBS Broadcasting.

31   'UN Inspector: Iraqis Cooperative', *Philadelphia Inquirer*, 5 August 1991.

32   'The Iraqi Connection', David Rose, *Observer*, 11 November 2001.

33   'A Nation Challenged: The School; Defectors Cite Iraqi Training for Terrorism', Chris Hedges, *New York Times*, 8 November 2001.

34   *War on Iraq*, Scott Ritter and William Rivers Pitt, p. 46, London 2002.

35   'Germ warfare team ends work', Walter Putnam, Associated Press, 7 August 1991.

36   *Saddam's Secrets*, Tim Trevan, p. 35, London 1999.

37   'Irradiation of *Bacillus anthracis* using a Cobalt source', S. Watson and B. Patience, *Salisbury Medical Bulletin*, 68 (January 1990), Special Supplement.

38   'Germ Warfare Inspection Team Ending Work in Iraq', *Tulsa World*, 8 August 1991.

39   Smithson, p. 52.

40   *Ibid.*, p. 53.

41   *Ibid.*, p. 54.

42   *Ibid.*, p. 51.

43   'UN Weapon Inspectors Gave Briefings on Iraq: Talks with Military Officials Violate Formal Policy of Special Commission', *Wall Street Journal*, Daniel Pearl (who would be kidnapped and executed by Pakistani militants in 2003), 11 February 1998.

44   Alastair Campbell would later use the exact same phrase ('above his pay grade') to exonerate his office from the obvious spin one of his underlings would put on the draft of a dossier Campbell denied existed at a meeting he claimed not to know about. In the event, as writer Peter Oborne has observed, (*The Triumph of the Political Class*, p. 173, London 2007), Campbell's

press officer, Danny Pruce, had more input into the September Dossier than the entire Foreign Office. The draft in question was dated 9 September and published in 2008. The meeting occurred at two o'clock in the afternoon on that same day, and Campbell had already acknowledged it in a memo he wrote that morning, which was subsequently released at Hutton.

45 'UN Weapons Inspectors Gave Briefings on Iraq: Talks with Military Officials Violate Formal Policy of Special Commission'.

46 Hansard, 11 March 1999, col. 352.

7 INTENT

1 *Germ Gambits*, Amy Smithson, p. 41, Stanford 2011.

2 'Verification of Biological and Toxin Weapons Disarmament', Matthew Meselson, Martin M. Kaplan and Mark A. Mokulsky, *Science and Global Security*, vol. 2 (1991).

3 *Germs*, Judith Miller, Stephen Engelberg and William Broad, p. 50, New York 2001.

4 *Plague Wars*, Tom Mangold and Jeff Goldberg, p. 155, London 1999.

5 *The Soviet Biological Weapons Program*, Milton Leitenberg and Raymond Zalinskas, p. 640, Harvard 2012.

6 *The New Spies*, James Adams, p. 273, London 1994.

7 Statement by Ambassador Ronald F. Lehman II, Head of the United States Delegation, Biological and Weapons Convention, Third Review Conference, 10 September 1991.

8 WE NEED A CRISIS BY THURSDAY

1 'UN Experts Now Say Baghdad Was Far from Making an A-Bomb before the Gulf War', Paul Lewis, *New York Times*, 20 May 1992.

2 'UN: Iraq Nuclear Activity Over', *Sarasota Herald-Tribune*, 4 September 1992.

3 Interview with openDemocracy, 9 July 2003. www.opendemocracy.net

4 'There Are No More Gaps Left: Expert, Iraq's Compliance with Resolutions on Biological Weapons', *Khaleej Times* (Bahrain), 29 April 1994.

5 The claim originated with National Security Advisor Brent Scowcroft, and the figure was precisely 200 Scuds. When President George H. W. Bush wrote a letter to Congressional leaders on 15 November 1991, this figure had become simply 'several hundred others'. By February, some journalists were quoting anonymous intelligence sources who said Iraq had as many as 800, although Colin Powell said he would be 'surprised' if it was more than a third of that. The real figure was zero.

6 'US Official Says Saddam Hussein Lying about Weapons', United States Information Agency, 10 August 1991.

7 *Iraqi Confidential*, Scott Ritter, p. 61, New York 2005.

8 *Saddam's Secrets*, Tim Trevan, p. 58.

9 *Disarming Iraq*, Hans Blix, p. 22, London 2004.

10 *Against All Enemies*, Richard A. Clarke, p. 69, New York 2004.

11 *Ibid.*, p. 69.

12 The documents were summarised briefly in the (sixth) site-inspection report but never mentioned in the formal semi-annual or annual IAEA papers.

13 *Iraqi Confidential*, Scott Ritter, p. 14.

14 *Ibid.*, pp. 43–5.

15 Muayad Hassan Naji al-Janabi, for example, was a nuclear physicist shot in Amman in December 1992. A few years later, microbiologist Jawad al-Aubaidi, who had formerly worked at the Plum Island Animal Disease Center in the US, was apparently hit by a truck. The driver was never identified. At least two more Iraqi biologists disappeared around the same time: several UNSCOM inspectors suggested they had been murdered by the Mukhabarat, while senior Iraqis believed they had defected to the US.

16 'Chance of US-led strikes', Ocala *Star-Banner*, 26 July 1992.

17 Trevan, p. 185.

18 *Ibid.*, p. 193.

19 'US said to plan raids on Iraq if access is denied', Patrick E .Tyler, *New York Times*, 16 August 1992.

20 'Bush's strategy to split Iraq', *Albany Herald*, 19 August 1992.

21 'Jesse: voice of the Christian left', John Nichols, *Toledo Blade*, 17 August 1992.

22 'Saddam Hussein to the Rescue', William Safire, *The Dispatch (Lexington)*, 17 August 1992.

23 'White House shifting policy on Iraq', Mary Curtius, *Boston Globe*, 21 August 1992.

24 Attempting to total the civilian deaths that Britain and America inflicted on Iraq, and how, is a grim, arduous and unpleasant task. It is naturally best left to groups of independent experts who can pool resources and man hours, although all such entities are liable to be labelled politically biased. Nevertheless, simply because it has gone generally unreported elsewhere: Operation Southern Watch, the long air campaign against Iraq's air defences in the Shia segments of the no-fly zones (neither of which was mandated by a UN resolution; Boutros Boutros-Ghali called them illegal), went on for eleven years. During that time, French, British and American pilots entered the southern no-fly zone on over 150,000 occasions; David Kay called it 'maintenance bombing'. In 1999, this amounted to three air strikes a week. To the best knowledge of the Office of the UN Humanitarian Coordinator in Iraq, in these twelve months alone this activity resulted in 144 civilian deaths and 446 civilian injuries. A confidential report to this effect was issued by the UNOHCI, welcomed by the UN Secretary General, and condemned by both the British and the American governments as a dereliction of duty that aided the enemy.

25 'A Case Not Closed', Seymour Hersh, *New Yorker*, 1 November 1993.

26 Prior to this it was reported that several of them were actually released on bail, although the Kuwaiti Attorney General denied it. *The Terrorist List: The Middle East*, vol. 1, Edward F. Mickolus, p. 216, Praeger Security International, Westport 2009.

27 'Ex-CIA Aides Say Iraq Leader Helped Agency in 90s Attacks', Joel Brinkley, *New York Times*, 9 June 2004.

28 'CIA backed Iraqi bombers', Patrick Cockburn, *Independent*, 26 March 1996.

29 *Hide and Seek*, Charles Duelfer, p. 168, New York 2009.

30 *Failing Intelligence*, Brian Jones, p. 6, London 2010.

31 [Written] statement of Dr Brian Francis Gill Jones for the Hutton Inquiry. When Jones came to be cross-examined at the hearing, Hutton never once asked him about Kelly's SIS connections.

32 *Iraqi Confidential*, Scott Ritter, p. 192.

33 This was UN Security Council Resolution 707, which had been brought about largely by Iraq's reluctance to disclose the entirety of its nuclear research programme.

34 *Germ Gambits*, Amy Smithson, p. 68.

35 *Iraqi Confidential*, Scott Ritter, p. 137.

36 *Ibid.*, p. 138.

37 Duelfer, p. 158.

38 *Ibid.*, p. 94.

39 *The Weapons Detective*, Rod Barton, p. 132, Melbourne 2006.

40 Smithson, p. 182.

41 *Out of the Ashes*, Andrew Cockburn and Patrick Cockburn, p. 12, London 1999.

42 This was Amy Smithson. Smithson, p. 183.

43 Duelfer, p. 95.

44 'Iraq Hides Germ Weapons, Inspectors Say', *Observer*, 25 December 1994.

45 See Cryptome www.cryptome.org

46 Duelfer, p. 97.

47 Barton, p. 139.

48 'A Futile Game of Hide and Seek', Barton Gellman, *Washington Post*, 11 October 1998.

49 Duelfer, p. 121.

50 Trevan, p. 294.

51 'Biological program in Iraq larger than believed', *Baltimore Sun*, 28 February 1995.

52 Barton, p. 148.

53 Smithson, p. 88.

54 'Iraq's Ton of Germs', William Safire, *New York Times*, 13 April 1995.

55 'Iraqis Try to Build a Better Chicken at Former Weapons Plant', Dilip Ganguly, Associated Press, 22 April 1995.

56 'Sanctions don't harm Saddam', Steve Platt, *New Statesman*, 4 November 1995.

57 *A Different Kind of War*, H. C. von Sponeck, p. 93, New York 2006.

58 *Invisible War*, Joy Gordon, p. 236, Harvard 2012.

59 *The Impact of the Oil-for-Food Programme on the Iraqi People*, p. 20, Working Group established by the Independent Inquiry Committee, 7 September 2005.

60 'The Health of Baghdad's Children', S. Zaidi and M. C. Fawzi, *Lancet*, 350 (8988), December 1995.

61 'Book recounts toll of sanctions on Iraq', Raymond A. Schroth, *National Catholic Reporter*, 24 November 2010.

62 Duelfer, p. 105.

63 Smithson, p. 91.

64 Duelfer, p. 104.

65 *Ibid.*, p. 104.

66 Trevan, p. 328.

67 Barton, p. 158.

68 Ambassador Madeleine Albright, Statement to the UN Security Council, US Department of State press release 5 July 2005.

69 'World waits for final piece in Iraq's weapons jigsaw', Scripps News Service, 21 July 1995.

70 Smithson, p. 99.

71 'Iraq's Weapons Not Effective, America Admits', Patrick Cockburn and Charles Glass, *Independent*, 7 March 1998.

72 'US Missiles Knock Down Nine SCUDS over Israeli cities', *Washington Post*, 21 January 1991.

73 'Bioterror', interview with PBS Broadcasting, aired in the US 12 February 2002.

74 United Nations UNMOVIC Compendium, p. 906.

75 Duelfer, p. 110.

76 Barton, p. 165.

77 Duelfer, p. 487.

78 Smithson, p. 128.

79 'The Defector's Secrets', John Barry, *Newsweek*, 3 March 2003.

80 United Nations UNMOVIC Compendium, p. 969.

81 *War on Iraq*, Scott Ritter and William Rivers Pitt, p. 39, London 2002.

82 'Scott Ritter's Private War', Peter Boyer, *New Yorker*, 9 November 1998.

83 *Out of the Ashes*, Andrew Cockburn and Patrick Cockburn, p. 197, London 1999.

84 *Weapons of Mass Destruction: Additional Russian Co-operation Needed to Facilitate US Efforts to Improve Security at Russian Sites*, US General Accounting Office, released 24 March 2003.

85 Duelfer, p. 166.

86 *Iraq–US Confrontations*, Kenneth Kratzman, Alfred Prados and Clyde Mark, Congressional Research Service, Washington, DC, 5 December 1996.

87 The three Turkish invasions of Iraqi Kurdistan are as follows: Operation Steel, 20 March to 4 May 1995; Operation Hammer, 12 May to 7 July

1997; Operation Dawn, 25 September to 15 October 1997. These operations were in addition to smaller, ongoing incursions and air strikes.

88 'Saddam's Best Friend', Seymour Hersh, *New Yorker*, 5 April 1999.

89 'Iraqi opposition opens office in Jordan', *Washington Times*, 19 February 1999.

90 'Ex-Saddam defense minister set to be executed', Robert Windrem, NBC News, 12 October 2007.

91 'UN discovers banned arms in Baghdad', *Star-Ledger*, 25 April 1997.

92 United Nations UNMOVIC Compendium, p. 849.

93 *Ibid.*, p. 854.

94 'Issues at UN Again: Iraq, Nerve Gas, and Weapons Inspections', *New York Times*, 23 October 1998.

95 'UN Experts Report Finding Mustard Gas in Iraqi Shells', *New York Times*, 29 April 1998; 'The Republic of Iraq, Permanent Mission to the United Nations', press release, 30 April 1998.

96 'Obstacles not new for inspectors in Iraq', *Austin American-Statesman*, 9 November 1997.

97 Cockburn and Cockburn, p. 165.

98 Denis Halliday, Ghandi International Peace Award acceptance speech, 2003.

99 'Saddam's Best Friend', Seymour Hersh, *New Yorker*, 5 April 1999.

100 *Saddam Defiant*, Richard Butler, p. 75, London 2000.

101 Duelfer, p. 138.

102 *Plague Wars*, Tom Mangold and Jeff Goldberg, p. 297, London 1999.

103 *Fourth Report of the Chairman of the Special Commission following the adoption of Security Council Resolution 1051*, 6 October 1997.

104 'For Iraq, a Dog House with Many Rooms', Barbara Crossette, *New York Times*, 23 November 1997.

105 Chris Cobb-Smith interviewed for *In Shifting Sands*, Five Rivers 2001.

106 *Iraqi Confidential*, Scott Ritter, p. 272.

107 'Saddam's anthrax in our duty frees', *Sun*, 24 March 1998.

108 'Propaganda Drive against Iraq: As Weapons Crisis Mounted Briefings and Intelligence Leaks Increased', Richard Norton-Taylor and Ian Black, *Guardian*, 25 March 1998.

109 Roger Hill interviewed for *In Shifting Sands*, Five Rivers 2001.

110 von Sponeck, pp. 192–3.

111 Butler, p. 221; von Sponeck, p. 193.

112 'Iraq hiding germ agents, inspectors say', William Broad and Judith Miller, *New York Times*, 17 December 1998.

113 *This Week*, ABC News, 16 November 1998.

114 'Iraq's Weapons Not Effective, America Admits', Patrick Cockburn and Charles Glass, *Independent*, 7 March 1998.

115 'Bacterial Agents: The Use of Biologic [*sic*] Agents in Warfare', Leon A. Fox, *Military Surgeon*, vol. 72 (March 1933), no. 3.

116 'Letters to the Editor', *Financial Times*, 6 February 1998.

117 'Iraq's Weapons Not Effective, America Admits', Patrick Cockburn and Charles Glass, *Independent*, 7 March 1998.

118 'Blair Calls Attack a Job Well Done', *Washington Post*, 20 December 1998.
119 von Sponeck, p. 203.
120 Butler, p. 212.

9 APPOINTMENT IN SAMARRA

1 Interview with Charles Duelfer, 2012.
2 *A Different Kind of War*, H. C. von Sponeck, p. 231, New York 2006.
3 'Russia Acquiesces to Destruction of Toxic Agents in Iraq', *Monitor*, vol. 5 (July 1999), no. 146, p. 29.
4 *The Mirage Man*, David Willman, p. 90, New York 2011.
5 *Against All Enemies*, Richard Clarke, p 163, New York 2004.
6 'US falls short in anti-terrorist preparedness', *Deseret News*, 29 April 1998.
7 *The Good, the Bad, and the Wasteful in the Defense Budget*, Federation of American Scientists, vol. 51 (May/June 1998), no. 3.
8 *60 Minutes*, CBS News, 11 February 2009.
9 Commission on the Intelligence Capabilities of the United States Regarding Weapons of Mass Destruction, Report to the President of the United States, p. 92, 31 March 2005.
10 'Germans accuse US of Iraqi weapons claim', *Guardian*, 2 April 2004.
11 Commission on the Intelligence Capabilities of the United States Regarding Weapons of Mass Destruction, Report to the President of the United States, p. 48, 31 March 2005.
12 Commission on the Intelligence Capabilities of the United States Regarding Weapons of Mass Destruction, Report to the President of the United States, p. 85, 31 March 2005; *Curveball*, Bob Drogin, p. 155, London 2008.
13 Drogin, p. 111.
14 Interview with author, 2012.
15 Both the Smith–Mundt Act of 1947 and the Foreign Relations Act of 1987 were passed with the rather quaint intention of preventing the American government from misinforming its own population. It is, for example, why Voice of America radio is not disseminated inside the continental US. The Department of Defense also has its own rules prohibiting domestic psychological operations. There is no equivalent legal protection in the UK.
16 *Hide and Seek*, Duelfer, p. 173, New York 2009.
17 *The Weapons Detective*, Rod Barton, p. 187, Melbourne 2006.
18 Duelfer, pp. 172–3.
19 'The Lessons and Legacy of UNSCOM: An Interview with Richard Butler', *Arms Control Today*, June 1999.
20 'Why I'm certain my friend Dr Kelly was murdered', Andrew Malone, *Daily Mail*, 3 August 2010.
21 'Dead British weapons expert had ties on Central Coast', Kevin Howe, *Monterey Herald*, 3 September 2003.
22 'American was Kelly's spiritual mentor', James Bone, *The Times*, 9 September 2003.
23 Barton, p. 188.

24 United Nations Security Council Resolution 1284.

25 *Disarming Iraq*, Hans Blix, p. 149, London 2004.

26 'US Germ Warfare Research Pushes Treaty Limits', *New York Times*, 4 September 2001.

27 Goulty to McKane, 20 October 2000 letter and attachment *Iraq: Future Strategy*, Declassified Documents, Iraq Inquiry.

28 'Vet school scientists work on vaccine', *Roanoke Times*, 9 June 2000.

29 'More re-enlistment options', Rod Hafemeister, *Air Force Times*, vol. 61 (28 May 2001), no. 44.

30 Letter from David Kelly to Paul Taylor, Director DSTL, 17 April 2000, MOD/3/0140, Hutton Inquiry.

31 Cambone's notes were discussed extensively by the 9/11 Commission. They were also mentioned in Bob Woodward's book *Plan of Attack*, and broken as a story by CBS News. After a request under the US Freedom of Information Act, they were released to the public in redacted form, and are freely available on the Internet. This quotation comes from the unredacted portion of the notes.

32 'The Downing Street Memo', as originally reported in the *Sunday Times*, 1 May 2005.

33 According to the widely published opinion of Christopher Meyer, then British Ambassador to the US. At the time of writing, the documents to support his view have been withheld from the Iraq Inquiry, an action which tends to support this judgement.

34 This was originally reported by the Wisconsin Institute itself on its IraqWatch website. It has since been taken down but it is still accessible through the Wayback Machine Internet Archive.

35 'Rumsfeld, in break with State Department, says Iraq would deceive and deny weapons inspectors', Associated Press, 16 April 2002.

36 Barton, p. 192.

37 This document is referred to, and Electronic Warfare Unit 113 specifically mentioned, in the following CIA report: *Intelligence Related to Possible Sources of Biological Agent Exposure during the Persian Gulf War*, Robert D. Walpole, Special Assistant to the Director of Central Intelligence for Persian Gulf War Illnesses, August 2000.

38 'US says Baghdad is hiding anthrax', Bill Gertz, *Washington Times*, 8 November 2002.

39 'CIA hunts Iraq Tie to Soviet Smallpox', Judith Miller, *New York Times*, 3 December 2002.

40 *The Soviet Biological Weapons Program*, Milton Leitenberg and Raymond A. Zilinskas, p. 481, Harvard 2012.

41 Susan Watts, BBC *Newsnight*, 2 June 2003.

42 Duelfer, p. 228.

43 The Deputy Chief of DIS is the one that does the real work; the actual Chief is always a serving senior military officer rotated out on a revolving-door basis.

44 *Failing Intelligence*, Brian Jones, p. 83, London 2010.
45 *Ibid.*, p. 114.
46 *The Way of the World*, Ron Suskind, p. 185, New York 2008.
47 Hutton Inquiry, TVP/3/0136.
48 'Gentle man with core of steel', BBC News, 19 July 2003.

10 HARROWDOWN

1 Mr A was subsequently revealed to be the ex-UNSCOM chemical inspector Rod Godfrey. *The Strange Death of David Kelly*, Norman Baker, p. 175, London 2007.

2 *The End of the Party*, Andrew Rawnsley, p. 216, London 2010.

3 *Ibid.*, p. 369.

4 'Mystery of Tony Blair's money solved', David Leigh and Ian Griffiths, *Guardian*, 17 December 2009 (rather a bold title: it's nowhere near solved).

5 *Germs*, Judith Miller, Stephen Engelberg and William Broad, p. 135, New York 2001.

6 John Clark of the Foreign Office rang him all afternoon but his phone was off. James Harrison from the Ministry of Defence tried him a little before six and it was back on again, but no one answered. Hutton Inquiry testimony.

7 The Baha'i faith, I'm told, lays down no funeral rites of its own. It is happy to accept the rituals of the community to which the deceased belongs.

8 'UN bugging scandal widens', BBC *News*, 27 February 2004.

9 'Secret swinger at nuclear weapon HQ', Alex West, *Sun*, 16 October 2009.

10 When the Intelligence and Security Committee sacked its first and last Investigator, John Morrison, for disparaging Blair's claims over WMD in a *Panorama* documentary, Davies appointed him a senior fellow.

11 'MoD spy expert is net sex perv', Ben Ashford and Veronica Lorraine, *Sun*, 28 November 2008.

12 *Hide and Seek*, Charles Duelfer, p. 113, New York 2009.

13 The death was later ruled accidental. Steven Rawlings was the astrophysicist, Devinder Sivia the mathematician.

14 'Urgent appeal to save Iraq's academics', press release, 2006, BRussells Tribunal, www.brussellstribunal.org

15 *Iraq to release Saddam Hussein's last WMD scientist*, Agence France-Presse/NEWCORE, 15 April 2012.

BIBLIOGRAPHY AND FURTHER READING

Aaronovitch, David, *Voodoo Histories: The Role of the Conspiracy Theory in Shaping Modern History* (London, 2009)

Abse, Leo, *Tony Blair: The Man Behind the Smile* (London, 2001)

Adams, James, *The New Spies* (London, 1994)

Ahmed, Nafeez Mosaddeq, *Behind the War on Terror: Western Secret Strategy and the Struggle for Iraq* (Forest Row, 2003)

Alibek, Ken, *Biohazard* (London, 1999)

Arnove, Anthony (editor), *Iraq Under Siege: The Deadly Impact of Sanctions and War* (London, 2000)

Baker, Norman, *The Strange Death of David Kelly* (London, 2007)

Barton, Rod, *The Weapons Detective: The Inside Story of Australia's Top Weapons Inspector* (Melbourne, 2006)

Blix, Hans, *Disarming Iraq* (London, 2004)

Braithwaite, Rodric, *Across the Moscow River* (Yale, 2002)

Bulloch, John and Morris, Harvey, *No Friends but the Mountains: The Tragic History of the Kurds* (London, 1992)

Bulloch, John and Morris, Harvey, *Saddam's War: The Origins of the Kuwaiti Conflict and the International Response* (London, 1991)

Butler, Richard, *Saddam Defiant: The Threat of Weapons of Mass Destruction, and the Crisis of Global Security* (London, 2000) (published in the US under the title *The Greatest Threat: Iraq, Weapons of Mass Destruction, and the Growing Crisis of Global Security*)

Cahn, Anne H, *Killing Détente: The Right Attacks the CIA* (Pennsylvania, 1998)

Carter, G B, *Chemical and Biological Defence at Porton Down 1916–2000* (London, 2000)

CIA, *The Pike Report with an introduction by Philip Agee* (Nottingham, 1977)

Clarke, Richard A, *Against All Enemies: Inside America's War on Terror* (New York, 2004)

Clarke, Robin, *We All Fall Down: The Prospect of Biological and Chemical Warfare* (London, 1968)

Cockburn, Andrew and Cockburn, Patrick, *Out of the Ashes: The Resurrection of Saddam Hussein* (London, 1999) (later reprinted in the US under the title *Saddam Hussein: An American Obsession*)

Cole, Leonard A, *Clouds of Secrecy: The Army's Germ Warfare Tests over Populated Areas* (Maryland, 1988)

Cole, Leonard A, *The Eleventh Plague: The Politics of Biological and Chemical Warfare* (New York, 1996)

Collins, Tony, *Open Verdict: An Account of 25 Mysterious Deaths in the Defence Industry* (London, 1990)

Cook, Robin, *The Point of Departure: Diaries from the Front Bench* (London, 2003)

Curtis, Mark, *Web of Deceit: Britain's Real Role in the World* (London, 2003)

Davies, Nick, *Flat Earth News* (London, 2009)

Domaradskij, Igor V, *Biowarrior: Inside the Soviet/Russian Biological War Machine* (New York, 2003)

Drogin, Bob, *Curveball: Spies, Lies and the Con Man Who Caused a War* (New York, 2007)

Duelfer, Charles, *Hide and Seek: The Search for Truth in Iraq* (New York, 2009)

Endicott, Stephen and Hagerman, Edward, *The United States and Biological Warfare: Secrets from the Early Cold War and Korea* (Indiana, 1999)

Evans, Grant, *The Yellow Rainmakers: Are Chemical Weapons Being Used in Southeast Asia?* (London, 1983)

Finlan, Alastair, *The Gulf War 1991* (Oxford, 2003)

Glantz, David, *The Siege of Leningrad 1941–44: 900 Days of Terror* (Wisconsin, 2001)

Gordon, Joy, *Invisible War: The United States and the Iraqi Sanctions* (Harvard, 2012)

Grubard, Stephen R, *Mr Bush's War: Adventures in the Politics of Illusion* (London, 1992)

Harris, Robert and Jeremy, Paxman, *A Higher Form of Killing* (London, 1982)

Hedges, Chris, *War Is a Force That Gives Us Meaning* (London, 2003)

Hersh, Seymour M, *Chain of Command: The Road from 9/11 to Abu Ghraib* (London, 2004)

Hiro, Dilip, *Neighbours, Not Friends: Iraq and Iran after The Gulf Wars* (London, 2001)

Hitchens, Christopher, *Regime Change* (London, 2003)

Hoffman, David E, *The Dead Hand: Reagan, Gorbachev and the Untold Story of the Cold War I* (New York, 2009)

Jones, Brian, *Failing Intelligence* (London, 2010)

Kampfner, John, *Blair's Wars* (London, 2003)

Karsh, Efraim, *The Iran-Iraq War 1980–1988* (Oxford, 2002)

Kelly, Michael, *Martyr's Day: Chronicle of a Small War* (London, 1993)

Khmelnizky, Dmimitry, *Stalin and Architecture* (Russia, 2010)

Klotz, Lynn C and Sylvester, Edward J, *Breeding Bio Insecurity* (Chicago, 2009)

Kouzminov, Alexander, *Biological Espionage* (London, 2005)

Lawrence, T E, *Seven Pillars of Wisdom* (London, 1926)

Leitenberg, Milton and Zilinskas, Raymond A, *The Soviet Biological Weapons Program: A History* (Harvard, 2012)

Lockwood, Jeffrey A, *Six-Legged Soldiers: Using Insects as Weapons of War* (Oxford, 2009)

Lowther, William, *Iraq and the Supergun, Gerald Bull: The True Story of Saddam Hussein's Dr Doom* (London, 1991)

Macarthur, John R, *Second Front: Censorship and Propaganda in the 1991 Gulf War* (London, 2004)

Maclean, Alistair, *The Satan Bug* (London, 1962)

McManners, Hugh, *Gulf War One* (London, 2010)

Mangold, Tom and Goldberg, Jeff, *Plague Wars: A True Story of Biological Warfare* (London, 1999)

Mantius, Peter, *Shell Game: A True Story of Banking, Lies, Politics and the Arming of Saddam Hussein* (New York, 1995)

Matthias, Willard C, *America's Strategic Blunders: Intelligence Analysis and National Security Policy 1936–1991* (Pennsylvania, 2001)

Miller, Judith; Engleberg, Stephen; Broad, William H, *Germs: Biological Weapons and America's Secret War* (New York, 2001)

Mitchell, Marcia and Thomas, *The Spy Who Tried to Stop a War: Katherine Gun and the Secret Plot to Sanction the Iraq Invasion* (Sausalito, 2008)

Murakami, Haruki, *Underground* (London, 2002)

Murray, Craig, *Murder in Samarkand: A British Ambassador's Controversial Defiance of Tyranny in the War on Terror* (Edinburgh, 2006)

Oborne, Peter, *The Triumph of the Political Class* (London, 2007)

Parenti, Christian, *The Freedom: Shadows and Hallucinations in Occupied Iraq* (New York, 2004)

Pearson, Graham S, *The UNSCOM Saga: Chemical and Biological Weapons Non-Proliferation* (London, 1999)

Preston, Richard, *The Cobra Event* (New York, 1998)

Preston, Richard, *The Demon in the Freezer* (New York, 2002)

Preston, Richard, *The Hot Zone* (New York, 1994)

Purkitt, Helen E and Burgess, Stephen F, *South Africa's Weapons of Mass Destruction* (Bloomington, 2005)

Rawnsley, Andrew, *The End of the Party: The Rise and Fall of New Labour* (London, 2010)

Regis, Ed, *The Biology of Doom: The History of America's Secret Germ Warfare Project* (New York, 1999)

Reid, Anna, *Leningrad: The Tragedy of a City Under Siege: 1941-44* (London, 2011)

Ride, David, *In Defence of Landscape: An Archaeology of Porton Down* (Stroud, 2006)

Ritter, Scott, *Endgame: Solving the Iraq Problem – Once and for All* (New York, 1999)

Ritter, Scott, *Iraqi Confidential: The Untold Story of the Intelligence Conspiracy to Undermine the UN and Overthrow Saddam Hussein* (New York, 2005)

Ritter, Scott and Rivers Pitt, William, *War on Iraq: What Team Bush Doesn't Want You to Know* (London, 2002)

Rogers, Simon (editor), *The Hutton Inquiry and Its Impact* (London, 2004)

Ross, Carne, *Independent Diplomat: Dispatches from an Unaccountable Elite* (London, 2007)

Rusbridger, James, *The Intelligence Game: Illusions and Delusions of International Espionage* (London, 1989)

Saeed, Mahmoud, *Saddam City*, (London, 2004)

Sagan, Carl, *The Demon-Haunted World: Science as a Candle in the Dark* (New York, 1997)

Said, Edward W, *Orientalism* (London, 1978)

Salinger, Pierre with Laurent, Eric, *Secret Dossier: The Hidden Agenda Behind the Gulf War* (London, 1991)

Short, Clare, *An Honourable Deception? New Labour, Iraq, and the Misuse of Power* (London, 2004)

Smith, Michael, *The Spying Game: The Secret History of British Espionage* (London, 2004)

Smithson, Amy E, *Germ Gambits: The Bioweapons Dilemma, Iraq and Beyond* (Stanford, 2011)

Stewart, Rory, *Occupational Hazards* (London, 2006)

Suskind, Ron, *The Way of the World* (New York, 2008)

Sweeney, John, *Trading with the Enemy: Britain's Arming of Iraq* (London, 1993)

Synnott, Hilary, *Bad Days in Basra* (London, 2008)

Timmerman, Kenneth R, *The Death Lobby: How the West Armed Iraq* (New York, 1991)

Trevan, Tim, *Saddam's Secrets: The Hunt for Iraq's Hidden Weapons* (London, 1999)

Turner, Stansfield, *Secrecy and Democracy: The CIA in Transition* (Boston, 1985)

Ungar, Craig, *The Fall of the House of Bush: The Untold Story of*

How a Band of True Believers Seized the Executive Branch, Started the Iraq War, and Still Imperils America's Future (New York, 2007)

Urban, Mark, *UK Eyes Alpha* (London, 1996)

Von Sponeck, Hans C, *A Different Kind of War: The UN Sanctions Regime in Iraq* (New York, 2006)

Willman, David, *The Mirage Man: Bruce Ivins, the Anthrax Attacks, and America's Rush to War* (New York, 2011)

Wright, Lawrence, *The Looming Tower: Al-Qaeda's Road to 9/11* (London, 2006)

ACKNOWLEDGEMENTS

All books should be journeys, for the reader but for the author too. This certainly was. I am grateful to Mike Jones at Simon & Schuster for giving me the opportunity to reach a stage of meaningful closure over a mesh of suspicion, doubt and anger that has entrapped me for ten years.

I never believed in the claims that Iraq had weapons of mass destruction. I knew from the moment Blair announced the September Dossier would be issued that it would be a piece of propaganda that almost entirely suborned the real purpose and the true competence of Britain's substantial intelligence community. I was heartened that somebody from within that community spoke out, although when the Ministry of Defence offered him up as a 'mole', my heart sank. I knew it would only be for him to retract his claims. I expected others, but there has only been Brian Jones, now also dead, and John Morrison, who was promptly sacked (I would be interested to know more about Morrison's subsequent departure from the Brunel Centre for Intelligence and Security Studies, but I have been unable to contact him). Everyone else has stayed silent.

When Kelly was found, I spent the next few years of my life waiting for the other shoe to drop. If war and government are at stake, lies and corpses are, after all, endemic. But the story of his suicide, like the story of the Iraq War, cannot be reduced to an Oxfordshire murder mystery. The conspiracy stretches further than that, beyond the mere realms of conspiracy, in fact, into something that indicates a dysfunctional democracy, and something akin to Mackay's madness of crowds.

The former Ambassador to Uzbekistan, Craig Murray, once

told me he had spoken about Iraqi WMD with a friend at the Foreign Office. Murray was told that everyone knew there weren't really any weapons of mass destruction in Iraq, but it was an institutional mindset. 'It's like when I'm playing Championship Manager,' his friend said. 'I know, when I'm sat at my computer, I'm not really managing a football team. When I go into the Foreign Office, I know there aren't any weapons, and it's just my job. Like Championship Manager is just a game.'

To speak out against that, it seems, is a rare thing. The rest of us have to pick the truth as best we can. The same can be said for the secretive, hyperbolic world of biological weapons. It is a field filled with stark warnings, bold claims and hungry budgets, yet there are still a few neutral, expert voices to be heard.

When I started this book I had no more than a GCSE B in biology. I couldn't have explained the differences between viruses and bacteria. That too was part of my journey, and I was helped along it by a number of individuals worthy of praise. There are two I would like to single out in particular: Milton Leitenberg, and Julian Perry Robinson, who is now (I hope) enjoying his retirement. I doubt they will agree with every observation, detail and argument laid out here, but they are helpful, industrious and truly authoritative academics. Their presence and their work reminds us that we do not have to blindly accept the unsourced claims of politicians, or our own intelligence agencies, and nor should we. Sadly, at time of publication, the future of the Harvard Sussex Programme, which Julian Perry Robinson co-founded, appears uncertain. Its archive, a more valuable research resource than ever, is in storage. I hope Sussex University or some other institution will give it the support that it needs.

Thanks are also due to Sue Philpott, an excellent copy-editor, and Jo Whitford, my project editor, who both had to endure an author who was too obsessed to let go. Antony Topping at Greene and Heaton also helped me put this all to rest. Any errors in this book are entirely my own.

Lastly, my apologies and best wishes go to the Kelly family

themselves, for I have trod on your memories. I was driven to. I hope you are at peace, and happy, and that one day, should you wish, you will add your voices to history.

Rob Lewis
Cardiff, 2013
rob@robertlewis.com

The Moving Finger writes; and, having writ,
Moves on: nor all thy Piety nor Wit,
Shall lure it back to cancel half a Line,
Nor all thy Tears wash out a Word of it.

Omar Khayyám

INDEX